Portfolio & Investment
M A N A G E M E N T

State-of-the-Art Research, Analysis and Strategies

EDITOR
FRANK J. FABOZZI

Visiting Professor
Alfred P. Sloan School of Management
Massachusetts Institute of Technology
and Managing Editor
The Journal of Portfolio Management

PROBUS PUBLISHING COMPANY
Chicago, Illinois

Library of Congress Cataloging-in-Publication Data Available

ISBN 1-55738-027-9

Printed in the United States of America

1   2   3   4   5   6   7   8   9   0

Preface

In seeking to achieve a client's financial goals, an investment manager can choose from a broad range of financial instruments and numerous portfolio strategies. The purpose of *Portfolio and Investment Management* is twofold. First, the major financial instruments and their risk/return characteristics are described. Second, the latest equity and fixed income portfolio strategies are explained. In describing these strategies, the practical problems of implementation are discussed.

Given the high degree of specialization within the investment management business, information from a wide range of experts is more useful than just a single author's viewpoint. I have chosen some of the finest financial minds to write for this book. All contributors are recognized experts in their area.

OVERVIEW OF THE BOOK

In Chapter 1, I review the investment management process, the fundamentals of capital market theory and its implications for investment management, and the role of options and futures in investment management. Robert Arnott reflects on the investment world of the 1990s in Chapter 2. In Chapter 3, Robert Arnott and Roger Clarke discuss strategies for asset allocation. In Chapter 4, Daniel Coggin outlines the various active equity management styles and models commonly used for equity valuation. Eric Sorensen in Chapter 5 builds on the foundation developed by Daniel Coggin to show how using active valuation disciplines a portfolio should be constructed.

Mark Zurack describes the various forms of portfolio insurance in Chapter 6. Stock index trading strategies employing stock index futures (program trading, stock index arbitrage, and portfolio insurance) are described by Joanne Hill and Frank Jones in Chapter 7. Dean D'Onofrio explains how dynamic hedging can be used as a risk control management tool in Chapter 8.

The motivations and benefits of indexing an equity portfolio are discussed by Donald Luskin in Chapter 9. In Chapter 10, Bruce Collins focuses on the investment management of index funds, with emphasis on the use of stock index futures.

The number of products in the fixed income market has grown dramatically in the 1980's, particularly in the mortgage-backed securities market. In Chapter 11, Dessa Fabozzi and I provide an overview of the U.S. fixed income securities markets. Ravi Dattatreya and I provide a framework for active fixed income portfolio management in Chapter 12. The case for indexing fixed income portfolios and the strategies that can be employed are the subject of Chapter 13, written by Sharmin Mossavar-Rahmani. In Chapter 14, Llewellyn Miller, Uday Rajan and Prakash Shimpi describe liability funding strategies. Frank Jones and Beth Krumholtz discuss how derivative instruments can be used to manage fixed income portfolios in Chapter 15. Jo Ann Corkran explains in Chapter 16 how corporate pension plan sponsors can best respond to FASB 87.

The difficulty with assessing investment performance is selecting an appropriate benchmark. In Chapter 17, Jon Christopherson describes the role of "normal" portfolios and their construction. Ron Surz then describes the various methodologies employed for measuring and evaluating performance in Chapter 18.

The international equity and bond markets and their historical performance are described in Chapter 19 by Gary Brinson and Richard Carr.

ACKNOWLEDGEMENTS

I would like to express my deep personal appreciation to the contributors. The following individuals gave generously of their time to read portions of this book: Robert Arnott (First Quadrant), Anand Bhattacharya (Underwood Neuhaus & Co.), John Carlson (Security Pacific Bank), Daniel Coggin (First Union National Bank of North Carolina),

Mark Dunetz (Kidder, Peabody), Sylvan Feldstein (Merrill Lynch Capital Markets), William Marshall (Franklin Savings Bank) and Chuck Ramsey (Bear Stearns).

Michael Ryder, Director of Production Services for Probus Publishing Company, provided invaluable support throughout all phases of this project.

Last, but certainly not least, I wish to thank my wife Dessa for her patience and the sacrifice of weekends and evenings so that I could complete this project.

Frank J. Fabozzi

CONTENTS & CONTRIBUTORS

CHAPTER 1

Introduction

FRANK J. FABOZZI, PH.D., CFA
VISITING PROFESSOR OF FINANCE
SLOAN SCHOOL OF MANAGEMENT
MASSACHUSETTS INSTITUTE OF TECHNOLOGY

The focus of this book is portfolio and investment management. This chapter describes the investment management process, the implications of capital market theory for the investment manager, and the role of options and futures in managing a portfolio.

THE INVESTMENT MANAGEMENT PROCESS

There are five main steps in investment management:

1. Setting investment objectives.
2. Establishing investment policy.
3. Selecting the portfolio strategy.
4. Selecting the assets.
5. Measuring and evaluating performance.

Setting Investment Objectives

The first main step in the investment management process is setting investment objectives. For institutions such as pension funds and life insurance companies, these objectives may be a cash flow specification to satisfy a liability due at some future date or a series of liabilities due at different future dates. A guaranteed investment contract (GIC) sold by a life insurance company is an example of the former; the projected benefit payout to beneficiaries of a pension plan and an annuity policy sold by a life insurance company are examples of multiple liabilities. For institutions such as banks and thrifts, the objective may be to lock-in a minimum interest rate spread over the cost of their funds. For others, such as mutual funds and some trust accounts, the investment objective may be to maximize return.

Establishing Investment Policy

The second main step is establishing policy guidelines to satisfy the objectives. Setting policy begins with asset allocation among the major asset classes—the products of the capital market. The major asset classes include equities, fixed income securities, real estate, and foreign securities. Client and regulatory constraints must be considered in establishing an investment policy. For example, state regulators of insurance companies (life insurance companies and property and casualty insurance companies) may restrict the amount of funds allocated to certain major asset classes. Even the amount allocated within a major asset class may be restricted based on the characteristics of the particular asset.

So too must tax and financial reporting implications be considered in adopting investment policies. For example, life insurance companies have certain tax advantages that make investing in tax-exempt municipal securities generally unappealing. Since pension funds are exempt from taxes, they too would not usually be interested in tax-exempt municipal securities. Property and casualty insurance companies will vary their ownership of tax-exempt municipal securities depending on projected profits from underwriting operations. Commercial banks at one time were major buyers of municipal securities; however, the 1986 tax act made investing in municipal bonds somewhat less attractive to commercial banks.

Financial reporting requirements, in particular Statement of Financial Accounting Board Nos. 87 and 88 and the Omnibus Budget Reconcilation Act of 1987 (a legislative initiative which reinforces the FASB 87 interpretation of liabilities), affect the way in which pension funds establish investment policies. Unfortunately, sometimes financial reporting considerations force institutions to establish investment policies that may not be in the best interest of the institution in the long run.

Selecting a Portfolio Strategy

Selecting a portfolio strategy that is consistent with the objectives and policy guidelines of the client or institution is the third step in the investment management process. Portfolio strategies can be classified as either active strategies or passive strategies. Essential to all active strategies are expectations about the factors that are expected to influence the performance of an asset class. For example, with active equity strategies this may include forecasts of futures earnings, dividends or price-earnings ratios. With active fixed income portfolios this may involve forecasts of future interest rates, future interest rate volatility or future yield spreads. Active portfolio strategies involving foreign securities will require forecasts of future exchange rates.

Passive strategies involve minimal expectational input. The most popular type of passive strategy is indexing. The objective in indexing is to replicate the performance of a predetermined index. While indexing has been employed extensively in the management of equity portfolios, the use of indexing for managing fixed income portfolios is a relatively new practice.

Between these extremes of active and passive strategies have sprung strategies that have elements of both. For example, the core of a portfolio may be indexed with the balance managed actively. Or a portfolio may be primarily indexed but employ low risk strategies to enhance the indexed return. This strategy is commonly referred to as "enhanced indexing" or "indexing plus."

In the fixed income area, several strategies classified as *structured portfolio strategies* have been commonly used. A structured portfolio strategy is one in which a portfolio is designed so as to achieve the performance of some predetermined benchmark. These strategies are frequently used in funding liabilities. When the predetermined benchmark is to have sufficient funds to satisfy a single liability regardless of the course of future interest rates, a strategy known as *immunization* is used. When the predetermined benchmark is multiple future liabilities that must be funded regardless of how interest rates change, the strategies that can be used are immunization or *cash flow matching*.

Even within the immunization and cash flow matching strategies, low risk active management strategies can be employed. One immunization strategy, *contingent immunization*, allows the portfolio manager to actively manage a portfolio until certain parameters are realized. If those parameters are realized, the portfolio is then immunized.

Indexing can be considered a structured portfolio strategy where the benchmark is to achieve the performance of some predetermined index. Portfolio insurance strategies—where the objective is to insure that the value of the portfolio does not fall below a predetermined amount—is also viewed as a structured portfolio strategy.

Selecting Assets

Once a portfolio is selected, the next main step is the selection of the specific assets to be included in the portfolio. It is in this phase that financial theory tells us the investment manager attempts to construct an *optimal* or *efficient* portfolio. An optimal or efficient portfolio is one that provides the greatest *expected* return for a given level of risk, or equivalently, the lowest risk for a given *expected* return.

Measuring and Evaluating Performance

The measurement and evaluation of investment performance is the last step in the investment management process. (Actually, it is improper to say that it is the last step since investment management is an ongoing process.) This step involves measuring the performance and then evaluating that performance relative to some realistic benchmark.

While the performance of a portfolio manager when compared to some benchmark may demonstrate superior performance, this does not necessarily mean that the portfolio satisfied its investment objective. For example, suppose that a life insurance company establishes as its objective maximization of portfolio return and allocates 75% of the fund to stocks and the balance to bonds. Suppose further that the portfolio manager responsible for the equity portfolio of this pension fund earns a return over a one year horizon that is 4% higher than the Standard & Poor's 500 stock index (a benchmark used to evaluate equity performance). Assuming that the risk of the portfolio was similar to that of the S&P 500, it would appear that the portfolio manager performed well. However, suppose in spite of this performance the life insurance company cannot meet its liabilities. The failure was in establishing the investment objectives and setting policy, not with the manager responsible for managing the portfolio.

CAPITAL MARKET THEORY AND INVESTMENT MANAGEMENT

In our discussion of the investment management process, we have left several questions unanswered. First, which is the best investment strategy to use—active or passive? Since risk is a key element in the asset allocation decision, portfolio construction and portfolio evaluation, how should it be measured? How should an optimal or efficient portfolio be designed?

The theoretical breakthrough in helping us answer these questions came with the work of Harry Markowitz in 1952 in which he demonstrated how an optimal or efficient portfolio can be constructed[1]. The key insight offered by Dr. Markowitz's work is that the risk of any individual security, as measured by its standard deviation of return, is not what is important. Instead, it is the correlation (or covariance) of a security's return within a diversified portfolio that will determine its risk. Thus, while the expected return of a portfolio is the market-weighted average expected return of the securities comprising the portfolio, the risk of the portfolio is not a linear function of the standard deviation of the risk of the individual securities.

After the publication of the seminal work by Professor Markowitz, Professors William Sharpe, John Lintner and Jan Mossin independently developed a capital market theory using the Markowitz framework for constructing an optimal portfolio.[2] The Sharpe-Lintner-Mossin

---

[1] Harry M. Markowitz, "Portfolio Selection," *Journal of Finance* (March 1952), pp. 71-91. An expanded presentation appears in his book *Portfolio Selection: Efficient Diversification of Investment* (New York, N.Y.: John Wiley & Sons, 1959).

[2] William F. Sharpe, "Capital Asset Prices: A Theory of Market Equilibrium under Conditions of Risk," *Journal of Finance* (September 1964), pp. 425-442; John Lintner, "Security Prices, Risk, and Maximal Gains from Diversification," *Journal of Finance* (December 1965), pp. 587-616; and Jan Mossin, "Equilibrium in a Capital Asset Market," *Econometrica* (October 1966), pp. 76-83.

analysis demonstrated that a "market" portfolio offers the highest level of return per unit of risk in an *efficient* market. (We'll define an efficient market later.) By combining securities in a portfolio with characteristics similar to the market, the efficiency of the market would be captured. The theoretical "market" portfolio consists of all risky assets. The weight of each risky asset in the market portfolio is equal to the ratio of its market value to the aggregate market value of all risky assets. That is, the market portfolio is a capitalization-weighted portfolio of all risky assets.

The Sharpe-Lintner-Mossin analysis also showed how risk should be defined and the relationship between risk and return. Specifically, their analysis showed that the risk of a security as measured by the standard deviation of return can be partitioned into two components: nondiversifiable and diversifiable risk. Nondiversifiable risk is a measure of how a security's return is affected by factors common to all securities. The impact of these factors on a portfolio cannot be avoided, since they are common to all securities in the portfolio. For this reason, other names for nondiversfiable risk are *market risk* or *systematic risk*.

Diversifiable risk or unsystematic risk is the unique risk associated with an individual security. Examples of this risk include a strike or major litigation that will adversely impact the profit potential of the firm. This risk can be avoided by holding a diversified portfolio of securities. Empirical studies using randomly generated stock portfolios have shown that, by holding a portfolio of about 10 to 12 different stocks, an investor can diversify away virtually all unsystematic risk. Therefore, the only risk present in a well-diversified portfolio is nondiversifiable or market risk. It is only this risk that investors should be compensated for accepting.

The Sharpe-Lintner-Mossin analysis demonstrated that market risk can be measured by the product of the standard deviation of the return on the market and the "beta" of the security. The beta, estimated using historical data, measures the sensitivity of the return on the security to changes in the market (as measured by some market index such as the S&P 500). Since the standard deviation of the market is common to all securities, the beta of the security is a proxy for relative systematic risk.

Given that the only risk that investors should be compensated for is market risk and beta is a relative measure of market risk, the Sharpe-Lintner-Mossin analysis demonstrated the following relationship between risk and return for any asset:

Expected return = risk-free rate

+ beta x [expected market return - risk-free rate]

The above relationship is referred to as the *capital asset pricing model* (CAPM) and states that the expected return from a security should equal the risk-free rate of return plus a risk premium.

While the capital asset pricing model has been the foundation of the theory of finance since its introduction, the arbitrage pricing theory (APT) developed by Professor Stephen Ross in 1976[3] has challenged it as a workable theory. Basically, APT allows for more than one factor that systematically affects the price of all securities. Investors want to be compensated for accepting each of these different systematic factors. Mathematically, APT can be expressed as follows when there are k systematic factors:

Expected return = risk-free rate

$$+ beta_1 \times [\text{risk premium for factor 1}]$$
$$+ beta_2 \times [\text{risk premium for factor 2}]$$
$$+ \ldots \ldots$$
$$+ beta_k \times [\text{risk premium for factor k}]$$

The APT states that the expected return is a composite of the compensation for each source of risk. The beta of the factor is the sensitivity of the security to the particular risk factor. As in the CAPM, the expected return is not determined by unsystematic (diversifiable or unique) risk. Notice also that if there is only one systematic factor, the APT is consistent with the CAPM.[4]

The practical problem with using the APT in investment management has been in identifying the systematic factors. However, some recent progress has been made in this area. For example, one study found that there are five economic factors that affect equity returns: unanticipated changes in default risk, unanticipated changes in the term structure of interest rates, unanticipated changes in inflation, unantici-

---

[3]Stephen A. Ross, "The Arbitrage Theory of Capital Asset Pricing," *Journal of Economic Theory* (March 1976), pp. 342-363.

[4]For a further discussion, see Edwin Elton and Martin Gruber, *Modern Portfolio Theory and Investment Analysis* (New York: John Wiley & Sons, 1987), pp. 352-354.

pated changes in the long-run growth rate of profits for the economy, and residual market risk.[5] Statistical techniques for measuring these risk factors have been developed.[6]

MARKET EFFICIENCY AND PORTFOLIO STRATEGIES

The term *efficient capital market* has been used in several contexts to describe the operating characteristics of a capital market. Professor Richard West draws a distinction between an *operationally* (or *internally*) efficient capital market and a *pricing* (or *externally*) efficient capital market.[7]

In an operationally efficient market, investors can obtain transaction services as cheaply as possible given the costs associated with furnishing those services. Transaction costs include commissions and market maker spreads. For the equity markets, since the elimination of fixed commissions on May 1, 1975, the commission structure has moved closer to the competitive level dictated by the cost of providing brokerage services. As for the market maker spread, the jury is still out. Barriers to market making on the New York Stock Exchange, for example, historically has prevented spreads from being competitive. Competitition from the over-the-counter market and regional stock exchanges have forced specialists on the exchange to be more competitive.

Pricing efficiency refers to a market in which prices at all times fully reflect all available information that is relevant to the valuation of securities. When a market is price efficient, active strategies will not *consistently* produce superior returns after adjusting for (1) risk, (2) transaction costs, and (3) management advisory fees.

There are three forms of market efficiency—weak, semistrong and strong. The distinction between these forms is the relevant set of

---

[5]See Nai-Fu Chen, Richard Roll and Stephen A. Ross, "Economic Forces and the Stock Market," *Journal of Business* (July 1986), pp. 383-403; and Edwin Burmeister and Kenneth D. Wall, "The Arbitrage Pricing Theory and Macroeconomic Factor Measures," *The Financial Review* (February 1986), pp. 1-20.

[6]See Michael A. Berry, Edwin Burmeister and Marjorie B. McElroy, "Sorting Out Risks Using Unknown APT Factors," *Financial Analysts Journal* (March-April 1988), pp. 29-42.

[7]Richard R. West, "Efficiency of the Securities Market," Chapter 2 in Frank J. Fabozzi and Frank G. Zarb (editors), *The Handbook of Securities Markets: Securities, Options, and Futures* (Homewood, IL: Dow Jones-Irwin, 1986).

information that is believed to be impounded into the price of the security at all times. *Weak efficiency* means that the price of the security fully reflects price and trading history of the security. *Semistrong efficiency* means that the price of the security fully reflects all public information (which, of course, includes historical price and trading patterns). *Strong efficiency* exists in a market in which the price of a security reflects all information regardless of whether or not it is publicly available.

For the equity markets, the preponderence of empirical evidence is that the market is efficient in the weak form, although there have been recent studies challenging this position.[8] While most of the empirical studies suggest that the market is efficient in the semistrong form, anomalies such as the small firm effect, January effect, week-end effect, and neglected firm effect, suggest that there may be pockets of inefficiency.[9] In these empirical tests, the measure of risk used to determine risk-adjusted returns is beta. Studies of the strong form of market efficiency have looked at the performance of professional money managers. These studies do not suggest that professional money managers can consistently earn superior returns.

Studies investigating the efficiency of the bond market have examined one of the following questions:

1. Are there market participants who have superior interest rate forecasting ability?
2. Do active money managers consistently outperform popular indexes?
3. Are bonds priced such that there are arbitrage trading opportunities?
4. Does the market use all publicly available information to value an issue?

Studies examining the first question are tests of the weak form of the efficiency of the bond market. The overwhelming evidence suggests

[8]See for example Andrew W. Lo and A. Craig MacKinlay, "Stock Market Prices Do Not Follow Random Walks: Evidence from a Simple Specification Test," *The Review of Financial Studies* (Spring 1988), pp. 3-40; and Stephen W. Pruitt and Richard E. White, "Who Says Technical Analysis Can't Beat the Market?" *The Journal of Portfolio Management* (Spring 1988), pp. 55-58.

[9]For a review of the empirical evidence on market anomalies, see Diana Harrington, Frank J. Fabozzi and Russell Fogler, *Stock Market Evidence* (Chicago: Probus Publishing, 1989).

that interest rate movements cannot be predicted with a degree of consistency and accuracy sufficient to generate superior investment performance. As for the second question, several studies suggest that on average money managers have not done better than some popular indexes. However, these studies are deficient because they do not properly reflect the risk accepted by the money manager surveyed in the studies.

There are a few studies that have focused on the third question. These studies have been limited to the government bond market for three reasons: (1) price data are more readily available than other sectors of the bond market; (2) the price data are more reliable than for other sectors of the bond market, and; (3) tests can be conducted without being concerning with the impact of credit risk.

Studies of the government bond market suggest that it is efficient, yet there are instances where trading opportunities to enhance returns occur.[10] As for the corporate, municipal and mortgage-backed securities market, there is insufficient evidence to draw any conclusion about market efficiency.

This brief review of the efficiency of the equity and bond markets does not do justice to the extensive research on the topic. There are no perfect studies. All empirical studies are flawed due to either methodological limitations (or errors) or lack of good data. Suppose that after evaluating the empirical evidence an investment manager or fund sponsor believes that inefficiencies exist in a particular market sector. Active portfolio strategies can be employed to exploit that inefficiency. What strategy should be pursued by an investor who believes that a market sector is sufficiently efficient so that superior risk-adjusted returns can not be consistently realized after accounting for transaction costs and management advisory fees? In this case, a passive approach should be followed—but what is the best passive approach to pursue?

Recall from our earlier discussion of the Sharpe-Lintner-Mossin analysis (CAPM) that in an efficient market the "market" portfolio offers the highest level of return per unit of risk because it captures the efficiency of the market. The theoretical market portfolio should be a capitalization-weighted portfolio of all risky assets. As a proxy for the theoretical market portfolio, an index that is representative of the

---

[10]See for example Robert M. Conroy and Richard J. Rendleman, "A Test of Market Efficiency in Government Bonds," *The Journal of Portfolio Management* (Summer 1987), pp. 57-64.

market should be used. But this is nothing more than indexing. Thus, there is strong theoretical support for an indexing strategy in an efficient market.

ROLE OF OPTIONS AND FUTURES IN INVESTMENT MANAGEMENT

With the advent of options and futures on financial instruments, active and offensive-minded portfolio risk management strategies, in the broadest sense, assumed a new dimension. The investment manager can achieve new degrees of freedom. It is now possible to alter the market profile of an equity or fixed income portfolio economically and quickly. They offer investment managers risk and return patterns that were either previously unavailable or to costly to obtain.

Options and Futures Defined

An option is a contract in which the writer of the option grants the buyer of the option the right to purchase from or sell to the writer an underlying instrument at a specified price (called the exercise or strike price) within a specified period of time.[11] The underlying instrument may be a security such as a common stock or a bond, a foreign currency, a commodity such as a precious metal, a futures contract, or a financial index such as the Standard & Poor's 500. When the underlying instrument is something that cannot be delivered, such as a financial index, the contract is settled in cash.

In exchange for the option, the buyer pays the writer (seller) of the option a certain sum of money called the option premium or option price. When an option grants the buyer the right to purchase the underlying instrument, it is called a *call option*. When the option buyer has the right to sell the underlying instrument to the writer, the option is called a *put option*.

A futures contract is an agreement between a buyer and seller in which the buyer agrees to take delivery and the seller agrees to make

---

[11]When an option may be exercised at any time up to and including the expiration date (the date after which the option is void), the option is called an *American option*. If the option only allows the buyer to exercise the option at the expiration date and not before, the option is called a *European option*.

delivery of something at a specified price at the end of a designated period of time (called the *settlement date*). There are futures contracts on agricultural products, precious metals, foreign currencies, fixed income securities, and stock indexes.

Both options and futures are highly leveraged investment vehicles. Viewed in isolation, an option or a futures contract is a highly speculative instrument. However, the lesson we learned from the work of Dr. Markowitz is that the risk of an instrument is not its risk in isolation but within a portfolio context. The prudent use of derivative instruments can reduce the overall risk of a portfolio or control the risk of a portfolio.

There are differences between options and futures contracts that determine their risk-reward characteristics and thereby their use in investment management. In a futures contract, both the buyer and the seller are obligated to perform at the settlement date. For options, the buyer has the *right*, but not the obligation, to perform. It is the option seller (writer) who has the obligation to perform. In addition, in a futures contract the buyer does not pay the seller to accept the obligation as in the case of an option where the buyer pays the seller the option price. How these differences impact the risk and return characteristics is discussed below.

Risk and Return Characteristics of Options and Futures

The maximum amount that an option buyer can lose is the option price. The maximum profit that the option writer (seller) can realize is the option price. The option buyer has substantial upside return potential while the option writer has substantial downside risk. At the expiration date, the profit or loss of an option position depends on the price of the underlying instrument.

To see how the risk-return pattern of an option on an underlying instrument differs from that of a cash market position in the same underlying instrument, let's compare the purchase of a call option (long call option position) with the purchase of the underlying instrument (long cash position) at the expiration date. Suppose that the price of the underlying instrument is $100, the price of the call option is $3 and the strike price is $100.

Both positions will increase in value as the price of the underlying instrument increases. The long cash position realizes a dollar for dollar gain when the price rises. In contrast, the gain on the long call position will be equal to the dollar gain on the cash market instrument minus the cost of the option (i.e., the option price). So, for example, if at the expiration date the price of the underlying instrument increases by $12, the gain on the long call position is only $9. Thus, the long call position reduces the upside potential by an amount equal to the option price. In exchange for the option price, the investor is purchasing downside protection. If the underlying instrument decreases, the long cash position realizes a dollar for dollar loss. The long call position, however, loses at most the option price regardless of how much the underlying instrument decreases by.

To see how an option combined with a cash market position can change a portfolio's risk-return pattern, consider a portfolio that includes a long position in some cash market instrument. This position will gain dollar for dollar for every dollar increase in the price of the cash market instrument. However, it will also lose dollar for dollar for every dollar decrease in the price of the cash market instrument. Suppose that a put option with a strike price equal to the current market price of the cash market instrument is purchased. At the expiration date of the option, if the price of the cash market instrument has increased, the gain in the position will be equal to the gain in the cash market instrument less the option price. Thus, once again, the upside potential is reduced by the option price. The benefit of the put option is that if the price of the cash market instrument falls, the lowest price that the investor will receive is the strike price. This is because the investor can exercise the option and sell the cash market instrument at the strike price which we assumed in this example is equal to the price of the cash market instrument at the time the put option was purchased. Thus, the minimum price that the investor will realize for the cash market instrument is the strike price minus the put option price. This strategy is commonly referred to as a *protective put strategy*.

In contrast to options, a long (short) futures position will realize a dollar for dollar gain (loss) and realize a dollar for dollar loss (gain) depending on whether the futures price at the settlement date increases (decreases). The key point is that the risk-return pattern is symmetrical for a rise or fall in the futures price, as is the case for a cash market position in the underlying instrument. So, if the futures price at the settlement date is $12 greater than the futures price at which the futures contract was purchased, the long futures position will gain $12. However, if the futures price at the settlement date is $40 lower, the long futures position will lose $40. There is no downside protection with the futures contract.

Let's compare a protective put strategy which can be used for hedging a portfolio with the sale of a futures contract for hedging a portfolio. Since the objective of a hedge is to protect the portfolio value, the sale of a futures contract is appropriate because a loss on the underlying cash market position if there is a price decline can be offset by a gain realized on a short futures position. With an appropriately constructed short futures position a loss in one position (long cash market position or short futures position) will be offset by the other. There is no upside potential for the combined position. In contrast, as we explained earlier, for the protective put strategy, the portfolio will be protected for a cost equal to the option price. If the cash market position increases, the portfolio will realize the increase less the option price. If there is a decline in the cash market position, the decline in the portfolio value will be limited to the strike price minus the option price.

Pricing of Options and Futures

The implementation of portfolio strategies using options and futures requires that the investment manager be capable of identifying whether they are properly priced. The theoretical price of both options and futures are determined using arbitrage arguments. This means that it possible to construct a portfolio using a risk-free instrument and the underlying instrument that will have an identical risk and return characteristic as the option or futures contract. To avoid pure arbitrage profits, the price of the option or futures contract must be equal to the value of the portfolio used to replicate its risk and return profile.

The basic futures price relationship can be expressed as:

$$\text{futures price} = \text{current market price}$$
$$+ \text{current market price (cost of financing - yield earned)}$$

The futures price depends on the current market price, the cost of financing the underlying instrument if purchased today and the yield earned on the underlying instrument. The difference between the cost of financing and the yield earned is called the *net financing cost* because it adjusts the financing cost for the yield earned. The net financing cost is more commonly called the *cost of carry* or, simply, *carry*. Positive carry means that the yield earned is greater than the financing cost; negative carry means that the financing cost exceeds the yield earned. The futures price can be equal to, less than, or greater than the current market price depending on whether there is zero carry, positive carry or negative carry, respectively. Modifications to the basic futures relationship are necessary to take into consideration the nuances of the different futures contracts.

While the price of a futures contract is relatively straightforward, options are more complicated to price. The most popular option pricing model for common stock is the Black-Scholes option pricing model.[12] An alternative option pricing model that is more adaptable to pricing options on dividend paying stocks, bonds and futures is the *binomial option pricing model*.[13]

All option pricing models based on the arbitrage or riskless hedge argument require the following six variables as input to determine the theoretical or "fair" option price: (1) current price of the underlying instrument, (2) strike price, (3) time to expiration, (4) short-term risk-free interest rate over the life of the option, (5) coupon rate, and (6) volatility of the underlying instrument over the life of the option. Of these six variables, the only one not known is volatility. Regardless of how good an option pricing model an investment manager uses, the option price derived will only be as good as the estimate for volatility.

Applications of Options and Futures

Holding aside the pure speculative uses of options and futures, listed below are some of the investment management applications of options and futures.

1. They may be used to create a synthetic instrument that offers a higher return than a cash market instrument or an index.
2. Options and futures can be used to adjust the risk exposure of a stock or bond portfolio quickly. For a stock portfolio, this means

---

[12]Fischer Black and Myron Scholes, "The Pricing of Corporate Liabilities," *Journal of Political Economy* (May-June 1973), pp. 637-659.

[13]John Cox, Stephen Ross and Mark Rubinstein, "Option Pricing: A Simplified Approach," *Journal of Financial Economics* (September 1979), pp. 229-263; Richard Rendleman and Brit Bartter, "Two-State Option Pricing," *Journal of Finance* (December 1979), pp. 1093-1110; and William Sharpe, *Investments* (Englewood Cliffs, N.J.: Prentice-Hall, 1981), Chapter 16.

adjusting the beta of the portfolio. For a bond portfolio, this means adjusting the duration of the portfolio. In the special case where an investment manager wants to hedge a portfolio, this means adjusting the beta of a stock portfolio or the duration of a bond portfolio to zero.

3. Options and futures can be used for asset allocation to alter the stock/bond mix of a portfolio quickly.

4. Futures contracts can be used to reduce the transaction costs of creating an index fund.

SUMMARY

In this chapter, the investment management process, capital market theory and its implications for selecting a portfolio strategy, and the role of options and futures in investment management were reviewed. The 18 chapters that follow tie together the fundamental principles described in this chapter.

CHAPTER 2

The Investment World of the 1990s: Reflections on the Future*

ROBERT D. ARNOTT
PRESIDENT &
CHIEF INVESTMENT OFFICER
FIRST QUADRANT CORP.

With the many recent advances in investment theory and practice, we have seen a proliferation of new products, new strategies, and even new investment assets. Along with these new products, strategies, and assets, the role of the pension sponsor, the role of the investment manager, and the state of investment theory are all changing.

This chapter is an attempt to step back from the specifics in order to explore the implications of all this change for the investment world of the 1990s. The principal focus is on the quantitative arena, for most of the growth in our industry in the past decade (and most of the growth in the coming decade) stems directly from the strides made in quantitative theory and application.

---

*Adapted and expanded from Robert D. Arnott, "The Future for Quantitative Investment Products," *Journal of Portfolio Management*, Winter 1988.

THE HISTORIC CONTEXT: EVOLUTION OR REVOLUTION?

If we are to assess the future direction for investment management in general and for quantitative management (see Exhibit 1) in particular, it is necessary to ask, What is amiss in the investment world today? A brief look at the developments of the past three decades may give us an indication of the challenges that we now face in investment management.

EXHIBIT 1:
A PRACTITIONER'S VIEW OF QUANTITATIVE INVESTING

What is quantitative investment management, anyway? Quantitative investment management is more a matter of process than anything else. The differentiating feature is that the quantitative manager lets the computer do the dirty work in finding investments that have certain target characteristics. For example, in equity management, the process imposes discipline on the security selection process. A quantitatively derived portfolio cannot fail to match the intended portfolio characteristics. These additional facts need emphasis:

1. Quantitative investment management does not guarantee success. A bad discipline, quantitatively implemented, will perform badly. Indeed, it may do worse than a similar qualitative process, because there may be less slippage.
2. There is no basis for believing that a quantitative approach is superior to a qualitative approach, de facto.
3. As more investors engage in quantitative investment management, an historically effective discipline will not suffice. The quantitative manager must have a disciplined process that is superior to other investment approaches, *including other quantitative approaches*.

Therein lies today's challenge. It is no longer enough to be quant. It is necessary to be a better quant.

The role of the pension sponsor has evolved considerably, as summarized in Exhibit 2. In the 1950s, the management of pension assets was handled as a small part of the responsibilities of the Assistant Treasurer. In the 1960s, a growing asset base, coupled with disappointing results for the bond assets that had been the asset class of choice in the 1950s, prompted increased awareness of the importance of pension management. In the 1970s we saw the building of a pension management staff.

The vast unfunded liability and the mandate of ERISA focused more attention on pension management and on performance. A growing awareness of the asset/liability mismatch led to the exploration of alternative asset classes and increased the complexity of the choices faced by the pension sponsor.

EXHIBIT 2:
A SIMPLIFIED LOOK AT RECENT HISTORY: ROLE OF THE SPONSOR

1950s—Part-Time Assistant Treasurer

1960s—Growing More Interested Due to:
  —Growing Asset Base
  —Disappointing Bond Results

1970s—Building of Pension Management Staff
  —Increased Importance of Performance
  —Vast Unfunded Liability
  —Complexity of Choices
  —Growing Awareness of Asset/Liability Mismatch

1980s—Crises of Complexity
  —Too Many Choices
  —Too Few Tools

1990s—Clear Perspective on the Asset/Liability Match/Mismatch?
  —Use of Tools to Control Aggregate Characteristics of Pension Plan.

There has been a parallel evolution in the role of the pension plan manager, detailed in Exhibit 3. In the 1950s, the pension manager was typically a bond manager; this individual's mandate, to paraphrase Keith Ambachtsheer[1], was to act as a buffer between the pension sponsor and the stormy uncertainty of the capital markets. In the 1960s, sponsors became more interested in stocks because of dreadful bond results, and the balanced manager came into existence. In the 1970s, with a growing dissatisfaction at the ineffectual management of balanced portfolios, index funds emerged. After all, relative performance is a zero-sum game by definition. If one active manager is to beat the market, then someone else must be losing relative to the market,

---

[1]Keith P. Ambachtsheer, *The Pension Fund and the Bottom Line*, Dow Jones-Irwin, 1985.

otherwise the market place would be beating the market, which is tautologically impossible. For sponsors who were losing confidence in their ability to choose superior managers, passive strategies affected a safe haven.

EXHIBIT 3:
A SIMPLIFED LOOK AT RECENT HISTORY: ROLE OF THE MANAGER

1950s — Bond Manager, acting as "buffer" between sponsor and markets

1960s — Balanced Manager, acting as "buffer"

1970s — Specialized Managers, hawking specialized products. Emergence of Passive Management

1980s — Blizzard of Choices: Active, Passive, or Core Management; Derivative-Based Strategies

1990s — Tools for Sponsors: Active or Passive "Tilted" Portfolios, Fulfillment Funds, Rebalancing, Asset Allocation

---

This shifting roles of the pension sponsor and the investment manager reflect a changing array of asset class choices employed by the money managers and sponsors. In the 1950s, as Exhibit 4 suggests, bonds were the asset of choice. In the 1960s, stocks were added to the spectrum of assets. In the 1970s, there was growing interest in what might be characterized as "covariance assets." Real estate, overseas investments, venture capital, and other asset classes tend to behave independently of stocks and bonds. Thus, they can reduce the risk of a portfolio without necessarily reducing the return. Indeed, the portfolio which uses these covariance assets tends to find the return increased at any given level of risk. In the current decade there has been a surge of interest in the use of derivative securities. Arbitrage strategies, tactical asset allocation strategies, and other override strategies are surging in popularity.

Not surprisingly, investment theory has also moved in new directions. In the 1950s, the state of the art in investment theory consisted of a general awareness of the linkage between risk and reward. The 1960s

EXHIBIT 4:
A SIMPLIFIED LOOK AT RECENT HISTORY: ASSET CLASSES

1950s — Bonds

1960s — + Stocks

1970s — + Covariance Assets (Real Estate, International, . . .)

1980s — + Derivative Securities (Portfolio Insurance, Arbitrage, Tactical Asset Allocation)

1990s — + ? ? ?

---

saw the emergence of theories such as the Capital Asset Pricing Model and the Dividend Discount Model. At this juncture, no one was actually foolish enough to *run money* based on the models, but academia and some on the fringes of money management began to explore these concepts as a matter of theoretical interest. In the 1970s, arcane ideas of the prior decade gained acceptance, and managers began to use beta, alpha, and dividend discount models. At the same time, duration emerged as a basis for bond management. Once again, few managers were so foolish as to rely solely on these disciplines, but a number of managers found them to be useful tools in the security selection process. Covariance became recognized as an important issue in the management of the total pension plan. Alternative assets such as real estate and international investments were explored for their covariance implications, in order to control the total risk of the pension portfolio. As with every decade, the 1970s saw the arrival of certain gimmicks. Option-based Ponzi schemes proliferated under the pseudoscientific name of "option overriding." With the proliferation of low covariance assets, art and rare coins were discussed in investment conferences as serious alternatives for the pension sponsor.

THE CHOICES WE FACE—AND WISH WE DIDN'T

In the 1980s, managers face a blizzard of choices. Unfortunately, there is a dearth of effective tools for controlling the attributes or characteristics of the portfolios under management. Exhibit 6 dramatizes this "Crisis of Complexity." There is active management, passive management, and, for those who want just a little active management, there is

EXHIBIT 5:
A SIMPLIFIED LOOK AT RECENT HISTORY: QUANTITATIVE THEORY

1950s—None

1960s—Beta/Alpha and Dividend Discount Model as Theory

1970s—Beta/Alpha DDM as tool Duration-based Bond Management awareness of importance of Covariance option-based Ponzi Gimmicks

1980s—Multivariate Issue Selection Multivariate Risk Measurement Reshaping Return Distributions (e.g., Portfolio Insurance Asset Allocation Disciplines)

1990s—Unified Pricing Model? Long-Term/Short-Term Models?

---

core management. There are bond managers, stock managers, international managers, and managers of alternative and synthetic assets that fit each of these characteristics. Some of these strategies permit the portfolio manager and the owner of the assets to reshape the entire return distribution of the portfolio.

In response, there has been a rapid increase in the sophistication of quantitative theory and a shortening of the time between development of theory and application. Multivariate issue selection, which was on the fringes of money management as recently as 1980, is becoming a mainstream portfolio management approach. Multivariate risk management, based on theories such as the Arbitrage Pricing Theory, is becoming recognized as an important tool for controlling the risk attributes of a portfolio. Asset allocation disciplines have jumped from the academic pages to large-scale implementation in less than five years.

Today's complexity breeds opportunity for those who have the staff and the time to exploit it. The owner of the assets, such as a corporate pension sponsor, typically does not have the time to explore the proliferation of opportunities and improvement strategies without running the risk of changing the return and risk attributes of the portfolio in unintended and dangerous ways. Alternatively, the owner can choose multiple specialty managers; he can employ managers with a demonstrated aptitude for using derivative securities; he can employ alternative asset classes with attractive covariance attributes; and/or he can

EXHIBIT 6:
THE TRANSITION: 1960s to 1980s

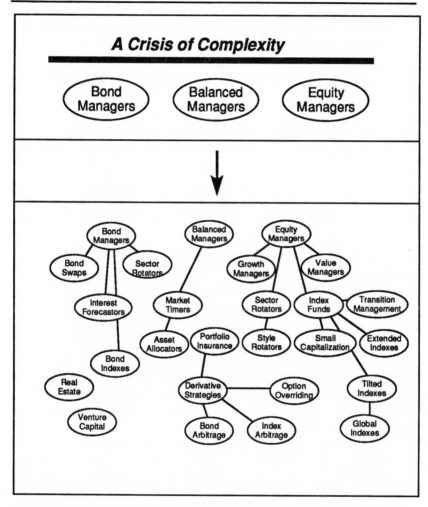

employ active or passive managers for the management of the core holdings of the pension plan.

What is the end product, once all of these are put together? What measure of control does the owner have over these attributes? Unfortunately, the more an owner employs these new disciplines, new tools, and new strategies, the less control the owner has over the aggregate portfolio.

NEEDS AND RESPONSES IN THE 1990s

The direction for the 1990s is clear. The sponsor and other owners of portfolio assets will move toward a deeper understanding of the nature of the asset/liability match or mismatch. The sponsor will have access to tools to control the aggregate risk characteristics of the total pension plan. In the 1990s, investment managers will turn their attention away from exploring the next fashionable niche in the marketplace and toward developing products that can *exploit* a complex world by helping the sponsor to bring that complexity under control.

Perhaps the pension executive will be given a role in the organization equivalent to the role of the manager of a corporate profit center. After all, if the pension executive adds just 100 basis points to the long-term return on the pension assets, then he or she will have added just as much to the bottom line of the company as will the manager of a similarly-sized operating division who boosts its ROE by 100 basis points. It is ironic that most corporations fail to give adequate recognition or attention to this opportunity.

How will the investment management community respond to these client needs?

Control Tools

First and foremost, we will see the development of tools that can help the owners of assets develop a consolidated total plan with attributes matching their needs. These tools will offer a badly needed measure of control over the complexity facing the investor.

The concept of the fulfillment or completeness fund is one example. A fulfillment fund enables the owner to assemble a list of active or passive managers with certain style attributes and use *one* fulfillment manager to control the normal style stance of the total pension plan. This is achieved without disrupting the management of the other portfolios and without offsetting the value that the other managers can add through active investment decisions. Indeed, with a fulfillment fund, asset owners need no longer be concerned about whether a new active manager's style is complementary to those of the other managers. The fulfillment portfolio sharply reduces the importance of this consideration by explicitly complementing the style of a multiply managed portfolio, thereby simplifying the control of the total portfolio.

Passive asset mix rebalancing tools that use futures to control the asset allocation of the pension plan to match the intended long-term normal asset mix will continue to be developed. In unpublished research by Walter Dec of General Motors, this "passive" rebalancing strategy is actually a powerful source of return enhancement. The typical portfolio can benefit by some 30 basis points annually on the *total* portfolio with a simple rebalancing process, instead of allowing the mix to drift with the whims of the capital markets. This added value is still more dramatic when compared with the 67 basis points annually forfeited by the typical pension sponsor.[2] This 67 basis point loss is due to untimely "rear-view mirror" asset allocation, which led many sponsors to slash equity exposure in late 1974 and cut bond exposure in mid–1981. These rebalancing disciplines will likely be linked with active asset allocation strategies that control the aggregate asset allocation stance of the total pension plan.

What do you do with the 5% of equity assets that are *always* idle in cash? Futures can be used to put those assets to work. What of the soaring popularity of portfolio insurance? Strategies can and will be offered that will exploit the futures mispricing triggered by these strategies. Such strategies will include explicit selling of portfolio insurance as well as rebalancing and tactical asset allocation, which implicitly tends to take the other side of the portfolio insurance trades.

Will these products increase or decrease the complexity of pension management? Ironically, the ultimate effect of this particular increase in the number of products will be a decrease in the complexity that the sponsor faces, because *these* products are targeted to control the character of a total portfolio, regardless of the variety of its pieces. These investment tools will cleanly separate the management of the asset allocation decision from the management within an asset class. Many of the products for the 1990s will integrate the management of derivative securities with the behavior of the underlying assets.

Opportunistic Trading Strategies

Another likely direction for asset management is toward the area of opportunistic trading strategies that segregate long-term and short-term

[2]Gary P. Brinson, L. Randolph Hood and Gilbert L. Beebower, "Determinants of Portfolio Performance," *Financial Analysts Journal*, July/August 1986, pp. 39–44.

models. Risk and return models, such as price to book value, tend to be "slow" models that evince their influence and contribute to investment performance only over a long horizon. Other models, such as earnings surprise, suggest that the attractiveness of a security shifts rapidly from quarter to quarter, or even day to day. These "fast" models are not practical for issue selection, because they tend to add little value after transaction costs. Nonetheless, as a screen for marginal trades, triggering, or blocking trades based on the "fast" discipline, these could add considerable value. Comparatively few practitioners are actively exploring this kind of strategy. In any event, an awareness of the time horizon of portfolio strategies is likely to play an important role in defining the growth areas for investment management in the 1990s.

The Outlook for Theory

What do the 1990s have in store for quantitative theory? The industry has made tremendous strides over the past decade in redefining the nature of capital market risk. It would not be surprising to see some evolution in the direction of a Unified Pricing Model, which links together multiple asset classes. The Arbitrage Pricing Theory (APT) was a first, but incomplete, step in this direction.

Peter Bernstein[3] suggests this kind of linkage. Is not a junk bond simply a combination of a series of zero coupon bonds coupled with a short put option? Can we not make the same characterization for preferred stock? Does not an individual stock consist of issue-specific risk coupled with equity market risk and assorted factor exposures? Would not many of these factor exposures cross over to alternative asset classes, such as real estate and venture capital?

Two other developments in quantitative theory that are likely to arrive in the coming decade lie in the areas of global asset allocation and in the expanded role of fixed-income management.

FASB 87 forces the pension sponsor to reflect the net present value of pension liabilities directly on the balance sheet. One of the unfortunate attributes of this accounting standard is that the sensitivity of liabilities to interest rates is reflected on the bottom line, while sensitiv-

---

[3]Peter L. Bernstein, "Asset Allocation: Things Are Not What They Seem," *Financial Analysts Journal,* March/April 1987, pp. 6–8.

ity to other economic factors is not.[4] The Omnibus Budget Reconciliation Act of 1987 (OBRA) magnifies this pressure severalfold, by creating direct cash flow consequences for any sponsor which permits their pension to become underfunded.

By implication, the pension sponsor faces considerable exogenous pressure to neutralize interest rate sensitivity of the asset/liability mismatch. Because OBRA also prevents contributions to any well-funded plans, this pressure can only be expected to grow with time. This means increased use of long duration bonds.[5] Long duration bonds may not be the best asset class for pension sponsors because their long-term real returns tend to be modest. Nonetheless, it is fair to anticipate that long-term bonds will play a more important role in pension management in the next decade than they have in the past decade. As a result, we should see significant strides in a more fully developed understanding of the nature of bond management over the next decade, as an indirect result of FASB 87.

With the globalization of securities markets, we can surely expect a greater understanding of the interplay among the various international capital markets. International investing is widely understood to be a means of reducing the risk of a total pension portfolio through covariance effects, without decreasing returns. Indeed, history suggests the prospect of actually increasing returns. While it is unlikely that we will see a unified risk model for the international arena in the coming decade, we will see an increased understanding of the quantitative features and attributes of international markets.

Passive Management

Without question, we must anticipate growing and broadening activity in the passive arena. Passive indexes have beaten the median equity manager in seven of the ten years 1977–86, while passive bond indexes have outpaced the median bond manager in eight of those years. This relative performance is not surprising, for any active manager can add

[4]Robert D. Arnott and Peter L. Bernstein, "The Right Way to Manage Your Pension Fund," *Harvard Business Review,* January/February 1988.

[5]Martin L. Leibowitz, "Total Portfolio Duration: A New Perspective on Asset Allocation," *Financial Analysts Journal,* September/October 1986.

value only if another active manager underperforms. Nevertheless, it is a compelling case for passive management for any organizations that do not believe they have the "Midas touch" in choosing active managers.

The applications of passive management will also be broadened to cover convertibles, international stocks, international bonds, and other asset classes, particularly as new indexes are developed for these assets. A passive bond fund need not be matched to a bond index; it can be matched to the shape of the pension liability stream. A passive equity fund need not be matched to the S&P 500, but may be matched to a broader index, to an index targeted to offset the risks of the sponsor organization, or to an index targeted to complement the active managers employed by a sponsor. Passive strategies can be deliberately tilted in the direction of intended factor exposures, which offers intriguing opportunities. We may well see corresponding strategies emerge on the fixed-income side and even in the management of global and non-traditional assets.

WHAT ABOUT ACTIVE MANAGEMENT?

This description of a changing world leads us to ask, once again, "Is active management dead?" In the past decade, we have moved from a world in which institutional investors were a major part of the market to an environment in which institutional investors essentially *are* the market.

If active managers on average cannot beat the market, what hope is there for any investor to outperform? Money managers are the market; the market cannot beat itself; therefore money managers, in aggregate, cannot beat the market. The fallacy in this argument is simple. It proves only that the money management community *as a whole* cannot beat the market. One cannot interpret this as evidence that the markets are efficient, or that manager selection is a futile exercise. Indeed, there is compelling evidence to the contrary.

Pension consultants, such as SEI and Frank Russell, have occasionally published material demonstrating that the manager who succeeds in one year has essentially a fifty-fifty chance of succeeding in the subsequent year. Roughly one out of four investment managers are above average two years in a row, and roughly one out of eight are above average three years in a row.

Does this prove that manager selection does not matter? On the surface it would appear so, but this analysis once again masks a subtle yet important reality: More managers exhibit significantly above average or significantly below average results than chance alone would predict.

Exhibit 7 shows the year-by-year dispersion of investment results achieved by equity managers from 1976 to 1985. If relative results were a random process, then the spread between the best-performing managers and the worst-performing managers should converge gradually as we examine more and more years of performance. As Exhibit 7 demonstrates, this convergence does occur, but not nearly as much as probability theory would suggest. The pattern observed in long-term performance is not consistent with the idea that manager skill is random. Rather, the pattern of relative performance is more consistent, with half of all managers adding 1.5% annually because of superior skill, and the other half losing 1.5% annually because of inferior skill.

Exhibits 8 and 9 show a similar evaluation of SEI results for the consistency of manager success during the years 1981–85. If it were impossible to exhibit skill in money management, then one out of thirty-two managers would outpace the median in all five years, and a like number would have lagged in all five years. A survivor bias in the data weeds out many in this latter category, but the five-time winners occur roughly four times as often as they should if skill played no role. Indeed, the results are more consistent with a world in which half of all managers are "winners" (with a 65% chance of above average results), and half are "losers" (with a 65% chance of below average results). These results are far more powerful than most active investment managers would expect.

In short, there *are* investors with an ability to add value *vis-a-vis* the markets. As relative performance is, by definition, a zero-sum game, the corollary must also hold true: There are managers with "negative skill," or a tendency to lag the markets.

What we cannot know in advance is which managers have skill and which do not. Statistical tools are too weak to isolate the successful investor before many years have passed. This results in one of the key ironies in pension plan management: The sponsors who have the sophistication, analytic systems, and staffing to carry out manager selection with some likelihood of finding these superior managers are precisely the sponsors who have the greatest interest in passive management. They fully recognize how difficult it is to select superior

EXHIBIT 7:
ARE SOME INVESTORS "SKILLFUL"? AN EVALUATION OF EQUITY MANAGER QUARTILES

SEI 1-Yr. Results	1985	1984	1983	1982	1981	1980	1979	1978	1977	1976
25th Percentile	33.3%	6.2%	24.1%	25.8%	3.1%	37.2%	24.7%	10.1%	(3.7)%	20.8%
75th Percentile	27.3	(1.9)	16.0	17.6	(6.6)	24.3	16.2	4.6	(8.5)	13.7
Range[a]	6.0	8.1	8.1	8.2	9.7	12.9	8.5	5.5	4.8	7.1

Cumulative Results Since		1984	1983	1982	1981	1980	1979	1978	1977	1976
25th Percentile		18.1%	19.9%	20.8%	17.0%	19.4%	20.1%	18.8%	16.7%	17.3%
75th Percentile		11.9	14.7	16.9	12.6	15.9	16.1	15.1	12.6	13.5
Range[a]		6.2	5.5	3.9	4.4	3.5	4.0	3.7	4.1	3.8
Theoretical Range—Random Results[b]		5.0%	4.3%	3.8%	3.6%	3.7%	3.4%	3.1%	2.8%	2.6%
Theoretical Range—Skill Exists[c]		5.5	5.0	4.6	4.5	4.6	4.4	4.1	4.0	3.8

[a]Spread between 25th and 75th percentile managers.
[b]Assumes that no "skill" exists: All managers have results which are median plus some random "value-added" (with a standard deviation of 1.5 times the range in each calendar year).
[c]Assumes that "skill" exists: Half of all managers are "winners," with results which are normally 1.5% above the median; half are "losers," with results which are normally 1.5% below the median; all managers still exhibit some random variability in "value-added."

EXHIBIT 8:
IS THERE SKILL IN INVESTMENT MANAGEMENT?

	Percent of Managers	
	Actual	Theoretical
Balanced 5 Years Top Quartile	1.3%	0.1%
Balanced 5 Years Above Median	8.5	3.1
Balanced 5 Years Below Median	2.0	3.1
Equity 5 Years Top Quartile	1.7	0.1
Equity 5 Years Above Median	11.5	3.1
Equity 5 Years Below Median	2.1	3.1

EXHIBIT 9:
IS THERE SKILL IN INVESTMENT MANAGEMENT?

	Percent of Managers Beating Median:		
	0/5 or 5/5 Year	1/5 or 4/5 Years	2/5 or 3/5 Years
SEI Equity Funds	13.6%	35.0%	51.4%
SEI Balanced Funds	10.5	31.6	57.9
Theoretical:			
Random 50/50	6.2	31.3	62.5
3 Yr. Survivor Bias	4.2	25.0	70.8
Skill 65/35	8.8	33.6	57.5

managers. The sponsors who lack the operational wherewithal to effectively select superior managers have a strong bias against passive management, and they are the most committed to employing active managers.

SUMMARY AND CONCLUSION

The investment world is evolving rapidly. The pace of change is reflected in the role of the owners of assets (especially the corporate sponsor), in the role of the investment manager, in the nature of investment markets, and in the character of investment products. Today, ideas become operational products in a fraction of the time that the process took twenty years ago. For organizations positioned to take advantage of few opportunities, the world offers prospects for great success.

Much of this change has been in the area of quantitative disciplines and techniques. While major opportunities exist in the quantitative arena, in the passive arena, and in the use of derivative securities, other pockets of opportunity can readily be identified in active management, and even in the more conventional asset management techniques. These merit further exploration.

Perhaps the most telling conclusion is that this proliferation of techniques, products, and asset classes confronts the asset owner with a myriad of choices. Perhaps the greatest challenge for the money manager is to define and develop tools that can help the sponsor to control and to reshape the attributes of the pension plan. Here lie the greatest need and the greatest opportunity.

CHAPTER 3

Active Asset Allocation

ROBERT D. ARNOTT
PRESIDENT &
CHIEF INVESTMENT OFFICER
FIRST QUADRANT CORP.

ROGER G. CLARKE, PH.D.
MANAGING DIRECTOR &
CHIEF INVESTMENT OFFICER
TSA CAPITAL MANAGEMENT, INC

THE SEMANTICS OF ASSET ALLOCATION

Active asset allocation is a subject which has attracted enormous interest in recent years. But asset allocation means different things to different people. Before we can begin to review asset allocation issues, it is important to open with a discussion of semantics. No single name for any of these concepts is "right" or "wrong," but, because of the confusion surrounding asset allocation issues, we must define our use of these terms before we begin. As shown in Exhibit 1, this discussion must center on three distinct classes of asset allocation.

33

EXHIBIT 1:
ASSET ALLOCATION OBJECTIVE

Long-Term Asset Allocation
- Establish policy mix consistent with long-term portfolio objectives

Tactical Asset Allocation
- Add value; opportunistically respond to changing patterns of reward
- Buy low, sell high

Portfolio Insurance
- Protect against unacceptable performance
- Sell low, buy high

Long-term asset allocation or *policy asset allocation* is the evaluation of the needs of a pension plan or endowment and the assessment of the appropriate asset mix required to meet those needs. Long-term asset allocation is not an active strategy. Rather, it is the identification of the normal policy asset mix policy which will represent the best compromise between a need for stability and a need for performance. This is sometimes called *strategic asset allocation*.

Active asset allocation encompases a number of strategies. *Tactical asset allocation* refers to an active management process in which the investor seeks to opportunistically respond to the changing patterns of the capital markets. The objective of tactical asset allocation is to make money by shifting the asset mix in response to changing opportunities. This is also sometimes called either *strategic asset allocation* or *dynamic asset allocation*.

Portfolio insurance is also an active asset allocation strategy. The intent in portfolio insurance is not to make money by responding to opportunities in the marketplace. Rather, the objective of portfolio insurance is to protect against adverse consequences. The synthetic put is the best know example of a portfolio insurance process. This is also sometimes known as *dynamic asset allocation*. The reason for this discussion of semantics is clear. The same words are often used for two or more concepts.

The intent of long-term or policy asset allocation is to shape the normal risk profile of a portfolio to meet the long-term needs of a plan.

This involves careful balancing of the need for return versus the aversion to risk.

The objective in tactical asset allocation is performance. The intent is to shift the asset mix to respond to the changing patterns of opportunity which are available in the markets. Tactical asset allocation is an inherently "buy low, sell high" process.

Practitioners of portfolio insurance don't like to think of it this way, but protection strategies are an inherently "sell low, buy high" strategies, at the margin. Portfolio insurance is really designed for the primary purpose of protecting against unacceptable adverse consequences, or to reshape the distribution of likely returns. This chapter will focus primarily on the issues which affect the management of tactical asset allocation.

ATTRIBUTES OF TACTICAL ASSET ALLOCATION

As Exhibit 2 suggests, tactical asset allocation has several key attributes. In one sense tactical asset allocation is comparable to sector rotation, except that instead of rotating among the economic sectors of the equity market we are rotating among the sectors of the capital markets, or asset classes. It is based on a strategy which objectively measures the likely relative returns of the major liquid asset classes, typically stocks, bonds and cash. Some organizations use fewer asset classes, while others use more. Nonetheless, the strategy involves a disciplined, quantitative structure for measuring available returns. Tactical asset allocation is designed to exploit shifts in the relative attractiveness among these asset classes.

Most important, tactical asset allocation is a strategy which provides the discipline to take a contrarian position. In each of the tactical asset allocation strategies currently employed by various practitioners, the

EXHIBIT 2:
TACTICAL ASSET ALLOCATION

- Analogous to sector rotation.
- Objectively measure available returns.
- Change asset mix in response to changing opportunities.
- Key attribute: inherently contrarian.

tendency will be to buy the out-of-favor asset class. In late 1974, the returns available in the equity markets were most impressive *vis-á-vis* bond or cash returns. There was a reason for this—equities were severely out of favor. It takes a great deal of courage to buy stocks in that environment. A tactical asset allocation discipline can give an investor the confidence to take that contrarian stance.

THE CHALLENGE OF SYSTEMATIC MANAGEMENT OF ASSET ALLOCATION

How do most organizations handle asset allocation? As noted in Exhibit 3, the long-term asset allocation is typically established based on a careful analysis. The tradeoffs between uncertainty and performance are carefully weighed in light of the long-term needs of the pension plan. Short-term adjustments are typically handled through cash flows with little or no formal analysis. Indeed, short-term adjustments are often handled in a way which is far from contrarian. Many organizations were slashing equity exposure in late 1974 and slashing fixed income exposure in mid 1981. The most important attribute of tactical asset allocation is that it can provide a disciplined framework to prevent such errors. The advent of futures represents an interesting opportunity. They facilitate these short-term adjustments with very low transaction costs.

In looking at tactical asset allocation, perhaps the first question to be addressed is whether or not it is possible to add value by shifting the asset mix. One way to look at this question is to consider the flows between the markets. If Digital Equipment becomes severely undervalued relative to IBM, money can and will flow readily from IBM into

EXHIBIT 3:
HOW IS ASSET ALLOCATION HANDLED?

- Most organizations base long-term asset allocation decision on a careful evaluation of the needs of the plan.
- Active asset allocation handled through cash flows; may be ad hoc.

—but—

- Is successful active asset allocation possible?
- How can it be effected?

Digital Equipment to exploit the opportunity. This pattern of capital flows helps to keep securities from straying very far from fair value. Intriguingly, we observe far less fluid capital flows between asset classes. If yields soar, stock market portfolio managers typically do not rush to buy bonds. That is "not their job." If cash yields rise sharply, as occurred in mid-1983, bond and stock managers typically do not rush to sell their holdings in order to capture those cash yields. In short, while there are some flows between asset classes, they tend to happen gradually and in relatively modest size. If capital flows do not occur, then markets can stray far from fair value. This is the fundamental reason that asset allocation may represent the single greatest opportunity to enhance performance available in the capital markets today.

THE NATURE OF THE ASSET ALLOCATION DISCIPLINE

The second key question to be addressed is how an asset allocation process might be implemented. A disciplined structure for asset allocation is generally predicated on three key assumptions, summarized in Exhibit 4. First, the capital markets indicate what rates of return are available in the various asset classes. We *know* the yield on cash. We *know* the yield to maturity on long bonds, and we know the price/earnings ratio on the stock market, which can give us some indication of the long-term rewards available in stocks. The second key assumption is that there is a normal relationship among these implied returns. The third and most critical assumption is that the capital markets correct disequilibrium conditions when they occur. As equity returns stray from their normal relationship *vis-á-vis* fixed income returns, the forces of the capital markets will pull them back into line towards normalcy.

This normal relationship is illustrated in Exhibit 5. In April of 1981, the return available in the equity markets stood 2% below the normal

EXHIBIT 4:
TACTICAL ASSET ALLOCATION—KEY ASSUMPTIONS

- The markets tell us what rewards are available.
- There are normal, equilibrium relationships in these rewards.
- When rewards offered by the asset classes stray from normal, market forces will pull them back into line.

EXHIBIT 5:
THE EQUITY RISK PREMIUM AND STOCK MARKET RETURNS,
APRIL 1981 TO DECEMBER 1982

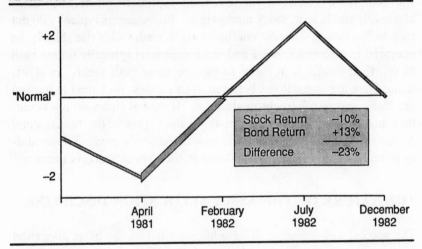

Stock Return	−10%
Bond Return	+13%
Difference	−23%

relationship *vis-á-vis* fixed income. This represented an opportunity because the capital markets had strayed from equilibrium. It took nine months for the capital markets to correct this disequilibrium. This disequilibrium was corrected through a 23% differential in returns between stocks and bonds. The bond market rose 13%, the stock market fell 10%.

A few months later, equity returns stood nearly 2% above the normal relationship *vis-á-vis* bonds, as illustrated in Exhibit 6. It took five months for the capital markets to correct this disequilibrium. It was corrected through a 16-percentage-point difference between stock returns and bond returns. Stock returns outpaced bonds because of this unusual return opportunity presented by the capital markets.

All tactical asset allocation processes function essentially in this fashion. There are subtle differences which make some tactical asset allocation processes more effective than others. For example, there are differences which lead to biases towards one asset class or another over an extended period of time. Also, there are subtle differences which lead some asset allocation processes to time market tops and bottoms rather poorly. The best asset allocation strategies combine several key decisions, noted in Exhibit 7. Such strategies begin with a systematic evaluation of these kinds of market opportunities. The measurement of

EXHIBIT 6:
THE EQUITY RISK PREMIUM AND STOCK MARKET RETURNS,
APRIL 1981 TO DECEMBER 1982

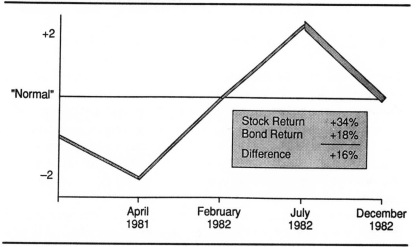

Stock Return	+34%	
Bond Return	+18%	
Difference	+16%	

EXHIBIT 7:
TACTICAL ASSET ALLOCATION PROCESSES

The best tactical asset allocation processes combine:

- A measurement of disequilibrium conditions— where do the opportunities lie?
- An evaluation of economic implications— can the markets sustain a return to equilibrium?
- Considerations of patterns of sentiment— is the opportunity now or later?

how far the markets have strayed from equilibrium relationships must lie at the foundation of any successful asset allocation approach. However, it is important to recognize that opportunities lie not only in markets which have strayed from equilibrum, but also in economic conditions which can sustain a *return to* equilibrium. It is this tendency to return to equilibrium that is the profit mechanism of any asset allocation strategy. It can also be useful to assess the sentiment at work in the marketplace. Will the markets move *now* or *later*?

Nonetheless, most tactical asset allocation products share this fundamental process. In so doing, most tactical asset allocation processes share a highly disciplined structure and an inherently contrarian nature. Finally, most tactical asset allocation processes share in the fact that they have enhanced performance by a startling margin.

TACTICAL ASSET ALLOCATION: WHY BOTHER?

The next question confronting us is whether it even makes sense to contemplate active shifts in asset mix. But consider the alternative: should we make no active shifts in mix in response to changing market opportunities? Is it preferable to permit the shifting of asset mix to be driven by the wandering movements of the market or by a systematic structure designed to exploit opportuniites? Exhibit 8 demonstrates the rationale for a systematic approach to managing the asset allocation decision.

Suppose that a portfolio can return 10% per annum over the next decade. What happens with a simple rebalancing mechanism? In other words, what happens if the normal asset allocation for the pension plan is simply rebalanced back to that norm every month? When stocks go down we buy more stocks to boost the stock market exposure back to its normal level. When bonds go up, we cut bond exposure back to its normal level. History suggests that this simple passive strategy would historically have added approximately 30 basis points per annum. Though this doesn't seem like much in the short run, it can result in a substantial dollar gain over time. For example, boosting the performance from 10% per annum to 10.3% per annum would boost the value of a $100 million pension plan at the end of a decade by some $8 million. Let's further suppose that by introducing a 20% active asset allocation range, just 1% more could be added to the annual return. This translates into an additional $25 million at the end of a decade.

EXHIBIT 8:
TACTICAL ASSET ALLOCATION—ALTERNATIVES

- No active shifts; drifting mix
  $100M becomes $259M in 10 years at 10%.
- "Passive" rebalancing; constant mix
  $100M becomes $267M in 10 Years at 10.3%
- Tactical asset allocation
  $100M becomes $292M in 10 years at 11.3%.

Results obviously depend on the size of the asset base and length of the horizon. Even so, simple asset allocation changes can result in substantial benefits over time.

Enough about the concepts. How about implementation? First and foremost, it should be noted that implementation *must* be as disciplined as the investment decision process itself. Without a disciplined implementation process, one should not even consider managing asset allocation decisions.

THE "PORTFOLIO UPGRADE" PHENOMENON

With a disciplined implementation process, asset allocation can be affected either with or without the use of futures. Implementation of asset allocation is significantly improved if futures are used. The transactions incurred by both tactical asset allocation and portfolio insurance are considerable. Any avenue for cutting transaction costs is important. Nonetheless, implementation without futures is not without merit. If stock or bond holdings are actively managed, not indexed, implementation without futures forces the continual upgrading of the holdings within each asset class.

Let's go through an example. As Exhibit 9A shows, the typical portfolio is made up of holdings which might be categorized by an investor as buy candidates or hold candidates. The hold candidates are issues which are not attractive enough to be buy candidates, but not unattractive enough to justify the transaction costs which would be incurred in selling the stock. Thus, the typical portfolio consists of holdings which are deemed to be quite attractive and holdings which are deemed to be only mildly attractive. Active asset allocation forces the improvement of the portfolios within the asset classes. Why is this so? If the asset allocation decision prompts a shift *into* stocks, the investor most assuredly will not add stocks that are deemed only marginally attractive. The investor will buy stocks which are deemed to be quite attractive, namely the buy candidates. If an asset allocation decision prompts a sale of stocks, the stocks sold will most assuredly not be the buy candidates, as shown in Exhibit 9B. They will come from the marginally attractive sector of the portfolio, or the hold candidates. In so doing, the remaining stocks in either case will generally be the buy candidates.

EXHIBIT 9A:
ASSET ALLOCATION IMPLEMENTATION PORTFOLIO UPGRADE
PHENOMENON

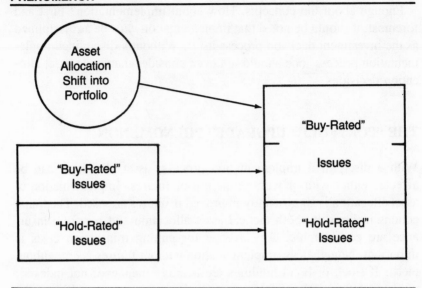

EXHIBIT 9B:
ASSET ALLOCATION IMPLEMENTATION PORTFOLIO UPGRADE
PHENOMENON

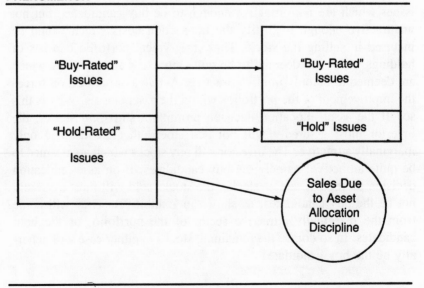

As a result, the equity holdings will be subject to a continual process of upgrading and will contain more issues from the most attractive portions of the market than equities held in an account which is not subject to asset allocation. The same holds true for the bond holdings or for the holdings of any other asset class subject to asset allocation.

Clearly, this does not assure that the stocks in an asset allocation portfolio will outpace the stocks in a portfolio which does not engage in asset allocation. It only implies that the *merits or demerits* of the stock and bond selection disciplines will be magnified by the asset allocation process. The stocks and bonds held in an asset allocation portfolio will be dominated by issues which are judged by the investor to be more attractive.

THE ROLE OF FUTURES

Transaction costs represent the principal disadvantage of active asset allocation without the use of futures. Transaction costs have been estimated to be at any of a number of levels. Let's suppose that transaction costs are 200 basis points for equities and half that for bonds. Both a tactical asset allocation and a portfolio insurance strategy will likely force turnover amounting to perhaps 100% per annum. This means that an asset allocation discipline must add 150 basis points per annum or it is not worth employing. Most tactical asset allocation disciplines do indeed offer rewards several times that. Therefore, tactical asset allocation does not *require* the use of futures. It can be implemented effectively and very profitably without resorting to the use of futures. Portfolio insurance, on the other hand, is not really designed to add value. So a 150 basis point per annum transactions cost, on top of the considerable cost implicit in the nature of portfolio insurance, is a serious penalty for implementation of portfolio insurance.

What about implementation through futures? As Exhibit 10 suggests, the merits of futures in asset allocation trading are considerable. The commissions on a futures trade are trivial. $20 round-trip commission for purchase and subsequent sale of $100,000 worth of stock market exposure is fairly typical. This amounts to 2 basis points for a round-trip transaction. The market impact can also be trivial, since buying or selling $100 million worth of exposure in the stock market or bond market will represent 1-2% of an average days' volume of the futures exchanges. Thus, transaction costs are slashed to very low

EXHIBIT 10:
ASSET ALLOCATION IMPLEMENTATION— ADVANTAGES OF FUTURES

- Transaction costs minimized.
- Excellent liquidity; rapid execution.
- One day settlement; simultaneous trades.
- Does not disrupt management of underlying assets.
- Stabilizes portfolio income stream.
- Potential for favorable mispricing.

levels. Instead of an asset allocation discipline having to add 150 basis points, it need only add 10 to 20 basis points to cover the transaction costs.

Second, these markets are very deep and liquid. Stock index futures now trade some $5-10 billion each day. Bond futures are the most liquid single market in the world, routinely trading over $25 billion daily. As such, an investor can execute a $100 million asset allocation shift in minutes with relative ease.

For example, Exhibit 11 illustrates the growth in equity index futures in recent years relative to the dollar volume of equities traded on the New York Stock Exchange. Stock index futures were first introduced in 1982. By 1983, the average daily dollar volume traded in equity index futures surpassed that traded on the NYSE itself. Now the stock index futures trade as much as twice the volume of the stocks on the NYSE.

Third, futures permit simultaneous trades. If investors want to sell $100 million worth of bond exposure and buy $100 million worth of stock market exposure without using futures, they can eliminate the bond exposure in minutes, since the Treasury markets are highly liquid. However, on the equity side, they will have to carefully craft a buy program consistent with their investment management disciplines, and have their trading desk and brokers work the order carefully— all of which can take days.

This is mitigated to some extent if the trades are managed through index funds, where a program trade can be effected quickly. But even with index funds the manager can still run into a thorny problem with the differences in settlement times. The stocks settle in five days while Treasury bonds settle in a day. This would mean that there would be $100 million completely uninvested for four days in order to synchronize settlement dates. Investors can make a $100 million shift in their

EXHIBIT 11:
NEW YORK STOCK EXCHANGE VS. FUTURES DOLLAR VOLUME (DAILY AVERAGE: JANUARY 1982–APRIL 1987)

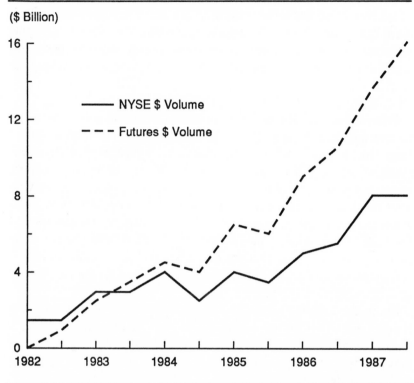

asset mix in minutes using futures, without any concern for settlement or other operational difficulties.

Fourth, a shift in mix implemented by futures is not disruptive to the management of the underlying assets. If investors want to sell $100 million stocks and buy $100 million in bonds, they have to carefully design a sell program which will not alter the characteristics of the equity portfolio in unintended ways. This step alone can take days. They then have to execute the trade, carefully working the order in conformity of available liquidity. Then they have to do the same thing on the bond side. The whole process could take many days. With futures, the underlying stock and bond portfolios are not disrupted. *Indeed, the futures strategy can be overlayed on top of another manager without the other manager even being aware of the trades.*

This separation of the futures positions from the asset managers has another advantage. If the active asset managers are outperforming the index, the use of futures permits the investor to fully capture the value added by management *within* the asset classes. The futures only reflect the index return, while the assets are earning the index return plus something extra. Thus, any excess returns stay with the portfolio, regardless of shifts in mix effected through futures. However, the reverse is also true: any *underperformance* within the asset classes, relative to the index, also stay with the portfolio.

Fifth, for organizations where income is a consideration, the use of futures does not disrupt the income stream. If the portfolio is shifted from stocks into bonds, the income rises, which is nice. If a few months later it is shifted back to stocks, the income drops, which might be an unpleasant dose of reality. With the use of futures, the underlying asset mix need not change, and the income stream generated by those assets need not change, either. However, the value of the futures will fluctuate as the markets move, resulting in gains and losses on the futures position. These changes might be considered more as capital gains then as income; when accounted for in this way, the income can remain stable even though the asset mix is shifting.

Sixth, the futures may be favorably mispriced. If a futures trading strategy uses the futures mispricing as part of the decision rule, a strategy can be designed which benefits from any ongoing pattern of futures mispricing. Futures some times do stray from the fair value *vis-á-vis* the underlying assets.

Let's look a little closer at the issue of futures mispricing, which is often called the *basis risk*. Our research suggests that many times the future are favorably mispriced when tactical asset allocation shifts are made. Thus far, they have *never* been mispriced to an extent which would justify the transaction costs of making an asset allocation shift via the stock and bond markets. In short, the mispricing has been highly advantageous for most conventional tactical asset allocation processes.

Most tactical asset allocation disciplines are inherently contrarian. It is often a buy low, sell high discipline. When equities sag, equity exposure is boosted sharply. This usually happens at a time when, due to the drop in the stock market, there is a good deal of pessimism and the futures are underpriced *vis-á-vis* fair value. Equity exposure is often cut after significant market rallies. This is typically a period of euphoria in which the futures are overpriced *vis-á-vis* fair value. In short, asset allocation disciplines, because they are contrarian, reap considerable benefit from futures mispricing.

THE MECHANICS OF IMPLEMENTATION THROUGH FUTURES

To illustrate the asset allocation decision consider the following two examples. In the first example shown in Exhibit 12, we accomplish asset allocation by using the underlying assets. In this case, we start with the portfolio of $50 million of equity and $50 million of bonds. If we want to shift the asset alloction mix from 50% equity and 50%bonds to 60% equity and 40% bonds, we would sell $10 million worth of

EXHIBIT 12:
ASSET ALLOCATION SHIFT USING UNDERLYING ASSETS

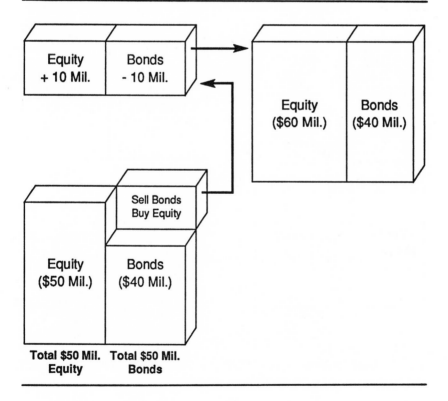

bonds and buy $10 million worth of equity exposure. The resulting portfolio would be shifted to $60 million worth of equity and $40 million worth of bonds.

Now, consider the asset allocation shift using futures. First, the use of futures requires a liquidity reserve in order to fund the margin requirements for the futures positions. In the second example in Exhibit 13 we begin with a portfolio totaling $100 million composed of $45 million worth of equity and $45 million worth of bonds, and $10 million in cash equivalents. The cash reserve is used as collateral for the futures positions. In order to accomplish the asset allocation shift it is required that we buy $15 million worth of equity exposure and sell $5 million worth of bond exposure. With these futures transactions equity exposure in the portfolio would total $60 million. This is achieved by

EXHIBIT 13:
ASSET ALLOCATIONS SHIFT USING FUTURES

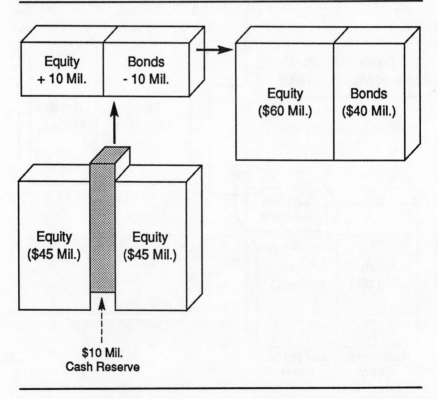

having $45 million of equity exposure in the underlying stocks and $15 million of equity exposure through the futures market. The bond exposure in the portfolio would be reduced to $40 million from the initial $45 million by the short position in $5 million worth of bond futures. As a result of the futures transactions, the total portfolio exposure has been changed to 60% equities and 40% bonds, while leaving the underlying assets in place.

THE PITFALLS OF FUTURES

Though having important advantages, the use of futures for asset allocation does have some disadvantages. In the first place, even though the use of futures often allows for favorable mispricing, there is the potential for unfavorable mispricing. These periods of unfavorable mispricing will increase the cost of the asset allocation move using futures relative to making the shift using the underlying assets. However, the mispricing would have to be quite severe before it would actually be more advantageous to trade the underlying securities. With current arbitrage activity it is unlikely that such levels would occur very often, if at all.

A second disadvantage of using futures for asset allocation comes about because of the back office work which is required on a daily basis to mark to market the futures positions. Any gains or losses in the futures contracts are required to be settled daily, requiring transfers of funds between the investor and the broker. This daily back office work requires constant attention and can be both costly and time consuming.

A third disadvantage of using futures is that a cash liquidity reserve is necessary to accommodate the margin requirements and daily settlement of the futures positions. Funding this liquidity reserve often forces the investor to liquidate some assets currently invested in stocks and bonds. Though the underlying reserve is invested in cash equivalents, a full investment exposure can be achieved by buying equity index or bond futures to overlay the cash position. This replaces the active asset returns which might be had from investing in actual stocks and bonds with index-like performance tied to the futures contracts. To the extent that active asset management can add value relative to the index, this differential return is sacrificed because of the necessity to fund the liquidity reserve and achieve full exposure indirectly using a futures overlay.

THE FUTURE FOR TACTICAL ASSET ALLOCATION

In closing, we might observe that the capital markets are exhibiting a pattern of "telescoping." The time horizon between the development of an effective concept, the translation of that concept into effective, differentiated product, and the popularization of that product is growing ever shorter. Even so, active asset allocation strategies appear to offer an intriguing opportunity. In the past five years active allocation disciplines have moved from essentially no assets, to approximately $25-30 billion in assets in the United States. This amounts to just over 1% of total institutional assets.

As long as these disciplines are employed to manage a relatively small pool of assets, and as long as *most* asset allocation decisions continue to be made on a somewhat *ad hoc* basis, this kind of process should continue to offer significant and relatively consistent opportunities for value-added. History suggests that this kind of discipline can add 600 basis points per annum. Even if the coming decade only provides half as great an opportunity, the cumulative impact of that kind of return enhancement is staggering. Indeed, it would be fair to say that an asset allocation discipline is far more important than either effective manager selection or security selection for the long-term performance of a pool of assets.

CHAPTER 4

Active Equity Management

T. Daniel Coggin, Ph.D.
Vice President
Capital Management Group
First Union National Bank

Active equity management begins with the notion, explicitly stated or implied, that the stock market is not totally "efficient." Put another way, active equity management assumes that all historical and current information is not "fully and correctly" reflected in the current price of every stock.[1] Hence, there exist stocks which are "under-valued," "fairly-valued," and "over-valued." The task of the active equity manager is, therefore, to decide which stocks are which and invest accordingly. This chapter presents an outline of the process and begins with a brief discussion of the primary active investment styles.

ACTIVE EQUITY INVESTMENT STYLES

The primary styles of active equity management are "top-down" and "bottom-up." Even though there are few pure examples of these two

---

[1] Some active managers would argue that the stock market is "short-term efficient" with respect to the near-term prospects for a company, and "long-term inefficient" with respect to a company's longer-term trends and prospects. This is a highly debatable issue which will not be pursued here.

styles, they serve as a useful point of reference. The top-down manager begins with an assessment of the overall economic environment and a forecast of its near-term outlook. Given this forecast, he determines the relative attractiveness of the various financial markets (e.g., stocks, bonds, real estate, and cash equivalents) and makes an *asset allocation* decision. The process of making this decision is described in detail in Chapter 3. Once the top-down manager has decided how much of his portfolio is to be allocated to equities, he then analyzes the stock market in an attempt to identify economic sectors and industries that stand to gain or lose from his economic forecast. After identifying attractive and unattractive sectors and industries, the top-down manager finally selects a portfolio of individual stocks. Exhibit 1 presents this process as a diagram. Subgroups of this management category include "market timers" and "group rotators."

The bottom-up manager de-emphasizes the significance of economic and market cycles and focuses on the analysis of individual stocks. Using financial analysts and/or computer screening techniques, the bottom-up manager seeks out stocks that have certain characteristics

EXHIBIT 1:
THE TOP-DOWN INVESTMENT PROCESS

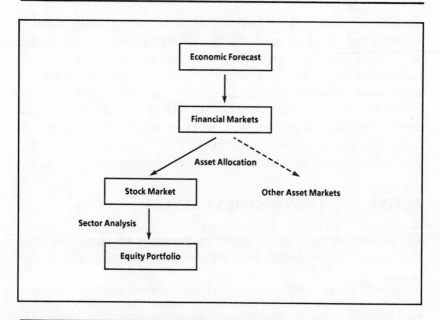

that are deemed attractive (e.g., low Price/Earnings ratio, small capitalization, low analyst coverage). A variety of management styles can be subsumed under the general bottom-up management category. Notable active equity managers who fit this basic style include Dean Le-Baron (Batterymarch Financial Management), Peter Lynch (Fidelity Magellan Fund), and Warren Buffett (Berkshire Hathaway, Inc.). Having defined the two major styles of active equity management, we will discuss some of the major sub-categories in the next section.

SUB-CATEGORIES OF ACTIVE EQUITY MANAGEMENT

Value Managers

The value manager seeks to buy stocks that are at a discount to their "fair value" and sell them at or in excess of that value. Value managers can fall into either the top-down or the bottom-up category. Value managers use dividend discount models, Tobin's q (the ratio of a firm's market value to the replacement cost of its assets), P/E ratios, "earnings surprise," and other similarly motivated constructs. Value managers are sometimes called "contrarians" because they see "value" where many other market participants apparently do not. In terms of portfolio characteristics, value managers have relatively lower betas and P/E ratios, and higher dividend yields.

Growth Managers

The growth manager seeks to buy stocks that are typically selling at relatively high P/E ratios due to high earnings growth, with an expectation of *continued* high (or higher) earnings growth. Growth managers can be classified as either top-down or bottom-up. Growth managers are often divided into large capitalization and small capitalization subgroups. The portfolios of growth managers are characterized by relatively higher betas, P/E ratios, returns on equity and growth rates, and lower dividend yields.

Group Rotation Managers

The group rotation manager is in a subcategory of the top-down management style. While there are few pure group rotation managers, many investment firms use this technique to a degree. The basic idea behind group rotation is that the economy goes through reasonably well-defined phases of the business cycle. Some generic names for these (sequential) phases are: recession, recovery, expansion, and credit-crunch. The group rotator belives he can discern the current phase of the economy and forecast into which phase it will evolve. He can then select those economic sectors and industries that are about to benefit. For example, if the economy were perceived to be about to move from recession to recovery, the group rotator would begin to purchase stocks in the appropriate sectors (e.g., credit cyclicals, consumer cyclicals, technology, and transportation) and specific industries (e.g., building materials, savings and loans, autos, electronics, and trucking) that are sensitive to a pickup in the economy. Thus the portfolio of the group rotation manager is characterized by concentrations in a small number of "economically timely" industries.

Technicians

Perhaps the boldest assault on the notion of an efficient market comes from the technicians. Technicians (sometimes called technical analysts or chartists) discern market cycles and pick stocks solely on the basis of historical price movements as they relate to projected price movements. In the words of Edwards and Magee from their classic text:

> *Technical analysis* is the science of recording, usually in graphic form, the actual history of trading (price changes, volume transactions, etc.) in a certain stock or in "the averages" and then deducing from that pictured history the probable future trend.[2]

Exhibit 2 presents some examples of classic "point-and-figure" charts which form the basis of the "science" of technical analysis. By reading a chart of the price action of a stock (or a group of stocks) and artfully discerning patterns such as those in Exhibit 2, the technician hopes to be able to predict the future path of that price action.

Even though numerous academic studies have shown technical anal-

---

[2]Robert D. Edwards and John Magee, *Technical Analysis of Stock Trends*, 5th ed. (Boston, Mass.: John Magee, Inc., 1966), 5.

EXHIBIT 2:
MAJOR POINT-AND-FIGURE CHART PATTERNS

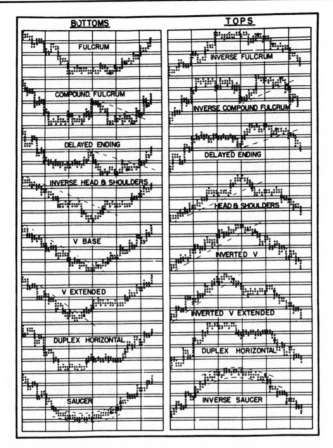

Source: Investment Research Library, First Union National Bank, Charlotte, N.C.

ysis to be of little or no value in predicting common stock returns,[3] it still survives as a technique that deserves mention in any survey of contemporary active equity management styles. There are still some pure technical analysts around, and many investment management firms have a "token" technician on staff.

[3]See Edwin J. Elton and Martin J. Gruber, *Modern Portfolio Theory and Investment Analysis,* 3rd ed. (New York, N.Y.: John Wiley, 1987), Chapter 15, for a summary of these studies.

Market Timers

The market timer is typically in a subcategory of the top-down investment style and comes in many varieties. However, the basic notion of the market timer is that he can forecast when the stock market will go up (or continue to go up) and when it will go down (or continue to go down). In this sense, the market timer is a not-too-distant relative of the technical analyst. The portfolio of the market timer is not always fully invested in common stocks. Rather, he moves in and out of the stock market as his economic, analytical, and technical work dictates. While academic studies of market-timing ability suggest that it rarely exists, many investment managers still feel compelled to attempt it in varying degrees. A successful example of combining modest market timing with the value approach is the Capital Management Group at First Union National Bank (Charlotte, N.C.). Market timing is viewed by some as an essential ingredient to the solution of the asset allocation problem discussed in Chapter 3.

Hedgers

The hedger seeks to buy common stocks, but also to place well defined limits on his investment risk. One popular hedging technique involves simultaneously purchasing a stock and a protective put option on that stock. The put option sets a floor on the amount of loss that can be sustained (if the stock price goes down), while the potential profit (if the stock price goes up) is diminished only by the original cost of the put. This is an example of a relatively simple "hedge." The types of hedges quickly get rather complicated and are beyond the scope of this chapter.

Having discussed some of the various styles of active management, we turn now to a discussion of some of the actual models of equity valuation used by active equity managers.

MODELS OF EQUITY VALUATION

The DDM[4]

The dividend discount model defines the current price of a stock as the discounted present value of its projected dividend stream. In theory, the

EXHIBIT 3:
THE GENERALIZED THREE-PHASE DDM

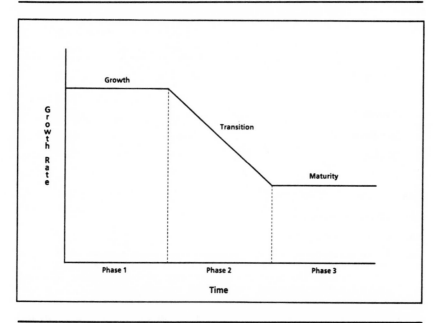

DDM is unbiased and thus rationally reflects the consensus of market participants for the value of a stock. However, proponents of the DDM argue that market "inefficiencies" such as superior information and market psychology *do* exist and can be translated by the DDM to reveal over- and underevaluation.

The version of the DDM most commonly used by practitioners is the *three-phase* DDM. This model assumes that all companies go through three phases, analogous to the concept of the "product life cycle." In the *growth* phase, a company experiences rapid earnings growth as it produces new products and expands market share. In the *transition* phase, the company's earnings begin to mature and decelerate to the rate of growth of the economy as a whole. At this point, the company is in the *maturity* phase, in which earnings continue to grow at the rate of the general economy. Exhibit 3 presents a graph of this relationship.

---

[4]For an expanded discussion of the DDM as a tool for active equity management, see the entire November/December 1985 issue of the *Financial Analysts Journal* and T. Daniel Coggin, "The Dividend Discount Model and the Stock Selection Process," in D. E. Logue, ed., *Handbook of Modern Finance, 1986 Update* (Boston, Mass.: Warren, Gorham & Lamont, 1986).

EXHIBIT 4:
ACTUAL TOTAL RETURNS BY DDM EXPECTED RETURN QUINTILE RANK, 1973–1986 (N=250 STOCKS)

	Actual Return	Annual Rate
Quintile 1	819.2%	17.2%
Quintile 2	584.5	14.7
Quintile 3	361.0	11.5
Quintile 4	194.9	8.0
Quintile 5	99.8	5.1
Total Sample (equal-weighted)	348.6	11.3
S&P 500 (equal-weighted)	586.8	14.8
S&P 500 (market-weighted)	287.6	10.2

Note: The quintile returns are equal-weighted and based on annual rebalancing. Quintile 1 contains the stocks with the highest expected returns from the DDM and Quintile 5 contains the stocks with the lowest expected returns.

Different companies are assumed to be at different phases in the three-phase model. An emerging growth company (e.g., Genentech) would have a longer growth phase than a more mature company (e.g., Proctor & Gamble). The inputs to the DDM are provided by professsional financial analysts who forecast company-level earnings, growth rates, and dividend payout rates.[5] An example of an application of the DDM in the equity valuation process is presented in Exhibit 4.

Exhibit 4 shows the results of a study of the use of the three-phase DDM, using a sample of 250 large to medium capitalization stocks over the fourteen-year period, 1973–1986. This DDM used the current price (P_0), a forecasted dividend stream (D_n), and solved for the expected return (k) in the equation:[6]

$$P_0 = D_1/(1+k) + D_2/(1+k)^2 + \ldots + D_n/(1+k)^n$$

---

[5]A description of the techniques of security analysis is beyond the scope of this chapter. For more on this topic, see Jerome B. Cohen, Edward D. Zinbarg, and Arthur Zeikel, *Investment Analysis and Portfolio Management*, 5th ed. (Homewood, Ill.: Richard D. Irwin, 1987), Part 4, *Security Analysis*.

[6]See Richard W. Taylor, "Make Life Easy: Bond Analysis and DDM on the PC," *The Journal of Portfolio Management* 12 (Fall 1985): 54–57, for a handy computer program for the PC that will solve for the expected return or the price in the three-phase DDM.

The entries in Exhibit 4 are actual total returns (assuming no transaction costs) that would have resulted from buying the stocks ranked by expected return once a year on January 1, holding them for the entire year, and rebalancing at the beginning of the next year. Each expected return quintile contained fifty stocks. The results presented in Exhibit 4 are striking and illustrate the potential utility of the DDM as a stock valuation tool. A number of current investment managers use the DDM (in varying degrees) as an input to the equity valuation decision.

The Benjamin Graham Low P/E Model

The legendary Benjamin Graham proposed a classic investment model in 1949 for the "defensive investor"—one without the time, expertise, or temperament for aggressive investment. The model was updated in each subsequent edition of his book, *The Intelligent Investor.*[7] Some of the basic investment criteria outlined in the 1973 edition are representative of the approach:

1. A company must have paid a dividend in each of the last 20 years.
2. Minimum size of a company is $100 million in annual sales for an industrial company and $50 million for a public utility.
3. Positive earnings must have been achieved in each of the last ten years.
4. Current price should not be more than one and one half times the latest book value.
5. Market price should not exceed fifteen times the average earnings for the past three years.

Graham considered the P/E ratio as a measure of the price paid for value received. He viewed high P/Es with skepticism and as representing a large premium for difficult-to-forecast future earnings growth. Hence, lower P/E, higher quality companies were viewed as having less potential for earnings disappointments and the resulting downward revision in price.

A study by Oppenheimer and Schlarbaum reveals that over the

---

[7]This model is fully described in Benjamin Graham, *The Intelligent Investor,* 4th rev. ed. (New York, N.Y.: Harper & Row, 1973), Chapter 14.

period 1956–1975 significant risk-adjusted excess returns were obtained by following Graham's strategy, even after allowing for transaction costs.[8] While originally intended for the defensive investor, a variation of Graham's low P/E approach is currently followed by a number of professional investment advisors.[9]

The Relative Strength Model

The notion of relative strength was made popular by the doctoral dissertation of Robert Levy written in 1966 and his article in the *Financial Analysts Journal* in 1967.[10] Relative strength models come in several varieties, but the basic idea is that stocks that have had better than average price action over the recent past will continue (for some time in the future) to have above average price action. These models generally calculate percent change in stock price over some recent period, rank-order the percentages from high to low, and purchase the stocks with the largest percent increases.

While not a pure version of the relative strength model, the well-known Value Line Timeliness ranking system includes a relative strength component in its calculation.[11] The record of the Value Line Timeliness rank is impressive. Assuming no transaction costs, the stocks ranked in the top group had a total return of 11,797% over the period 16 April 1965 to 30 December 1986 (allowing for changes in rank during the year) and a total return of 2,071% (if ranks are changed only once a year). A study by Copeland and Mayers documents the existence of significant abnormal performance (based on the market model) for Value Line predictions over the period 1965–1978, before transaction costs.[12] A recent article by John Brush demonstrates the

[8]Henry R. Oppenheimer and Gary G. Schlarbaum, "Investing with Ben Graham: An *Ex Ante* Test of the Efficient Markets Hypothesis," *The Journal of Financial and Quantitative Analysis* 16 (September 1981): 341–60.

[9]For a thorough presentation of the low P/E investment strategy, see David Dreman, *The New Contrarian Investment Strategy* (New York, N.Y.: Random House, 1982).

[10]Robert A. Levy, "Random Walks: Reality or Myth," *Financial Analyst Journal* 23 (November/December 1967): 129–32. See also the comment by Michael C. Jensen in the same issue and the reply by Levy in the January/February 1968 issue.

[11]See Arnold Bernhard, *Value Line Methods of Evaluating Common Stocks* (New York, N.Y.: Arnold Bernhard & Co., 1979), pt. 4, for a complete description of the Value Line Timeliness Rank.

[12]Thomas E. Copeland and David Mayers, "The Value Line Enigma (1965–1978)," *Journal of Financial Economics* 10 (November 1982): 289–321.

predictive ability of eight *pure* relative strength models of varying complexity over the period 1969–1984.[13]

Homogenous Group/Group Rotation Models

The homogenous group model of James Farrell serves as the prototype for all subsequent work in this area.[14] Farrell's model uses *cluster analysis*, a statistical technique which identifies clusters of stocks whose returns are highly correlated within each cluster and relatively uncorrelated between clusters. Using this technique, Farrell determined that there are at least four clusters of stocks in the market: growth, cyclical, stable, and energy.

Managers who use the group rotation approach can apply cluster analysis to define homogenous groups of stocks whose returns strongly co-vary. As Farrell shows, a substantial reward awaits the manager who can select valid clusters and then correctly forecast those the market will favor. Specifically, in a study spanning the period 1970–1977, Farrell found that the net advantage to perfect group rotation over a buy-and-hold S&P 500 portfolio was 289%. While it is highly unlikely that any manager was able to forecast *exactly* which groups would be in favor during this (or any other) period, it is clearly demonstrated that reasonable accuracy can produce attractive returns.

A recent study by Coggin and another by Sorensen and Burke use the notion of relative strength to show that a group rotation strategy of buying industry groups with superior relative price performance results in superior returns.[15] The Coggin study shows evidence of persistence of superior returns for subsequent periods of one year, while the Sorensen and Burke study demonstrates superior returns for periods of at least two quarters.

---

[13]John S. Brush, "Eight Relative Strength Models Compared," *The Journal of Portfolio Management* 13 (Fall 1986): 21–28.

[14]See James L. Farrell, Jr., "Homogenous Stock Groupings: Implications for Portfolio Management," *Financial Analysts Journal* 31 (May/June 1975), and *Guide to Portfolio Management* (New York, N.Y.: McGraw-Hill, 1983), ch. 8.

[15]See T. Daniel Coggin, "On the Persistence of S&P 500 Industry Group Returns, 1975–1985," Working Paper, Capital Management Group, First Union National Bank, Charlotte, N.C., 1986; and Eric H. Sorensen and Terry Burke, "Portfolio Returns from Active Industry Group Rotation," *Financial Analysts Journal* 42 (September/October 1986): 43–50.

Multifactor Models

The idea that common stock prices can be described by an econometric model with a small number of well-chosen explanatory variables dates back at least to the late 1930s. This concept is currently experiencing a resurgence of interest by both academics and practitioners. The purpose here is not to recite all the models or trace their histories,[16] but to describe four examples of multifactor models of equity valuation in current use that illustrate the technique and its potential.

The first model is the *Multiplex Model* of Trinity Investment Management Corp. (Bellefonte, Pa.). This model attempts to address the problem, well known to practitioners, that "no single model works well all the time." There are eight separate valuation models that are combined through a proprietary weighting scheme to produce the Multiplex Model: a "cashflow plowback" model, a return on equity model, a dividend discount model, Graham and Dodd's "central value" model, two P/E models, and two earnings models. Surprisingly, for the sixteen years ending 31 December 1986, each one of the eight submodels has an annualized total return that exceeds that of the S&P 500. The Multiplex Model has the highest annual return of 17.5% (assuming no transaction costs), versus 10.9% for the S&P 500. Trinity Investment Management Corp. has available performance figures (including transaction costs) for actual portfolios managed with the Multiplex Model.

The second example is the multifactor model developed by the Quantitative Research Department headed by George Douglas at the New York brokerage firm of Drexel Burnham Lambert, Inc. Douglas and his associates are working with a seven-factor model that includes the following sources of valuation: P/E, P/Book value, dividend yield, return on equity, P/Cash flow, P/Sales, and forecast risk (the predicted change in an analysts' consensus estimate of current year EPS). The initial results are encouraging, and the model shows promise as a tool to predict common stock returns. One particularly interesting feature of the Drexel product is that it allows clients to specify and test their own multifactor models using the Drexel computer and database. Some important work in this area is also being done at two other New York brokerage firms: Goldman Sachs (under the leadership of Steven Einhorn) and Salomon Brothers (under the leadership of Eric Sorensen).

---

[16]See Michael Keenan, "Models of Equity Valuation: The Great SERM Bubble," *The Journal of Finance* 25 (May 1970): 243–73, for a good summary and evaluation of this literature.

The third example is the multifactor model of Chen, Roll, and Ross.[17] Their model is consistent with the arbitrage pricing theory (APT) developed by Stephen Ross and expanded by several others.[18] The basic model proposed by Chen, Roll, and Ross asserts that asset prices depend upon their exposure to the "state variables" which describe the economy. Their testing revealed four economic variables that are significant in explaining monthly stock returns over the period 1958–1984: the monthly growth rate in industrial production, unanticipated inflation (defined as the monthly first difference in the logarithm of the CPI minus a variable representing the expected inflation rate), unanticipated change in the term structure of interest rates (defined as the spread between long- and short-term bond returns), and unanticipated change in the risk premium (defined as the spread between low- and high-grade bond returns). Stephen Ross and Richard Roll have started their own money management firm (Ross and Roll Asset Management, Gwynedd, Pa.), which uses a proprietary version of this basic model.

The final example of the multifactor approach to equity valuation is presented in a recent paper by Aruna Ramamurti, president of Triangle Portfolio Associates (Pittsburgh, Pa.).[19] Ramamurti's three-stage model first removes the return on a stock attributable to its covariance with the overall market by calculating the excess return from the single-factor CAPM (capital asset pricing model), for a sample of 900 companies. The second stage then regresses the excess return for each stock onto three variables assumed to be priced by the market: size, E/P, and return on equity. The third stage calculates expected returns for the companies using the regression coefficients for the three variables. Ramamurti found a significant positive correlation between expected and actual monthly returns for the period 1978–1986, and plans to incorporate the model into a product to be offered by her firm.

---

[17]This model is described and tested in Nai-Fu Chen, Richard Roll, and Stephen A. Ross, "Economic Forces and the Stock Market," *The Journal of Business* 59 (July 1986): 382–403.

[18]See Stephen A. Ross, "The Arbitrage Theory of Capital Asset Pricing," *Journal of Economic Theory* 13 (December 1976); and "Risk, Return and Arbitrage," in I. Friend and J. L. Bicksler, eds., *Risk and Return in Finance, Vol. I* (Cambridge: Ballinger, 1977). A summary of recent developments in the APT is given in Gur Huberman, "A Review of the Arbitrage Pricing Theory," Working Paper No. 166, Center for Research in Security Prices, University of Chicago, 1986.

[19]Aruna S. Ramamurti, "A Systematic Approach to Generating Excess Returns Using a Multiple Variable Model," in Frank J. Fabozzi (ed.), *Institutional Investor Focus on Investment Management* (Cambridge, MA: Ballinger Publishing, 1989).

Market Anomaly Models

If the stock market were totally efficient, then there should be no systematic gain from investing in stocks with certain easily identifiable characteristics, such as low P/E, small capitalization, and low analyst coverage. However, numerous academic studies have shown that such "market anomalies" do in fact exist. A recent summary by Donald Keim discusses five sources of anomalous return in the stock market: high dividend stocks, small capitalization stocks, low P/E stocks, abnormally high returns for the month of January, and abnormally high returns for stocks rated "1" in the Value Line Timeliness rank.[20] Other studies have noted abnormally low returns for stocks on Monday, as compared to the rest of the week.

The low P/E strategy and the Value Line Timeliness rank were mentioned earlier. There is a growing interest in active investment strategies that attempt to capture excess returns available to other stock market anomalies as well. Dimensional Fund Advisors, Inc. (Santa Monica, Calif.) now has available small capitalization stock funds that invest in the U.S., Japan and the U.K. Several money managers now use "extent of coverage by Wall Street analysts" (sometimes called the "neglect effect") as one of their investment criteria. The strategy in this case is to buy attractive stocks which are under-followed by Wall Street and hence have (potentially) undiscovered value. Time will tell whether or not these anomalies persist as more market participants become aware of them. For now at least, their existence presents appealing investment opportunities.

The CAPM

No discussion of models of equity valuation would be complete without including the Sharpe-Lintner capital asset pricing model (CAPM).[21] The CAPM has been for over 20 years the premier model of equilibrium asset pricing in a competitive market. While its promise has not been fully realized, and the APT (arbitrage pricing theory) looms on the

---

[20]Donald B. Keim, "The CAPM and Equity Return Regularities," *Financial Analysts Journal* 42 (May/June 1986): 19–34.

[21]Many current investment textbooks contain a discussion of the CAPM and its empirical tests. One particularly good example is by Edward J. Elton and Martin J. Gruber, *Modern Portfolio Theory and Investment Analysis*, 3d ed. (New York, N.Y.: John Wiley, 1987), Part 2.

horizon as its successor, some money managers still employ its basic insights. As explored in Chapter 9, the use of index funds as a tool for passive equity management is supported by the central prediction of the CAPM—that the market portfolio is *the* mean-variance efficient port-folio for all risk-adverse investors.

Those who use the CAPM for active equity management employ its prediction that, in equilibrium, the expected return on a stock is an exact linear function of the risk-free rate, the beta for the stock (i.e., its expected covariance with the market portfolio), and the expected return on the market portfolio. This linear relationship is called the *security market line*, described by the equation:

$$E(R_{CAPM}) = r_f + \beta_i[E(R_M)-r_f]$$

where $E(R_{CAPM})$ is the expected return on stock i (sometimes called the *required* return) predicted by the CAPM, r_f is the risk-free rate, β_i is the beta for stock i, and $E(R_M)$ is the expected return on the market portfolio.

In theory, a stock whose expected return from a valuation model (such as the DDM) equals the expected return from the CAPM is said to be "in equilibrium." If the expected return from the DDM were greater than the expected return from the CAPM, then the market would adjust the price of the stock upward and hence lower its expected return. If the expected return from the DDM were less than the expected return from the CAPM, then the market would adjust the price of the stock down-ward and hence raise its expected return. Exhibit 5 presents this rela-tionship in the form of a graph.

The 45-degree dotted line in Exhibit 5 represents the equilibrium condition where $E(R_{DDM}) = E(R_{CAPM})$ for a stock. Following this log-ic, stocks X, Y, and Z are undervalued; stocks A, B, and C are fairly valued; and stocks R, S, and T are overvalued. Hence, *ceteris paribus*, the CAPM manager would buy stocks X, Y, and Z; hold stocks A, B, and C; and sell stocks R, S, and T. A variation of this basic approach has been successfully implemented by First Chicago Investment Advi-sors (Chicago, Ill.).

But How Have They Done Lately?

A recent study by Robert Jones of Goldman Sachs summarized in *The Wall Street Journal* (15 September 1987) sheds some light on this

EXHIBIT 5:
THE RELATIONSHIP BETWEEN E(R_{DDM}) and E(R_{CAPM})

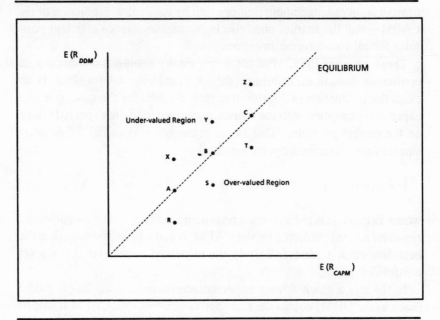

EXHIBIT 6:
HISTORICAL AND RECENT PERFORMANCE OF SEVEN POPULAR MODELS OF EQUITY VALUATION

Model	Annualized Total Return Relative to S&P 500	
	30 June 1968– 30 June 1987	30 June 1986– 30 June 1987
Dividend Discount Model	+7.0%	−6.8%
Low P/E	+4.7	−8.6
Price Momentum	+7.6	−5.0
Historical EPS Growth	+4.7	−12.0
Low Earnings Uncertainty	+1.3	−6.4
Low Analyst Coverage	+7.0	−1.0
Small Capitalization	+9.3	−1.7

Source: Goldman Sachs and *The Wall Street Journal* (15 September 1987)
Note: Returns are defined as annualized total return percentage for the top 20% of stocks ranked by each model in excess of (+) or less than (−) the return on the S&P 500 stock index.

question. Exhibit 6 shows the record of seven historically popular equity valuation models over the nineteen years prior to 30 June 1987, and over the twelve months ending 30 June 1987.

As revealed in Exhibit 6, none of the seven models continued its historical track record in the year ended 30 June 1987, and none of the seven outperformed the S&P 500 stock index for the period. According to Jones, this never happened before in the nineteen-year history of his backtests. The stocks that did outperform the S&P index over the twelve-month period were overvalued, large capitalization, low earnings growth, high P/E, low dividend, high analyst coverage stocks. These stocks as a group fit no single investment style currently in use! None of the commentators interviewed in the article could explain this phenomenon. However, they did agree that the market is unlikely to continue to ignore "value" for long—undervalued stocks must eventually come back into favor. The vast majority of active equity managers underperformed the S&P 500 index for this period. One can safely wager that those managers (and their clients) eagerly await a return to "sanity" in the stock market. The stock market crash of October 1987 is viewed by some as "correcting" the market's overvaluation.

CAN ACTIVE EQUITY MANAGEMENT ADD VALUE?

Keith Ambachtsheer and James Farrell asked this question in 1979 and concluded that the answer is yes.[22] Many current critics would disagree. With regard to the market technicians, Exhibit 7 presents the results of a survey conducted by *Investors Intelligence* and reported on the popular TV financial commentary, "Wall Street Week." While technical analyst Robert Prechter and his investment newsletter (*The Elliott Wave Theorist*) currently bask in the limelight,[23] Exhibit 7 suggests that the majority opinion of technical market analysts has been a "negative indicator" for the stock market over the period 1963–1987. A recent study by researchers at the University of Calgary reported in the *Wall Street Journal* (13 November 1987) indicates that a market timer must get at least 72% of his calls right to beat a buy-and-hold stock portfolio!

---

[22]Keith Ambachtsheer and James L. Farrell, Jr., "Can Active Management Add Value?" *Financial Analysts Journal* 35 (November/December 1979): 39–47.

[23]See Cynthia Crossen, "Wave Theory Wins Robert Prechter Title of Wall Street Guru," *The Wall Street Journal*, 18 March 1987.

EXHIBIT 7:
INVESTORS INTELLIGENCE **SURVEY OF MARKET ADVISORS REPORTED ON "WALL STREET WEEK" (3 APRIL 1987)**

Date	Dow	% Bullish	% Bearish	Subsequent Dow Move	Over Next # Months
8/02/63	689	8.6	91.4	+250 (+36%)	21
1/12/73	1047	61.6	38.4	−470 (−45%)	23
12/13/74	577	36.5	63.5	+425 (+74%)	14
1/14/77	983	78.8	21.2	−235 (−24%)	14
8/13/82	784	34.3	65.7	+500 (+64%)	15
10/03/86	1774	33.3	66.7	+948 (+53%)	11
8/25/87	2722	60.8	39.2	−984 (−36%)	2
10/19/87	1738	47.5	52.5	?	?

Note: "% Bearish" includes Bears plus those advisors forecasting a market correction. Data for 25 August 1987 and 19 October 1987 obtained directly from *Investors Intelligence* as of 21 August 1987 and 16 October 1987, respectively.

According to the popular financial media, active equity managers have fared little better.[24] Using one of the largest investment manager databases available, the 1985 edition of the annual Consistency Study conducted by the SEI Funds Evaluation Service (Chicago, Ill.) found:

1. No equity portfolio included in the study outperformed the S&P 500 stock index in any of the preceding ten years (1976–1985).
2. Only 45% of the equity portfolios outperformed the S&P 500 in six or more of the preceding ten years.
3. Less than 1% of the equity portfolios outperformed the median return for all equity managers in each of the preceding ten years.

Bar charts of the complete data are presented in Exhibits 8 and 9.[25]

---

[24]See, for example, the cover story "Why Money Managers Don't Do Better," *Business Week*, 4 February 1985, 58–65.

[25]The reader should note that the full 1985 SEI Consistency Study includes results for balanced portfolios and bond portfolios as well. Extracted here are some highlights of the equity segment of the study. The results for the balanced portfolio segment and the bond portfolio segment are very similar to those for the equity segment.

EXHIBIT 8:
EQUITY FUNDS: TOTAL FUND RETURNS CONSISTENTLY ABOVE S&P 500
ANNUAL PERIODS 31 DECEMBER 1975 THROUGH 31 DECEMBER 1985

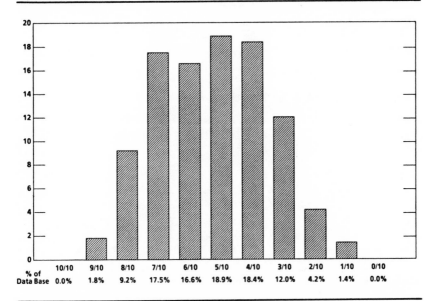

% of	10/10	9/10	8/10	7/10	6/10	5/10	4/10	3/10	2/10	1/10	0/10
Data Base	0.0%	1.8%	9.2%	17.5%	16.6%	18.9%	18.4%	12.0%	4.2%	1.4%	0.0%

Source: SEI Funds Evaluation Service, Chicago, Ill.

What does all this mean? Some would argue that this proves active equity management is a "loser's game."[26] Hence, it is sometimes viewed as fruitless, senseless, and even hypocritical to try to beat the market. Nonetheless, active equity management continues to thrive with literally thousands of participating firms in the U.S. alone. Funds contributed to passive management schemes ebb and flow—typically, more funds flow in after a year or two of weak stock market performance, while fewer funds flow in after a year or two of strong market performance. Active equity managers continue getting contributions because individuals, pensions funds, and endowments continue to believe that the right manager can deliver outperformance. As shown in Exhibits 8 and 9, *some* of them actually do.

[26]For an often cited exposition of this view, see Charles D. Ellis, "The Loser's Game," *Financial Analysts Journal* 31 (July/August 1975). One of Ellis's main points is that it is very difficult for institutional money managers to beat the market because (in effect) they *are* the market.

EXHIBIT 9:
EQUITY FUNDS: TOTAL FUND RETURNS CONSISTENTLY ABOVE MEDIAN
ANNUAL PERIODS 31 DECEMBER 1975 THROUGH 31 DECEMBER 1985

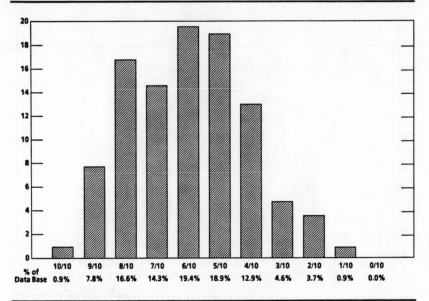

% of	10/10	9/10	8/10	7/10	6/10	5/10	4/10	3/10	2/10	1/10	0/10
Data Base	0.9%	7.8%	16.6%	14.3%	19.4%	18.9%	12.9%	4.6%	3.7%	0.9%	0.0%

Source: SEI Funds Evaluation Service, Chicago, Ill.

A reasonable view appears to be that there is room for both active and passive equity managers in the investment profession. The active manager serves the more risk-accepting investor (whether it be all or a part of his portfolio), while the passive manager serves the more risk-adverse (perhaps, more skeptical) investor. Both management styles perform a valuable service to the community of investors.

Program Trading

There is a relatively new market phenomenon: large-scale program trading which involves the simultaneous buying and selling of stocks and stock index futures by arbitrageurs and portfolio insurance programs. Chapter 7 explores this topic in more detail. Program trading has allegedly spawned a more volatile stock market than was previously the norm. Some fear that the validity of traditional models of equity valuation and active management will be weakened as a result. However, it is the considered opinion of other market observers that program trading has *not* made the stock market more volatile.

A study of stock market volatility reported on a recent airing of "Wall Street Week" (22 May 1987) indicated that (to date) the 1980s is one of the less volatile decades of this century, while the 1930s was the most volatile. Using market volatility data for the period 1970–1987, Jack Schwager argues that any increases in volatility caused by program trading are isolated and short-lived, and concentrated on contract expiration dates.[27] Furthermore, Schwager contends that the arbitrage activity underlying program trading actually serves to make the stock market more stable and efficient. The real impact of program trading will come more clearly into focus as it matures into a more routinized market activity. The debate surrounding this issue has intensified since the stock market crash of October 1987.

Quantitative Methods

A final comment concerns the general state of the use of quantitative methods in investment management. Two recent national surveys indicate that only a small percentage of investment managers use quantitative techniques to manage money. A survey reported in *Pensions & Investment Age* (10 November 1986) reported that only 8% of respondents use quantitative methods to manage stocks; and a survey conducted by Arthur D. Little, Inc. (Cambridge, Mass.) in March 1987 reported that only 30% of respondents indicated intensive use of quantitative methods in their overall money management effort.[28]

While both of these surveys are based on small sample sizes, their basic conclusions are probably representative of money managers today. Twenty years after the "quantitative revolution" of the late 1960s, most managers apparently continue to rely on conventional (i.e., non-quantitative) methods of investment management. In the case of stocks, this generally means that financial analysts perform fundamental security analysis and make recommendations to portfolio managers about which stocks to buy and sell. A relatively large subjective component is then applied to the final investment decision. No doubt, this process has been successful (and will continue to be successful) for some investment management firms.

---

[27]Jack Schwager, "Program Trading: Does It Really Distort Markets," *Futures*, April 1987, 50–51, 72. See also G. J. Santoni, "Has Programmed Trading Made Stock Prices More Volatile," *Review*, Federal Reserve Bank of St. Louis 69 (May 1987): 18–29.

[28]"Quantitative Methods and Information Technologies for Investment Advising," Arthur D. Little, Inc. (Cambridge, Mass.), April 1987.

Perhaps, as the Arthur D. Little survey suggests, quantitative methods are considered misleading, inadequate, and too complex by most managers. However, the success of those managers who do use them (several having been mentioned in this chapter) is evidence that quantitative investment methods *can* enhance the investment process. The proper blend of impartial and unemotional quantitative analysis with human investment experience and intuition (plus a little luck now and then) can be a powerful combination. It is a reasonably safe bet that an increasing number of investment managers will come to this conclusion.

CHAPTER 5

Constructing Portfolios with Equity Valuation

ERIC SORENSEN, PH.D.
DIRECTOR OF QUANTITATIVE ANALYSIS
SALOMON BROTHERS INC

Considerable theoretical and empirical research is in place which describes the portfolio construction paradigm: expected return is maximized (or expected risk is minimized); the standard model reduces to a mean/variance framework; covariance is highlighted as a crucial input; and historical data are called upon to furnish the bulk of the critical estimates of risk and return.

We owe much to those who have made conceptual and empirical contributions to our understanding of modern portfolio theory. Nevertheless, from a practical standpoint this work is far from the zenith of its potential implementation. In this chapter we describe a process for assessing stock valuation and for integrating the results into an active management strategy.[1]

---

[1] This valuation work is embodied in our development of the E-MODEL. See Eric H. Sorensen and Steven B. Kreichman, "Valuation Factors: Introducing the E-MODEL," Salomon Brothers Inc, May 12, 1987.

73

JOB ONE—EKE OUT AN ALPHA

Modern portfolio theory has perked our interest in quantifying return and risk. In the previous chapter Daniel Coggin reviews all the ways in which managers are currently exploiting modeling techniques to earn extra returns in a competitive environment—or eke out an alpha.

It is apparent that managers have increased their dependence on disciplines for relative rankings of stocks, sectors, and markets.

Valuation tools have become an integral part of the investment process. We can make two generalizations about the usage of these models: 1) the predominant usage is to find relative attractiveness (as opposed to measure relative risk), and 2) only infrequently is the usage of valuation employed in isolation from other disciplines and/or traditional techniques.

Active managers focus on stock or investment ideas. The goal is to find opportunity. If the stock idea turns out to be a good one, then risk is secondary. Since the important dimension appears to be return potential, most managers tend not to reduce the process to just one single valuation ranking. This is because valuation disciplines have times of good performance and times of poor performance. Therefore, managers often diversify across strategies or selection techniques.

Many valuation models are "slow models" in that their timing is inexact. Therefore, some managers use a "technical overlay" in the investment process. "Technical" can translate into various manipulations of price patterns, or into "momentum" in earnings trends.

There exists a host of drawbacks associated with pure implementation of valuations disciplines: 1) value indicators experience dry spells; 2) there is often no risk analysis; 3) there is often unwanted exposure in the tails of the distribution (high ranked or low ranked stocks); and 4) there is no modeling of the compatibility across other asset classes (such as cash or bonds). In sum—*modern portfolio theory tells us little about how to implement expected return and risk into an active management strategy.*

THE MARRIAGE OF A GRACEFUL MODEL WITH CRASS DATA

To fully incorporate valuation work into the investment process is to unearth artful procedures in "marrying" the elegant portfolio model with the often rough data. The extreme choices of how to combine quantitative disciplines are to "optimize" or to "eclecticize." Most managements choose something closer to the latter. That is, they go beyond traditional stock picking, but stop far short of full optimization.

Thus, the profession has made progress in application of formal quantitative techniques. The progress has been to replace the *old stock selection art of "interior decorating"* (a little steel, a little food, a little technology, etc.) with the *new model selection art of "interior decorating"* (a little value, a little earnings momentum, a little industry betting, etc.).

A more formidable process would be to build a *bona fide* modern portfolio theory optimization structure. However, this requires a realistic marriage between the model and the fundamental data which are subjected to the model. In many instances, this marriage is far from "love at first sight." Indeed, in some investment management organizations where any pre-nuptial romance is clearly absent, the marriage has been a "shot-gun wedding." Quantitative disciplines have sometimes been forced on what would otherwise be called traditional organizations.

VALUATION ON A LEVEL PLAYING FIELD

The first priority of combining real data with a model structure is to generate "expected return" estimates. It is imperative that the process overcome several obstacles. First, the stock valuation model should translate this into changes in expected return for stocks. When rates are 10%, PE's should be 20, and vice versa. Moreover, given that the duration of one stock differs from the duration of another stock, the dynamics of the model should be reflected in rankings of stocks under a variety of interest rate assumptions.[2]

Second, the modeling should make adjustment for risk. At the equity market level, the appropriate risk premium should provide a sense of equilibrium for stocks. At the security level, valuations must reflect differences across securities. The art of valuation modeling should inject a dose of realism in the manner in which market participants price fundamental differences across firms.

---

[2]See Martin L. Leibowitz, Eric H. Sorensen, Robert D. Arnott, and H. Nicholas Hanson, "A Total Differential Approach to Equity Duration," Salomon Brothers Inc, September 1987.

Third, the model should give consideration to the appropriate time horizon. If the model is a "slow" valuation model, then it should not purport to provide month-by-month timing. On the other hand, a timely process for normalizing earnings can improve the short-term results of the model.

THE E-MODEL APPROACH TO CONSTRUCTING PORTFOLIOS

At this point it is instructive to describe the E-MODEL (E for earnings), an earnings-based valuation model developed at Salomon Brothers Inc. The E-MODEL is a 3-phase growth model that provides a theoretical valuation for any stock. (The formulations are in the chapter appendix.) The E-MODEL valuations incorporate specific factors and market conditions.

We model market conditions in accordance with accepted capital market theory. As in the Capital Asset Pricing Model, our estimates of required return reflect the risk-free rate plus a risk premium. The E-MODEL uses a base discount rate that is equal to the combination of the 10-year government bond rate and a measure of the equity market risk premium. (In valuing specific stocks, we also adjust the discount rate for each stock to account for firm-specific factors.)

Exhibit 1 presents a typical display of the E-MODEL distribution of the percent undervaluation. The model calculates the theoretical value of each stock and determines the return required to move a stock's price to the E-MODEL valuation.

In constructing the distribution of expected returns in November 1987, we used a base discount rate of 12.95%. This rate is the combination of an 8.75% bond rate and a 4.2% equity market risk premium. Exhibits 2 and 3 present a history of the base discount rate and its components. When we aggregate the valuation results, slightly fewer than one half of the stocks are undervalued.

BASICS OF THE E-MODEL

The E-MODEL is a present value model that provides fundamental valuations, or target prices. These target prices can be translated into

EXHIBIT 1:
DISTRIBUTION OF E-MODEL VALUATIONS

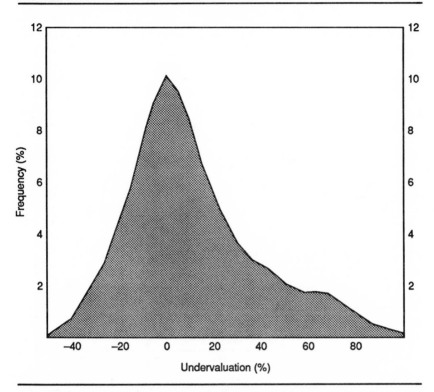

expected returns.[3] The model is thus a relative value model, in that each target price leads to a measure of undervaluation or overvaluation.

THE CHALLENGE OF NORMALIZING EARNINGS GROWTH

The E-MODEL attempts to overcome several deficiencies that sometimes characterize dividend discount models and earnings valuation models. One example is normalizing earnings.

---

[3]The expression of relative value can take several forms. For example, we previously used the ratio of value to market price to rank stocks on relative value. In essence, this calculation equals 1 plus the expected return assuming that the stock converges to theoretical value at the end of one year.

EXHIBIT 2:
HISTORICAL MARKET DISCOUNT RATE, 1976-86

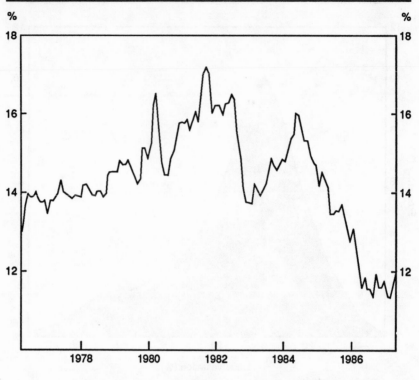

Valuation theory assumes that stock prices are continually converging to normal levels. Portfolio managers are aware of the importance of normalizing the valuation parameters, even though the task of normalizing can be difficult.

The E-MODEL addresses the issue of normalizing earnings for each stock. We use computer algorithms to assess the historical profitability, historical revenues, historical patterns of price-to-sales relationships, and consensus earnings data.[4] In valuing each stock, the current level

---

[4]In addition, we normalized current earnings by averaging the historical earnings with the consensus forecasts. This technique proved less than perfect in many instances. Currently, the E-MODEL uses a series of statistical techniques and logical cross-checks to arrive at normalized earnings for all of the stocks in our universe.

EXHIBIT 3:
HISTORICAL COMPONENTS OF DISCOUNT RATE: INTEREST RATES
AND RISK PREMIUM, 1976-86

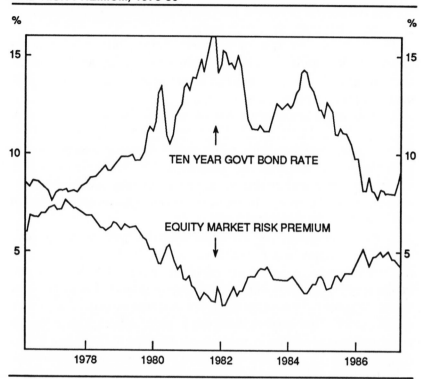

of normalized earnings and the near-term growth in earnings are important inputs.

Through the process of normalizing, the model avoids relying strictly on a string of forecasted dividend payments. The model values a future pattern of normalized flows and is, therefore, useful in valuing all types of stocks. The E-MODEL is consistent in its approach to valuation across securities including growth stocks, cyclical stocks, and stocks that currently pay no dividends.

The model generates a 3-phase growth pattern of future normalized earnings. The model uses a normalized payout ratio that the company could maintain while sustaining the assumed growth rate. Thus, only a portion of the earnings growth pattern is discounted in valuing the stock of the company.

STOCK FACTOR ADJUSTMENTS

The market often assigns different values to two stocks with similar normalized growth prospects. For example, bank stocks are, in general, valued differently than drug stocks.

To adjust for firm (and/or industry) factors, the model assesses several stock-specific parameters. In addition to near- and intermediate-term growth assumptions, the model incorporates factor adjustments to prevent biases in valuation.

To make factor adjustments, the discount rate includes the results of a cross-sectional factor model. The factor model analyzes how firms' capitalization rates vary with a variety of firm-specific elements. For example, the model generates valuations that are sensitive to such important firm characteristics as earnings variance, dividend payout, industry group, earnings momentum, revenue momentum, forecast variance, firm size, and leverage.

In our earlier research we accomplished risk adjustment by calculating a fundamental beta for each stock.[5] In the E-MODEL we use multiple regression to assess the valuations accorded to stocks in relation to specific variables while accounting for growth. The stock factor model captures the market premium or discount associated with each specific stock. The variation in the stock-specific discount rate may be positive or negative relative to the overall market discount rate. Other things being equal, a positive adjustment to the discount rate lowers the E-MODEL valuation.

MODEL OUTPUT

Exhibit 4 presents the results of the E-MODEL. The output includes target price, target price/earnings ratio, normalized growth assumptions, expected return, and duration estimates. The expected return is determined by assuming that the price of the stock converges to theoretical price. For modeling purposes, we chose a 12-month time horizon, during which the price is assumed to normalize.[6]

---

[5]See Eric Sorensen and David Williamson, "The Value of Dividend Discount Models," *Financial Analysts Journal,* Nov.-Dec. 1985. We used several variables to adjust the discount rate to capture the firm-specific risk. These included dividend yield, financial strength, leverage, average return on equity, and the historical variance in return on equity.

[6]In reality, the time that it takes for the stock price to converge to true value varies from stock to stock. It is possible to model this by making the time horizon dependent on stock characteristics that are related to price behavior.

EXHIBIT 4:
E-MODEL DYNAMICS

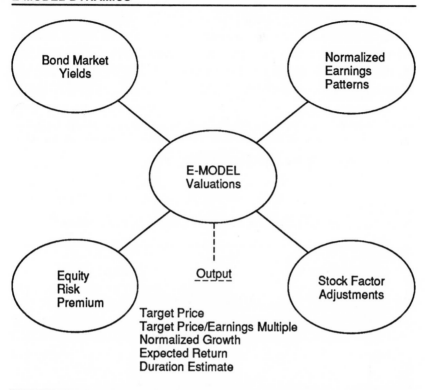

CHARACTERISTICS OF MODEL RESULTS

The E-MODEL identifies stocks that have a present value that departs from current price. The model/price earnings ratio reflects growth and risk for each stock.

To emphasize the importance of the growth and risk assumptions, consider the following: (1) if we replaced the normalized earnings with trailing reported earnings; (2) replaced future growth with a constant, which was the same for each stock; and (3) asserted that all stocks had equal risk, then the E-MODEL ranking would be equivalent to a simple low/price earnings ranking.

In contrast, the E-MODEL serves as an "intelligent low price/earnings approach." The E-MODEL is not concerned with "high" or "low" price/earnings. Rather, the model measures what the theoretical multiple should be as determined by the characteristics of the firm, and then finds opportunity by comparing the model with current market pricing.

The E-MODEL is an appropriate medium through which one can examine valuation. Exhibit 5 presents a scatter diagram of the E-MODEL results versus the price of each stock. This view differs slightly from the distribution of expected returns in Exhibit 1. The most attractive stocks are to the right of the diagonal. These stocks have valuations that exceed their current prices. For stocks to the right of the diagonal, some combination of growth, risk or normalized earnings supports higher valuations than are reflected in price.

EXHIBIT 5:
PREDICTED VALUATIONS—E-MODEL VERSUS ACTUAL MARKET PRICES

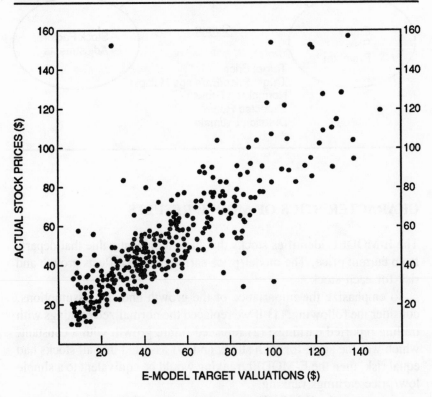

ADJUSTED VERSUS UNADJUSTED RESULTS

An important feature of the model is the adjustment for pricing factors other than growth. Allowing for a set of factor adjustments helps to avoid several problems:

1. Models that do not incorporate risk adjustment are subject to error. Prior studies have indicated that the price earnings ratio is a function of growth and such factors as quality and risk.[7]
2. Valuation models without adjustments for specific factors are prone to errors in market timing. Under certain market conditions, prices may converge rather quickly to theoretical value. Valuation tools tend to be long-term strategies, and portfolio managers who adhere to a rigid model subject themselves to "slow" performance results during some market environments.
3. Unadjusted valuation models often lead to industry biases. If the model does not distinguish between the market's assessment of the earnings across industries, the result may lead to an overconcentration in particular groups. Our empirical results demonstrate that, for extended periods, higher discount rates are applied to particular groups. If this phenomenon is very slow to change, and if our model does not incorporate the proper adjustments, then the model may lead us erroneously to "cheap" stocks.

To make the third point, we ran valuation models with and without factor adjustments. That is, we valued a large set of stocks with the E-MODEL and simultaneously valued the same set of stocks with an unadjusted present value model.

To contrast the results on the basis of sector and industry, we analyzed the composition of the top 50, 100, and 200 stocks from both models with the S&P 500 as the universe. Exhibit 6 illustrates the sector concentrations for the 50 most undervalued stocks in both groups, as of May 1987. In addition, it includes the S&P weightings. In all three cases the portfolios are weighted by market capitalization.

---

[7]The first published paper that correlated a price/earnings ratio with firm characteristics was V. S. Whitbeck and M. Kisor, "A New Tool in Investment Decision Making," *Financial Analysts Journal*, May-June 1963. Whitbeck and Kisor also identified the importance of normalizing earnings, although they did not explain their procedure for normalization.

EXHIBIT 6:
SECTOR WEIGHTINGS FOR THE TOP-RANKED 50 STOCKS—E-MODEL
VERSUS UNADJUSTED MODEL

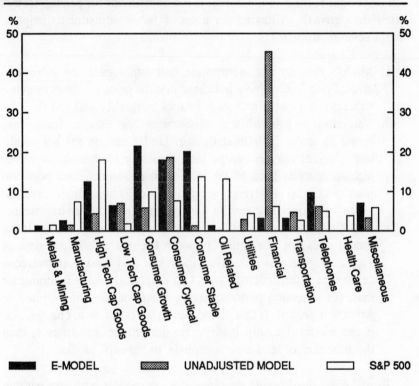

Exhibits 7 and 8 present sector-weighting comparisons for the top 100 and the top 200 stocks for both models. The most striking result is the overconcentration in financial stocks for the unadjusted model. With no adjustment for stock-specific earnings risk, financial stocks comprised almost 50% of the weighting of the top 50 portfolio.

In Exhibit 8, we extended the comparison between the two models to 200 stocks. The unadjusted model continued to overweight the financial sector. In contrast, the E-MODEL top-50 rankings tended to favor consumer stocks and telephone issues.

As expected, when we increased the size of the portfolio to 100 and 200 stocks, the contrasts diminished. For the top 200 stocks, the E-MODEL overweighted manufacturing, consumer growth, oil-related,

EXHIBIT 7:
SECTOR WEIGHTINGS FOR THE TOP-RANKED 100 STOCKS—E-MODEL
VERSUS UNADJUSTED MODEL

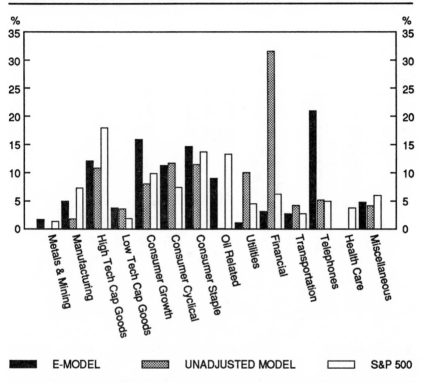

| E-MODEL | UNADJUSTED MODEL | S&P 500 |

and telephone stocks. Conversely, the E-MODEL underweighted utilities and technology stocks.

PROFILES OF E-MODEL RANKINGS

Exhibits 9, 10 and 11 present a set of profiles for stocks ranked by the E-MODEL. The top panel in Exhibit 9 shows the average percentage of undervaluation of the 2,000 stocks arrayed in five quintiles. Quintile 1 comprises the top 400 stocks. The bar graph shows the average degree of undervaluation in this quintile, as well as the other four quintiles. Each of the bar graphs that follow demonstrate various similarities within the same quintile groupings of stocks.

EXHIBIT 8:
SECTOR WEIGHTINGS FOR THE TOP-RANKED 200 STOCKS—E-MODEL
VERSUS UNADJUSTED MODEL

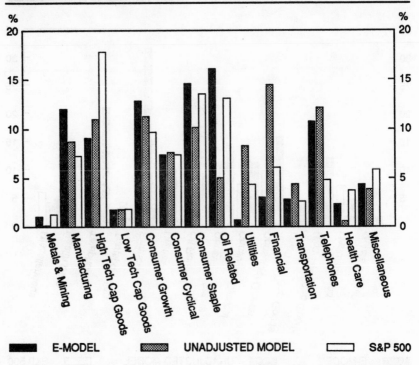

For example, based on the E-MODEL ranking, stocks in the top quintiel have the lowest actual price/earnings ratios (see Exhibit 9). Lower E-MODEL quintiles have higher average price/earnings ratios.

In a similar fashion, other relationships can be observed by comparing E-MODEL rankings with various security attributes. Exhibit 10 shows that the top quintile of E-MODEL stocks has an average growth rate of 18.6%. The lower quintiles have lower growth rates. There appears to be a slight bias in favor of earnings growth. At the same time, when we divide the price/earnings ratio by growth, we see that the model provides a rational structure. In Exhibit 10, the top quintile comprises stocks that have price/earnings ratios that are slighlty lower than their forecasted growth rates. The lowest-ranking quintile comprises stocks which, on average, have price/earnings ratios that are 2.24 times their respective growth rates.

Percent Undervalued Quintile Ranking

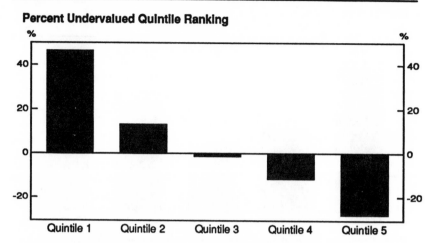

Price/Earnings Ratio: Current Price/Forecast Earnings

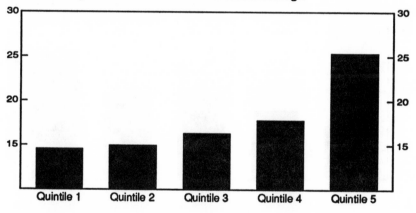

Price Earnings Ratio: Model Price/Normalized Earnings

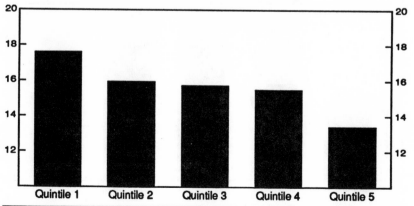

EXHIBIT 10:
E-MODEL QUINTILES

Growth Rate

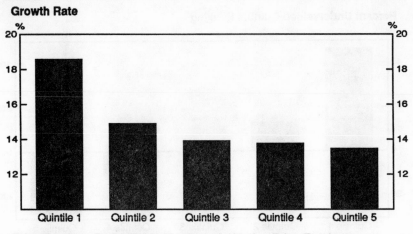

Price/Earnings Ratio Divided by Growth: Market Price/Earnings Ratio/Consensus Growth

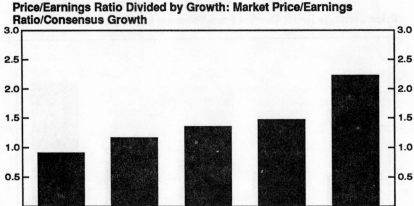

Market Capitalization

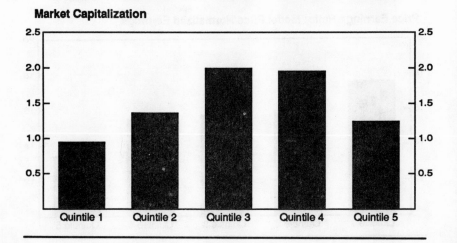

EXHIBIT 11:
E-MODEL QUINTILES

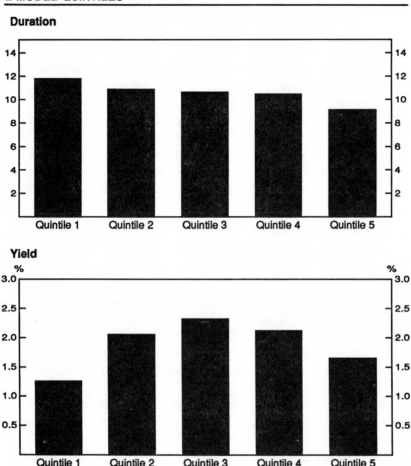

Duration

Yield

Completing our review of the quintile graphs, Exhibit 11 shows that the E-MODEL predicts small-capitalization stocks to be more attractive. In addition, Exhibit 11 illustrates that the most attractive stocks tend to have longer durations and lower dividend yields.

STOCK VALUATIONS

Exhibit 12 presents stock valuations for a list of stocks. The model assumptions for Aluminum Co. of America (AA) are: 1) normal earnings—$3.71; 2) growth rate—9.81%; and 3) discount rate—12.14%.

The first column of numbers in Exhibit 12 represents the assessment of undervaluation. The E-MODEL indicates that AA is undervalued by 13.25%, based on a valuation of $482.7 and a price of $42.62. The stock should carry a PE of 13.02, and if growth remains in tact, then the stock is expected to earn 24.36% over a 1-year horizon.

As we can see from the results in Exhibit 12, the range of valuations is quite wide. The expected returns on the individual stocks depend on the market pricing of the stocks in comparison to the valuation results. If the stock experiences earnings momentum, and the price also rises, this does not necessarily mean that the stock becomes more or less undervalued. The model is sufficiently dynamic to capture changes in fundamentals, expectations, and the risk structure of stocks. Changes in relative attractiveness depend on changes in price *and* fundamentals.

DYNAMIC VALUATION

The E-MODEL presented in Exhibit 12 is static. This particular run of the model assumes that interest rates are 8.75%, the equity market risk premium is 4.2%, and the growth in gross national product (GNP) is 1% in the intermediate term.

At the top of the "percent undervalued" column, we see that capitalization-weighted valuation of the entire universe of 2000 stocks is 2.92% undervalued. This column gives us the valuation ranking input for portfolio construction.

We might ask, What if the world changes? What if interest rates rise? What if the economy slows? What if we enter a period of adverse earnings momentum? Despite our E-MODEL adjustments, which are intended to account for risk, a change at the macroeconomic level can quickly result with erroneous rankings.

The portfolio construction process must be dynamic. For example, if rates change we would expect that the duration (or interest rate sensitivity) will be an important risk factor.[8] Exhibit 13 diagrams the potential effects of a macroeconomic shock on the valuation of equities.

Suppose that inflation rises and the economy accelerates at the same time. This will have a number of direct and interactive effects on the valuation of equities. First, a rise in interest rates will cause capitalization rates to rise in the equity markets. Other things being equal, this

---

[8]For a detailed discussion of the meaning of stock duration, see "A Total Differential Approach to Equity Duration" and Chapter 12 for a general discussion of duration.

EXHIBIT 12:
E-MODEL—SLOW GROWTH

Ticker	Name	Model Results						Model Assumptions					Industry
		Percent Undervalued	Present Value	Market Price 11/6/87	Target Price 1 Year	Expected Return 1 year	Model PE	Normal EPS	Growth Rate	Discount Rate	Dividend Yield	Cap ($Million)	
	Universe Average Cap Weighted	2.92				12.95	14.07		9.61	11.94	2.90		
	Universe Average Equal Weighted	1.65				11.84	13.46		9.72	12.27	2.35		
AA	Aluminum Co. of America	13.25	48.27	42.62	53.01	24.36	13.02	3.71	9.81	12.14	1.95	3734	Aluminum
AAPI	Apple Computer, Inc.	26.28	47.67	37.75	54.88	45.37	17.71	2.69	15.11	11.62	0.42	4745	Computer & Business Equip.
ABS	Albertson's, Inc.	12.97	28.24	25.00	31.34	25.36	15.69	1.80	10.97	11.50	1.49	837	Retail (Food Chains)
ABT	Abbott Laboratories	-0.20	47.90	48.00	54.65	13.85	16.81	2.85	14.08	11.65	1.69	10929	Health Care Diversified
ACCOB	Coors (Adolph) Co-Cl B	-26.55	14.51	19.75	15.35	-22.30	11.62	1.25	5.79	12.26	2.00	721	Beverages
ACK	Armstrong World Inds. Inc.	38.46	39.46	28.50	43.26	51.79	15.00	2.63	9.62	11.56	2.14	1352	Miscellaneous
ACV	Alberto-Culver Co.	-4.36	18.05	18.88	20.37	7.90	14.99	1.20	12.82	11.87	0.99	263	Cosmetics
ACY	American Cyanamid Co.	-8.15	36.28	39.50	40.33	2.10	14.59	2.49	11.15	11.75	2.12	3618	Chemicals (Diversified)
ADM	Archer-Daniels-Midland Co.	25.37	23.04	18.38	25.57	39.18	14.84	1.55	11.01	11.62	0.38	3173	Foods
AEG	Allegis Corp.	-28.30	51.98	72.50	55.39	-23.60	11.89	4.37	6.56	12.12	1.00	4229	Air Transport
AEP	American Electric Power	-34.10	17.30	26.25	17.70	-32.57	9.72	1.78	2.31	12.86	8.51	5080	Electric Utilities
AET	Aetna Life & Casualty Co.	-13.91	44.87	52.12	48.44	-7.06	9.85	4.55	7.96	13.65	4.55	5927	Multi-Line Insurance
AGC	American General Corp.	21.49	39.18	32.25	43.54	35.00	11.45	3.42	11.12	13.05	3.29	4204	Multi-Line Insurance
AHC	Amerada Hess Corp.	32.57	34.63	26.13	36.33	39.07	12.62	2.74	4.90	-11.89	1.70	2172	Oil (Integrated Domestic)
AHM	Ahmanson (H.F.) & Co.	-21.66	12.53	16.00	13.55	-15.32	7.16	1.75	8.10	15.50	4.32	1567	Savings & Loan
AHP	Amer. Home Prod.Corp.	1.73	72.61	71.37	78.89	10.53	14.82	4.90	8.65	11.46	3.90	10462	Health Care Diversified
AIG	American Int'l Group	-4.52	60.39	63.25	69.34	9.63	12.46	4.85	14.81	13.21	0.31	10330	Multi-Line Insurance
AIT	Amer. Information Tech.	-12.06	77.06	87.62	81.00	-7.56	12.50	6.17	5.12	11.55	5.24	12300	Telephones
AL	Alcan Aluminum Ltd.	28.51	30.84	24.00	32.93	37.20	13.30	2.32	6.76	11.59	1.67	3785	Aluminum
ALD	Allied Signal, Inc.	-35.27	21.20	32.75	22.70	-30.69	11.53	1.84	7.08	12.37	3.95	5622	Miscellaneous
AMB	American Brands Inc.-Del	28.01	56.16	43.87	60.78	38.54	14.23	3.95	8.22	11.57	3.73	4834	Tobacco
AMD	Advanced Micro Devices	-5.11	9.96	10.50	11.29	7.55	16.25	0.61	13.35	11.63	0.00	614	Electronics (Semiconductors)
AMH	Amdahl Corp.	15.76	35.02	30.25	39.15	29.42	14.53	2.41	11.80	11.94	0.42	1561	Computer & Business Equip.

EXHIBIT 12:
E-MODEL—SLOW GROWTH—continued

		Model Results						Model Assumptions					
Ticker	Name	Percent Undervalued	Present Value	Market Price 11/6/87	Target Price 1 Year	Expected Return 1 year	Model PE	Normal EPS	Growth Rate	Discount Rate	Dividend Yield	Cap ($Million)	Industry
AMI	American Medical Int'l	-24.82	9.12	12.13	9.58	-20.98	9.27	0.98	5.10	13.56	4.40	1061	Hospital Management
AMP	Amp, Inc.	1.59	46.98	46.25	53.52	15.72	17.44	2.69	13.91	11.47	1.31	5002	Electrical Equipment
AMR	AMR Corp.-Del.	9.91	39.02	35.50	41.91	18.06	12.04	3.24	7.42	12.15	0.00	2086	Air Transport
AMT	Acme-Cleveland Corp.	-32.47	7.09	10.50	7.52	-28.38	10.48	0.68	6.05	12.86	2.74	66	Machine Tools
AMX	Amax, Inc.	-4.24	16.40	17.13	17.89	4.44	10.53	1.56	9.07	14.15	0.00	1628	Metals (Misc.)
AN	Amoco Corp.	0.02	68.52	68.50	72.45	5.77	14.04	4.88	5.75	11.56	4.04	17528	Oil (Integrated Domestic)
ANDW	Andrew Corp.	-1.44	12.07	12.25	13.46	9.85	15.45	0.78	11.45	11.56	0.00	123	Communications (Equip/Mfrs)
APD	Air Prod. & Chem., Inc.	-24.50	25.29	33.50	27.31	-18.49	10.88	2.32	7.96	13.10	2.04	1876	Chemicals
AR	Asarco, Inc.	58.23	36.39	23.00	38.42	67.02	11.89	3.06	5.55	12.45	0.00	653	Metals (Misc.)
ARC	Atlantic Richfield Co.	1.31	72.94	72.00	77.44	7.56	13.79	5.29	6.18	11.52	4.24	12853	Oil (Integrated Domestic)
AS	Armco, Inc.	40.58	13.71	9.75	14.20	45.61	10.83	1.27	3.58	12.17	0.00	844	Steel
ASC	American Stores Co.-New	18.55	72.91	61.50	84.13	36.79	17.62	4.14	15.39	11.52	1.12	1904	Retail (Food Chains)
AST	American Standard, Inc.	-26.74	26.56	36.25	28.29	-21.96	11.55	2.30	6.53	12.28	3.58	1135	Building Materials
AUD	Automatic Data Proc.	25.17	50.69	40.50	58.23	43.78	17.34	2.92	14.86	11.50	0.88	3064	Computer Data Service
AVP	Avon Products	-6.83	22.59	24.25	24.42	0.71	11.76	1.92	8.10	12.38	5.69	1707	Cosmetics
AXP	American Express	-4.00	24.00	25.00	26.58	6.31	10.57	2.27	10.74	13.58	2.12	10737	Financial (Misc.)

EXHIBIT 13:
E-MODEL—ROBUST GROWTH

		Model Results						Model Assumptions					
Ticker	Name	Percent Undervalued	Present Value	Market Price 11/6/87	Target Price 1 Year	Expected Return 1 year	Model PE	Normal EPS	Growth Rate	Discount Rate	Dividend Yield	Cap ($Million)	Industry
	Universe Average Cap Weighted	26.45				41.05	14.14		11.51	12.62	2.90		
	Universe Average Equal Weighted	29.77				45.53	13.72		11.93	12.90	2.35		
AA	Aluminum Co. of America	56.24	64.84	41.50	72.55	74.83	13.19	4.92	11.90	12.79	1.95	3636	Aluminum
AAPI	Apple Computer, Inc.	50.14	54.05	36.00	63.35	75.97	17.86	3.03	17.20	12.29	0.42	4525	Computer & Business Equip.
ABS	Albertson's, Inc.	18.48	30.06	25.38	33.73	32.93	14.89	2.02	12.20	12.32	1.49	849	Retail (Food Chains)
ABT	Abbott Laboratories	8.53	53.45	49.25	61.89	25.67	16.81	3.18	15.80	12.32	1.69	11213	Health Care Diversified
ACCOB	Coors (Adolph) Co-Cl B	10.25	20.53	18.62	22.16	18.96	13.13	1.56	7.90	12.37	2.00	680	Beverages
ACK	Armstrong World Inds. Inc.	48.35	43.21	29.13	47.92	64.52	14.39	3.00	10.90	12.33	2.14	1381	Miscellaneous
ACV	Alberto-Culver Co.	29.52	23.96	18.50	27.68	49.60	16.73	1.43	15.50	12.26	0.99	257	Cosmetics
ACY	American Cyanamid Co.	30.85	49.40	37.75	56.41	49.43	15.82	3.12	14.20	12.28	2.12	3458	Chemicals (Diversified)
ADM	Archer-Daniels-Midland Co.	57.13	28.68	18.25	32.52	78.18	15.48	1.85	13.40	12.28	0.38	3151	Foods
AEG	Allegis Corp.	1.30	73.95	73.00	80.75	10.62	11.98	6.17	9.20	12.85	1.00	4258	Air Transport
AEP	American Electric Power	-1.08	25.84	26.13	26.72	2.29	10.39	2.49	3.40	12.94	8.51	5056	Electric Utilities
AET	Aetna Life & Casualty Co.	28.19	64.89	50.63	72.10	42.41	10.32	6.29	11.10	14.24	4.55	5757	Multi-Line Insurance
AGC	American General Corp.	26.71	41.34	32.63	46.30	41.91	10.70	3.86	12.00	14.14	3.29	4253	Multi-Line Insurance
AHC	Amerada Hess Corp.	82.58	46.56	25.50	49.58	94.45	12.93	3.60	6.50	12.38	1.70	2120	Oil (Integrated Domestic)
AHM	Ahmanson (H.F.) & Co.	22.00	19.67	16.12	22.01	36.52	7.83	2.51	11.90	15.75	4.32	1579	Savings & Loan
AHP	Amer. Home Prod.Corp.	8.05	77.26	71.50	84.67	18.42	14.07	5.49	9.60	12.29	3.90	10480	Health Care Diversified
AIG	American Int'l Group	0.65	67.94	67.50	79.15	17.26	12.18	5.58	16.50	14.07	0.31	11024	Multi-Line Insurance
AIT	Amer. Information Tech.	-3.51	85.16	88.25	90.35	2.38	11.53	7.39	6.10	12.57	5.24	12388	Telephones
AL	Alcan Aluminum Ltd.	72.36	40.29	23.38	43.88	87.70	13.16	3.06	8.90	12.40	1.67	3686	Aluminum
ALD	Allied Signal, Inc.	2.23	33.48	32.75	36.96	12.86	13.52	2.48	10.40	12.41	3.95	5622	Miscellaneous
AMB	American Brands Inc.-Del	34.01	58.46	43.62	63.66	45.93	13.31	4.39	8.90	12.38	3.73	4807	Tobacco
AMD	Advanced Micro Devices	58.39	17.23	10.88	20.77	91.02	19.22	0.90	20.60	12.33	0.00	636	Electronics (Semiconductors)
AMH	Amdahl Corp.	69.77	49.23	29.00	56.96	96.42	15.64	3.15	15.70	12.58	0.42	1496	Computer & Business Equip.

EXHIBIT 13:
E-MODEL—ROBUST GROWTH—continued

| | | | | Model Results | | | | Model Assumptions | | | | | |
| | | | Market | Target | Expected | | | | | | | | |
Ticker	Name	Percent Undervalued	Present Value	Price 11/6/87	Price 1 Year	Return 1 year	Model PE	Normal EPS	Growth Rate	Discount Rate	Dividend Yield	Cap ($Million)	Industry
AMI	American Medical Int'l	16.38	13.53	11.63	14.54	25.10	9.52	1.42	7.50	14.18	4.40	1017	Hospital Management
AMP	AMP, Inc.	18.12	53.15	45.00	61.61	36.90	17.31	3.07	15.90	12.21	1.31	4867	Electronics (Semiconductors)
AMR	AMR Corp.-Del.	75.77	61.30	34.87	67.98	94.93	13.08	4.69	10.90	12.64	0.00	2049	Air Transport
AMT	Acme-Cleveland Corp.	−24.55	8.49	11.25	9.12	−18.89	8.97	0.95	7.50	14.81	2.74	71	Machine Tools
AMX	Amax, Inc.	25.39	19.44	15.50	21.69	39.94	9.94	1.96	11.60	15.46	0.00	1474	Metals (Misc.)
AN	Amoco Corp.	13.75	78.77	69.25	84.45	21.94	13.62	5.78	7.20	12.36	4.04	17720	Oil (Integrated Domestic)
ANDW	Andrew Corp.	20.34	13.99	11.63	15.86	36.47	15.44	0.91	13.40	12.27	0.00	117	Communications (Equip/Mfrs)
APD	Air Prod. & Chem., Inc.	24.69	39.59	31.75	44.22	39.28	12.23	3.24	11.70	13.29	2.04	1778	Chemicals
AR	Asarco, Inc.	124.33	46.83	20.88	50.06	139.81	11.27	4.16	6.90	13.41	0.00	592	Metals (Misc.)
ARC	Atlantic Richfield Co.	37.24	105.85	77.12	114.32	48.22	13.39	7.91	8.00	12.39	4.24	13768	Oil (Integrated Domestic)
AS	Armco, Inc.	70.33	15.97	9.38	16.69	78.00	9.65	1.66	4.50	13.55	0.00	812	Steel
ASC	American Stores Co.-New	30.48	76.98	59.00	89.76	52.14	16.51	4.66	16.60	12.36	1.12	1827	Retail (Food Chains)
AST	American Standard, Inc.	18.34	40.98	34.62	44.91	29.70	12.71	3.22	9.60	12.62	3.58	1084	Building Materials
AUD	Automatic Data Proc.	33.35	54.51	40.88	63.23	54.68	16.50	3.30	16.00	12.33	0.88	3093	Computer Data Service
AVP	Avon Products	17.39	28.17	24.00	30.91	28.77	12.52	2.25	9.70	12.68	5.69	1689	Cosmetics
AXP	American Express	11.30	28.10	25.25	31.64	25.32	10.55	2.66	12.60	14.35	2.12	10844	Financial (Misc.)

will lower the E-MODEL valuations of stocks. This is the traditional dividend discount model (DDM) duration. Second, if the equity market risk premium rises it will accentuate the duration impact. If the risk premium falls it will dampen the duration impact. Third, the fundamentals of some companies may improve, and the fundamentals of other companies may deteriorate. Companies which respond more favorably to price increases and economic expansion will have earnings momentum, which tends to offset the downward pressure on valuations. These are companies which have a relatively high "earnings flow through" characteristic.

Assume for the moment that interest rates rise from 8.75% to 10.0%; GNP growth rises from 1% to 3%; and that the equity market risk premium falls from 4.2% to 3.7%. Exhibit 14 presents the E-MODEL results under this new scenario. Note that now the precent undervalued is 26.45% on a capitalization-weighted basis. However, not all stocks responded by the same degree to the new macroeconomic assumptions. For example, AA has gone from 13.25% undervalued to 56.24% undervalued—a big rise. At the same time, Albertson's (ABS) has experienced a very minor improvement in attractiveness.

The model has accounted for each firm's sensitivity to economic activity. AA earnings growth has improved by 21% (rising form 9.81% to 11.9%). On the other hand, ABS earnings growth has improved by only 11% (rising from 10.97% to 12.2%). Thus, AA has a greater response to an increase in economic activity. The discount rate rose considerably for both stocks, but on net AA has, by far, the greatest improvement in relative attractiveness.

AGGREGATE VALUATIONS AND DURATION

The valuation modeling must be sensitive to the differential impact of economic activity on different stocks and sectors. In addition, it is possible to aggregate the stock results to value the entire equity market across various scenarios.

Exhibit 14 presents a matrix of the valuations of the 2,000 stocks (individual stocks, not an index) for five GNP forecasts and seven long-term interest rate forecasts. The top row of the exhibit shows how undervalued the market is under various interest rate assumptions, a stable economy, and robust growth of 3% GNP growth.

As we shift down each row in Exhibit 14, we reduce our outlook for

EXHIBIT 14:
E-MODEL VALUATIONS FOR ALTERNATIVE ECONOMIC SCENARIOS (STOCK PRICES AS OF NOVEMBER 6, 1987)

Economic Scenario	Growth 3 Years	Real GNP	Percent Undervalued—Cap Weighted (Top) and Equally Weighted (Bottom) — Market Risk Premium						
			6.00%	7.00%	8.00%	9.00%	10.00%	11.00%	12.00%
Economic Growth	3.70%	3.00%	67.84%	53.51%	41.21%	30.53%	23.25%	12.99%	5.72%
	1.50%		41.26%	29.25%	18.89%	9.92%	2.07%	-4.84%	-10.94%
Economic Slowdown	4.20%	0.00%	9.94%	0.97%	-6.81%	-13.62%	-19.55%	-24.75%	-29.40%
	-1.50%	-4.10%	18.57%	-11.89%	-23.14%	-24.38%	-29.48%	-33.97%	-37.99%
Economic Decline	-4.70%	-3.00%	-16.72%	-23.14%	-28.71%	-33.59%	-37.90%	-41.72%	-45.13%
			-16.72%	-23.14%	-28.71%	-33.59%	-37.90%	-41.72%	-45.13%

Methodology: We have measured each company's economic sensitivities. Regression analysis of historical sales growth is measured against real GNP and interest rate changes. Each company's operating and financial leverage magnifies the impact of changes to earnings per share growth. Under each scenario, the company has an alteration to its normalized earnings and its three- to five-year growth rate. Each stock is then valued in accordance with the E-MODEL methodology at various interest rate assumptions.

real GNP growth. A shift down to the middle row shows that the market is overvalued by 13.62% (cap-weighted) if we enter a period of flat growth in GNP. This valuation assumes a stock price as of November 6, 1987 (an S&P level of 240), and a long-term interest rate of 9%. However, this GNP scenario is perhaps consistent with a lower interest rate level. If rates fall to 7%, the market is fairly valued.

The valuation matrix provides a measure of duration for the stock market. If GNP is growing at 3%, and interest rates are 8%, then a 100-basis point rise in rates increases stock valuations by approximately 11% (41.21% − 30.53%). This scenario assumes no change in economic growth. Stock market duration in this case would be 11.

Assume, however, that the interest rate rise was a rise in real rates, and that as a result the economy slowed as a result. With rates rising to 9% and GNP growth slowing to 1.5%, the market would have a duration of approximately 30 (41.21 − 9.92).

CONSTRUCTING PORTFOLIOS

The optimal solution to the portfolio maximizes an E-MODEL-type expected return while minimizing risk or unwanted exposures. One way to solve the portfolio problem is to construct a full-blown optimization with a complete covariance structure. This solution requires a substantial data set and the implementation of a quadratic program.

On purely theoretical grounds one must assume that either 1) investor utility functions are quadratic, or 2) security returns are normally distributed. Given the nature of the world, neither of these conditions represent reality. Consider the normality condition. Historical return distributions for individual stocks are not normal. The distributions have rather high peaks around the mean, and rather fat tails. One can "fix" the distribution by some standardization or ordinal ranking process.

From a practical standpoint, these theoretical conditions may not be as inhibiting to rational portfolio construction as some have suggested. It is far more important that the model which produces the expected returns be compatible with input data so as not to create biases or "clumps" of unwanted exposures in the tails of the distribution. This was, in part, the intention of the E-MODEL.

MINIMIZING RISK

Someone once asked Will Rogers how he had achieved success in the stock market. He said, "I buy when the stocks have small prices and sell when the stocks have big prices." At which point the inquisitor responded, "What if the small prices don't become big prices?" Mr. Rogers answered, "Then I don't buy them.

Clearly, Will Rogers should be credited with those who claim to have "invented" portfolio insurance. Perhaps his comments also reflect the pragmatic view of return and risk: if it's going up that's return; if it goes down, that's risk.

To construct a full covariance matrix for a 500-stock portfolio, one must produce 125,500 covariance estimates (each stock compared with every other stock). That's a lot of work. In addition, for those of us who have constructed such data sets with historical return data, we have discovered that the covariance matricies are not good predictors of *future* covariance matrices. Using pairwise comparisons to construct historical returns correlations have proven to be too tedious, and inaccurate for *ex ante* risk measures. The errors found in using historical correlations to estimate risk can easily average 30 to 50%.

Other covariance techniques include the single index model and multifactor models, which are shortcut methods to create a covariance structure.[9] The single index model relates the risk of any security to the "market," and assumes that all the covariance between any two securities is fully explained by each security's market covariance (beta). In formal terms, the extra-market covariance between securities is minimal. This approach reduces the 500-stock data requirement of 125,000 estimates to 1,500 estimates. However, it is perhaps too simplistic to deal with the complexities of the real world.

MULTIFACTOR RISK MODELS

With or without optimization, multifactor models provide a workable solution to active portfolio construction. Multifactor analysis is manageable in that it reduces the covariance problem to a tractible level, and at the same time has the potential for more precise risk analysis. The multifactor framework expresses the risk of a security as a linear

---

[9]See Edwin J. Elton and Martin J. Gruber, *Modern Portfolio Theory and Investment Analysis*, John Wiley & Sons, 1984.

combination of a plurality of factors (or attributes) which are common to all securities. For example, each stock has a growth rate, a momentum component, an identifiable industry, and so on.

With the multifactor model, the covariance matrix is generated by first producing a covariance matrix of common factors (10 to 20 factors is sufficient). Pairwise correlations between stocks are then determined quantitatively by assessing each stocks' sensitivities to the several factors.

Perhaps the greatest advantage of this approach to portfolio construction is the intuitive appeal of the factors to traditional portfolio managers. For example, manager style (i.e., growth manager versus value manager) provides categorization of factors associated with investor behavior and market cycles. In addition, major industries can be represented as factors.

Industry exposure and industry rotation are critical decisions for almost all active managers. Relative performance is often determined by "industry bets," either intentional or otherwise. Optimization without regard to industry exposure would be seemingly unacceptable to most active managers.

The incorporation of industry factors requires at least two assumptions. First, we must assume that industry-specific effects cause price movements to differ from one group to another. This is analogous to assuming that the win-loss records of the baseball teams in the American League East, say, will result in an array of team standings that will change throughout the course of a season.

Second, group rotation assumes that the firms within an industry exhibit some homogeneity in their relative price movements, aside from overall market influences. Carrying the athletic analogy further, we expect the individual players on, say, the New York Yankees to have a style of play that distinguishes them from players on the Boston Red Sox.

Most prior research on the covariation of security returns across industries has concentrated on homogeneity of returns for firms within an industry. That is, it has observed a player and tried to predict which team he is on.

At the same time, some research exists which evaluates industry rankings.[10] Do the top "teams" remain top teams for extended periods

---

[10]See Eric H. Sorensen and Terry Burke, "Portfolio Returns from Active Industry Group Rotation, *"Financial Analysts Journal,* September-October 1986.

of time? Or do "league standings" vary randomly from season to season. Evidence is in favor of persistence in industry leadership, which is a departure from random walk, much the same as we observe in major athletic leagues.[11]

Empirical evidence lends support for industry factors for predicting stock-by-stock covariances as well as for understanding industry bets within a portfolio. First, the correlations between any two securities within a defined industry are, in general, 5 to 15 times greater than correlations between firms across industries. Indeed, one of the better predictors of covariance between two securities is the average covariance between the two industries in general. Second, industry returns are not random over time. In ranking industry performance each quarter over quarter, there is an average 15% correlation in the rankings over the period 1972 to 1984.[12] In some adjacent quarters the rankings are as high as 38%, and as low as −20%.

ACCEPTANCE OF OPTIMIZATION TECHNIQUES

Few active managers use formal optimization. Nevertheless, as the securities industry continues its trend toward commodity-type trading of portfolios, there will be an increasing need to marry subjective (or quantitative) estimates with formal portfolio construction techniques.

Optimization techniques have already received wider utilization in passive strategies, as well as in asset allocation strategies. The reasons for wider acceptance with these techniques, as opposed to traditional stock picking, are twofold. First, the data requirements of asset allocation and indexing are less heroic than for active stock picking. With asset allocation there are fewer assets (typically 3 to 9 asset categories). As such, the covariance framework is much more stable over time. The objective function is better specified with respect to indexing since the technique is oriented toward minimization of tracking error as opposed to maximizing of alpha. (Expected returns for individual securities are subject to rather large errors due to the size of the nonsystematic component.)

---

[11]See Eric H. Sorensen and Terry Burke, "Portfolio Returns from Active Industry Group Rotation."

[12]Ibid.

Second, acceptance of more complete quantitative techniques will only occur when traditional managers and plan sponsors become comfortable with the process. Comfort will spread as the quantitative techniques for evaluating expected return begin to assimilate the factors that traditional managers and analysts know to be important, such as earnings trends, risk differentials, sustainable growth, and so on.

SOME GENERAL CONCLUSIONS

The trend toward quantification of the active management process will continue with or without the vote of traditionalists. Quantification will become more important in both domestic portfolios and international portfolios.

The critical dimension of advancement in this area is not which type of optimization algorithm is "best." With the proper constraints, it may be that a linear program provides solutions which are equal to those of a quadratic program, despite the fact that the "portfolio problem" is presumed to be a nonlinear optimization over a covariance domain.

On the other hand, as we learn more about estimation of covariance structures we can better implement nonlinear optimization in the classical portfolio model. Advances will occur as the models which we use in assessing relative return and optimal portfolio construction begin to mesh. It is incumbent upon those who design quantitative disciplines to focus on two aspects of model building. The first is that the models intelligently fit the data. This embraces the responsibility to understand the quality, distribution, and information value in a given data series. The second is that the marriage of model and data not only succeeds in producing synergy, but also succeeds in the "look and feel" realm of attracting the active portfolio manager.

APPENDIX

The E-MODEL is an earnings growth valuation. The valuation parameters include systematic (or macroeconomic) inputs and stock-specific inputs.

At the foundation, the E-MODEL originates with the intrinsic notion of present value:

$$V = \sum_{t=1}^{\infty} \frac{E_t}{\pi_{i=1}^{t}\left(1+K_i\right)} \tag{1}$$

where:

V = intrinsic value

E_t = estimated cash flows in period t. This is the amount that the firm could pay out of normal earnings and maintain the assumed growth rate

K_t = the appropriate discount rate for period t

Using standard procedures, this general model is transformed into a more workable framework, which is based on normalized earnings, normalized payout, growth rates, interest rates, market risk premium, and factor adjustments. The formal result for the expression of the E-MODEL is below.

The E_t parameter breaks down into several components. At any point in time,

$$E_t = f(E_0, G_A, G_B, g)$$

1. E_0 is the portion of normal earnings that could be available for payment to current shareholders. This is based on the earnings level that the company is capable of generating under normal operational assumptions. Normalization is accomplished by a series of algorithms incorporating actual earnings, actual revenue patterns and trends in price-to-sales relationships. In addition, we use consensus earnings estimates to assess the levels of E_0.
2. G_A is the near-term earnings growth. It is the compound annual growth in future earnings. The growth horizon is typically over the next three to eight years. The time horizon of near-term growth depends on the particular growth rate that is used. We make small adjustments in the growth assumption for those firms with extremely high or extremely low growth rates to avoid biases.
3. G_B is second-phase earnings growth. It is the transition period, and earnings growth will move toward long-term growth.

4. g is the long-term growth assumption. It is assumed to be the same for all stocks. The long-term growth rate is measured in relation to the long-term discount rate. The long-term discount rate, k, is assumed to be constant at the beginning of the steady-state growth phase.

The k_t parameter represents the discount rate that is used to discount the normalized stream to present value. The components of k_t are:

$$k_t = f(R, I, U(f))$$

5. R is the equity market risk premium. As seen in Exhibit 3, the risk premium historically is in a range of about 2%-7%.
6. I is the 10-year Government bond rate.
7. U(f) represents a series of factor adjustments that reflect risk, quality of earnings, and current behavioral forces in equity pricing.

Equation (1) can be expressed as:

$$V = \sum_{t=1}^{\infty} \frac{E_t}{(1 + R + I + U(f))^t} \tag{2}$$

$$V = E_o \sum_{t=1}^{A} \frac{(1 + G_A)^t}{(1 + R + I + U(f))^t}$$

$$+ E_A \sum_{t=A+1}^{B} \frac{(1 + G_B)^{t-A}}{(1 + R + I + U(f))^t} \tag{3}$$

$$+ E_B \sum_{t=B+1}^{\infty} \frac{(1 + g)^{t-B}}{(1 + R + I + U(f))^t}$$

After some manipulation, expression (3) becomes:

$$
V = \frac{E_o\left(1 + G_A\right)\left[1 - \left(\dfrac{1 + G_A}{1 + R + I + U(f)}\right)^A\right]}{R + I + U(f) - G_A} \tag{4}
$$

$$
+ \frac{E_A\left(1 + G_B\right)\left[1 - \left(\dfrac{1 + G_B}{1 + R + I + U(f)}\right)^{B-A}\right]}{\left(R + I + U(f) - G_B\right)\left(1 + R + I + U(f)\right)^A}
$$

$$
+ \frac{E_B(1 + g)}{(k - g)\left(1 + R + I + U(f)\right)^B}
$$

CHAPTER 6

The Many Forms of Portfolio Insurance*

MARK A. ZURACK, CFA
VICE PRESIDENT
GOLDMAN, SACHS & CO.

Investment managers always face the difficult task of allocating assets among capital markets. Although the stock market has outperformed long bonds and Treasury bills over the last 60 years, there have been periods when stocks have underperformed bonds and cash.

To diversify the risk of being fully invested in stocks, investors have typically allocated portions of their portfolio to different asset classes. An alternative risk-reduction strategy is the purchase of portfolio insurance, that is, the ownership of an equity portfolio with limited downside risk and unlimited upside market participation. Its most basic form is a portfolio with a protective put (see Exhibit 1).

*This chapter has been adapted by the editor based on a Goldman, Sachs' report prepared by the author in October 1984. The principles of portfolio insurance described in this chapter, however, are equally applicable today.

EXHIBIT 1:
RETURN CHARACTERISTICS FOR A PORTFOLIO WITH
A PROTECTIVE PUT

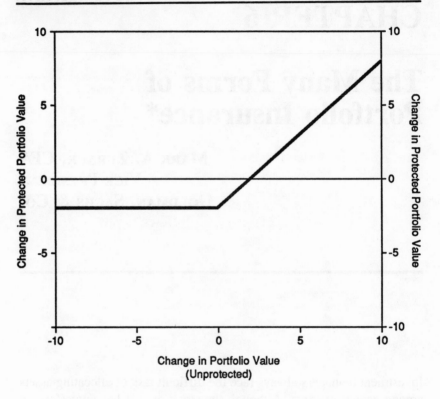

Over the last few years portfolio insurance has been a much talked about strategy. Before the October 1987 decline, estimates of $90 billion in underlying assets were managed using the techniques described in this chapter. Since then, the strategy has lost popularity for reasons that would require a whole chapter to explain adequately. Still there are investors who desire the risk/return characteristics of portfolio insurance. For that reason, in this chapter we will not discuss the reasons why you should or should not enter into a portfolio insurance program but rather focus on the different ways the strategy can be put into place.

DIFFERENT FORMS OF PORTFOLIO INSURANCE

A portfolio insurance strategy can be created in many ways. In this section, we focus on the most common. An investor entering a portfolio insurance program should first determine the type of insurance desired; only then can the investment strategy that efficiently provides the needed protection be selected. In most cases, the insured portfolio's payoff pattern will take the form of an option, either directly by using listed options to limit risk or indirectly by using a combination of assets with pricing similar to an option.

The cost of portfolio protection will depend on the degree to which the investor requires full downside protection and unrestrained upside return. Full protection, the most costly form of portfolio insurance, requires that the option's strike price be close to the portfolio's value. If the manager is willing to accept some decline in investment value before obtaining full protection or is willing to sacrifice some upside participation, the cost of protection will decline. The first strategy involves purchasing an out-of-the-money put, the second an in-the-money put. Exhibit 2 compares the cost of an in-, at-, and out-of-the-money index put for the S&P 100.

EXHIBIT 2:
COMPARATIVE PREMIUMS FOR THREE-MONTH S&P 100 INDEX PUTS*

Type of Put	Put Premium as a % of the Index
$5 in-the-money	1.05%
At-the-money	2.79
$5 out-of-the-money	1.67

*Market volatility is set at 15% per year, interest rate at 9.5%, the index at 160 and the dividend yield at 4.5%.

A portfolio insurance strategy can be transacted in the market with stocks and listed options or by actively shifting assets to and from cash to create a position with the risk profile of an option. This position, referred to as a *synthetic option*, is established by a process called *dynamic hedging*.[1]

---

[1] Leland O'Brien Rubinstein Associates, "Dynamic Allocation Strategies: Why LOR?," March 1984, Berkeley, CA.

A dynamic hedging program involves creating an insured equity position by adjusting a portfolio's weighting in stocks, cash, and stock index futures as the portfolio changes in value. In such a program, the investor systematically purchases stocks and/or index futures as the market rises and sells them as the market falls.

Portfolio insurance strategies also differ in the extent to which they expose the investor to the relative performance of a specific portfolio and the market. When a portfolio of stocks is combined with stock index futures or puts, the performance of the program will depend on the relative return of the portfolio and the index (unless the portfolio is the index). In contrast, a protection program that combines listed index calls or stock index futures with money-market securities does not involve the ownership of specific stocks, and its performance thus hinges only on movements of the underlying market index. Exhibit 3 summarizes the advantages and disadvantages of different strategies.

Buying Index Puts

One way to insure a portfolio is to purchase an index put on a broad market index. A diversified group of stocks, when combined with an index put, protects the portfolio from market decline while reducing the portfolio's potential appreciation only by the premium paid. The cost of the put premium depends on market conditions: It increases as dividends rise and market volatility increases, and declines with rising interest rates. (See Exhibit 4.)

There are distinct advantages to using index puts to insure a portfolio. First, unlike synthetic puts, which are discussed later, the cost of an index put can be determined in advance. Second, the portfolio manager can still actively manage his equity position. And third, index put premiums are lower than put premiums on individual stocks. The disadvantage of using index puts to hedge a portfolio is the lack of any liquid listed put contract with a life of more than one or two months. A portfolio manager constructing a longer than two-month hedge with listed index puts must therefore roll over one- and two-month contracts.

Buying Puts on Individual Stocks

Another way to insure an equity position is to purchase puts against each individual stock in a portfolio. A collection of individual insurance policies, as it were, provides added protection relative to a put on

EXHIBIT 3:
DIFFERENT FORMS OF EQUITY PORTFOLIO INSURANCE*

Strategy	Advantages	Disadvantages
Buying index puts against a portfolio	Insurance cost determined in advance. Investor captures portfolio nonmarket return.	Listed puts do not trade with expirations greater than 4 months. Must accept the pricing risk of subsequent option purchases.
Buying puts on individual stocks	Portfolio positions protected against decline on a stock-by-stock basis.	Premiums greater than for index puts. Not every stock has a listed put.
Buying index calls and money market securities	Can vary fixed income strategy around the call position; call performance tied to a diversified index.	Cannot capture nonmarket return on a portfolio of stocks. Must accept the pricing risk of subsequent option purchases.
Buying calls on individual stocks and money-market securities	Full participation in all gains from individual stock movement.	Premiums greater than for index calls. Not every stock has a listed call.
Selling stock index futures to create a synthetic put	Can create strike price and expiration date. Will capture portfolio alpha.	Actual cost cannot be predetermined. Must accept pricing risk of the futures contract.
Raising cash by selling stocks to create a synthetic put	No futures pricing risk.	Higher transaction costs and market impact costs in most instances.
Buying stock index futures to own a synthetic call	Can vary fixed income investment. Equity performance tied to a common index such as the S&P 500.	Cost cannot be predetermined. Position is exposed to index futures pricing risk.

*In addition to the insurance strategies using listed options and stock index futures, it is possible to create an over-the-counter European or American index option with a longer life than that available in the listed markets.

EXHIBIT 4:
VALUE OF A 2¾ MONTH AT-THE-MONEY S&P 100 INDEX PUT AT
VARIOUS LEVELS OF MARKET VOLATILITY AND INTEREST RATES

Market Volatility[a]		Interest Rates[b]	
Annualized Rate	Put Premium as a % of Index Value	Annual Rate	Put Premium as a % of Index Value
14%	2.1%	8%	2.35%
16	2.4	10	2.21
18	2.8	12	2.09
20	3.1	14	1.97
22	3.5	16	1.77
24	3.9		

[a]The risk-free rate is set at 9.5% annually, the dividend yield at 4.5% annually.
[b]Market volatility is set at 15% annually, the dividend yield at 4.5% annually.

EXHIBIT 5:
COMPARISON OF A PUT ON EACH STOCK IN AN INDEX VERSUS FIVE
PUTS ON THE INDEX ITSELF

	Beginning Value	Ending Value	Put Value
Stock 1	100	105	0
Stock 2	100	95	5
Stock 3	100	110	0
Stock 4	100	90	10
Stock 5	100	102	0
Index	100	100.4	0

Total value of puts on individual stocks = 15.
Total value of puts on the index = 0.

an entire portfolio. The owner of a portfolio of puts will exercise those with value while allowing the balance to expire worthless. In contrast, the value of an index put depends on the aggregate move of all holdings in the index and may expire worthless even if many of the stocks in the index decline in value. Exhibits 5 and 6 show that the return for a collection of at-the-money puts on a five-stock portfolio can differ significantly from the return of five puts on the entire portfolio.

EXHIBIT 6:
TOTAL RETURN ON A FIVE STOCK INDEX VS. EACH INDIVIDUAL
SECURITY

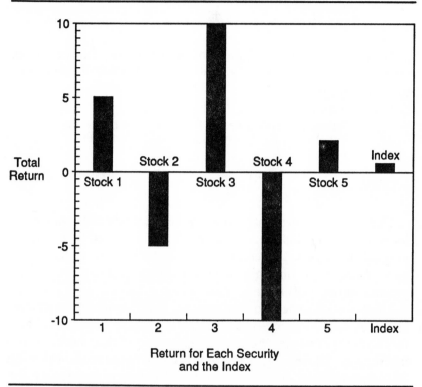

There are disadvantages to purchasing puts on individual stocks. Put premiums on individual stocks are higher than on market indices. In addition, trading costs are higher for individual puts. This strategy requires more time to manage, and implementation is constrained by the availability of stocks with liquid put contracts. However, in a volatile market where individual stocks are not moving up and down together, a strategy of purchasing equity puts on individual stocks should be more beneficial than other portfolio insurance strategies.

Buying Index or Individual Equity Calls

A well-known strategy using options involves reproducing a stock or index position with a combination of calls and puts.

$$\text{Change in Call Price} - \text{Change in Put Price} =$$

$$\text{Change in Stock Price} + \text{Dividends} - \text{Interest Financing Cost}$$

Through algebraic substitution, the above relationship can be extended to equate a stock/put combination with a call/money-market security strategy.

$$\text{Change in Call Price} + \text{Interest Rate Carrying Cost} = \text{Change in Stock Price}$$

$$+ \text{Change in Put Price} + \text{Received Dividends}$$

This formula shows that an investor can purchase calls to create an investment very similar to an equity portfolio insured with puts.[2] A long call/money-market security investment is not a new idea; investment management companies have been investing in so-called "90-10" programs using calls on individual stocks.

There are advantages to this strategy. Portfolio managers who believe they can add incremental return by trading the "yield curve" have the flexibility of varying the quality and maturity of their money-market investments. The manager can choose between equity and stock index calls depending on the type of market participation desired. By purchasing index calls, he gains immediate equity exposure with one transaction. Alternatively, he can buy a portfolio of equity calls to take advantage of price increases in individual stocks. The incremental cost of buying equity calls is the increased call premium for individual stocks.

SYNTHETIC OPTIONS AND DYNAMIC HEDGING

The previous section described four portfolio insurance strategies using calls and puts on listed options. Puts are combined with stocks on an

---

[2]All listed options can be exercised any time before expiration. There are times when a put would be exercised while a call would not and vice versa, so the two insurance strategies are not identical.

individual or portfolio basis, and calls are purchased along with money-market securities. Underlying all four approaches is the assumption that calls will increase in value as the market goes up while puts will decline, and vice versa. An option pricing model allows us to measure the change of the call and put price for a small change in value in the underlying stock or index. This change in the price of an option for a small change in the underlying security's price is called an *option delta* or *hedge ratio*.

To illustrate how the hedge ratio of an option would affect total return for the strategies described so far, we assume that the option deltas for an index call and put equal 0.5. If the portfolio and the index move in tandem, when the market increases $10, the owner of the portfolio hedged with an index put will earn $10 on his stocks and lose $5 on his puts, for a net gain of $5. The index call/money-market securities owner will also earn $5, reflecting the delta on his call position. In both cases, total return is directly comparable to the return on a portfolio of stocks and cash with an allocation of 50% stocks and 50% cash.

By properly measuring an option's hedge ratio, it is possible to create a synthetic option contract with a combination of stocks and cash. In a dynamic hedging program, the stock/cash position is adjusted as the option's hedge ratio changes. Hedge ratios change with changes in security prices, interest rates, and stock market volatility. Exhibit 7 illustrates how such changes affect hedge ratios; it also shows the stock/cash allocation required to maintain the proper synthetic options position.

To balance a synthetic option position, the allocation between stocks and cash should be adjusted for small changes in the hedge ratio. Typically, most dynamic hedging postions are adjusted for 5%-10% movements in the hedge ratio.

As we mentioned earlier, the owner of the synthetic call or put will buy stocks when the market is up and sell them when it is down. In a choppy market, this strategy can prove costly. Thus, the effective cost of a synthetic option is a function of the frequency of purchases and sales needed to balance the hedge. Transaction frequency depends on the volatility of the market during the life of the synthetic option. In contrast, the buyer of a listed put or call knows his cost in advance because it is based on the market's anticipated volatility. *Therefore, the cost of a listed option is a function of expected volatility, while the cost of a synthetic option depends on experienced volatility.*

EXHIBIT 7:
EFFECT OF CHANGING MARKET FACTORS ON A DYNAMIC HEDGING STRATEGY

	Change in Hedge Ratio		Appropriate Action to Rebalance a Synthetic Options Position	
Change	Calls	Puts	Calls	Puts
Stock market up	+	–	Buy stock/decrease cash	Buy stock/decrease cash
Stock market down	–	+	Sell stock/increase cash	Sell stock/increase cash
Interest rates up	+	–	Buy stock/decrease cash	Buy stock/decrease cash

Implementation of a dynamic hedging program forces the manager to make a market transaction every time an adjustment is needed. The cost of transacting becomes an important consideration in determining whether a synthetic option program makes sense. We recommend that a portfolio manager in a dynamic hedging program adjust his equity position with stock index futures or systematically purchase or sell percentages of the entire portfolio. A portfolio manager can change his equity and cash positions by purchasing and selling stock index futures. Using index futures rather than buying and selling individual stocks should reduce trading costs. However, the investor who integrates stock index futures in a dynamic hedging program must enter and exit from the futures market at certain times, depending on movements in the cash market. The timing of these transactions is not dependent on the relative value of the stock and futures market.

Therefore, the investment manager who uses stock index futures to create a dynamic hedging position runs the additional risk that he will have to sell cheap and buy rich futures. Stock index futures pricing risk has lessened in recent years due to increasing efficiency in the market, but it can still reduce total return for the equivalent cash position.

For very large dynamic hedging programs ($500 million to $1 billion), we suggest that the investment manager consider adjusting stock/cash positions in a formal portfolio restructuring program. In such a program, the investment manager transacts a stock portfolio through a broker with specific agreements made in advance. The total cost of transactions in very large portfolios may not differ significantly between the stock and the futures market. In addition, by raising cash in the stock market, the portfolio manager is not exposed to the pricing risk of the index futures market.

As there are tradeoffs among different portfolio insurance strategies using listed options, a portfolio manager should consider different dynamic hedging strategies in deciding how to establish a protected position.

Synthetic Index Puts

The creation of a synthetic index put requires changing the portfolio's allocation in cash and stocks from a fully-invested equity position. The amount of the portfolio invested in cash depends on the type of put

EXHIBIT 8:
EXAMPLE OF THE CREATION OF A SYNTHETIC PUT POSITION

1. An investor starts with a $10-million investment in equities.

2. He measures the hedge ratio for a one-year at-the-money put to equal 0.5; the S&P 500 index is at 160.

3. He sells 63 S&P 500 futures to reduce his portfolio's exposure to the stock market to $5 million.

4. 0.5 hedge ratio times $10 million equals $5-million desired cash position.

$$\frac{5 \text{ mil}}{160 \times 500} = \text{Approx. 63 S\&P 500 futures contracts reduce equity exposure by } \$5 \text{ million.}$$

desired and is calculated by measuring the delta of the synthetic position. The cash/stock allocation is adjusted as the delta changes, reflecting the changing characteristics of the put contract. Exhibit 8 shows how a portfolio manager would use index futures to create a synthetic put position.

The return on the portfolio hedged with futures will differ from the interest rate on cash to the extent that the portfolio's performance differs from that of the index and the futures are mispriced in the creation and unwinding of the position.

$$\begin{matrix} \text{Hedged} \\ \text{Portfolio} \\ \text{Return} \end{matrix} = \begin{matrix} \text{Risk-Free} \\ \text{Return} \end{matrix} + \begin{matrix} \text{Excess} \\ \text{Return} \\ \text{Due to} \\ \text{Futures} \\ \text{Under- or} \\ \text{Over-} \\ \text{Valuation} \end{matrix} + \begin{matrix} \text{Portfolio} \\ \text{Nonmarket} \\ \text{Return} \end{matrix}$$

Synthetic Index Calls

The creation of a synthetic index call/money-market strategy starts with a portfolio of interest-bearing securities with specific quality and duration characteristics. Exhibit 9 shows how a call position is established by the purchase of stock index futures or stocks to gain an exposure to the stock market equal to the call's hedge ratio. The

EXHIBIT 9:
EXAMPLE OF THE CREATION OF A SYNTHETIC CALL POSITION USING STOCK INDEX FUTURES

1. An investor starts with a $10-million investment in money-market securities.

2. He measures the hedge ratio for a one-year at-the-money call to equal 0.5; the S&P 500 index is 160.

3. He buys 63 S&P 500 futures contracts to establish a $5-million exposure in the stock market.

---

manager who uses index futures to synthetically create index calls will have a stock market exposure directly equivalent to the underlying index.

IMPLEMENTING A PORTFOLIO INSURANCE PROGRAM

In the previous section, we outlined the different ways a portfolio insurance strategy can be created. We believe three major factors should influence how an insurance program should be executed: liquidity; the type of protection desired; and the futures and options prices prevailing at the time of the trade.

Liquidity

Successful implementation of a portfolio insurance program requires the creation and adjustment of large stock index futures, equities, and options positions. To limit transaction costs in the program, positions should be taken only in the most liquid markets. Exhibit 10 shows that the size of the insurance program constrains the options and futures contracts that can be considered.

Shorter Versus Longer Expiration Options

The desired average life of the option position influences the structuring of a portfolio insurance program. Listed index options trade most actively in the near expiration months. A manager seeking to use a longer-term option to protect the portfolio is limited to synthetic or

EXHIBIT 10:
LIQUID FINANCIAL INSTRUMENTS FOR PORTFOLIO INSURANCE
PROGRAMS

Transaction Size	Index Puts and Calls	Index Futures	Portfolio Restructuring Programs
Under $50 million	S&P 100, NYSE	S&P 500, NYSE	Yes
$50-100 million	S&P 100	S&P 500, NYSE	Yes
$150-500 million	S&P 100	S&P 500	Yes
$500 million-plus	None	S&P 500	Yes

over-the-counter options. Thus, the decision to use listed or synthetic options is influenced by the relative attractiveness of shorter- and longer-term options.

Options with a longer life are definitely cheaper than short-term options in terms of total premium paid per year. However, the investor owns more protection with 12 1-month puts than with one 12-month put or four 3-month puts.

An owner of shorter-term at the money puts profits in a vacillating market by hedging downturns while only losing the option premium in months with positive market return. By comparison, the owner of a longer put may lose his entire premium in a volatile market if the net effect is a flat market return. Based on earlier tests, we found that no one strategy consistently dominated another. Therefore, *we do not accept the argument that longer puts should always be used because they are a cheaper form of protection.*

However, there may be circumstances in which the desired future payoff pattern of the investor warrants use of synthetic longer-term options, as outlined in the examples below:

- *Example 1:* An investor needs $1 million to pay off a liability in one year. The current market value of his equity portfolio is $1.01 million. He realizes that he must hedge his portfolio from market decline to meet the obligation, but he wants to participate in the stock market should it go up. He determines that a one-year deep in-the-money put is required to achieve the protection he desires. By measuring the hedge ratio on a deep-in-the-money put, he can sell enough index futures to create a one-year synthetic put.

- *Example 2:* An investor has a $1-million position in stocks. He is bullish on the market over the next year, but cannot allow his equity balance to decline below $900,000. He decides that a one year out-of-the-money synthetic put is required to insure the position properly. By selling enough futures to maintain an equity exposure consistent with the put's hedge ratio, the investor maintains his stock market position while adding an effective stop loss should his portfolio decline below $900,000.

When the investor needs a specific amount of cash at the end of the hedging period, it makes sense to use a dynamic hedging strategy to tailor a European option with an expiration date meeting the investor's requirements.

Valuation

If the investment manager is unconstrained by the need for a specific portfolio payoff, we believe he should use as many investment tools as possible to build an insurance product. We have showed how equities, listed stock and index options, and stock index futures can enter into a portfolio insurance program. The prevailing prices at the time of the trade in the stocks, options and futures should be considered in comparing the relative attractiveness of one insurance program over another. Exhibit 11 provides a systematic approach to evaluating strategies based on relative value between equities, options, and futures.

A portfolio manager who trades between stocks, options, and futures when running an insured portfolio should consider trading costs and valuation error when evaluating a switch from one asset to another. Trading costs include commissions and the impact of transacting in the market. Trading costs are higher for a swap from stocks to futures or stocks to options than for a switch from futures to options.

A swap among cash, futures, and options is only effective if the fair value estimate for each asset is correct. Exhibit 12 lists the market factors that affect the valuation of stock index futures and options. We believe that one can be more confident in a fair value estimate for an index future than for an index option. The only variable in a futures

EXHIBIT 11:
COMPARISON OF DIFFERENT PORTFOLIO INSURANCE STRATEGIES BASED ON VALUATION

Strategy	When Most Attractive
Buy index calls and money-market securities	Call premiums are low relative to put premiums and fair value.
Buy stock index futures and money-market securities	Index futures price below fair value; call and put premiums are at fair value or high.
Buy stocks and sell index futures	Index futures are expensive; put and call premiums are at fair value or high.
Buy stocks and index puts	Puts are low relative to call premiums and fair value; futures are undervalued.
Buy and sell stocks to raise and use cash	Futures and options are unattractively priced relative to the desired position, or position size is large.

EXHIBIT 12:
EXTERNAL MARKET CONDITIONS INFLUENCING VALUE OF STOCK INDEX FUTURES AND OPTIONS

Futures	Options
Interest rates	Interest rates
Future dividends	Future dividends
	Future market volatility

model requiring estimation is the projection of future dividends. In contrast, the market volatility estimate required to calculate fair value for an index option is constantly changing and very difficult to predict.

CONCLUSION

Portfolio insurance is an equity strategy that allows a stock portfolio to participate in a bull market while protecting the position against market decline. In its most straightforward form, portfolio insurance involves the purchase of a protective put against an equity position. In addition, the economic equivalent of an equity portfolio and long put can be created using index calls, index futures, individual stock calls, individual stock puts or by trading in portfolios of stocks. The major attraction of portfolio insurance is that it limits downside portfolio risk without capping potential upside return.

There are many ways to construct a portfolio insurance strategy, including buying puts on individual stocks, buying index puts against a portfolio, buying index or individual calls with money-market securities, and using stock index futures or portfolio restructuring programs to create synthetic options positions. A portfolio manager looking to implement a portfolio insurance strategy should define the period for which he wants to own insurance and consider the costs and benefits of using short- or long-term options. The liquidity of listed index puts, calls, and futures will determine the index used for a given strategy. The manager should evaluate the current prices of index calls, puts, and futures to choose his insurance strategy. By determining the most attractively priced instrument, a portfolio manager can improve the performance of the protected portfolio.

CHAPTER 7

Stock Index Trading: Techniques and Applications*

JOANNE M. HILL, PH.D.
VICE PRESIDENT
PAINEWEBBER

FRANK J. JONES, PH.D.
DIRECTOR
BARCLAYS DE ZOETE WEDD

The purpose of this chapter is to explain the nature of strategies and trading techniques used by institutional investors for enhancing the return and managing the risk of diversified stock portfolios. Attention is focused on program trading techniques as well as on stock index arbitrage, portfolio insurance, and asset allocation strategies that utilize these techniques.

*This chapter is based on a publication of the Financial Futures Department of Kidder, Peabody & Co. entitled *Program Trading, Portfolio Insurance and the Stock Market Crash*. The authors wish to thank Steven Bodurtha, Bernard A. Kroll and R. Steven Wunsch of Kidder, Peabody & Co. for their assistance in preparing this chapter.

PROGRAM TRADING

Program trading is a trading technique (not an investment strategy) for trading lists of stocks, very often in amounts designed to represent some stock index. This technique has evolved to meet the large-scale trading needs of pension funds and money managers. Originally, program trading was designed to allow index funds to buy or sell a package of stocks at closing prices. Many index funds embraced this technique since they were evaluated on how well they tracked the closing prices of their target index. Program trades have also been used in the fixed-income markets for several years; for example, when a pension fund wants to acquire a package of bonds in order to satisfy future cash flow obligations, a dedication or an immunization strategy may be employed.[1]

Stock trading desks that handle program trading have portfolios stored on their computers which they can send to the floor via computer with a few simple commands. These portfolios have stocks and shares designated in the appropriate weights used in the index for portfolios of various sizes, e.g., $10-25 million. Some portfolios purchased and sold in program trades do not resemble indices at all, but rather are lists of stocks than an investment manager wishes to sell or buy in conjunction with an actively managed portfolio being revised, a switch from one money manager to another, or a large injection or withdrawal of cash in the equity market.

Program trades are often, but not always, executed via electronic systems. All program trades, computer-assisted or not, depend on human decision making. Program trading was originally, and, in some cases still is, done by hand by carrying preprinted order tickets quickly to the specialist posts in an attempt to execute the list of stock orders as simultaneously as possible. However, program trading is more efficient and less costly to implement using the automated order execution facilities that have been made available by the various exchanges and NASD. In the NYSE's Super DOT (Designated Order Turnaround) System, orders are transmitted simultaneously and electronically to the appropriate specialist post in a fashion similar to electronic mail. This system is also used for retail orders which, if under 2,099 shares, are executed within 2 minutes of entry.

---

[1]See Chapter 14.

Program trading serves as an efficient and cost-effective order entry system for house traders and customers who want to trade portfolios of stock simultaneously. When program trades occur, all the OTC dealers or relevant specialists on the exchange floor begin receiving buy or sell orders almost simultaneously and the impact on stock quotes is faster than if the same orders were entered one at a time through individual stock orders or via block trading desks. Since the same amount of stock gets sold (or bought) whether done in concert or separately, the net impact on the index should be the same at the time when all trades have been executed. This point in time, however, is likely to occur sooner with program trading facilities than without them. Also, the execution cost tends to be significantly lower if the portfolio is traded in a program fashion. Program trading can take advantage of economies of scale in computer-based order entry and confirmation facilities. Also, in the cases where the customer desires a guaranteed execution price, the risk to the dealer is lower and the risk is more manageable if the portfolio is traded simultaneously rather than as individual stock positions. This lower risk on the part of the dealer can be passed along in a lower commission charge.

Applications of Program Trading

The Stock Market as a Commodity: Many critics of stock index futures and program trading take issue with the fact that these trading vehicles and trading strategies treat the stock market as a commodity. In fact, there are some good reasons for treating the equity market as an integrated unit rather than just as the sum of its parts. Advances in investment theory over the last 20 years have concluded that the risk of a portfolio's general equity market exposure should be separated from the risk of specific stock holdings for purposes of portfolio construction, risk management and performance evaluation. These principles of modern investment theory argue that the most efficient risk reduction can be achieved by diversifying investments across stocks. Portfolios should be selected that meet the objective of achieving the greatest risk reduction for a given return level. The portfolios that meet this criteria tend to be well-diversified, often resemble market indices, and thereby effectively view the stock market as a commodity.

Even for very actively managed equity portfolios, a large portion of price movement can be attributed to movements in the value of the overall equity market as defined by a market index. Given that many equity managers think of their risk and return as having an overall market component and a specific stock issue component, it is not unreasonable to think of risk management as most effectively implemented by treating these components separately. Therefore, the overall stock market exposure component of a diversified equity portfolio is a commodity to the same extent that the general level of interest rates is a central component of a fixed-income portfolio and thus a commodity.

Further, there are large groups of U.S. investors who think of stock indexes when they think of the U.S. equity market. Many investment products are specifically designed to trade the U.S. equity market as a whole. Index fund or passive equity management is based on the notion that it is very difficult or costly to achieve consistent returns in excess of that achieved by a market index. Very large institutional investors are forced by their very size to hold widely diversified portfolios that behave very similarly to the overall market indices. By explicitly investing the funds in a portfolio designed to track an index rather than in one or several actively managed portfolios, the institution can pay a lower investment management fee. This lower fee for passive management is possible because no specific stock research is necessary, and because trading and portfolio accounting can be streamlined, particularly if program trading facilities are used. By the end of 1987, some 30% of the total defined benefit assets of the 200 largest pension funds was indexed. Half of these 200 pension funds had some funds under passive index management, while 32% used stock index futures.

Passive or index management is also growing in international investment management; investors actively (or passively) select country allocation and then invest in an index portfolio within that country. In all of these cases, the stock market is effectively treated as a commodity or single unit, and the lowest cost means of trading this single unit is typically with a program trade or a stock index future, if available.

Specific Applications of Program Trading: Probably the largest users of program trading are pension funds and money managers acting in their capacity. Many of these institutions have become comfortable trading stocks in combination with the following purposes:

1. Managing portfolios invested in indexes.
2. Moving funds from one market to another, most commonly be-

tween the stock and bond market, between sectors of the stock market, or from one country to another.

3. Moving funds from one money manager to another.
4. Handling large contributions, withdrawals, or other cash flows of pension funds.
5. Moving out of one set of unattractive stocks to a new set of stocks deemed as undervalued.
6. Modifying the equity exposure of a well-diversified portfolio, e.g., in connection with a portfolio insurance, tactical asset allocation, or strategic asset allocation strategy.
7. Implementation of a stock index arbitrage trade.

Broker-dealers also use program trading for stock index arbitrage, for managing their trading desk risk, and for hedging their contingent index obligations. The applications of program trading techniques by user are shown schematically in Exhibit 1. As can be seen in Exhibit 1 and the list above, most of these applications of program trading are motivated by traditional investment management approaches and practices. Pension beneficiaries and owners of these institutional funds have benefitted from the lower commissions and lower execution risk of program trading. Program trading commissions are typically under $.05 a share, and market impact can be minimal compared to buying or selling the equivalent amount with individual stock trades, especially when trading is done on a market-on-close basis. Commissions of $.10 per share or more are common on stock trades, and the market impact charges and bid-ask spreads are usually wider. Many portfolios which are traded as packages have a very high correlation with the market indices on which index futures and options are based and are therefore more easily hedged by the stock trading desks of brokerage firms. Program trades can also be executed on a guaranteed basis in which the investors agree to pay a somewhat higher commission to shift the market impact risk of the trade to the broker/dealer.

Many pension funds and money managers utilize stock index futures for the same cost reasons that they use program trading—cost savings that are passed along to the claimants and owners of the funds. In the circumstances in which it makes sense to do a program trade, a trade in index futures could serve as a short-term substitute. Execution costs in index futures are typically even less than in a program trade and the liquidity of the index futures markets is in aggregate 150-200% of that

EXHIBIT 1:
PROGRAM TRADE APPLICATIONS

Institutional Investor*	
Overall Fund or Plan	**Asset allocation**
	Portfolio insurance
	Moving funds from one manager to another
	Handling large contributions or withdrawals
	Terminating plans
Stock Segment	**Passive equity management**
	Investing cash flows and dividends
	Swapping between stocks and cheap stock index futures
	Active equity management
	Purchasing a list of attractive issues
	Disposing of a list of unattractive issues
Cash Segment	**Cash management**
	Buy stocks and sell futures to create synthetic cash (arbitrate)

Broker/Dealer	
Arbitrage Desk	**Buy index/sell futures**
	Short index/buy futures
Block Desk	**Hedge a guaranteed portfolio execution**
Risk Management Desk	**Hedge a short or a long OTC index option obligation**

*Pension fund, mutual fund, money manager, insurance, endowment, non-profit institution.

of the stock market as measured by the underlying value of index contracts traded on an average day. Keeping in mind the goal of implementing a strategy for the lowest transaction cost, many institutional investors have turned to index futures markets for execution cost savings that are ultimately passed on to the small investors who are beneficiaries and indirect holders of these institutional equity assets. Thus, small investors, who have been cited as being damaged by program and index futures trading, are among the main beneficiaries of the cost savings achieved by these techniques, because of their use by the pension funds in which they have significant indirect holdings of stocks.

Impact of Program Trading and Greater Institutional Participation in Markets

There have been a number of developments in recent years that have resulted in changes in the composition of trading and the associated demands placed on market-making systems. In the last 20 years the proportion of stock trading activity from institutional investors has been increasing due to the growth of pension assets and indirect investment by individual investors in mutual funds. (See Exhibit 2.)

This growth in insitutional participation has lead to a concentration of investment decision-making authority in fewer hands. In addition, forces within money management institutions have led to more centralization in the investment decision-making process, and therefore in the trading process. The increased use of quantitative decision techniques, a shift toward less decision-making authority on the part of individual portfolio managers, and the centralization of the trading desk and trading authority at large money management institutions, have contributed to the growth of the average trade size from 224 shares in 1965 to 2,112 shares in 1987, as shown in Exhibit 2. Many of these changes have been motivated by the desire to reap the benefits of economies of scale in trading costs and to improve trading efficiency; that is, many money management firms have taken steps to aggregate trading requirements so that the demand and supply of stock from the portfolio managers at each institution could be collected and integrated before they are brought to the marketplace. A byproduct of this greater concentration has been that market-makers, even in the absence of program trading, must be able to handle larger trades at a given point in time. The role of block trading desks has become more important for

EXHIBIT 2:
STOCK TRADING ACTIVITY FROM INSTITUTIONAL INVESTORS

	1965	1977	1987
NYSE daily volume (000 shares)	6,176	20,928	188,937
Average number of block trades	9	215	3,651
Block trades as % of volume	3.1%	22.4%	49.9%
Average trade size in shares	224	641	2,112

Source: New York Stock Exchange.

accommodating these larger trading demands. The move to passive (index) management accentuates this trend to large scale investment management. Not only has trading volume in specific issues become more concentrated, but also more trading is done on a portfolio basis. With the growth of portfolio or program trading, there is a greater likelihood that a specialist will be exposed at the same time on the same side of the market in all of the stocks covered at that specialist post. Offsetting this "nondiversifiable" risk is the fact that in a program trade the trader is less likely to be acting on specialized information regarding a specific stock issue.

Index futures and program trading techniques have been popular in managing these large pools of funds because of the trading cost savings and greater efficiency involved; however, many market makers on the floors of both the futures and stock exchanges have accepted these changes in their environment with some reluctance and caution. The large demands for liquidity that these institutions require, especially when they all desire to trade simultaneously, have always had the potential to place great strains on the capital and operational systems of the marketplace. The system whereby specialists diversify their risk by making markets in stocks representing different industries does not deal with the risk they face when they are called on to take the other side of trades in which investment institutions wish to trade diversified portfolios (indexed or non-indexed) at a single point in time. Essentially, the innovations that have been instituted to minimize trading costs and money management fees—e.g., passive management—have changed the way in which stocks are traded. Liquid stock index futures markets have helped to accommodate some of these trading requirements as have program trading facilities at brokerage firms. The NYSE has made significant trade automation improvements, including the opportunity for greater use of the Super DOT system. However, the risk of providing market making services from the perspective of the specialist has increased due to this greater concentration and integration of investment decision-making authority.

STOCK INDEX ARBITRAGE AND ITS RELATION TO PROGRAM TRADING

Stock index arbitrage is a trading strategy through which offsetting trades are made in a stock index portfolio and index futures based on a perceived price discrepancy between the two markets that is in excess of the cost of executing the offsetting trades. Stock index arbitrage traders can include any investors who are natural holders of diversified stock portfolios or money market security positions, including pension funds, brokerage firms, financial institutions and private investors.

Prices in the futures and stock market can become misaligned from time to time for several reasons. Because futures markets are more liquid, allow for adjusting overall equity exposure with a single trade, and have lower trading costs and greater leverage potential, news or information is often first reflected in futures market prices. If and when futures prices become sufficiently out of line with stock index prices, arbitrage and traders step in to execute offsetting trades in both markets, thereby profiting and bringing prices more in line with fair values. As long as there is sufficient capital available to conduct the arbitrage, index futures prices will usually move quickly back within a band reflecting the cost and risk of executing the arbitrage trade. The side of the trade is executed in the stock market utilizes program trading techniques. Because the future is based on an index, the offsetting trade to an index futures trade involves trading a list of the stocks as comprised in that index. When an arbitrage trade is executed, a program trade in the underlying index must be executed as close in time as possible to the trade in the index future, the price of which is perceived to be out of line with the aggregate price of the component stocks. One must be able to get a reading on the prices in both markets simultaneously and have confidence of executing in both markets within a small margin of the prices as seen on the computer screen.

Stock index arbitrage trades do not occur in a vacuum. Stock index futures become mispriced in relation to stocks primarily because certain investors choose to implement their investment strategies mainly in one market or the other; that is, they have natural investment habitats. As mentioned above, many investors find the most cost-effective executions in index futures for revising their overall equity exposure based on a changing outlook regarding the aggregate equity market or economy. This is especially true if the change in equity exposure is anticipated to be short-term in nature. Many of these trades would be executed in the stock market if the futures market did not exist.

The upper panel of Exhibit 3 shows the process whereby information, analysis, and sentiment changes are transmitted to stock prices in the absence of a stock index futures market. Trades occur when the expected profits are in excess of the costs of trading on the information.

When a liquid stock index futures market exists in which trading costs are significantly lower than in stocks, the system is altered in three ways. First, the number of trades that occur becomes larger because trading costs are lower, as shown in the lower panel of Exhibit 3. Also, since trading costs are the same whether a two-way trade is completed

EXHIBIT 3:
MECHANISM LINKING STOCK AND FUTURES MARKETS

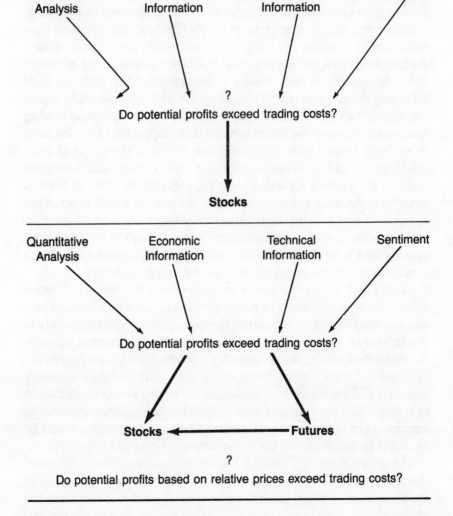

in two weeks or two years, more trading based on anticipated short-term moves in price become feasible when index futures exist. These incremental trades tend to be executed in the index futures market. Second, some trades that would otherwise be executed in the stock market shift to the futures market. These trades would be those that are large in dollar size and are based on a broad market view rather than on a specific stock or group of stocks. Finally, competition from the stock index futures market can help to lower commissions on stock trades, particularly program trades, and thereby increase the amount of information that results in stock trades as well.

Without stock index arbitrage, as designated by the arrows connecting futures and stocks in Exhibit 3, there is no mechanism to insure prices in the two markets reflect the same aggregate view of equity market value. Investors engaging in arbitrage evaluate whether the markets are out of line by looking at *relative* prices across the two markets. It is extremely difficult to say which market comes closest to showing the correct price at any point in time, but it is clear that they should move toward some equilibrium in terms of relative value. If futures are reflecting a more bullish view, prices there will be higher than their fair values given the index level and arbitrage traders will sell futures and buy stock to bring prices in line. If futures are underpriced relative to index values, traders will buy futures and sell stock.

The entities that engage in stock index arbitrage include broker/dealers in their trading accounts as well as institutional investors and large corporations. A long stock portfolio and short index futures position can replace a money market position and provide higher returns (net of transaction costs) when futures are overvalued. Some examples of institutions that have used hedged stock portfolios to replace Treasury bills, certificates of deposit or Eurodollar positions include nonfinancial corporations, money managers specializing in short-term cash management, savings and loans, mutual funds, endowment funds, and internally managed public and private pension funds. The combination of a long index futures position and a money market position creates a "synthetic" index fund with a return that exceeds that of the index to the extent that index futures are undervalued (net of transaction costs). Entities that have participated in this trade are any natural holders of indexed portfolios including index money managers, internally managed pension funds, mutual funds, endowments funds, and insurance companies.

In most cases, the sale or purchase of stock in a stock index arbitrage trade is a transaction that would have occurred anyway in the stock market if index futures contracts did not exist. Evidence of this is provided by the fact that many large investment institutions, which were faced with significantly underpriced stock futures on the days of the stock market crash (October 19 and 20 of 1987), chose to sell stock rather than futures as a means of reducing their equity exposure. If futures had been trading closer to fair value, they may have sold futures instead; their desire to move funds out of equities would have been transmitted into the stock market via a stock index arbitrage trade. From the point of view of the public and media, it may have appeared that the arbitrage trade was responsible for the decline in stock prices; in fact it was the original desire of large institutions to sell stocks in lieu of trades that would have been occurred in the futures markets. Placing constraints on program trading and, thereby, the stock index arbitrage mechanism would not necessarily reduce the amount of selling or buying except to the extent that the costs of execution are higher. It merely forces those trades that pass trading costs criteria to be executed in the stock rather than futures market.

The availability of index futures markets also permits speculative investors to trade stock indexes with less initial capital than would be required to purchase a comparable amount of stock on margin. These speculative investors have been estimated to represent only 10-15% of the volume in the S&P 500 futures market. Initial margin in futures, however, does not represent a down payment on a loan as it does in securities markets. Rather it serves as a good faith deposit indicating that the trader will engage in the transaction at the future date specified in the contract. Forward markets in currencies or mortgage securities are similar, but typically function without this initial security deposit. Other market participants are sheltered from the risk of fatal losses on the part of these speculators by the capital of the clearing members, by the exchange clearinghouse, by position limits, and by the requirement that all traders mark-to-market each day. That is, any losses on positions must be made whole in cash at the end of each trading day. Risk, therefore, from the point of view of the clearing members or clearinghouse is limited to the loss that can be incurred in a single day. In the equity market, mechanisms for avoiding the accumulation of large unrealized losses are less immediate and less effective. Not all speculative trades in index futures are necessarily transmitted into stock prices because arbitrage only occurs when index futures prices move outside of a transaction cost band around index values. Therefore, index futures prices trading at fair values must move in relation to index levels by approximately .5% or more before arbitrage trading will occur and transmit the move in index futures markets into equity prices.

Stock index arbitrage traders are unique users of futures markets because their futures trades are always accompanied by an offsetting stock portfolio or program trade. Thus, they have no stake in the prior or future direction of stock prices, only in the convergence of the futures price to the index value at expiration of the futures contract. When arbitrage brings stock prices in line with futures prices, it should always be the case that the new stock price will be within the bounds of the original index futures value and index value. For example, if an index is at 100 and futures are overvalued at 103 compared to their fair value of 102, the buying of stocks and selling of futures should ultimately result in an index value higher than 100 but lower than 102. The fact that arbitrage involves buying or selling large quantities of stock without a view on future price direction contributes to suspicions about the economic function of this strategy. In fact, the function of this arbitrage is to insure that both the stock and index futures markets are consistent in their valuation despite the fact that different investors choose to implement their investment strategies in one or the other markets.

An Analogy from Basic Economics

One way of understanding the means by which price determination occurs across two related but separate markets like the stock and stock index futures markets is to use a very basic example from economics. Think of two neighboring towns that have regional markets selling apples. People go to the market in the nearest town to buy apples, but the demand is greater in one town than in the other so that the prices rise in that town to $.59 pound vs. $.49 in the other. At a $.10 difference, it makes sense for a farmer who already owns a truck to buy them in the $.49 town, truck them to the other town, and try to sell them for $.59. As apples are shifted to the high demand town, the price in that town will fall and rise in the other, perhaps to settle at $.55 pound, at which point the farmer stops trucking the apples. The price differential between the two markets has to be high enough (exceed transportation costs) to make it worthwhile to redistribute the apples from one town to another.

The basic question here is, what is the real price of apples—$.49, $.59, or $.55? One could argue that the existence of the market in which apples can sell for $.59 causes the price to rise in the $.49 town to $.55. The existence of the farmer transporting the apples does, therefore, cause price volatility in both towns. However, would eliminating the market in which apples sell for $.59 mean the apples would still sell for $.49 in the other town? Probably not. Some people without access to apples in their neighboring town would drive the extra distance to purchase apples in the next town, creating demand such that the price would no longer stay at $.49. Therefore, with the two markets, each consumer gets to go to the closest town, and the farmer in the truck keeps the supply consistent with demand in both towns. With only one market, some consumers must drive a greater distance and therefore aggregate demand will be less than if there were two markets, but it is likely the price will lie somewhere between $.49 and $.59.

Some fundamental questions arise from this simple example that illustrate several of the issues involved in the role of index futures markets. Does the farmer/trucker provide a useful economic function? Answer: It depends what town you are from. Which town has the mispriced apples? Answer: It depends what town you are from. What happens if we close the lower priced market? Answer: Some of the suppliers will bring their apples to sell at the higher priced market and the price will fall there. What happens if we close the higher priced market? Answer: Some consumers from that market will drive to the lower priced market, increase demand there, and cause the price to rise there.

The analogy to index futures and stock markets is not perfect because the basic unit through which an equity position can be established is larger in the index futures market than it is in the stock market. One S&P 500 futures contract represents $125,000 of stock value with the index at 250, while 100 shares of an average stock priced at $40 per share represents $4,000. The difference in the size of units, in the market-making mechanisms (specialist versus competitive open outcry), in market entry costs, and in market regulations serves to differentiate the markets in somewhat the same manner as does the distance from one town to another in the example used above.

PORTFOLIO INSURANCE

Portfolio insurance refers to an investment strategy that attempts to alter the payoff pattern of a portfolio of risky assets, such as stocks or bonds, to reduce or eliminate downside returns while still allowing for the potential for upside returns. This alteration of returns involves significantly reducing the chance of returns below a minimum or floor level over some preselected horizon. In most cases portfolio insurance programs are defined in terms of some return floor and some horizon, e.g., 0% floor, three-year horizon. The cost of the strategy refers to the expected or realized underperformance of the strategy relative to the portfolio that is being protected. This cost should only be positive when the portfolio returns exceed those of the floor return, that is, in flat or up markets.

Portfolio insurance strategies have been frequently undertaken to increase the portion of funds that are allocated to investments with higher returns, such as equities, especially in rising markets. This higher exposure to equities may not be tolerated in the absence of portfolio insurance because of the potential for large losses on the equity position. These strategies have been most popular among large private pension funds which have seen their pension assets grow in relation to their pension liabilities. Many of these funds have instituted portfolio insurance strategies to protect their asset values against a cyclical decline in equity prices. In some cases, portfolio insurance strategies are applied with the goal of maintaining minimum ratios of pension assets to liabilities or a minimum surplus (asset minus liabilities). In this application, the fund is protected against increases in liabilities, e.g., from falling interest rates or rising inflation, that are not matched by gains in pension assets; however, the fund can still benefit from gains in assets relative to liabilities. Part of the appeal of portfolio insurance has been that it could be implemented as an overlay strategy with index futures or options; that is, a separate external manager or in-house manager can be used to administer the portfolio insurance program without interfering with the stock or bond management process, which may be being handled by multiple external managers. In an overlay strategy, the portfolio insurance manager is required to monitor any changes in the market value or risk characteristics of the assets being protected, but does not need to be in control of their selection.

Portfolio insurance strategies can be implemented by trading in the equity or index futures markets with the goal of creating a payoff pattern that mimics the changes in value of an option through a trading strategy often referred to as *dynamic hedging*. These strategies can also be executed in the options market by purchasing index put options along with the stock portfolio or by purchasing index call options along with a money market security like a Treasury bill. In dynamic hedging, the stock portfolio is hedged with stock index futures or has a mix of stocks and cash, where the portion of the portfolio hedged or held in cash varies between 0% and 100%. The stock allocation depends on the difference between the market value of the portfolio and the floor value as well as on the length of the portfolio insurance program. Operationally, as the market value of the portfolio rises in a rising stock market, the size of the hedged portion is reduced by buying stock index futures or stocks in a program trade; as the market value falls, the size of the hedged position or amount held in cash is increased by selling stock index futures or stocks in a program trade. Often the term of the portfolio insurance program is beyond a year, in which case the hedged portion or reserve asset is not cash but a fixed-income security with a term to maturity based on the length of the program. In this case, the portion held in equities depends on the relative movement of stocks and the reserve (fixed-income) asset. Dynamic hedging has been the most widely used implementation mode primarily because the types of strategies that have been most appealing in terms of cost and conformity to pension fund investment objectives have been those having horizons that extend beyond the time frame of listed option contracts. The over-the-counter and listed option markets have been too restrictive in terms of liquidity and position limits to accommodate the size of positions required to implement these programs on a large scale. A summary of the means by which portfolio insurance can be implemented is provided in Exhibit 4.

As described above, for portfolio insurance implemented via dynamic hedging, the stock portfolio being protected or index futures are traded in varying amounts in an attempt to duplicate the gains and losses that would actually have been achieved by holding a put or call option if one were available with the terms desired. The trades associated with dynamic hedging are typically on the same side as the direction of the market, e.g., selling when indexes are falling and buying when indexes are rising. They therefore are considered to be destabilizing trades that can contribute to higher volatility. However, except in the

EXHIBIT 4:
PORTFOLIO INSURANCE AND PROGRAM TRADING

Portfolio Insurance Implemented Through		
Options	*Futures*	*Stocks*
on Stock Index or on Futures on Stock Index	on Stock Index	Stocks only (implemented as a program trade)
Does not have to be managed as market moves (or is managed less aggressively)	Managed as market moves. With trades in the same direction as price changes.	
Does not require adjustment so not destabilizing (or requires much less adjustment)	Requires adjustment so marginally is destabilizing	Requires adjustment so marginally is destabilizing
Paid upfront based on Implied Volatility	Paid as trades occur and dependent on realized volatility and path of prices	
Can be handled as overlay strategy	Need control of stocks to trade	
Futures (and Options on Futures), Options on Stock Indexes and Stocks have different market maker systems		

case of large index moves, these trades are designed to gradually reduce the equity exposure of a portfolio as compared to what might otherwise have been an objective decision to move a large amount of funds out of equities in one large lump. The index futures market has been widely used as a means of executing dynamic hedging strategies because of its liquidity, low cost, and ease of execution compared to that of trading portfolios of stocks. Some portfolio insurance managers have the flexibility to implement in any of the index futures, options, or stock markets. Others implement the strategy in an "overlay" fashion—without controlling the stocks, they do their trading exclusively in the futures and options markets. Since a dynamic hedging trade is designed to change the exposure to the aggregate equity market, it is often implemented as a program trade when it is executed in the stock market.

The Role of Computer Models in Portfolio Insurance

Portfolio insurers that implement their strategies with dynamic hedging use mathematical modelling techniques processed on computers to arrive at a recommended equity exposure given the current level of the index, interest rates, volatility expectations, and trading costs. This use of computer programming techniques for quantitative modelling may lead some observers to refer to portfolio insurance as program trading. However, the computer models simply recommend an equity exposure consistent with both current market conditions and the design of the portfolio insurance strategy. It is up to the strategist and trader to determine how and when to implement that exposure. Some managers implement quickly after the need to adjust exposure is determined, some wait for several hours or days. Some managers adjust exposure frequently in small amounts for small changes in the value of their portfolios; others do it in larger amounts and less frequently. Some managers move toward but not all the way to the target equity exposure. Some manage exposure with stocks, others with futures, or with short-term options. The role played by perceived trading costs and market conditions in the decision to trade varies across managers.

In addition, each client has his or her own unique floor and horizon for the portfolio insurance program. Very different trading requirements are called for depending on the term and floor return of the portfolio insurance program. In general, strategies with short horizons in which the portfolio is close to its floor value have the largest trading requirements per index percentage move in a dynamic hedging framework. When a manager is using index options in a portfolio insurance strategy, no trading is required unless the floor or term of the strategy is changed or when the index options expire (in the circumstance in which short-term options are used to replicate longer-term options).

Implementation Risks

The three largest risks in implementation of a dynamic hedging strategy as a form of portfolio insurance are volatility that turns out to be higher than originally anticipated; discontinuous markets; and mispriced index futures. In the first case, trading requirements are higher than anticipated and more trades need to be reversed, raising the cost of the downside protection program above expected levels. Clients are warned that they will incur insurance charges based on realized volatility rather than expected volatility and that therefore the actual cost cannot be predicted with certainty. However, most managers show the client the level of costs that could be incurred in a highly volatile market in discussing whether to undertake a portfolio insurance strategy.

The second problem—discontinuous markets—is the risk that the stock or stock index futures market will not be available to execute the trades needed to bring the portfolio to the level of equity exposure consistent with the insurance strategy. A discontinuous market is one in which there are large changes in price between sequential trades, in particular between the close of a market and its open the following day. Should large price discontinuities occur, a portion of the portfolio will be underhedged and subject to the risk of the decline in stock values over the period during which there has been no opportunity to trade. The only solution to this problem is round-the-clock trading in liquid markets, no price limits, and no market halts. Another possibility is for the insurer to purchase options with far out-of-the-money strike prices that would appreciate in value and thereby adjust equity exposure if gaps in trading should occur. This latter solution would be quite costly.

Third, the risk of having to sell undervalued futures or buy over-priced futures can also add to the cost of the program but, except in extreme circumstances, the impact of mispricing is small compared to the other effects. This is true because there is already a trading cost savings from using futures that helps to offset some of the futures mispricing and because only a portion of the portfolio need be traded at any given point in time. In addition, many portfolio insurance managers have the alternative of trading the stock portfolio when it is disadvantageous to implement the dynamic hedge in the index futures market.

A final risk of portfolio insurance through dynamic hedging is the potential for so-called "cascade" effects in which portfolio insurers themselves might contribute to these falling stock prices to which they then respond by further stock selling. This risk arises because of the time pressure that is uniquely faced by portfolio insurers using dynamic hedging in bringing their portfolio into conformity with the appropriate equity allocation. The risk is positively related to the size of funds protected by portfolio insurance, and the proximity of existing protection programs to their termination and to their floor values. The existence of other strategies that call for offsetting stock trades under similar market conditions helps offset this risk only to the extent that investors employing these strategies happen to be trading at exactly the time that portfolio insurance activity exists in the marketplace. Such potential buyers would be value-based investors who tend to purchase stocks as prices fall; these investors, however, have no direct incentive to place their orders to buy or sell when portfolio insurers are placing theirs and should in fact be better off waiting until portfolio insurers have completed their trading. In the absence of these value-based investors on the other side, the liquidity for the portfolio insurance trades must come from the market-making facilities available off and on the exchange floors. This risk is also increased when market-makers have incomplete information about potential participants on the other side of the market or about the magnitude of potential selling associated with portfolio insurance strategies. Market-makers who are not aware of the price at which buyers are willing to step in may set a price too high and incur losses as further portfolio insurance selling occurs to the point where these market-makers deplete their capital to dangerously low levels. If they set the prices too low because of inaccurate estimates of the size of portfolio insurance selling or buying demands, the portfolio insurers will need to respond to the low price by selling more than they would have needed to if a clearing price had been previously determined. The basis for the effectiveness of dynamic hedging strategies is that those implementing such strategies do not influence prices by their trading activity. This assumption is most likely to be violated when changes in equity values are large and sudden, as was the case on October 16, 19, and 20th of 1987.

THE ROLE OF COMPUTER MODELS

Computers are used for computation in investment management much as calculators were used 10 years ago, and as hand calculations were used before that. They are also used for the speedy transmission of trading instructions and confirmations of trading events. Computers are used to maintain statistics describing price relationships over time and across markets. When these relationships reach critical points, as in a 30-day moving average crossing a 200-day moving average, or in stock index futures selling for more than the underlying stocks (taking into account financing costs, income effects, and trading costs), the trader takes notice of that disparity. He or she can decide whether to act and implement a trade based on the relationship moving back to a normal level. Many intervening events can cause a trader to ignore an opportunity which looks, based on computer calculations, to be profitable or advisable according to an investment strategy at a particular time, such as:

1. All funds available to the trader may be tied up in other strategies or positions.
2. Prices may be changing too fast for the trader to have confidence that the opportunity will still exist when the order arrives on the floor.
3. The trader may fear his or her trade will make the opportunity disappear because of its size relative to the order flow at that time in the market.
4. The trader thinks others will also see this opportunity and move more quickly to capitalize on it.
5. The signal is not strong enough to warrant taking on the execution risk.
6. The signal does not occur at the time the strategy is designed to monitor the relationship, e.g., intra-day vs. market close.
7. The trader has been given the discretion to delay trades if he or she feels better market conditions or a stronger signal will occur at a later date.

The basic point here is that human judgment is required to decide if and when to execute a trade that might be suggested by a model stored on a computer (or calculator or chartbook). The notion of computers trading a market into "meltdown" is not a reality. Human judgment is an essential element in interpreting trading signals given by computers. Computers are capable of determining when a pattern or statistic deviates from "normal," where normal is defined according to historical data or by relationships described by a model with assumptions stored in the computer. Historical data and model assumptions often give incomplete descriptions of events, such that human intervention is required to assess whether the data or model assumptions fit the reality at a particular point in time. For example, the stock of a firm facing potentially large liability lawsuits or the risk of bankruptcy, or with a terminally ill senior officer, may look tremendously undervalued when assessed by a computer model that cannot take these qualitative factors into account. However, any investor keeping up on current affairs would be aware of these issues and would be capable of integrating them into an analysis of the stock price.

THE INTERACTION OF ARBITRAGE, PORTFOLIO INSURANCE, ASSET ALLOCATION, AND OTHER INVESTMENT STRATEGIES

Another investment strategy that has grown in use in recent years is referred to as *asset allocation*. This strategy shifts exposures between stock, bonds, and cash depending on perceptions of relative value and risk in each of these asset classes. A specific form of asset allocation, called *tactical asset allocation,* implements these shifts on a more frequent basis than more traditional asset allocation and uses stock index and bond futures to effect the shift. Trading strategies such as portfolio insurance and tactical asset allocation have grown in size in recent years, in part because of the availability of low trading costs and liquid index futures markets in which these strategies can be executed. Not coincidentally future prices, with a few exceptions, traded within a 1-2% band around fair value thanks to the large supply of capital and efficient trading mechanisms available to conduct the arbitrage to keep prices in the two markets in line. Tactical asset allocators tend to be buyers of stocks in declining stock markets and sellers in rising markets, the opposite of the portfolio insurers. The feasibility and growth of this strategy has been furthered by the liquidity provided in index futures markets by portfolio insurance and stock index arbitrage. If this strategy had grown at the margin first, without the existence of portfolio insurance as an offset, it may have made markets less volatile because it is, on balance, a stabilizing strategy. Some of the destabilizing impact of portfolio insurance has been cushioned by asset allocation investment strategies and other purchases of stock that use fundamental value criteria as a basis for their investment decisions.

The strategies of portfolio insurance, tactical asset allocation, and stock index arbitrage can be categorized by their behavior in relation to stock market price trends and the speed with which they react to these trends, as summarized below.

Strategy	**Posture in Relation to Market Trend**	**Frequency of Monitoring**	**Time between Signal and Execution**
Portfolio Insurance	Trend supporting	Continuous or close of trading	Varies: intra-day or overnight
Asset Allocation	Trend reversing	Close of trading daily, weekly, or monthly	Overnight or longer
Stock Index Arbitrage	Trend neutral	Continuous	Immediate

Portfolio insurance implemented as a dynamic trading strategy tends to accentuate market trends by buying after prices have risen and selling after prices have fallen. The time frame for the trade response of portfolio insurance strategies is typically short because of the goal to maintain a floor return. Some managers monitor prices continuously and respond within minutes of a trigger being hit; others monitor only closing prices and respond some time within the following day with their trading requirements. With a few exceptions, most managers adjust their portfolios to the target equity exposure by the close of trading on the day following the point at which an adjustment was signaled.

Asset allocation strategies, on the other hand, are implemented with less urgency and are trend-reversing strategies. Many managers monitor prices and calculate fundamental values monthly and make their adjustments within the first few trading days of the subsequent month. Since these asset allocation managers are usually evaluated based on some performance benchmark, such as a balanced portfolio maintained at a constant mix, they have more flexibility in choosing when to implement mix changes subsequent to receipt of a buy or sell signal.

Tactical asset allocators utilizing futures usually monitor and make adjustments more frequently because of the ease of trading and low execution cost of stock index and bond futures. However, even these managers sometimes perceive an advantage in waiting when they observe many participants on one side of the market and rapidly changing prices. For example, if prices are falling sharply, asset allocators would typically be receiving a buy signal and may delay their purchase until they observe prices stabilizing with the expectation that they can purchase at lower prices at some later time. To the extent this delay in implementation does occur in periods of turbulent markets, the sequence of first portfolio insurers selling and then asset allocators buying in a down market would produce a whipsaw pattern in stock index levels. If, on the other hand, they both traded at the same time, the whipsaw would be eliminated but the net supply and demand impact on equities would be the same. In the former case, the market-maker becomes the buyer from the portfolio insurer and seller to the asset allocator to bridge the time gap; in the latter case, investors using these strategies would trade with one another directly.

Stock index arbitrage trades are neutral with respect to trend because they involve offsetting buy and sell orders in the stock and index futures markets. These trades may appear to influence the trend to the extent that the arbitrage opportunities are created because of portfolio insurance or tactical asset allocation trading activity. For example, as prices fall, selling by portfolio insurers in the index futures market could send futures to discounts from fair value and induce arbitrageurs to buy futures and sell stocks. From the perspective of the stock market, the arbitrage selling of stocks may appear to be destabilizing and trend-supporting, when the selling was in fact provoked by the demand for hedging by portfolio insurers implemented in the index futures market and transmitted to the stock market via the arbitrage activity. Trend-reversing activity in index futures from asset allocation traders may also be transmitted into the equity market by stock index arbitrage trades.

Exhibits 5 and 6 show several applications of stock index futures and the types of transactions that would occur in stocks, stock index futures, and bond or cash markets for different stock market moves. When prices increase, index futures or stock buyers include technical or momentum traders and portfolio insurers; index futures or stock sellers include value-based investors and asset allocators. Since index

EXHIBIT 5:
APPLICATIONS OF STOCK INDEX FUTURES

Applications	Central Variable	Types of Transaction	Related Stock Transaction	Substitute for Stock Transaction	Users
Portfolio insurance	Absolute level of stock price (or stock futures price).	Buy—when prices move up to trigger price. Sell—when prices move down to trigger price.	No	Yes	Pension Funds Endowments Non-profit institutions
Tactical allocation (base = balanced portfolio)	Relative stock/bond price/expected returns of cash.	Allocate from stocks to bonds when stock prices are high relative to bond prices and short-term returns and vice versa.	No	Yes	Pension funds Endowments Non-profit institutions
Momentum indicators technical analysis	Absolute level of stock price (stock index futures price).	Buy when prices increase. Sell when prices decrease.	No	Yes	Institutional and retail investors
Value-based strategies support/resistance		Buy when prices decrease. Sell when prices increase.	No	Yes	Institutional and retail investors

EXHIBIT 5:
APPLICATIONS OF STOCK INDEX FUTURES—continued

Applications	Central Variable	Types of Transaction	Related Stock Transaction	Substitute for Stock Transaction	Users
Arbitrage (long stock/short futures)	Futures price is rich relative to stock index.	Buy stock/sell futures: when futures are rich relative to fair value create synthetic cash instrument not limited by uptick rule.	Yes	No	Brokers Pension funds Endowments Corporations Banks
Arbitrage (short stock/long futures)	Futures price is cheap relative to stock index.	Buy futures/sell stock: when futures are cheap relative to fair value create synthetic stock portfolio short sellers limited by uptick rule index funds are major players.	Yes	No	Brokers Pension Funds Endowments Corporations Banks

EXHIBIT 6:
MARKET PHENOMENA DURING PRICE INCREASES AND DECREASES

	Value	Momentum	Portfolio Insurance	Tactical Asset Allocation	Arbitrage	Stock Futures
	Sell	Buy	Buy	Sell	Sell	Stocks
	Sell	Buy	Buy	Sell	Buy	Bonds or Cash*
			Sell	Buy		
Initial Price	Buy		Buy			
	Buy	Sell	Sell	Sell	Sell	Bonds or Cash*
		Sell	Sell	Buy	Buy	Stocks
				Buy		Stock Futures

*Can be executed in Futures or Cash.

futures tend to be overvalued in relation to the index in an up market, stock index arbitragers would be buying stock and selling stock index futures with offsetting trades in each market. In a declining price environment, the direction of these trades is reversed with technical, momentum and portfolio insurers selling and value-based investors, including asset allocators, buying. Arbitrage-traders would be sellers of stocks and buyers of cheap stock index futures. Note that the trades associated with stock index arbitrage that occur in the equity market are usually in the same direction as the price movement, and may apear to be destabilizing; however, there is always an offsetting stabilizing trade occurring in the stock index futures markets. Also, many of the strategies offset one another in the direction of their impact. The overall net effect depends on the magnitude of dollar trading volume in each strategy at a given point in time. For example, in an environment in which stock index arbitrage volume is small because of limits on the capital available for the trade or because of the speed with which prices are changing in both markets, a natural offset for portfolio insurers and technical (momentum) traders is not available. Alternatively, if tactical asset allocators trade several hours or days after portfolio insurers, the impact of trading by each group will be separately reflected in prices, the effect of which could be higher observed volatility.

SUMMARY

In this chapter, we explained the nature of strategies and trading techniques employed by the investment community for enhancing the return and managing the risk of diversified stock portfolios.

Program trading is a trading technique for trading lists of stocks simultaneously, very often in amounts designed to represent some stock index. This technique has evolved to meet the large-scale trading needs of pension funds and money managers. Program trades are often, but not always, executed via electronic systems. All program trades, computer-assisted or not, depend on human decision making. Many pension funds and money managers use program trading techniques and stock index futures markets for execution cost savings and flexibility that ultimately benefit the individuals who are the owners or claimants of these funds. The primary applications of program and stock index futures trading for these institutions include managing index funds, moving funds across asset classes or among managers, handling the investment of large cash flows, and conducting stock index arbitrage.

Stock index arbitrage is a trading strategy through which offsetting trades are made in a stock index portfolio and in index futures based on a perceived price discrepancy between the two markets that is in excess of the cost of executing the offsetting trades. Stock index arbitrage traders can include any investors who are natural holders of diversified stock portfolios or money market security positions, including pension funds, brokerage firms, financial institutions and private investors. A long stock portfolio and short index futures position can replace a money market position and provide higher returns when futures are overvalued. The combination of a long index futures position and a money market position creates a "synthetic" index fund with a return that exceeds that of the index to the extent that index futures are undervalued. Stock index arbitrage trades do not occur in a vacuum. Stock index futures become mispriced relative to stocks primarily because certain investors choose to implement their investment strategies mainly in one market or the other; that is, they have natural investment habitats. The fact that arbitrage involves buying or selling large quantities of stock without a view on future price direction contributes to suspicions about the economic function of this strategy. In fact, the function of this arbitrage is to insure that both the stock and index futures markets are consistent in their valuation, despite the fact that different investors choose to implement their investment strategies in one or the other markets.

Portfolio insurance refers to an investment strategy that attempts to alter the payoff pattern of a portfolio of risky assets, such as stocks or bonds, to reduce or eliminate downside returns while still allowing for the potential for significant upside returns. In most cases portfolio insurance programs are defined in terms of some return floor and some horizon, e.g., 0% floor, three-year horizon. The cost of the strategy refers to the expected or realized underperformance of the strategy relative to the portfolio that is being protected. Portfolio insurance strategies have been frequently undertaken to increase the portion of funds that are allocated to investments with higher returns such as equities, especially in rising markets. This higher exposure to equities may not be tolerated in the absence of portfolio insurance because of the potential for large losses on the equity position. These strategies have been most popular among large private pension funds who have seen their pension assets grow in relation to their pension liabilities, but have also been utilized by individual investors in mutual funds and via bank market-participation deposit certificates. Part of the appeal of portfolio insurance has been that it could be implemented as an overlay strategy with index futures or options; that is, a separate external manager or in-house manager can be used to administer the portfolio insurance program without interfering with the stock or bond management process, which may be handled my multiple external managers.

Portfolio insurance strategies can be implemented by trading in the equity or index futures markets with the goal of creating a payoff pattern that mimics the changes in value of an option through a trading strategy often referred to as *dynamic hedging*. These strategies can also be executed in the options market by purchasing index put options along with the stock portfolio or by purchasing index call options along with a money market security like a Treasury bill. Operationally in dynamic hedging, as the market value of the portfolio rises in a rising stock market, the size of the hedged portion is reduced by buying stock index futures or stocks in a program trade; as the market value falls, the size of the hedged position or amount held in cash is increased by selling stock index futures or stocks in a program trade. Portfolio insurers who implement their strategies with dynamic hedging use mathematical modelling techniques processed on computers to arrive at a recommended equity exposure given the current level of the index, interest rates, volatility expectations, and trading costs. This use of computer programming techniques for quantitative modelling may lead some observers to refer to portfolio insurance as program trading. However, the computer models simply recommend an equity exposure consistent with current market conditions and with the design of the portfolio insurance strategy. It is up to the strategist and trader to determine how and when to implement that exposure.

The three largest risks in implementation of a dynamic hedging strategy as a form of portfolio insurance are volatility that turns out to be higher than originally anticipated, discontinuous markets, and mispriced index futures. In the first case, trading requirements are higher than anticipated and more trades need to be reversed, raising the cost of the downside protection program above expected levels. The second problem, discontinuous markets, is the risk that the stock or stock index futures market will not be available to execute the trades needed to bring the portfolio to the level of equity exposure consistent with the insurance strategy. Third, the risk of having to sell undervalued futures or buy overpriced futures can also add to the cost of the program but, except in extreme circumstances, the impact of mispricing is small compared to the other effects. A final risk of portfolio insurance through dynamic hedging is the potential for so-called "cascade" effects in which portfolio insurers themselves might contribute to falling stock prices to which they then respond by further stock selling. This risk arises because of the time pressure that is uniquely faced by portfolio insurers using dynamic hedging to bring their portfolio in conformity with the appropriate equity allocation. The basis for the efficacy of dynamic hedging strategies is that those implementing such strategies do not significantly influence prices by their trading activity. This assumption is most likely to be violated when changes in equity values are large and sudden as was the case on October 16, 19, and 20th, of 1987.

Another investment strategy that has grown in use in recent years is referred to as *asset allocation*. This strategy shifts exposures between stocks, bonds, and cash depending on perceptions of relative value and risk in each of these asset classes. A specific form of asset allocation, called *tactical asset allocation*, implements these shifts on a more frequent basis than more traditional asset allocation and uses stock index and bond futures to effect the shift. The strategies of portfolio insurance, tactical asset allocation, and stock index arbitrage can be categorized by their behavior in relation to stock market price trends and the speed with which they react to these trends. Portfolio insurance implemented as a dynamic trading strategy tends to accentuate market trends by buying after prices have risen and selling after prices have fallen. The time frame for the trade response of portfolio insurance strategies is typically short because of the goal to maintain a floor return. Asset allocation strategies, on the other hand, are implemented with less urgency and are trend-reversing strategies. Stock index arbitrage trades are neutral with respect to trend because they involve offsetting buy and sell orders in the stock and index futures markets.

CHAPTER 8

Dynamic Hedging for Risk Control Management

DEAN D'ONOFRIO, CFA*
VICE PRESIDENT
BANKERS TRUST COMPANY

GENERAL DESCRIPTION

Dynamic Hedging (DH) is a conditional asset allocation strategy designed to attain at least a prespecified minimum result over a finite time period, yet provide a superior outcome if attainable. DH can also be defined as an investment strategy that will (at the conclusion of a finite period) provide the best result of N alternative outcomes.[1] In either case, DH is simply an asset allocation policy that is executed as a function of an investor's current wealth and risk tolerance. It is a

---

*With the help of Juli Blumenthal, Philip Green and Eric Lobben

[1]For a more detailed explanation, see Robert Geske, "The Valuation of Compound Options," *Journal of Financial Economics* 7 (1979):63–81. Also see Rene M. Stulz, "Options on the Minimum or the Maximum of Two Risky Assets," *Journal of Financial Economics* 10 (1982):161–85. Also see Richard Tanenbaum, "Beyond Portfolio Insurance, or the Poor Person's Portfolio Protective Put Pricing Paradigm," paper presented at the Investment Technology Association, May 1985, (New York Society of Securities Analysts, New York, NY).

"common sense" approach to asset allocation, quantified to precision.

The investment community has adopted the misleading term "portfolio insurance" for this technology because its most popular application to date has been protecting the value of equity portfolios. The label, portfolio insurance, is misleading for a number of reasons. Most notably, the term "insurance" implies pooling the risk of many diversified insureds. In truth, however, there is no such pooling of risk in so-called portfolio insurance. The investor bears all risks involved.[2]

An investor using portfolio insurance has simply decided to alter his risk exposure (i.e., through asset allocation changes) in tandem with changes in his wealth. There is no transfer of risk to a second party; there is merely a decision on the part of the investor to alter his risk exposure as a function of his current wealth.

For investors seeking similar results (i.e., a minimum future value or a greater value if possible) *and* assurance from a second party, there are alternatives, the most practical of which is the purchase of option contracts. Option contracts are instruments that give their holder the right to buy or sell securities at a pre-specified price on a particular date.[3] The owner of a stock and a put option on that stock owns an asset and an "insurance policy" on the future market value of that asset. Because a put option gives its holder the right to sell its underlying asset at a predetermined "strike price," an investor, if rational, would sell (or put) his asset at the strike price (to the seller of the option) should its market price fall below that level. Hence, owning a put option provides a floor value for an asset, or assurance of a minimum future market value.

What can an investor do if he wishes to maintain a minimum asset value, yet holds an asset or portfolio of assets for which there are no listed options? What can he do if the listed options that exist do not have suitable maturities, strike prices, or liquidity? Short of finding an investor willing to write a put or an insurer willing to underwrite a policy, he has two general choices. If he requires that results be assured by a second party, he can attempt to approximate owning the desired option contract by buying and selling a combination of the available

---

[2]If options are purchased instead of pursuing a dynamic hedging program, the investor bears only credit risk.

[3]Options, in this chapter, refers to Euro-style settlement contracts (i.e., exercisable at expiration only).

options.[4] The other alternative is to attempt to replicate the option strategy through careful execution of a dynamic hedging program. In this case, dynamic hedging can be (and often is) defined as a method of replicating the return of options or, similarly, a facility to create synthetic options.[5]

The primary value of dynamic hedging technology is the ability to create, synthetically, assets that otherwise would not exist. Armed with this ability, an investor can go beyond the "known world" of investment management and create investment strategies that offer a more precise match to the specified objectives and risk tolerances of the investor.

With this in mind, the reader is strongly encouraged to examine the motivation for traditional investment policies. What are the minimum goals of these strategies? How is risk defined? What is the cost of reducing or eliminating risk?

APPLICATIONS

In the preceding section we identified "portfolio insurance," or protecting one's previous gains, as the most popular application of DH. This, however, is neither the only application, nor, in many cases, the best application of DH. Since DH is a technique of providing investors with the better of N alternatives, it is then best applied in situations where the investor has defined a minimum goal, yet given the opportunity, would prefer a superior outcome.

Let's look at some examples. In the aforementioned case of using DH to protect gains, the rational investor has done so, because he has determined the amount of future wealth he requires to meet his goal or obligations; yet, he desires a greater amount of wealth if it is attainable. Therefore, he constructs a strategy that will, at some point in the future, attempt to provide him with the better of a) a predetermined amount of minimum wealth, or b) a greater amount of wealth if possible.

---

[4]It is possible to approximate the performance of an option through a combination of long and/or short positions in other options. However, if the desired option has a different expiration date than those available, then the replication process will require periodic rebalancing. Hence, it, too, is a form of dynamic hedging.

[5]See Mark Rubinstein and Hayne E. Leland, "Replicating Options with Positions in Stock and Cash," *Financial Analysts Journal* (July–August 1981):3-12.

Investors who commit their funds to guaranteed investment contracts, annuities, dedicated bond portfolios, and immunized bond portfolios are examples of investors who desire a minimum amount of future wealth. However, these investors have accepted a single outcome as their desired result. They have determined that they have no tolerance for a return on their assets even slightly below that which they have "locked up."

To the extent that the investors using these strategies can tolerate a slightly lower, yet pre-specified, minimum return, and assuming that they prefer higher returns when they are available, then a DH program may be a more suitable strategy. DH's relative attractiveness in this case stems from its ability to offer the better of a) a pre-specified minimum return, set at a tolerable level below that of the alternative immunization or dedication, or b) a substantially higher return than that available through immunization or dedication.

The above example can be labeled as a "synthetic convertible bond." That is, a slightly lower fixed return is accepted (as in convertibles) in exchange for the opportunity to achieve a significantly greater return (as through conversion).

The key point in determining whether DH is a suitable investment strategy lies upon one's ability to define risk as *the likelihood of achieving a definable goal within a finite time period*. Most pension funds maintain an asset allocation policy designed to achieve the highest expected return for a given level of risk. Traditionally, risk has been defined as variability (standard deviation) of return. If one believes that security returns are approximately log-normally distributed (a common assumption), then return volatility as a measure of risk would be depicted as in Exhibit 1.

However, return volatility alone may not explain risk. For many investors, risk is equivalent to the potential for loss or the likelihood of underperforming a specific fixed rate or benchmark return. In that case, risk could be generally depicted as in Exhibit 2.

Using pension funds as an example, we can define risk as the likelihood of not maintaining a minimum funding level or, similarly, the likelihood of being faced with a larger than expected minimum contribution. For pension funds, therefore, wealth may be defined as the surplus (or deficit) of assets over liabilities and risk may be depicted as in Exhibit 3.

Pension plan sponsors who can define risk as the probability of not

EXHIBIT 1:
VARIABILITY OF RETURN AS A MEASURE OF RISK

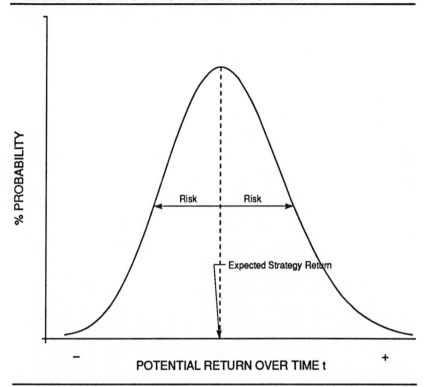

maintaining a minimum plan wealth should consider the use of DH.[6] This is because DH will continuously allocate assets *according to the fund's ability to meet its goal.* Without such a program, there will inevitably be times when the fund is at risk of violating its minimum goal, or even more likely, times when the fund will be overly conservative. The cost incurred in the former case is easily understood: having to make a larger than expected contribution, for example. The cost

---

[6]See William F. Sharpe, "Policy Asset Mix, Tactical Asset Allocation, and Portfolio Insurance," Chapter 7 in Robert Arnott and Frank J. Fabozzi (editors), *Asset Allocation* (Chicago, IL: Probus Publishing 1988). Also see Jay O. Light and Andre F. Perold, "Conditional Allocation Policies for a Self-Insured Pension Fund," Harvard Business School (December 1986). Also see Mark Kritzman, "What's Wrong With Portfolio Insurance?" *Journal of Portfolio Management* (Fall 1986):13–16.

EXHIBIT 2:
PROBABILITY OF UNDERPERFORMING AS A MEASURE OF RISK

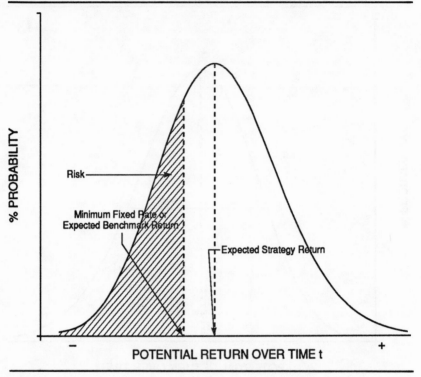

incurred in the latter case is the economic profit that is foregone because of an overly cautious investment policy.

Pension sponsors, of course, aren't the only investors for whom DH may be suitable. Participants in defined contribution plans are classic examples of investors who require a minimum return, yet would prefer higher returns if attainable. Typically, however, the majority of their assets is committed to fixed-rate instruments; moreover, their mix of investments is rarely changed, regardless of their ability to bear risk. DH, however, would provide them with the opportunity for greater returns, yet would protect them from loss by automatically increasing their risk when they can afford to, and decreasing it when they can't.

More esoteric applications of DH do not provide assurance of an *absolute* minimum value, but of a *relative* goal.[7] For example, a DH

_____

[7]See William Margrabe, "The Value of an Option to Exchange one Asset for Another," *Journal of Finance* 33 (March 1978).

EXHIBIT 3:
LIKELIHOOD OF VIOLATING MINIMUM FUNDING LEVEL AS A
MEASURE OF RISK

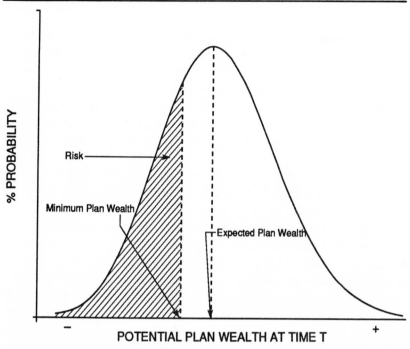

strategy can be created so that it will provide (less a slight premium) the better performance of either a) an actively managed portfolio, or b) an indexed portfolio.

This application of DH may be a more efficient method of managing funds that have traditionally been divided among multiple managers. Typically, in such an environment, although each individual manager may have his own style bias, it is most likely that each also maintains a certain level of diversification. This is to be expected, because even though a large fund with many managers is diversified as a whole, each manager sees only his component. Therefore, each maintains a certain level of diversification, which inevitably reduces his upside potential.

The motivation behind a multiple manager structure is usually two-fold: Multiple managers provide overall diversification to the total fund, yet each individual manager provides the potential for excess returns.

The fund as a whole will enjoy excess profits (over index funds) to the extent that the individual biases of the managers collectively add value. Conversely, the fund as a whole will underperform index funds to the extent that the collective active management biases do not pay off.

A more efficient method of achieving similar results may be available through the use of DH. Specifically, a program can be constructed which would provide the better of either a) the return of active management, less a premium, or b) the return of an index fund, less a pre-specified number of basis points. Within such a program, assets would be divided between an active component and a passive component. The allocation would change, subject to the fund's ability to meet its minimum goal.

The potential benefits of this strategy *vis-à-vis* a traditional multiple manager approach stem primarily from the following two facts. First, diversification would be provided by a passive vehicle, as opposed to the collective holdings of many managers. This, of course, is a less expensive method of providing a more exact form of diversification. Management fees are lower, transactions costs are less, and the amount of diversification is more precise. Second, since diversification is not a concern, individual managers need only concentrate on selecting their "best ideas." Reducing the workload of the active manager may make him more productive. In addition, as with all DH strategies, the overall risk of the fund would be dynamically altered according to its ability to meet the minimum goal. This means that the fund as a whole will take more risk automatically and efficiently when it can afford to, and take less risk when it cannot.

In summary, DH can be effectively used in any situation in which one is currently endeavoring to control or modify risk exposure as a function of absolute or relative wealth. Traditional risk controlling strategies are generally imprecise, requiring guess-work to determine the appropriate risk posture, and can result in less than optimal results. DH brings a greater level of precision to the task of maintaining risk posture, and gives the investor a reliable vehicle for controlling the acceptable outcomes.

PROGRAM MECHANICS

The first step in setting up a DH program is specifying its parameters. The items that must be specified are:

- the time horizon,
- the minimum acceptable outcome, and
- a reasonable, desired, alternative outcome.

A strategy's specification should result from its motivation. For instance, consider a strategy that was designed to fund a subset of pension liabilities as the minimum outcome, yet seeks to earn excess profits (i.e., fund a longer stream of liabilities) if attainable. In that case, the time horizon would equal the duration of the liabilities, and the minimum return is that which funds the liabilities. The portfolio would consist of two asset classes: a "hedge" asset, designed to attain at least the minimum outcome over the horizon, and a "risk" asset, which carries the potential for a substantially higher return than that of the hedge asset. In this situation, the hedge asset would most likely be a structured bond portfolio, while the risk asset would most likely be an equity portfolio.[8]

Mechanically, the fund would be divided and continously rebalanced between the two assets according to its ability to bear risk. (Risk, again, is defined as the likelihood of not achieving the minimum desired outcome within the specified time period.) Since it is the fund's preference to exceed the minimum outcome if possible, and since that is not possible through investment in the hedge asset, it is the objective of the strategy to maintain as much exposure as possible to the risk asset. The maximum amount of exposure to the risk asset that is tolerable is determined by the answers to the following questions:

- What has the portfolio earned to date, relative to its minimum desired result?
- As a result, what is the required minimum return from this point forward?
- What can we earn, "risk free," through investment in the hedge asset?
- How much time is remaining until expiration of the strategy?
- What is the likelihood that an investment in the risk asset will suffer a loss great enough to jeopardize the minimum outcome

---

[8]In any dynamic hedging program, the risk asset can be any asset other than the hedge asset. In the example cited, since the hedge asset is a structured bond portfolio, the risk asset could be, for example, equities, gold, bonds of different duration, or even T-bills. A structured bond portfolio, in this context, refers to a portfolio designed so as to mimic any change in present value of the liabilities in question.

before the next opportunity to sell units of the risk asset and to buy units of the hedge asset?

In general, as the portfolio's return exceeds its goal, it can afford to take more risk. Conversely, as the portfolio's return lags its goal, it must take action to prevent the likelihood of further slippage, that is, it must take less risk. Therefore, as the portfolio appreciates at a rate faster than its minimum desired pace, a greater percentage will be invested in the risk asset. Yet, as its return lags the minimum desired pace, more will be invested in the hedge asset. (Exhibit 4 in the appendix contains the chronology of events for a hypothetical program with a one-year horizon and a minimum return of −5%. The risk asset is an S&P 500 index fund, while the hedge asset is a one-year discount note.)

The astute reader will recognize the five factors listed above as the required inputs in most option pricing models.[9] Of course, this is no coincidence. (Recall our earlier definition of dynamic hedging as a method of creating synthetic options.) As is the case with options pricing, all but one of the required inputs for dynamic hedging are easily determinable. The one that is not is the variability of risk asset returns.

Estimating the variability of risk asset returns is the most difficult and the most important part of implementing a dynamic hedging strategy. This input is essentially a forecast. As with any forecast, it is unlikely that events will unfold exactly as predicted. Consequently, an investor embarking upon a dynamic hedging strategy cannot be completely assured of achieving the minimum desired outcome, nor can he exactly predict the degree to which the fund will participate in favorable risk asset returns.

It is important to note that DH strategies can fail if volatility estimates are grossly incorrect. Greater than expected volatility may cause a loss greater than that thought possible before the next trading opportunity. If the loss reduces the hedged portfolio's market value to a level

[9]See Fischer Black and Myron Scholes, "The Pricing of Options and Corporation Liabilities," *Journal of Political Economy* 81 (May–June 1973):637–59. Also see Robert C. Merton, "Theory of Rational Option Pricing," *Bell Journal of Economics and Management Science* 4 (Spring 1973):141–83. Also see John C. Cox, Stephen A. Ross, and Mark Rubinstein, "Option Pricing: A Simplified Approach," *Journal of Financial Economics* 7 (September 1979):229–63.

below the discounted value of the desired minimum, the strategy will have failed. This is because the minimum ending value cannot be assured, even through complete liquidation and 100% investment in the risk-free asset.[10]

There are a number of methods used to attempt to predict future volatility. Some rely on historical returns, some impute volatility from listed option prices, some use multi-factor regression models, while others involve examination of daily trading ranges. Unfortunately, there is no reliable method of exactly predicting volatility.

Fortunately, it is unlikely that estimates can be so wrong that they seriously jeopardize the desired minimum; it is likely, however, that experienced volatility will differ enough from expectations to cause some tracking error around the original expected result. Therefore, in executing a program, the prudent DH manager periodically (if not continuously) monitors the barometers of expected volatility and reacts appropriately.

Obviously, there are some remedies available to the DH manager that will reduce or eliminate the risk of volatility misestimation. For instance, the manager can take a conservative approach and use a very high estimate for volatility. As a result, the average exposure to the risk asset will be lower, making a floor violation less likely. However, participation in positive risk asset returns will be greatly reduced. That is, in exchange for greater assurance of achieving the floor return, the investor must pay a higher opportunity cost premium.

As mentioned earlier, an alternative to dynamic hedging altogether is an outright purchase of option contracts. If a protective put is purchased, the cost of the hedge is known in advance and the floor is assured because the contract holder can put his shares to the contract writer at the strike price. In essence, the investor in this case has transferred any volatility misestimation risk to the option writer. As a result, the only risk the investor bears is that associated with the creditworthiness of the option writer. Since the option writer is equally aware of the consequences of misestimating volatility, however, one should assume that he will demand an option price above that associated with his volatility prediction in order to be compensated for the risk he bears. Consequently, one would expect to pay more for options than for

---

[10]See the Appendix for an illustration.

DH, unless it is known in advance that the option writer's volatility estimate is too low.[11]

The reader may also recognize that each of the aforementioned factors determining the risk/hedge asset mix changes continuously; therefore, the optimal allocation between risk and hedge assets will change continuously. This raises two salient issues. First, because continuous trading per se is impossible, the actual risk/hedge asset mix (referred to as the *hedge ratio*) will almost always differ from the "optimal" mix. Second, frequent trading will generate a large amount of transactions cost, which will quickly erode the value of the portfolio.

Other than execution skills, coping with this tradeoff between "discrete replication error" and turnover is probably the only significant proprietary feature of the many dynamic hedging models available today. There are many rebalancing techniques employed (each designed to limit turnover while replicating options), too many to list here.[12] However, the important points to note are these:

a. Regardless of the method chosen, all methods require a forecast of risk asset return variability. Hence, the "optimal" hedge ratio as calculated by the forecast-dependent model will only be truly optimal if the current forecast of risk asset return volatility proves to be accurate.

b. Discrete replication error will be random in the long run, while transactions cost is always negative.

c. Simple "fix-it" techniques such as rebalancing trigger-point rules, trading with a one-day lag, or trading only a fraction of the "recommended" amount may be effective over isolated periods or in certain return distributions. However, it is prudent to recognize that every approach will have unwanted side effects. The objective is to choose an approach in accordance with each investor's willingness to tolerate that approach's specific side-effects.

---

[11]It is the author's assertion that at equilibrium, it is less expensive to self-insure (i.e., to use DH) than to buy insurance from a second party (i.e., to purchase options). Some assert, however, that at equilibrium the cost of self-insurance (i.e., the use of DH) will be *equal* to the purchase of insurance from a second party (i.e., the purchase of options).

[12]See Hayne C. Leland, "Option Pricing and Replication with Transactions Costs," *The Journal of Finance* 40 (December 1985):1283–1301.

IMPLEMENTATION VEHICLES

It is a widely held misconception that dynamic hedging is necessarily a futures trading strategy. It is not.

Stock index futures come into play in execution of these strategies for one primary reason. When equity and futures prices are at or near equilibrium (i.e., when one is a fair exchange for the other),[13] it is preferable to trade futures contracts because of their simplicity. In a single futures transaction, one can buy or sell a proportionate amount of exposure to 500 stocks. In the absence of stock index futures, the investor seeking to buy or sell a broadly diversified portfolio would have no choice but to trade each security. (The practice of simultaneously trading a number of stocks, usually a cross section of one's portfolio, is referred to by its users as "program trading.") Because stock index futures can reduce the number of transactions required from 500 to a single trade, they are economical trading vehicles, particularly in the execution of "portfolio insurance" strategies.

However, while it is true that stock index futures are usually close substitutes for stocks and that they are more liquid than stocks, it would be naive to assume that in volatile markets the liquidity offered by stock index futures can be had for free. There will be times when stock index futures are trading at a discount or a premium to their fair value.

Arbitrageurs are typically present in sufficient number to maintain a tight relationship between the stock index futures market and the stock market. As a result, stock index futures have traded as close substitutes for stocks. Consequently, most portfolio insurance managers have relied almost exclusively on stock index futures for program execution.

However, it appears that on "Black Monday," October 19, 1987, there was a tremendous imbalance between the selling pressure of portfolio insurers and their ultimate trading partners, arbitrageurs. As a

---

[13]A stock index futures contract is at "fair value" when an investor is indifferent to either holding the stocks or the futures contract. This is generally true when the following expression is satisfied:

Index Futures Price (less cost of trading)	=	Stock Index Price (less cost of trading)	−	Anticipated Dividend (over contract life)
		+	Investor's Risk-Free Rate (over contract life)	

result, futures prices fell to unprecedented discounts relative to stock prices.[14]

What are the implications for DH managers? Futures mispricing (or basis risk) is the enemy of all portfolio insurance programs that have no alternative but to use futures to execute their programs. Buying overpriced futures means earning a return on the risk asset below that earned by the index, while selling discounted futures means earning a hedge asset return below that which can be achieved through the cash markets.

If a manager elects to implement a strategy via trading stock index futures, he is, in effect, creating a synthetic option on the stock index future, *not* the stock index. As a result, the program is apt to be more expensive and/or more prone to floor violation (than if executed in the *better* of cash or futures markets) due to the higher volatility inherent in stock index futures *vis-á-vis* the cash index.

Hence, it is important to note that the potential problems of basis risk are greatly reduced for programs that can trade in the cash markets. In fact, futures mispricing presents these programs with the arbitrage opportunities that plague a "futures-only" implementation method. In light of this, it should be the program's ultimate objective to maintain the optimal mix of cash *and* derivative instruments in an attempt to avoid basis risk and potentially profit from it.

The final implementation factor that is worth noting is one that is often overlooked in dynamic hedging strategies: interest rate risk. Interest rate risk is incurred when the duration of the hedge asset does not match that of the strategy.

The hedge asset is, by definition, an asset that will earn the highest attainable fixed return over the strategy length, *risk free* (i.e., devoid of credit risk and interest rate risk). Any credit risk involved in holding fixed income securities can be easily eliminated via purchase of Treasuries. However, in order to eliminate interest rate risk, one must match the duration of the hedge asset to that of the strategy (i.e., immunize).

Shorting stock index futures and simultaneously holding an index fund will produce a fixed return through the futures contracts's expira-

---

[14]In theory, it is debatable as to whether or not futures prices were at a discount to "fair value" during this period, due to the relative inability or high cost of trading stocks.

tion.[15] However, assuming that the hedging strategy's length is beyond the expiration date of the current index future, the hedge asset return will not be immunized from interest rate risk. (It will be subject to reinvestment rate risk.) As a result, the return of the hedge asset, in this scenario, will not be immunized over the strategy's horizon but will vary with short-term rates. Should short-term rates decline, the hedge asset return will decline, making it more difficult to assure the strategy's minimum. The implication for DH managers is clear: if index futures have been shorted (unless the strategy expiration coincides with contract expiration), steps must be taken (e.g., using interest rate futures) to immunize the hedge asset.

COST

There is a basic cost associated with dynamic hedging or any other hedging strategy. It is the opportunity cost of not being fully invested in the risk asset, should the risk asset appreciate beyond the desired minimum. It is usually measured as the present value of the difference between the return generated by a DH strategy and that of the investor's "normal" portfolio. The normal portfolio in this case is the portfolio that would have existed had the investor not chosen to employ DH. For illustrative purposes, consider an investor whose portfolio is currently worth $100 and wants to assure himself that it will be worth at least $100 one year from now. To provide the appropriate protection, he buys a put option on his portfolio with a $100 strike price that expires in one year. Let's assume that this option costs $4, so that now he has $96 invested in his risk asset and $4 invested in the put option.

What will happen one year from now if his risk asset appreciates by 10%? Well, the $96 will grow to $10.60. The put option (with a $100 strike price) will be worthless. So, the total return of the strategy is $105.60–$100, or 5.6%.

With a return of 10%, the normal portfolio (i.e., 100% invested in

---

[15]From the expression in footnote 13, the cash flows are as follows:

Index Futures Price (receive)	−	Stock Index Price (pay)	+	Anticipated Dividends (receive)
	=	Investor's Risk-Free Rate (receive)		

the risk asset without the hedge) would have grown to $110. A simple method of calculating the present value of the difference in return between the option strategy and the normal portfolio is to take the ratio of the ending values and subtract it from one. In our example, the calculation would be as follows:

$$1 - \frac{\text{Strategy MV}}{\text{Normal Portfolio MV}} = 1 - \frac{105.6}{110.0} = 1 - .96 = .04$$

Notice that the cost in present value terms is 4%, which is equal to $4 on $100 or the original cost of the option. Of course, in this case, because our investor actually purchased an option, his cost was known at the start of the program. However, our investor could have executed a DH strategy instead of buying a put option in the hope of achieving similar results. Had he done so, and had the strategy produced these results, we would calculate "upside cost" in the same manner as above (i.e., upside cost = 4%). "Upside Capture," or the percent of the normal portfolio's value captured by the strategy is 96% in this case, or 100 minus upside cost.

As in the above example, calculating the cost of dynamic hedging after the fact is a simple task. However, how can one estimate the expected cost before embarking upon a hedging strategy?

Again, recall that DH is a systematic method of asset allocation designed to replicate the price behavior of options. As a result, options pricing formulae can be used to estimate the eventual cost of a DH program. However, among other things, options pricing formulae require an estimate of risk asset volatility in order to calculate price. Therefore, an estimate of the eventual cost of DH is only as good as the volatility prediction used in arriving at that cost estimate. In a previous section, it was shown that an inaccurate volatility forecast can potentially cause a floor violation. Similarly, it should be noted that misestimating volatility can also cause higher than expected opportunity cost.

In a general sense, higher than expected volatility will cause greater opportunity cost due to either high turnover, severe replication error, or both. (Recall the tradeoff between limiting turnover and continuous trading for better option replication.)

In truth, each of the implementation issues mentioned in this chapter will have an effect on upside cost. However, effects such as transactions cost, futures basis risk and interest rate risk can be controlled (to a degree) by the DH manager. Unexpected volatility risk, on the other hand, cannot be eliminated or reduced without either increasing cost or amplifying another source of risk.

PROGRAM ADJUSTMENTS

In a previous section, we stated that the parameters of each strategy should be determined by its application. The minimum goal, the time horizon, and the composition of the risk asset should be functions of the objectives and risk tolerance of the investor. It is important to realize, however, that the effective parameters will change as time passes and as market conditions change.

For example, a one-year strategy with a minimum return of -5% will evolve into a nine-month strategy after three months. The effective minimum at that point will depend on what the portfolio has earned to date. If we assume that the beginning portfolio value was $100, then the minimum value after one year will be at least $95. If, after three months, the portfolio's value has risen to $110, then the effective minimum return over the remaining nine months is -13.6%, because at that point the portfolio could afford to lose $15 and still satisfy the parameters of the program.

At that point, the investor must decide whether the effective parameters of his strategy are consistent with his objectives and risk tolerance. If $95 is truly the minimum amount the investor needs in order to be satisfied, then the effective changes to the DH program may not matter. However, if the $95 was somehow related to his total wealth at the time of inception, then it would appear that this is not an absolute goal, but a relative one. In that case, an effective minimum over nine months of -13.6% may not be appropriate.

Should our investor decide that the effective parameters of his current strategy do not fit his objectives and risk tolerance, he can easily alter them by adjusting his asset mix to one that conforms to a more appropriate strategy. However, before doing so, it is important that he consider the implied costs.

Let's assume in our example that the upside cost of the DH program after three months has been 2.8% (i.e., the normal portfolio or risk asset return to date has been 13.2%). Should our investor decide to stay with the current parameters, then the expected cost over the remaining nine months would be .8%. Hence, the total expected upside cost for the one-year program will be approximately 3.6%.[16]

Now, consider the consequences of restarting the program (adjusting the floor value to $104.5 and the horizon to one year hence). This would raise the expected upside cost over the total fifteen-month period to approximately 6.3%. Moreover, in this particular case, our investor would be selling out of an "out-of-the-money" strategy and buying into an "at-the-money" strategy. This will obviously generate additional transaction costs. As well, the new strategy will be more sensitive to market movements thereby generating additional trading and its inevitable cost.

So what's an investor to do? The decision whether to adjust one's strategy parameters or not is much like the cost/benefit analysis mentioned earlier with respect to turnover. Given one's objectives and risk tolerance, the investor must weigh the marginal utility of making an adjustment against its marginal cost.

SUMMARY

Dynamic hedging is an asset allocation scheme designed and implemented as a function of an investor's risk tolerance. Generally, DH strategies provide, at termination, the best of N alternative outcomes. However, most DH strategies can be described as attempting to replicate the return pattern of option contracts.

The primary usefulness of DH is that it allows an investor to quantify investment policy decisions in response to changing variables. As a result, it enables creation of previously unpursued investment strategies. A sample of these include synthetic protective put strategies, synthetic convertible bond strategies, dynamic asset/liability hedging, and dynamic active/passive management hedging.

Hedged portfolios are divided into a risk and a hedge asset. The hedge asset is that which will provide the minimum desired outcome, risk-free. The risk asset is any asset but the hedge asset.

The allocation between risk and hedge assets is generally a function of:

---

[16]This assumes the following: risk asset volatility = 20.0, risk-free rate = 6.85%.

1. results to date (price),
2. the minimum ending result (strike price),
3. time remaining (time to expiration),
4. the "risk-free" performance attainable from this point forward (risk-free rate), and
5. the likelihood of jeopardizing the minimum result through investment in the risk asset before the next opportunity to trade (relative volatility of the risk asset).

Of these factors, the one that *cannot* be determined is risk asset volatility. As a result, both the ability to assure a minimum result and the ability to predict participation in favorable risk asset returns are subject to error. This error cannot be eliminated unless volatility misestimation risk is transferred to another party via purchase of an option contract. Purchase of an option contract will be more expensive than DH unless realized volatility is greater than that assumed by the option seller.

When implementing a DH strategy, the manager is faced with replicating a continuous function in discrete steps. The trade-off he faces is frequent trading and high transactions cost versus infrequent trading and risk of greater replication error. This is one of the few areas where processes differ.

Program implementation is usually most economical in the futures market. However, in certain market environments, implementation in the cash markets is preferable. In any situation, proper implementation requires immunization of the hedge asset. Ultimately, best execution is only attained if the program maintains the optimal mix of cash and derivative instruments.

There is a cost associated with DH or any hedging strategy. It is the potential opportunity cost incurred as a result of devoting assets to a hedge that was not needed. The opportunity cost should be measured relative to the alternative investment strategy (i.e., that which would have existed in the absence of DH). An expected opportunity cost can be estimated for most DH strategies using options pricing formulae.

The effective parameters of a DH strategy change continuously. Investors should maintain awareness of the effective parameters of their strategies as both time passes and their wealth changes. Programs should be periodically adjusted to match the objectives and risk tolerance of the investor.

Lastly, it is most important to realize that dynamic hedging is merely common sense made complicated. With DH or any other investment strategy, you get what you pay for.

APPENDIX

Effects of Volatility Misestimation: An Example of "Whipsaw"

Assume a strategy's risk/hedge mix is 40/60% at the close of trading on Friday, the portfolio's current market value is $98, the minimum value one year hence is $100, and the risk-free rate attainable by the hedge asset is 7%. The 40/60% mix is in line with the manager's forecast of risk asset volatility. That is, with a risk-free rate of 7% and one year remaining, the manager must maintain a market value of at least $93.46 in order to assure a minimum value of $100 in a year. (If completely invested in the hedge asset at 7%, $93.46 will grow to $100 in a year.) For the portfolio value to drop from $98 to $93.46, the risk asset's value would have to drop 11.6% before the manager's next trade is executed.

However, over the weekend terrible events occur around the world, causing heavy selling pressure in world financial markets. Our DH manager is prepared and has orders in to sell his risk asset exposure at the open on Monday. Unfortunately, the risk asset opens 15% lower than it closed on Friday (i.e., the risk asset is much more volatile than predicted). As a result, the portfolio's value drops to $92.12, an amount too low to assure a value of $100 one year hence. (At 7%, $92.12 will grow to only $98.57.)

In the following days the market stabilizes. However, over the course of the remaining year, the manager has no choice but to remain 100% invested in the hedge asset. (If he invests at all in the risk asset, he risks causing an even greater floor violation.)

Unfortunately for our DH manager, the risk asset recovers all of its losses in the ensuing months and posts a return of 15% for the period. The return of the DH strategy, however, is -1.43%, producing an opportunity cost of over 15%, which is considerably greater than originally expected.

This example is intentionally extreme in order to illustrate the effects of volatility misestimation. While events of this magnitude are unlikely, it should be recognized that any amount of volatility misestimation will cause some tracking error around the original expectations of the program.

EXHIBIT 4:
SIMULATED RESULTS: ONE YEAR PROGRAM WITH
MINIMUM RETURN = −5%

	Up Market Scenario			Down Market Scenario			
Week	Risk Asset Index	Hedged Portfolio Index	Hedge Ratio	Risk Asset Index	Hedged Portfolio Index	Hedge Ratio	Week
52	100.00	100.00	0.68	100.00	100.00	0.68	52
51	101.78	101.25	0.71	100.31	100.26	0.68	51
50	104.17	102.98	0.76	100.22	100.24	0.68	50
49	104.43	103.21	0.76	99.78	99.99	0.67	49
48	105.50	104.05	0.78	98.41	99.11	0.64	48
47	106.32	104.71	0.79	98.25	99.05	0.63	47
46	106.93	105.22	0.80	98.86	99.49	0.64	46
45	107.60	105.77	0.81	98.45	99.28	0.63	45
44	107.47	105.70	0.81	98.41	99.30	0.63	44
43	108.60	106.62	0.83	99.28	99.91	0.65	43
42	109.79	107.62	0.85	99.13	99.86	0.64	42
41	110.14	107.93	0.85	99.68	100.27	0.66	41
40	111.42	109.02	0.87	99.30	100.06	0.64	40
39	111.31	108.95	0.87	98.65	99.69	0.63	39
38	110.83	108.56	0.86	97.57	99.05	0.60	38
37	113.36	110.71	0.89	98.46	99.65	0.62	37
36	111.80	109.37	0.88	97.79	99.28	0.60	36
35	111.62	109.23	0.88	97.78	99.33	0.59	35
34	113.35	110.73	0.90	97.85	99.43	0.59	34
33	114.05	111.36	0.91	97.83	99.48	0.59	33
32	113.58	110.96	0.90	96.79	98.90	0.56	32
31	113.54	110.93	0.90	96.97	99.07	0.56	31
30	114.53	111.83	0.92	97.37	99.36	0.57	30
29	114.36	111.69	0.92	97.03	99.22	0.56	29
28	115.89	113.07	0.93	97.47	99.53	0.57	28
27	116.54	113.67	0.94	97.07	99.36	0.55	27
26	116.09	113.27	0.94	97.47	99.65	0.56	26
25	115.33	112.58	0.93	98.13	100.08	0.58	25
24	114.07	111.44	0.92	98.19	100.18	0.58	24
23	115.11	112.39	0.94	97.41	99.78	0.55	23
22	114.33	111.69	0.93	98.29	100.33	0.57	22
21	116.04	113.25	0.95	98.11	100.29	0.56	21
20	118.46	115.50	0.97	98.44	100.54	0.57	20
19	118.45	115.50	0.97	98.00	100.34	0.55	19
18	118.53	115.58	0.97	97.46	100.10	0.53	18
17	118.51	115.56	0.97	97.62	100.25	0.53	17
16	117.24	114.36	0.97	97.23	100.10	0.51	16
15	117.47	114.58	0.98	97.42	100.27	0.51	15

EXHIBIT 4: (continued)
SIMULATED RESULTS: ONE YEAR PROGRAM WITH
MINIMUM RETURN = −5%

	Up Market Scenario				Down Market Scenario			
Week	Risk Asset Index	Hedged Portfolio Index	Hedge Ratio		Risk Asset Index	Hedged Portfolio Index	Hedge Ratio	Week
14	117.95	115.04	0.98		95.88	99.53	0.44	14
13	117.53	114.65	0.98		96.73	99.99	0.47	13
12	118.07	115.16	0.98		97.24	100.31	0.48	12
11	117.59	114.70	0.99		95.56	99.54	0.39	11
10	118.07	115.17	0.99		95.76	99.70	0.39	10
9	119.96	116.99	1.00		94.35	99.21	0.31	9
8	120.76	117.78	1.00		94.25	99.27	0.29	8
7	120.84	117.85	1.00		93.99	99.29	0.25	7
6	119.88	116.91	1.00		93.89	99.36	0.22	6
5	120.96	117.97	1.00		93.79	99.45	0.19	5
4	120.75	117.76	1.00		94.24	99.65	0.19	4
3	121.15	118.15	1.00		94.30	99.77	0.15	3
2	120.61	117.63	1.00		94.07	99.85	0.09	2
1	119.94	116.97	1.00		93.66	99.93	0.02	1
0	121.72	118.71	1.00		93.10	100.06	0.02	0

CHAPTER 9

Equity Indexing

DONALD L. LUSKIN
SENIOR VICE PRESIDENT
WELLS FARGO INVESTMENT ADVISORS

In *Investments*, a textbook for finance students, William Sharpe tells a fairy-tale about a land called Indicia. At the beginning of the story each Indician investor holds a perfect cross-section of all the securities of corporate Indicia. Then a casino owner persuades a group of bored money managers to begin to gamble with one another about the fortunes of particular corporations. The money managers enjoy the excitement, but as time goes by the investors who employ them began to notice that, on balance, more money is being lost than gained because the casino takes a small fee from each bet. Finally most investors become disgusted and set up "Indicia funds" to once again simply own a perfect cross-section of corporate Indicia. Sharpe concludes, "And everyone but the casino owner lived happily ever after."[1]

The residents of Indicia are, of course, practicing passive investment management, or indexing. They abandon the attempt to "beat the market" through active security selection or market timing, and instead seek optimal diversification by indexing their investment to the market portfolio.

Indexing began in 1970 when the Wells Fargo Bank introduced the Stagecoach Fund, a fund designed to track the New York Stock Exchange Composite Index by investing in every common stock listed on NYSE. This highly diversified fund proved to be too far ahead of its time, and was discontinued for lack of interest. Equity indexing didn't really catch on until 1973 when Wells Fargo introduced a fund designed to track the more widely followed S&P 500 Index.

Today, large indexed collective trust funds are administered by several national banks, and many of the largest govenmental, corporate, and charitable funds manage their own indexed portfolios. It is estimated in the press that as much as 10% of pension equity allocations are indexed.

WHY INDEXING?

Indexing has flourished because it is a successful response to both theoretical aspirations and practical needs.

On the theoretical side, indexing is a direct outgrowth of the academic concept of "efficient markets." In an efficient market, all relevant information is fairly reflected in securities prices—an investor can't hope to "beat the market" with research. Given this, an efficient investor will seek to maximize his risk-adjusted investment returns by buying and holding the most diversified possible portfolio. Ideally, like the residents of Indicia, he will hold the "market portfolio," a portfolio containing a capitalization-weighted investment in every security in the marketplace. In the real world, he will invest in a portfolio deemed to be a proxy for the market portfolio such as the S&P 500 Index.

On the practical side, as corporate, governmental, and union pension funds and savings plans, along with charitable and educational endowments, become increasingly large, strategies for managing their investments have become increasingly efficient and businesslike. Indexing has become the strategy of choice by which efficient institutions maximize control over investment outcomes and minimize investment costs.

To maximize control over investment outcomes, indexing begins by articulating an uncompromising standard of performance against which results will be judged—the returns of a benchmark index. Then the indexer follows the rigid discipline of buying and holding all the securities that make up the index in the same weights in which they are held in the index. Because no attempt at superior asset selection or market timing is made, the indexer is virtually assured of closely replicating the index's returns.

Indexing minimizes investment costs in three important ways. First, indexing minimizes brokerage commissons and market impact costs by minimizing the necessity to transact. Because it is almost entirely a buy-and-hold strategy, turnover is close to zero; the indexer need only transact to contribute or withdraw funds, reinvest income, or accommodate changes in the benchmark index. Second, when transactions must occur, their market impact is minimized. Because indexed portfolios are generally invested in securities in proportion to their market weights, the largest investments tend to be in those securities with the greatest liquidity. Third, because indexing dispenses with costly asset selection and market timing research, management fees can be significantly lower than those associated with "active" strategies.

The obvious appeal of maximizing control and minimizing cost are reinforced by the apparent failure of the average active manager to offer viable alternatives to indexing, as shown below:

	1980	1981	1982	1983	1984	1985	1986	1987
SEI Median	30.6%	−2.2%	22.4%	19.6%	1.5%	30.0%	16.7%	4.0%
S&P 500	32.4%	−0.5%	21.4%	22.5%	6.2%	32.1%	18.5%	5.1%

Indexing has been criticized for committing the investor to mediocrity by abandoning any attempt to outperform the market. It is true that indexing gives up the hope of outperforming the market, but it receives in exchange the assurance of not underperforming. Given the historical statistics on outperforming the market, this is more than a fair trade-off. The critics quote Alexander Pope: "Hope springs eternal in the human breast." But investment policies that depend on hope are merely gambling systems, and expensive ones at that. The prudent indexer is unashamed to quote Dante: "All hope abandon, ye who enter here!"

IMPLEMENTING INDEXING

Although indexing dispenses with the research often thought to be the core of investment management activity, its accurate implementation is not without its own difficulties and subtleties. In fact, the uncompromising standard of performance represented by the benchmark index focuses the indexer on details of the management process often swept under the rug by less disciplined active managers.

The first step in setting up an indexed portfolio is to select an appropriate benchmark index. If a given investor's goal is to find a proxy for the market portfolio, the selection is primarily driven by the desired depth of diversification. For example, many investors are satisfied with the S&P 500 Index, while others prefer broader-based indexes such as the Russell 3000 or the Wilshire 5000. If the goal is to index to a particular segment of the market portfolio, the selection is driven by the accuracy with which a given index represents the desired segment. For example, the S&P 500 represents the universe of mature, large-capitalization firms, while the Russell 2000 represents younger, smaller-capitalization firms.

The various indexes differ drastically in the ease and cost-effectiveness with which an investor can set up and maintain a successful indexed portfolio using them. For example, the S&P 500 consists of a manageable number of liquid stocks held in market-capitalization proportions and infrequently changed—it is highly feasible to buy and hold all of them with almost no ongoing adjustments. On the other hand, the Russell 2000 contains a large number of stocks which are frequently revised, and many of which are quite illiquid—it is considerably more expensive to buy and periodically revise them. One well-known index, the Value Line Average, simply cannot be used as a reasonable benchmark for an indexed portfolio. Its unusual construction gives each stock in the index an equal investment weight—there is no way to hold an actual portfolio that will replicate this characteristic.

Next, the indexer must decide how completely and perfectly he wishes to replicate the selected index. Ideally he will take a "census" approach, replicating it perfectly by buying and holding every stock in the index, and holding each in the same investment weight in which it is represented in the index. But under certain circumstances he might wish to take a "sampling" approach, selecting a subset of the index optimized to track the benchmark as closely as possible. Sampling is necessitated when certain securities in the index are prohibitively illiquid, or when the investor is restricted by policy from owning them.

Having chosen the benchmark index, and having chosen between census and sampling strategies, the indexer must set up and maintain the portfolio by transacting in the marketplace. When executing trades his challenges will be to minimize transaction costs and to minimize "tracking error," or deviations between the portfolio and the benchmark index.

Transactions necessitated by contributions to and withdrawals from the portfolio can be accommodated without creating tracking error provided that they are made simultaneously, and that measurement of the performance of the fund is appropriately time-weighted. Simultaneous transactions across a broadly diversified list of stocks are difficult to accomplish without considerable price impact in a marketplace which is presently geared to trading only one stock at a time. Consequently indexers and brokers have jointly developed several strategies through which impact can be reduced without sacrificing the immediacy and simultaneity of trading. Known generally as "package trading," these strategies are similar to the block-trading activities through which brokers facilitate large orders in individual stocks—the difference is that entire indexed portfolios are facilitated.

The most difficult trading situation the indexer will face is when stocks are deleted from and added to the benchmark index. The benchmark is calculated as though changes were made at closing prices, yet the changes are not publicly announced until the market has already closed. Consequently indexers must trade the following day at prevailing prices which are often far less advantageous than the previous day's close.

There are two strategies by which the indexer can enhance the returns of his portfolio without compromising the goal of tracking the benchmark index. First, he can lend securities in his portfolio to brokerage firms who need them to fulfill deliveries or effect short-sales. As with any lending activity, the returns from securities lending vary with the degree of credit risk the investor is willing to take. It is possible to earn meaningful returns even when demanding that loans be more than fully collateralized.

Second, indexers can engage in index futures arbitrage. Index futures are exchange-traded contracts similar to traditional futures on agricultural commodities. Their major difference is that, at maturity, they do not result in physical delivery of an underlying portfolio, but rather in cash settlement. It is a simple matter to calculate a trigger price for index futures contracts at which it would be profitable, after all costs, to sell an indexed portfolio and replace it with a position in the futures, reinvesting the cash proceeds in money market instruments until the futures mature. Since the index futures markets were introduced in 1982, it has been frequently possible to effect such arbitrages at significant profits. This strategy is discussed in more detail in the next chapter.

BEYOND INDEXING

Indexing can be more than an end in itself. The high level of control and economy realized through its disciplines can make an effective platform from which to launch other advanced investment strategies.

One popular advanced indexing strategy is "tilting," the deliberate introduction of biases into an otherwise perfectly indexed portfolio. For example, a manager may wish to emphasize such characteristics as high yield, low price/earnings ratio, or growth orientation. By tilting an index fund in favor of these characteristics, while holding all other characteristics constant, the manager makes an explicit, disciplined bet on only those elements, filtering out any other sources of non-market returns.

Another popular advanced strategy is "tactical asset allocation," in which a model determines periodic reallocations between an indexed equity fund, an indexed bond fund, and a money market fund. Because no active asset selection takes place within any of the funds, the strategy is a "pure play" between asset classes.

CHAPTER 10

Index Fund Investment Management

BRUCE M. COLLINS, PH.D.
MANAGER
INDEX PRODUCTS RESEARCH
SHEARSON LEHMAN HUTTON, INC.

The motivation and benefits of equity indexing were discussed in the previous chapter. The emergence of passive index funds was an outgrowth of the persistent underperformance of active money managers versus a performance benchmark like the S&P 500 index. Due to transaction costs associated with rebalancing, however, passive management has also fallen short. The introduction of index derivative products has provided managers with the tools that, when used correctly, can enhance the returns to an index fund. The replacement of stocks with undervalued futures contracts can add 50 to 100 basis points to an indexed portfolio's annualized return without incurring additional risk. In addition to incremental return, the portfolio itself can be tilted or biased toward a specific characteristic such as overweighting in a particular sector, or tilted in favor of a performance factor such as dividend yield or a price/earnings ratio. The creation of tilted index portfolios is a way to preserve a relationship with the benchmark while pursuing an active strategy. Furthermore, the indexed portfolio can also be combined with index options, individual equity options or convertible bonds to enhance returns. The basic strategy extends the concept of stock replacement by evaluating smaller slices of the portfolio or individual stocks.

This chapter focuses on investment management of index funds, with emphasis on the use of stock index futures.

CREATING AN INDEX FUND

The first step in creating an index fund is to select a bogey or performance benchmark. The choice of a benchmark may assume a multiple function. The fund performance may be measured against the "market" portfolio or a subset or sector of the market. For example, the fund may be interested in matching the performance of a technology sector or energy sector. Once established, this performance is measured against the market. A pure index fund, however, by definition, intends to perfectly replicate the market portfolio. The market portfolio in reality is not known with certainty. Nonetheless, the S&P 500 has served as the consensus representative of the market portfolio. Recently, the Wilshire 5000 and the Russell indexes have served as benchmarks for some index funds.

As an alternative to holding the underlying equities that make up the index, an index fund can be created by the purchase of futures contracts and Treasury bills. The two alternative methods will generate the same returns profile. Furthermore, the choice of a benchmark with a liquid futures contract is attractive because it makes a stock replacement program possible. Among the indexes with futures contracts are the S&P 500 Index, the Major Market Index, the Value Line Index, and the NYSE Composite Index. The latest equity index futures contracts are on the Russell 2000 and 3000 indexes.

The advantages and disadvantages of creating a synthetic index fund by holding long stock index futures and Treasuries, versus holding a long portfolio, are listed below.

The index fund has advantages relating to special events such as stock dividends. Otherwise, the decision to hold the index fund must be measured against the disadvantages of the synthetic index fund. There are two risks relating to holding futures contracts. First is the risk that

Index Fund	*Advantages*	*Disadvantages*
Long Stocks	Receive stock dividends	High initial transaction costs
	Restructurings often yield positive returns	Market impact
	Special dividends	Tracking error
	Stock replacement	Custodial costs
Synthetic	Low transaction costs	Variation margin risk
	No tracking error	Price risk
	No custodial costs	
	No cash drag due to dividend reinvestment	

the futures will be overpriced when purchased; or, because stock index futures expire quarterly, the position may need to be rolled out to the next contract. The risk is that the spread is overpriced. Both circumstances have a negative impact on the performance of the index fund and consequently its objective of matching the performance of the bogey may not be achieved.

The second factor that may influence the performance of a synthetic index fund is variation margin. Because futures are marked-to-the-market there are daily cash flows (referred to as variation margin) into or out of an account. Consequently, the futures position will outperform the index in an upmarket and underperform in a downmarket. This means the total dollar value of the investment may change due to variation margin. An underhedging technique is used to minimize the risk of misperformance due to variation margin. This involves purchasing fewer futures contracts to neutralize the trade-off between sustaining smaller losses in the futures position in a down market with an increased cash position due to satisfying the variation margin. The formula below is an adjustment factor for the number of futures contracts to purchase.

Adjustment Factor = 1/(1 + term interest rate)

To illustrate this, suppose there are 60 days remaining until expiration of an index futures contract on a $25,000,000 portfolio. Furthermore, suppose the index is at 326.80. The number of futures contract in a dollar equivalent position is 153 ($153 \times 500 \times 326.80 = \$25$ million). At a term interest rate of 1.068% (or 6½% annualized), the adjusted number of futures can be calculated as follows:

$$1/1.011 \times 153 = (approx.)\ 151$$

Should the market fall to 322, $367,000 ($4.8 \times 400 \times 153$) must be delivered to the account in cash. At expiration the loss due to foregone interest on the variation margin is $3,920 or $367,000 $\times 1.068\%$. The effect of an underhedged position would, in contrast, avoid the loss because 2 fewer contracts were purchased.

Further adjustments are required should interest rates significantly change prior to expiration. Additionally, the cost of financing variation margin falls with the time to expiration. Thus, the adjustment factor is influenced by the level of interest rates and time, and the number of futures contracts is adjusted accordingly. In both cases, the risk is that the futures contract is unfavorably priced when the adjustment is made.

A stock replacement strategy is an alternative to holding the index or a synthetic index fund, and involves the replacement of a long equity position with an equivalent exposure in the futures market and investing the proceeds from the stock sale in Treasury bills. By swapping between the portfolio of stocks which replicate an index and a combination of futures and Treasury bills when the futures are undervalued, an investor should be assured of equaling the market return and have a good chance of exceeding it. In 1987, index fund managers employing this strategy would have been able to outperform the S&P 500 index by as much as 150 basis points.

CONSIDERATIONS FOR CONSTRUCTING A REPLICATING PORTFOLIO OR BASKET

The objectives in basket construction are two-fold: (1) to minimize the cost incurred when trading in some of the smaller capitalized issues while (2) retaining the basket's ability to track the index. Designing the optimal replicating portfolio may involve holding all the stocks in the index or a subset. The size of the basket affects transaction costs, but holding fewer stocks than contained in the index generates tracking

EXHIBIT 1:
S&P 500 STOCK INDEX—TRACKING ERROR VS. SIZE

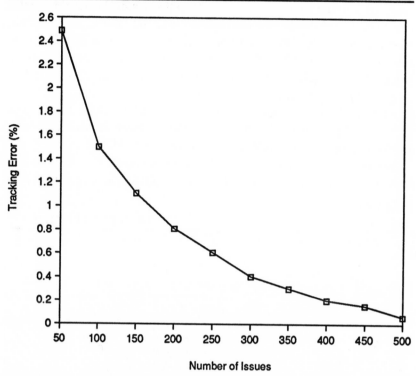

error.[1] The trade-off between basket size and tracking error is shown in Exhibit 1. The returns from a basket of 250 stocks, for example, will mistrack the S&P 500 by .6%. This means that there exists a 68% probability that the returns from the portfolio will fall within .6% of the returns from the S&P 500 on an annualized basis.

It is next to impossible for a portfolio's returns to exactly match the return on the index. Even if a portfolio is designed to exactly replicate an index, tracking error will result.[2] There are several reasons for this.

---

[1]Tracking error represents the risk that the replicating portfolio or basket will perform differently than the benchmark. Statistically, it is the standard deviation of the difference in expected returns.

[2]Positive tracking error holding all 500 stocks is a consequence of using historical returns in the estimation process and due to the changing composition of the index.

First, because odd-lot purchases are cumbersome, index funds are usually comprised of round lots, and as such the number of shares of each stock in the basket is rounded off to the nearest hundred from the exact number of shares indicated by the basket building algorithm. This rounding may affect the ability of smaller baskets (less than $25 million) to accurately track the index. Exhibit 2 shows the number of stocks that are included in the replicating portfolio for various dollar-sized baskets.[3] The resulting tracking error from rounding can be derived from Exhibits 1 and 2. As we see, a $10 million basket will reduce tracking error to an insignificant level. Even at this level, three stocks fall below the minimum round-lot threshold.

Second and more importantly, the composition of a stock index is a dynamic process: since most indexes are capitalization-weighted (with

EXHIBIT 2:
S&P 500 STOCK INDEX—NUMBER OF ISSUES PER $1MM INVESTED

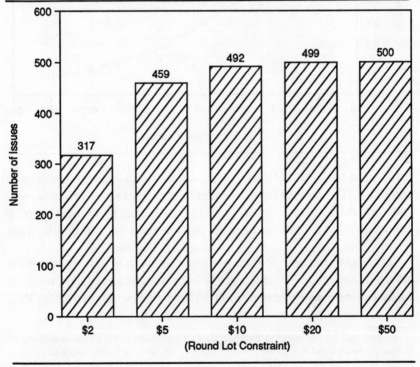

---

[3]Exhibit 2 is based on July 28, 1988 prices. The number of stocks may change as prices increase or decrease significantly.

the notable exception of the Major Market Index and the Value Line), the relative weights of individual issues are constantly changing. In addition, the list of stocks which comprises the index often changes. Thus, the cost of continually adjusting the portfolio, as well as timing differences, hinders a portfolio's ability to accurately track an index. The former problem is eliminated by holding all stocks in the index. The portfolio is then self-replicating, which simply means the weights are self-adjusting. If, however, the basket contains fewer stocks than the index, the weights are not self-adjusting and may require periodic rebalancing. Rebalancing is discussed in more detail in a later section.

The method used to construct a basket is to formulate a procedure to determine the weightings. There are two issues that must be addressed. First, the method of averaging must be determined and second, the method of weighting is important. In practice, there are two methods of averaging used in the calculation of popular indexes, arithmetic and geometric. Furthermore, there are three basic ways to look at weighting; market value or capitalization; price; and equal dollar weighting. The market value weighting for a single stock in an index is determined by the proportion of its value to the total market value of all stocks in the index. The typical price weighting scheme assumes equal shares invested in stock and the price serves as the weight. Equal dollar weights requires investing the same dollar amount in each stock. With capitalization-weighting, the largest companies naturally have the greatest influence over the index value. Consequently, under- or over-weighting in a large capitalization stock can lead to substantial mistracking. Also, these stocks tend to be the most liquid. Price weighting endows the stock with the highest price with the greatest influence on the index value. Equal dollar weighting does the opposite. In this case, the lowest priced stocks have the greatest potential to move the index for a given change in stock price, such as 1/8th. It is important to understand these properties when constructing an index fund.

An arithmetic index is simply the weighted average of all stocks that comprise the index where the weights are determined by one of the weighting schemes mentioned, that is.

Index = constant × sum (weight × price)

The constant represents an arbitrary number used to initialize the value of the index. Exhibit 3 illustrates the distinction between the three weighting schemes by presenting a hypothetical index using the three alternative weighting schemes. Exxon will have the greatest influence on the index value of a capitalization-weighted index because it has the largest market value, while 3M has the greatest influence in the price-weighted index. Notice that the share amounts are the same for a price-weighted index, while the weights are the same for the equal dollar-weighted index. The performance of one index versus another depends on the relative performance of the individual stocks that comprise the index. The price-weighted index will outperform the cap-weighted index should Merek and 3M outperform the other stocks. The reason is simply a matter of weightings. Furthermore, the same outcome would occur should Exxon and GE underperform the other stocks. The key, therefore, to understanding relative index performance is to understand the relative weights of the stocks.

Because each index is arithmetic, the index can be easily replicated regardless of the weighting scheme. This means as the price of a stock changes, the weights adjust automatically for consistency with the share amounts. This is true for any arithmetic index, regardless of the weighting scheme. Although the weights change, the share amounts do not. Consequently, no rebalancing is necessary. The implication for index funds is that holding the entire basket reduces the need for rebalancing. Even if the entire index is held, rebalancing may be necessary because changes in the weighting may occur for any of the reasons listed below.

- Some issues may cease to exist due to merger activity.
- A company may be added or deleted from the index should it meet or fail to meet capitalization or liquidity requirements for inclusion in an index or listing on an exchange.
- A company may split its stock or issue a stock dividend.
- New stock may be issued.
- Current stock may be repurchased.

Should any of these events occur, the constant term in the index valuation expression may require adjustment to avoid a discontinuous jump in the index value. The constant term is commonly known as the divisor.

A second method of averaging is geometric. Geometric averages are calculated as the n-th root of the product of returns or prices:

EXHIBIT 3:
BASKET SIZE: $1,000,000—JULY 27, 1988

	7/27	Total Shares (MM)	Total Cap ($MM)	S&P 500 Weight (%)	Cap Weight (%)	Cap Shares	Price Weight	Price Shares	Eq $ Weight	Eq $ Shares
AXP	26.625	420.802	11203.85	0.61	7.61	2858	11.54	4334	20.00	7512
GE	41.5	902.953	37472.55	2.03	25.45	6133	17.98	4334	20.00	4819
MMM	62.875	227.493	14303.62	0.78	9.72	1545	27.25	4334	20.00	3181
MRK	54.125	393.996	21325.03	1.16	14.48	2676	23.46	4334	20.00	3695
XON	45.625	1379	62916.88	3.41	42.74	9367	19.77	4334	20.00	4384
Totals:	230.75		$147,221.93	7.99	100.00	22580	100.00	21668	100.00	23591

$$\text{Index} = \text{constant} \times (\text{price}_1 \times \text{price}_2 \times \ldots \text{price}_n)^{\text{weight}}$$

This is similar to an arithmetic index except that the sums are products and the weights are exponents. In practice, only the Value Line Index is a geometric average.[4] It is also equally weighted such that the weights $= 1/n$. Although it is easy to construct a basket to track an arithmetic index by investing proportional dollars in each of the stocks, it is not possible to construct a portfolio that will continuously track a geometric index. However, an equally weighted arithmetic portfolio will best track a geometric index with the same component stocks. Thus, to best track the Value Line Index, equal dollars should be invested in each stock in the index.

It is also well known that a geometric average never exceeds an arithmetic average. This means that the replicating portfolio will always outperform the geometric index if all stocks in the index are held and the portfolio is continuously rebalanced. Because continuous rebalancing is not feasible, an element of risk is introduced in holding the replicating portfolio against the geometric index. Recall that this is not a problem with an arithmetic index. There is a known expression which measures the overperformance of the arithmetic portfolio versus the geometric index:

Overperformance $= \frac{1}{2}$ (average variance $-$ index variance)

This number is expected to be positive because the average variance of individual stock returns is greater than the variance of returns for a diversified portfolio. Recall that the best tracking portfolio against the Value Line is one which is an equally dollar-weighted arithmetic index. Two practical problems confront the holder of an index fund designed to track the performance of the Value Line. First, frequent rebalancing is required which is prohibitively expensive. Second, mistracking is a consequence of non-continuous rebalancing and overperformance. These two problems, combined with the difficulty of trading a large number of low-capitalization, low-price and illiquid stocks, present the investor with a fairly complex indexing problem. However, it is due to

---

[4]In January of 1988 Value Line began computing an arithmetic index using the same set of stocks contained in the traditional Value Line Index. Beginning with the September 1988 futures contract, all subsequent Value Line Index futures contracts are based on the arithmetic index.

the peculiarities of the index that opportunities may arise for attractive returns.

In summary, the first step in creating a stock index fund is simple but important: the manager must choose which index to replicate. To create a stock replacement program, the index chosen must have an actively traded futures contract. Furthermore, having chosen an index, the manager must then decide how closely to replicate it. As we have shown, not all indexes are calculated in the same way. The precise construction of the basket of stocks is related to the averaging and weighting method used to calculate the index. An arithmetic index can be tracked exactly by owning all stocks in the index in the proportions suggested by its weight in the index. Geometric averaged indexes, however, cannot be exactly replicated and introduce an element of risk into the construction of the best locally tracking basket of stocks.

Because the number of stocks that comprise an index can be substantial (see Exhibit 4), the cost of initializing an indexed portfolio can be high. In addition, the exchange listing may have performance implications for a stock replacement program. NYSE listed stocks can take advantage of the Designated Order Turnover (D.O.T) system, which may improve the speed and therefore the cost of execution. As an alternative to ownership of all stocks in the index, a set of smaller, but nevertheless efficient, portfolios are available. The selection of an indexed portfolio with fewer stocks than the index involves several factors. First, whatever portfolio is ultimately selected, it will be subject to residual risk. The manager must weigh-off the residual risk against the transaction costs related to maintaining a portfolio of all stocks in the index. The risk of course is that the portfolio will underperform the index. Second, once the manager decides on a level of residual risk and transaction costs, a method is required to construct a basket that meets this criteria.

The purchase or sale of a portfolio of stocks is known as *program trading*. The cost of executing a diversified portfolio should be less than executing each stock in the portfolio individually just as the risk of holding a diversified portfolio is less than that of holding an individual stock. Because the initiation of an index fund expresses an investor's desire to obtain broad market exposure, the purchase of any stock in the portfolio through a program trade is informationless, and therefore should cost less than a similar aggregation of "informed" trades. Furthermore, program trading allows the investor to transfer execution risk to the broker, which essentially provides the investor with an insurance protection option. The broker guarantees a price to the investor and in doing so provides the level of desired price protection. The cost of the option is negotiated with the broker. For these reasons, program trading provides a cost effective means of initiating an index fund or rebalancing an existing portfolio.

The cost of initiating and maintaining an S&P 500 Index Fund averages 10-15 basis points in commissions, 25 basis points in market impact and 5 basis points in rebalancing costs.[5]

METHODS OF CONSTRUCTING A BASKET

There are four methods used to build a basket designed to track an index. The first method simply involves purchasing all stocks in the index in proportion to their weightings in the index. The remaining three methods all involve constructing baskets with fewer stocks than the index. The first of these methods is a capitalization method which purchases a number of top capitalization stocks and equally weights the residual stock weightings across the basket. Thus, if the top 200 highest capitalization stocks are selected for the basket and this accounts for 85% of the total capitalization of the index, the remaining 15% is evenly proportioned among the 200 stocks.

The second method generates a stratified sample of the index defining each stratum by industry. The objective of this technique is to reduce residual risk by diversifying across industry sectors in the same proportion as the benchmark. Stocks within each industry sector are then selected using either capitalization ranking, valuation methods, or an optimization method.

The final method uses a quadratic optimization procedure to generate an efficient set of portfolios. The efficient set includes minimum variance portfolios for different levels of expected returns. The investor can select a portfolio among the set that satisfies his or her level of risk tolerance.

---

[5]The costs of rebalancing are directly related to turnover. Passive strategies, such as index fund investments, usually incur less turnover than active or dynamic strategies when the benchmark is dominated by large capitalization issues. Small capitalization stock index funds incur larger transaction costs because the stocks tend to be lower priced and less liquid. Historically, the average cost for small cap portfolios is 25 basis points in commissions, 75-125 basis points in market impact, and due to higher turnover, 10 basis points in annual rebalancing costs.

EXHIBIT 4:
INDEX COMPOSITION COMPARISON (JUNE 1988)

By Names:	Value Line	S&P 500	Russell 2000	Russell 3000
New York Stock Exchange	1149	462	549	1297
American Stock Exchange	95	9	327	363
Over-The-Counter	343	29	1124	1340
Toronto Stock Exchange	15	0	0	0

By Capitalization:	Value Line	S&P 500	Russell 2000	Russell 3000
New York Stock Exchange	77.16%	96.93%	36.62%	85.97%
American Stock Exchange	4.66	0.68	12.41	2.34
Over-The-Counter	17.54	2.39	50.97	11.69
Toronto Stock Exchange	0.64	0.00	0.00	0.00
	100.00	100.00	100.00	100.00

STOCK REPLACEMENT PROGRAM

Recall that a stock replacement program involves the replacement of stock with futures contracts. The dollar size of a basket, with a stock replacement program in mind, should be stated in terms of a number of futures contracts. An index fund will sell its stocks, replace them with a dollar equivalent of futures contracts and place the proceeds in a short-term investment fund. The dollar size of a basket should as a rule of thumb correspond to within .10 of a round number of futures contracts. The calculation of an appropriate number of equivalent futures is shown below.

Number of futures contracts $=$ Dollar value$/500 \times$ index

An algorithm is used that, for a given dollar value, generates the number of futures contracts that satisfies the tolerance level of .10. For example, suppose a manager is interested in creating a \$25,000,000 index fund designed to replicate the S&P 500. The number of futures contracts required to dollar match the stock position when the S&P 500 index is trading at 275 is given by \$25,000,000$/500 \times 275 = 181.81$. This does not satisfy our tolerance level. If \$25,000,000 represents an investment ceiling for the manager, the number of futures contracts is reduced to 181, otherwise it is rounded upward to 182. In either case, the initial dollar amount is adjusted to reflect the dollar value of the required number of futures contracts. There is no guarantee, however, that an optimal or efficient portfolio can be constructed at that dollar amount. This is not a significant problem at the \$25,000,000 level, but becomes more of a problem as the dollar value of the portfolio is reduced and when the portfolio is purchased in round lots. Therefore, the basket design evolves from the need to closely replicate the index and to closely reflect a round number of futures contract as part of a stock replacement program. There are programming algorithms that will satisfy these requirements and deliver the best tracking basket.

TRACKING ISSUES AND REBALANCING

Once the basket is purchased for a stock replacement program there are three central issues that must be managed. First, the integrity of the replication requirements must be maintained. This means monitoring the actual tracking performance of the portfolio versus the index. Recall that this is not a problem if the weights are self-adjusting. Should the basket represent a subset of the index, however, daily monitoring of the position is crucial to assure meeting the replication requirements (i.e., matching returns performance). A daily report should be generated that provides aggregate tracking information. Substantial mistracking will reflect a weighting imbalance between the basket and the index. Consequently, the basket may not reflect the prescribed number of futures contracts, which will jeopardize the stock replacement program. To manage this problem, periodic rebalancing is required. Because managing an index fund is a dynamic process, the manager is forced to periodically rebalance the portfolio and intuitively weight the transaction costs associated with rebalancing against the risk of increasing levels of tracking error.

The basket may require rebalancing should one of the following conditions arise: 1) additional exposure is desired; 2) the basket mistracks the index; 3) the composition of the index changes, or 4) capitalization change events.

The decision to rebalance is related to the anticipated impact of mistracking on returns. Once the decision is made, however, an optimization procedure is utilized to realign the basket at a minimum cost. Index funds are designed to avoid selection and market timing issues, but because the portfolio generates dividend income and with the possibility of cash inflows, the issue of timing cannot be entirely avoided. One solution is to invest the proceeds in money market instruments until sufficient amount of cash can be distributed across the entire portfolio. Another possibility is to combine the timing of investing additional cash with portfolio rebalancing, which may be less costly than treating the issues separately. The weightings are again determined using an optimization procedure. A new basket is created using the procedure described previously at a different dollar level. The procedure generates a list of buy and sell recommendations that will bring the basket back into line with the manager's objective at an acceptable cost. The rebalancing is often executing through a program trade on a negotiated price basis.

RETURN ENHANCEMENT

The importance of creating an index fund based on a round number of futures contracts becomes clear with the implementation of a stock replacement strategy. A stock replacement strategy is triggered when the futures are sufficiently mispriced to generate excess returns.

In theory, the price of an index futures contract should be equivalent to the cost of buying and holding the underlying cash index (i.e., the stocks which comprise the index) from today until contract settlement. Holders of stocks incur opportunity costs while simultaneously earning dividends. The difference between the two is called the cost of carry:

Theoretical futures price = Cash index (1 + cost of carry)

Cost of carry = (Cost of money − Annualized dividend yield)
× (Days of expiration/365)

Example:

Cash index = 275   Cost of money = 6.50%
Days to expiration = 60   Dividend yield = 2.00%
Theoretical futures price = 277.03

The difference between the cash index and the price of a futures contract on that index is called the *basis*. To the extent that the actual basis differs from the theoretical basis (theoretical futures price minus cash price), arbitrage opportunities exist. Index fund managers can enhance returns by substituting underpriced futures contracts for stocks in the portfolio and later repurchasing the stocks in the portfolio and unwinding the futures position when the actual basis falls back into line with the theoretical basis. Historically, there have been frequent opportunities to profit from this type of strategy. A second way to enhance returns is to buy the calendar spread when it satisfies the required excess return. At expiration of the near contract, the short futures position is replaced by selling stock.

To illustrate this using the assumptions in the theoretical futures example, suppose the futures trades down to 275.79 or 1.24 below fair value. By selling out their stocks, investing the proceeds in Treasuries at 6½% and buying futures at a $0.79 premium, an index fund can earn incremental return. If held until expiration, the amount of annualized incremental return is as follows:

$$\begin{aligned}\frac{\text{Increment}}{\text{Return}} &= \frac{\text{Interest}}{\text{on}} - \frac{\text{Dividend}}{\text{Yield}} - \frac{\text{Futures Premium}}{\text{Index}} - \frac{\text{Transaction}}{\text{Costs}}\\[6pt]\text{T-bills}\\[6pt]&= .011 - .0033 - .0029 - .0036\\[4pt]&= (.0012) \times (365/60)\\[4pt]&= 73 \text{ basis points}\end{aligned}$$

The index fund can pick up 73 basis points in annualized incremental return, or \$30,000, over 60 days assuming \$1 transaction costs. Transaction costs include commissions and market impact.

MARKET IMPACT

At any given time, the price at which a basket of stocks can be bought or sold will differ substantially from the cash index price, which is based on the prices at which each of the individual stocks comprising the index last traded. To sell a list of stocks at a given instant, the seller would receive the sum of the current bid prices of the individual stocks on the list (in the case of purchasing, the buyer would have to pay the current offer prices). The difference between the cash index and the cost of buying or selling a basket of stocks is generally referred to as market impact. Market impact, a major component of transaction costs, is a consequence of the stock bid/ask spread and any price concessions made due to the investor's demand for liquidity.

The level of market impact varies over time and depends upon several factors. Most prominent among these are the liquidity of the individual stocks in the basket and the size of the portfolio being transacted. Liquidity has a dual impact. The more liquid a security, the smaller the bid-ask spread and hence the smaller the difference in price between the last transaction and the desired one. Furthermore, the presence of buyers and sellers decreases the market impact of a large trade. Relatedly, market impact will increase as the size of the basket increases because of the likelihood of being unable to transact all of the shares at the current bid (or offering price). Whenever the difference between the actual basis and the theoretical basis exceeds the market impact of a transaction, the aggressive manager should consider replacing stocks with futures or *vice versa*. Returns can be enhanced significantly through such a strategy.

Once the strategy has been put into effect there are several subsequent scenarios that may unfold. First, should the futures become sufficiently rich relative to stocks, the futures position is sold and the stocks repurchased. Second, should the futures remain fair-valued the position is held until expiration, when the futures settle at the spot value and the stocks are repurchased market on close. Third, should the calendar spread become cheap, the current near futures position is sold and the next futures contract is purchased. In this case, nothing is done at the near expiration.

THE LINK WITH ACTIVE MANAGEMENT

Index fund management can be extended into active management to a fairly modest degree aimed at controlling risk. There are three methods that are worth mentioning. The first is the construction of a biased or "tilted" basket designed to emphasize a particular sector of the index or a performance factor such as earnings momentum, dividend yield, or price/earnings ratios. The basket is built to maintain a strong relationship to the benchmark by minimizing tracking error while creating a bias that is intended to enhance returns. The second method exploits the fact that indexes have different sector exposures. By combining the long basket with one or more short futures positions, sector exposure can be realized at a low cost and the potential exists for additional realized returns. By example, low capitalization exposure can be achieved when holding a portfolio indexed to the Russell 1000 by shorting the S&P 500 futures contract. The last method is an asset allocation model applied to the question of rebalancing. Simply put, additional cash is not added to the basket unless the expected return to stock exceeds that of the short-term investment fund or money market instrument (MMI). The decision can be made by purchasing an option to exchange one asset (the MMI) for the other. The cost of the choice is the price of the option. This strategy involves holding indexed equity and bond portfolios and using stock index futures and bond futures to implement the asset allocation decision.

CHAPTER 11

Survey of Bonds and Mortgage-Backed Securities

FRANK J. FABOZZI, PH.D., C.F.A.
VISITING PROFESSOR OF FINANCE
SLOAN SCHOOL OF MANAGEMENT
MASSACHUSETTS INSTITUTE OF TECHNOLOGY

T. DESSA FABOZZI, PH.D.
SENIOR SECURITY ANALYST
FINANCIAL STRATEGIES GROUP
MERRILL LYNCH CAPITAL MARKETS INC.

A bond is an instrument in which the issuer (debtor/borrower) promises to repay to the lender/investor the amount borrowed plus interest over some specified period of time. Prior to the 1970's, a typical ("plain vanilla") bond issued in the United States would specify (1) a fixed date at which the amount borrowed (principal) is due and (2) the contractual amount of interest that would be paid every six months. The date on which the principal is required to be repaid is called the *maturity date*. The annual interest rate that the issuer agrees to pay on the principal is called the *coupon rate*. Assuming that the issuer does

201

not default or redeem the issue prior to the maturity date, an investor who holds this bond until the maturity date would be assured of a known cash flow pattern.

The high and volatile interest rates that prevailed in the United States in the late 1970's and the early 1980's brought a wide variety of new types of "bonds" issued by corporations and municipalities designed to make them more attractive to investors. In the residential mortgage market, the pooling of individual mortgages to form mortgage pass-through securities began and increased dramatically. Derivative mortgage securities such as collateralized mortgage obligations and stripped mortgage-backed securities were created to meet the specific investment needs of a broadening range of institutional investors.

In the next four chapters, fixed-income strategies will be presented. The purpose of this chapter is to survey the various types of bonds and mortgage-backed securities. The securities are described and their investment characteristics are discussed. International bonds are discussed in Chapter 19.

RISKS ASSOCIATED WITH INVESTING IN BONDS

The investor in bonds may be exposed to one or more of the following risks: (1) interest-rate risk, (2) reinvestment risk, (3) credit risk, (4) call risk (prepayment risk in the case of mortgage-backed securities), (5) inflation risk, (6) foreign-exchange rate risk, and (7) marketability/liquidity risk.

Interest-Rate Risk

A bond's price moves in the opposite direction of the change in interest rates. As interest rates rise (fall), the price of a bond will fall (rise). For an investor who plans to hold a bond to maturity, the change in the bond's price prior to maturity is not of concern; however, for an investor who may have to sell the bond prior to the maturity date, an increase in interest rates subsequent to the time the bond was purchased will mean the realization of a capital loss. This risk is referred to as *interest-rate risk* or *price risk*. As explained in the next chapter, interest-rate risk of a bond is measured by its *duration*.[1]

---

[1]See pages 237-42 in Chapter 12.

Reinvestment Risk

The dollar return from investing in a bond comes from three sources: (1) coupon interest payments, (2) any capital gain (or capital loss) when the bond is redeemed, sold or matures and (3) interest earned from reinvesting the interim cash flows (coupon payments or principal repayments).[2] In order for an investor to realize a yield equal to the stated yield at the time the bond is purchased, these interim cash flows must be reinvested at an interest rate equal to that stated yield. The risk that interim cash flows will be reinvested at a lower rate than the stated yield at the time the bond is purchased such that the investor will earn a lower yield is called *reinvestment risk*. All coupon bonds expose the bondholder to reinvestment risk. Zero-coupon bonds do not have reinvestment risk.

Credit Risk

Default risk, also known as *credit risk*, is the risk that the issuer will default on its contractual payments of interest and/or principal. The obligations of the U.S. government are perceived to be free of default risk. For other issuers, the risk of default is gauged by quality ratings assigned by commercial rating companies such as Moody's Investor Service, Standard & Poor's Corporation, Duff & Phelps, and Fitch Investors Service, as well as credit research staffs of dealer firms and institutional investor concerns.

Call Risk

One of the provisions in the contract between the issuer and the bondholder might be that the issuer will have the right to retire or "call" all or part of the issue before the maturity date. The issuer wants this right so that at some time in the future if market interest rates have declined below the coupon rate on the issue, the issuer can retire the issue and replace it with new bonds at a lower interest rate. This early redemption is simply a corporation exercising an option to refinance its debt on more favorable terms.

---

[2]The importance of interest earned from reinvesting the interim cash flows was first highlighted in the now classic book by Sidney Homer and Martin L. Leibowitz, *Inside the Yield Book* (Published jointly: Englewood Cliffs, N.J.: Prentice-Hall, and New York: New York Institute of Finance, 1972).

From the investor's perspective, there are three disadvantages of the call provision. First, the cash flow pattern of a callable bond is not known with certainty. Second, because the issuer will only call the bonds when interest rates have dropped substantially below the coupon rate, the investor is exposed to reinvestment rate risk. That is, the investor will have to reinvest the proceeds received when the bond is called at lower interest rates than the yield when the bond was purchased. Finally, the capital appreciation potential of a bond may be reduced. For example, when interest rates fall, the price of a bond will rise. However, because the bond may be called, the price of a callable bond may not rise much above the price at which the issuer will pay if the bond is called. This characteristic of a callable bond is referred to as *negative convexity* or *price compression*.[3]

Holding aside credit risk, the key characteristic that distinguishes U.S. Treasury obligations, corporate bonds, municipal bonds and mortgage-backed securities is the degree of certainty of the cash flow pattern. In the case of Treasury securities, with the exception of some outstanding Treasury bonds that are callable, the cash flow is known with certainty. Since almost all long-term corporate and municipal bonds are callable by the issuer prior to maturity, the cash flow pattern of these securities is not known with certainty. Typically, however, the issue may have a provision prohibiting the issuer from calling or re-funding the issue until a specified number of years after issuance. Moreover, investors generally can expect that issuers will not call or refund an issue when the current market interest rate is greater than the issue's coupon interest rate.

For mortgage-backed securities, there also is uncertainty about the timing of the cash flow because the investor has effectively granted *each* borrower/homeowner in the pool of mortgages underlying the mortgage-backed security the option to prepay part or all of the mortgage at any time. The uncertainty of the timing of the cash flow is even greater for mortgage-backed securities than for corporate and munici-pal bonds because the option to prepay a mortgage will not depend solely on the current market interest rate. Instead, the exercise of the prepayment option will depend on the current market interest rate and unique circumstances facing each homeowner (such as relocations or defaults). The latter may cause principal prepayments when the current market interest rate is greater than the mortgage interest rate. Thus, the

---

[3] See pages 263-64 in Chapter 12.

decision to prepay a mortgage may be less of an economic decision than a chief financial officer's decision to refund corporate debt obligations.

Inflation Risk

Inflation risk or *purchasing power risk* is the risk that the return realized from investing in a bond will not be sufficient to offset the loss in purchasing power due to inflation. With the exception of adjustable or floating rate bonds, because the interest rate that the issuer promises to make is fixed, an investor is exposed to inflation risk.

Foreign-Exchange Rate Risk

A U.S. investor who purchases a bond in which the issuer promises to make payments in a foreign currency does not know what the resulting cash flow of the bond will be in U.S. dollars. The cash flow will depend on the foreign-exchange rate at the time the cash flow is received. Thus, the investor is exposed to *foreign-exchange rate or currency risk*.

Marketability Risk

Marketability risk (or *liquidity risk*) involves the ease with which an issue can be sold at or near a price corresponding to the prevailing market rate. The primary measure of marketability/liquidity is the size of the spread between the bid price (the price at which an issue can be sold) and ask price (the price at which an issue can be purchased) quoted by a dealer. The greater the dealer spread, the greater the marketability/liquidity risk. The number of active market makers will influence the size of the bid-ask spread; the more active market makers are in that particular issue, the smaller the bid-ask spread. For an investor who plans to hold the bond until the maturity date, marketability/liquidity risk is not a concern.

TREASURY SECURITIES

U.S. Treasury securities are backed by the full faith and credit of the United States government. Consequently, they are viewed by market participants as having no *credit* risk. Interest rates on Treasury securities are the benchmark interest rates throughout the U.S. economy, as well as in international capital markets. Interest income from Treasury securities is subject to federal income taxes but is exempt from state and local income taxes. Capital gains from the sale of Treasury securities may be taxed at the state and local level.

There are two categories of government securities—discount and coupon securities. The fundamental difference between these two types of securities is the form in which the holder receives interest and, as a result, the prices at which they are issued. Coupon securities pay interest every six months. Discount securities do not make periodic interest payments. Instead, the security holder receives interest at the maturity date, the dollar interest being the difference between the face value received at maturity and the purchase price.

The current practice of the Treasury is to issue all securities with maturities of one year or less as discount securities. These are called Treasury *bills*. All securities with maturities longer than one year are issued as coupon securities. Treasury coupon securities issued with original maturities between two and 10 years are called *notes*; those with original maturities greater than 10 years are called *bonds*. Although Treasury notes are not callable, many outstanding Treasury bond issues are callable within 5 years of maturity. The Treasury has not issued callable bonds since February 1985.

Treasury securities are typically issued on an auction basis. There are regular cycles in which the Treasury auctions and issues securities of specific maturities. The secondary market for Treasury securities is an over-the-counter market in which a group of U.S. government securities dealers continually provide bids and offers on outstanding Treasuries. The secondary market is the most liquid financial market in the world. In this market, the most recently auctioned Treasury issues for each maturity are referred to as "on the run" or "current coupon" issues. Issues auctioned prior to the current coupon issues are typically referred to as "off-the-run" issues and are not as liquid as on-the-run issues.

Bid and Offer Quotes on Treasury Securities

Bid and offers in the dealer market for Treasury bills are on a bank discount basis (in basis points), not on a price basis.

The yield on a bank discount basis is computed as follows:

$$\frac{\text{dollar discount}}{\text{face value}} \times \frac{360}{\text{number of days remaining to maturity}}$$

The quoted yield on a bank discount basis is not a meaningful measure of the return from holding a Treasury bill for two reasons. First, the measure is based on a face value investment rather than the actual dollar amount invested. Second, the yield is annualized based on a 360-rather than 365-day year, making it difficult to compare the yield with coupon securities that pay interest on a 365-day basis (such as Treasury notes or bonds).

Despite its shortcomings as a measure of return, this is the way that dealers in the market have adopted to quote Treasury bills. On many dealer quote sheets and some reporting services, however, two other yield measures are shown which attempt to make the yield comparable to a coupon bond and other money market instruments.

The measure that seeks to make the Treasury bill quote comparable to a coupon bond is called the *bond equivalent yield* (also called the *coupon equivalent yield*).[4] The *CD equivalent yield* (also called the *money market equivalent yield*) makes the yield on a Treasury bill more comparable to the way yields are quoted on money market instruments that pay interest on a 360-day basis, taking into consideration the price of the Treasury bill rather than its face value.

Prior to being auctioned, a new Treasury coupon issue is quoted on a yield to maturity basis (e.g., 8.52 or 11.23). The auction process determines the coupon rate. Thereafter the issue trades on a dollar price basis in price units of 1/32 of 1% of par (par is taken to be $100). For example, a quote of 92-14 refers to a price of 92 and 14/32. Thus, on the basis of $100,000 par value, a change in price of 1% equates to $1,000 and 1/32 equates to $31.25. A "plus" sign following the number of 32nds means that a 64th is added to the price. For example, 92-14+ refers to a price of 92 and 29/64 or 92.453125% of par value.

---

[4] The bond equivalent yield is found by doubling the semiannual interest rate that equates the present value of a coupon bond's cash flow to the price of the bond.

STRIPPED TREASURY SECURITIES

In August 1982, both Merrill Lynch and Salomon Brothers created zero-coupon Treasury securities. Merrill Lynch marketed these Treasury securities as "Treasury Income Growth Receipts" (TIGRs) and Salomon Brothers marketed them as "Certificates of Accrual on Treasury Securities" (CATS). The two investment banking firms did this by purchasing long-term Treasury bonds and depositing them in a bank custody account. They then issued receipts representing an ownership interest in each coupon payment on the underlying Treasury bond in the account and a receipt on the underlying Treasury bond's maturity value. The receipts created from the coupon stripping process were not issued by the U.S. Treasury, although the underlying bond deposited in the bank custody account was a debt obligation of the U.S. Treasury; thus, the cash flow from the underlying security was certain.

Other investment banking firms followed suit by creating their own receipts. These securities, as well as CATS and TIGRs, are referred to as *trademark* zero-coupon Treasury securities since they are associated with a particular firm. Because receipts of one firm were rarely traded by competing dealers, the secondary market was not liquid for any one trademark. To broaden the market and improve the liquidity of these receipts, a group of primary dealers in the government market agreed to issue generic receipts that would not be directly associated with any of the participating dealers. These generic securities are referred to as "Treasury Receipts" (TRs).

The problem with the trademark and generic Treasury receipts is that they clear by physical delivery, which is often cumbersome and inefficient. In August 1985, the Treasury announced its Separate Trading of Registered Interest and Principal of Securities (STRIPS) program. This program allows the stripping of designated Treasury issues for purposes of creating zero-coupon Treasury securities. The zero-coupon Treasury securities created under the STRIPS program are direct obligations of the U.S. government. Moreover, the securities clear through the Federal Reserve's book entry system. As a result of the STRIPS program, the origination of trademarks and generic receipts has stopped. Because of the greater marketability of the STRIPS, these securities now dominate the zero-coupon Treasury market.

FEDERALLY SPONSORED CREDIT AGENCY SECURITIES

Federally sponsored credit agencies are created by Congress as *privately* owned financial intermediaries whose purpose is to channel funds to particular sectors of the economy that Congress deems to require special assistance. There are five federally sponsored credit agencies. The *Farm Credit System* is responsible for the credit market in the agricultural sector of the economy. Three federally sponsored credit agencies—*Federal Home Loan Bank, Federal Home Loan Mortgage Corporation*—and *Federal National Mortgage Association* are responsible for providing credit to the mortgage and housing sectors. The *Student Loan Marketing Association* provides funds to support loans for higher education.

The federally sponsored credit agencies obtain their funds by issuing securities of two types: discount notes and bonds. Discount notes are short-term obligations, with maturities ranging from overnight to 360 days. Bonds are sold with maturities from 2 to 10 years, although some credit agencies may issue bonds with maturities of less than one year.

These securities are *not* backed by the full faith and credit of the U.S. government, as is the case with Treasury securities. Consequently, an investor who purchases a federally sponsored credit agency security is exposed to credit risk. The yield spread between these securities and Treasury securities of comparable maturity reflects differences in perceived credit risk and liquidity. The quality spread reflects the perceived financial burdens faced by the credit agency and the likelihood that the federal government will allow the credit agency to default on its outstanding obligations.

The price quotation convention for federally sponsored credit agency securities is the same as that for Treasury securities. That is, the bid and ask price quotations are expressed as a percentage of par plus fractional 32nds of a point.

CORPORATE BONDS

As the name indicates, corporate bonds are issued by corporations. They are classified by the type of issuer. The four general classifications used by bond information services are: (1) public utilities, (2) transportations, (3) industrials, and (4) banks and finance companies.

Either real property (using a mortgage) or personal property may be pledged to offer security beyond that of the general credit standing of the issuer. With a *mortgage bond*, the issuer has granted the bondholders a lien against the pledged assets. (A lien is a legal right to sell mortgaged property to satisfy unpaid obligations to bondholders.) *Debenture bonds* are not secured by a specific pledge of property, but that does not mean that they have no claim on property of issuers or on their earnings. Debenture bondholders have the claim of general creditors on all assets of the issuer not pledged specifically to secure other debt. They even have a claim on pledged assets to the extent that these assets have value greater than necessary to satisfy secured creditors. *Subordinated debenture bonds* are issues that rank after secured debt, after debenture bonds, and often after some general creditors in its claim on assets and earnings.

Credit Risk

Unlike Treasury securities, investors who own corporate bonds are exposed to credit risk. This is the risk that the issuer will default on its obligations. Most large institutional investors and investment banking firms perform their own credit analysis to assess the credit risk of an issuer. Most individual investors and some institutional bond investors rely primarily on commercial rating companies that perform bond analysis and express their conclusions by a system of ratings, which they publish. The four commercial rating companies are (1) Moody's Investors Service, (2) Standard & Poor's, (3) Duff and Phelps, and (4) Fitch Investors Service.

The two most widely used systems of bond ratings are Moody's and Standard & Poor's. In both systems the term *high grade* means low credit risk, or conversely, high probability of future payments. The highest grade bonds are designated by Moody's by the letters *Aaa*, and by Standard & Poor's by *AAA*. The next highest grade is *Aa* or *AA*; for the third grade both agencies use *A*. The next three grades are designated *Baa* or *BBB*, *Ba* or *BB*, and *B*, respectively. There are also *C* and *D* grades. In addition, Standard & Poor's uses a plus or a minus sign to provide a narrower credit quality breakdown within each class and Moody's uses 1, 2 or 3 to do this, 1 representing the highest quality within a class. Bonds rated triple A (AAA or Aaa) are said to be *prime;*

double A (AA or Aa) are *high quality*; single A issues are *upper medium grade*; and triple B are of *medium grade*. These four categories are referred to as containing *investment grade* issues. Lower rated bonds are said to have speculative elements or be *distinctly speculative*. They are also known as *junk bonds* or *high yield bonds*.

Call Risk

Most corporate issues have a call provision whereby the issuer has an option to buy back all or part of the issue prior to maturity. Some issues specify that the issuer must retire a predetermined amount of the issue periodically.[5] Whether the issuer has the choice to retire all or part of an issue prior to maturity or is required to do so, the bondholder is exposed to call risk.

Because of this risk, the bond issue usually includes a provision that denies the issuer the right to redeem bonds during the first 5 to 10 years following the date of issue with proceeds received from issuing lower-cost debt obligations ranking equal to or superior to the debt to be redeemed. This type of redemption is called *refunding*. While most long-term issues have these refunding restrictions, they are usually immediately callable, in whole or in part, if the source of funds comes from other than lower interest cost money. Cash flow from operations, proceeds from a common stock sale, or funds from the sale of property are examples of such sources. While the redemption price is often at a premium over par, there are many cases where the call price equals the par value.

Many bonds have some call protection. For example, they may not be called for the first three to seven years. Thereafter, the issue may be called for any reason. Investors often confuse refunding protection with call protection. Call protection is much more absolute in that bonds can not be redeemed *for any reason* during the protected period. Refunding restrictions only provide protection against the one type of redemption mentioned above. Failure to recognize this difference has resulted in unnecessary losses for some investors.

As a rule, corporate bonds are callable at a premium above par. Generally, the amount of the premium declines as the bond approaches

---

[5]For the most comprehensive coverage available on corporate call provisions, see Richard W. Wilson, *Corporate Senior Securities* (Chicago, IL: Probus Publishing, 1987).

maturity and often reaches par after a number of years have passed since issuance. The initial amount of the premium may be as much as one year's coupon interest or as little as coupon interest for half a year.

Corporate bond indentures may require the issuer to retire a specified portion of an issue each year. This is referred to as a *sinking-fund* requirement. Generally, the issuer may satisfy the sinking-fund requirement by either (1) making a cash payment of the face amount of the bonds to be retired to the corporate trustee who then calls the bonds for redemption using a lottery system, or (2) delivering to the trustee bonds with a total face value equal to the amount that must be retired from bonds purchased in the open market. Usually, the sinking-fund call price is the par value if the bonds were originally sold at par. When issued at a price in excess of par, the call price generally starts at the issuance price and scales down to par as the issue approaches maturity.

Many corporate bond indentures include a provision that grants the issuer the option to retire double the amount required for the sinking-fund provision. This *doubling option* effectively increases the call risk for the investor, since when interest rates decline, the issuer may find it advantageous to exercise this option at the special sinking-fund call price and retire a substantial portion of the high-cost outstanding issue. While the purpose of the sinking fund provision is to reduce credit risk by paying off the majority of the issue prior to maturity, this mandatory call provision increases call risk.

Options Granted to Bondholders

The call option granted to an issuer represents an option sold by the bondholder. In some issues, there are options that the issuer grants to the bondholder; that is, options that the bondholder purchases from the issuer when acquiring the bonds. Two examples of bonds with embedded options that are sold to bondholders are: (1) convertible or exchangeable bonds, and (2) putable bonds. A convertible or exchangeable bond allows the bondholder to obtain the stock of the issuer (in the case of a convertible bond) or the stock of a corporation other than the issuer (in the case of an exchangeable bond), by giving up the bond he is currently holding. Thus, a convertible or exchangeable bond is equal to a nonconvertible or nonexchangeable bond plus a call option on the stock or bond into which it can be converted.

A putable bond grants the bondholder the right to sell the bond back to the issuer at par value on designated dates. The advantage to the bondholder is that if interest rates rise after the issue date, thereby reducing the value of the bond, the bondholder can put the bond to the issuer for par and reinvest in higher yielding bonds. Thus, a putable corporate bond is composed of a non-putable corporate bond plus a long put option on the corporate bond.

Floating Rate Corporate Securities

The coupon interest on floating rate securities is reset periodically based on some predetermined benchmark. For example, the coupon rate may be reset every six months at a rate equal to 50 basis points above the six-month Treasury bill rate. Although the coupon on most issues resets on the basis of some financial index, there are some issues where the benchmark for the coupon rate is a nonfinancial index, such as the price of a commodity.

Floating rate corporate securities expose the bondholder to lower interest rate risk than fixed rate corporate securities, since their coupon resets to reflect the current market yield. In theory, a floating rate security with frequent resets should trade at par if the market views that the appropriate spread off the benchmark since the time of issuance has not changed. For example, suppose that an issuer offers a single-A rated floating rate security in which the coupon resets every three months to 40 basis points over the three-month Treasury bill rate. If the perceived credit quality of this issuer deteriorates such that investors at the reset date want 55 basis points over the three month Treasury bill rate for this bond, the price of the issue will sell below par. The opposite could occur if the credit quality improves and investors are willing to accept a lower spread. If the spread has remained constant, the issue should sell at par.

There may be other features in a floating rate issue. For example, many floating rate issues include a put option. Some issues are exchangeable either automatically at a certain date (often five years after issuance) or at the option of the issuer into fixed rate securities. A few issues are convertible into the common stock of the issuer.

MUNICIPAL BONDS

Municipal bonds are securities issued by state and local governments, and their creations such as "authorities" and special districts. There are tax-exempt and taxable municipal bonds. For tax-exempt municipal bonds, interest is exempt from Federal income taxation.[6] Interest may or may not be taxable at the state and local level. The large majority of municipal bonds outstanding are tax-exempt municipal bonds. For this reason, tax-exempt municipal bonds offer a lower yield than taxable bonds of the same maturity and comparable credit risk. Zero-coupon bonds, floating rate bonds and putable bonds are also available in the municipal bond market.

Municipal bonds are issued with one of two debt retirement structures or a combination of both. Either a bond has a *serial* maturity structure or a *term* maturity structure. With a serial maturity structure, a portion of the debt obligation is retired each year. When there is a term maturity structure, the debt obligation is repaid on a final date. Usually term bonds have maturities ranging from 20 to 40 years and retirement schedules (known as sinking funds) that begin 5 to 10 years before the final term maturity. Some municipal bonds may be called prior to maturity, as part of a mandatory sinking fund or at the option of the issuer. Thus, the bondholder may be exposed to call risk.

There are basically two types of municipal bond security structures: general obligation bonds and revenue bonds. Some securities share characteristics of both.[7]

General obligation bonds are debt instruments issued by states, counties, special districts, cities, towns, and school districts. They are secured by the issuer's general taxing powers. Usually a general obligation bond is secured by the issuer's unlimited taxing power. For smaller government jurisdictions such as school districts and towns, the only available unlimited taxing power is on property. For larger general obligation bond issuers such as states and big cities, the tax revenues are more diverse and may include corporate and individual income taxes, sales taxes, and property taxes. The security pledges for these larger issuers, such as states, are sometimes referred to as *full faith and credit obligations*.

The second basic type of security structure is found in revenue bonds. Such bonds are issued for either project or enterprise financings

---

[6]Congress grants this exemption to municipal issuers. The tax exemption is not a constitutional right.

[7]For a description of these securities, see Sylvan G. Feldstein and Frank J. Fabozzi, *Dow Jones-Irwin Guide to Municipal Bonds* (Homewood, IL: Dow Jones-Irwin, 1987).

in which the bond issuer pledges to the bondholders the revenues generated by the operating project financed. Examples include airport revenue bonds, college and university revenue bonds, hospital revenue bonds, single-family mortgage revenue bonds, multifamily revenue bonds, industrial development and pollution control revenue bonds, public power revenue bonds, resource recovery revenue bonds, seaport revenue bonds, sports complex and convention center revenue bonds, student loan revenue bonds, toll road and gas tax revenue bonds, and water revenue bonds.

Municipal securities issued for periods ranging up to three years are considered to be short-term in nature. Examples are tax anticipation notes (TANs), revenue anticipation notes (RANs), grant anticipation notes (GANs), bond anticipation notes (BANs), construction loan notes and tax-exempt commercial paper.

Municipal bonds are traded in the over-the-counter market. Markets are maintained on local credits by regional brokerage firms, local banks, and by some of the larger Wall Street firms. General names are supported by the larger brokerage firms and banks, many of whom have investment banking relationships with issuers.

As with corporate bonds, investors in municipal bonds are exposed to credit risk. In addition, investors who purchase tax-exempt munici-pal bonds are exposed to two types of risk which we shall refer to as tax risk. The first type of tax risk is the risk that the Federal income tax rate will be reduced. The higher the marginal tax rate, the greater is the value of the tax exemption feature. As the marginal tax rate declines, the price of a tax-exempt municipal bond will decline. The second type of *tax risk* is that a municipal bond that was issued as a tax-exempt issue is eventually declared by the Internal Revenue Service to be taxable. This may occur because many municipal revenue bonds have elaborate security structures that could be subject to future adverse congressional actions and IRS interpretations. As a result of the loss of the tax exemption feature, the municipal bond will decline in value in order to provide a yield comparable to similar taxable bonds.

MORTGAGE PASS-THROUGH SECURITIES

A mortgage pass-through security is created when one or more mort-gage holders form a collection (pool) of mortgages and sell shares or participations in the pool. A pool may consist of several thousand mortgages or only one mortgage. The cash flow of mortgage pass-through securities depends on the cash flow of the underlying mortgages. Because an understanding of mortgage pass-through securities requires an understanding of the cash flow characteristics of mortgages, we shall review the major types of mortgages that are used as collateral for mortgage pass-through securities.

Mortgages

A mortgage is a pledge of real estate to secure the payment of the loan originated for the purchase of that real property. The mortgage gives the lender (*mortgagee*) the right to foreclose on the loan and seize the underlying property in order to ensure that the loan is paid off if the borrower (*mortgagor*) fails to make the contractual payments. When the lender makes the loan based on only the credit of the borrower and on the collateral for the mortgage, the mortgage is said to be a *conventional mortgage*. Mortgage insurance may be obtained to guarantee the obligations of the borrower. The two forms of mortgage insurance which are guaranteed by the U.S. government if the borrower can qualify for them are Federal Housing Administration (FHA) and Veteran's Administration (VA) insurance. There are also private mortgage insurers.

The types of real estate properties that can be mortgaged are divided into two broad categories: residential and nonresidential properties. The former category includes houses, condominiums, cooperatives and apartments. Residential real estate can be subdivided into single-family (one-to-four family) structures and multifamily structures (apartment buildings in which more than four families reside). The second type of real estate property, nonresidential property, includes commercial and farm properties.

The mortgage loan specifies the interest rate of the loan, the frequency of payment, and the number of years to maturity. There are three types of mortgages underlying pass-through securities: level-payment fixed rate mortgages, graduated-payment mortgages and adjustable rate mortgages.

A *level-payment fixed rate mortgage* has the following characteristics: (1) the term of the loan is fixed (2) the interest rate is fixed, and (3) the amount of the monthly mortgage payment is fixed for the entire term of the loan (i.e., the mortgage is "level pay"). The level-payment fixed rate mortgage is the most common type of underlying mortgage for pass- through securities. The term of the mortgages is typically 30 years; however, in recent years an increasing number of 15-year mortgages have been securitized.

Each monthly mortgage payment for a level-payment fixed rate mortgage is due on the first of each month and consists of (1) interest of 1/12th of the fixed annual interest rate times the amount of the outstanding mortgage balance at the beginning of the previous month (interest "in arrears"), and (2) a scheduled repayment of a portion of the outstanding mortgage balance (principal). The difference between the total monthly mortgage payment and the interest portion equals the amount that is applied to reduce the outstanding mortgage balance. The monthly mortgage payment is designed so that after the last scheduled monthly payment is made, the amount of the mortgage balance outstanding is zero (i.e., the mortgage is fully repaid). The portion of the monthly mortgage payment applied to interest declines each month and the portion that goes to reducing the mortgage balance increases. The reason for this is that as the mortgage balance is reduced with each monthly mortgage payment, the interest on the mortgage balance declines. Since the monthly mortgage payment is fixed, a larger part of the monthly payment is applied to reduce the principal with each subsequent mortgage payment.

With a *graduated-payment* mortgage (GPM), the interest rate and the term of the mortgage are fixed, as with a level-payment fixed rate mortgage. However, the monthly payment for a GPM is smaller in the initial years (typically, the first five years) than for a level-payment fixed rate mortgage with the same mortgage rate. The level payments after the graduation period are higher or larger in the remaining years of the mortgage term than for a level-payment fixed rate mortgage.

The monthly payments in the earlier years of a GPM are generally not sufficient to pay the interest on the outstanding mortgage balance. The difference between the monthly mortgage payment and the accumulated interest (based on the outstanding mortgage balance) is then added to the outstanding mortgage balance. Thus, instead of amortizing the mortgage in the early years of a GPM, there is *negative amortization*. The higher level mortgage payments after the graduation period of the GPM are designed to fully amortize the outstanding mortgage balance by the end of the mortgage term which is, by then, greater than the original amount borrowed. The Federal Housing Administration (FHA) first introduced GPMs in late 1976. In 1979, GPMs first became eligible for pooling in certain types of pass-through securities.

An *adjustable rate mortgage* (ARM) is a mortgage in which the interest rate on the loan is adjusted periodically. The interest rate may be adjusted every six months, one year, two years or three years. The interest rate at the reset date is equal to a benchmark index plus a spread. The benchmark index used is either the interest rate on U.S. Treasury securities or a calculated measure such as a cost of funds index for a thrift. The benchmark for an ARM generally coincides with the term of adjustment. For example, for a one-year ARM, the benchmark would be a one-year Treasury rate or a cost of funds index for one year.

The basic ARM resets periodically and has no other terms that affect the monthly mortgage payment. Typically, however, ARMs do have other terms that affect the monthly mortgage payment, and hence the cash flow of the mortgage from the investor's perspective. These include: (1) periodic caps and (2) lifetime rate caps and floors.

Homeowners (borrowers) typically pay off all or part of their mortgage prior to the maturity date of the loan. Payments made in excess of the scheduled principal repayments are called *prepayments*. Effectively, the lender (mortgagee) has granted the homeowner (mortgagor) the right to prepay the mortgage balance at any time. Since the cash flow of a mortgage, and hence a mortgage-backed security, will depend on whether the homeowner exercises the option to prepay all or part of the mortgage prior to maturity and, if so, when those prepayments occur, it is important to understand the reasons why prepayments occur.

Prepayments occur for several reasons. First, most homeowners prepay the entire mortgage when they sell their home. The sale of a home may be due to (1) a change of employment that requires relocating, (2) the purchase of a more expensive home ("trading up"), or (3) a divorce in which the settlement requires sale of the marital residence. Second, if interest rates drop substantially after the time the mortgage was obtained, it may be beneficial for the homeowner to refinance the loan (even after paying all refinancing costs) at the lower interest rate. Third, in the case when homeowners cannot meet their mortgage obligations, the property is repossessed and sold. The proceeds from the sale are used to pay off the mortgage in the case of a conventional mortgage. For an insured mortgage, the insurer will pay off the mortgage balance. Finally, if property is destroyed by fire or another insured catastrophe occurs (such as the death of the mortgagor), the insurance proceeds are used to pay off the mortgage.

The risk that homeowners will prepay the mortgage at an inopportune time for investors (lenders)—generally, when interest rates fall and proceeds must be reinvested at a lower rate—is called *prepayment risk* or *call risk*. The latter term is used because the lender has effectively granted the homeowner a call option, much like the option bondholders grant corporations to call the bonds prior to maturity. An investor in a mortgage wants to be compensated for accepting prepayment or call risk. The question is, what constitutes fair compensation for accepting this risk?

Because of this call option, a valuation approach based on options theory has been advocated to value mortgage pass-through securities. While the approach is useful, it does have limitations because, in terms of option theory, homeowners may "irrationally" exercise the prepayment option or may not exercise it when it is rational to do so. More specifically, from an options' perspective, the rational exercise of the prepayment option by the homeowner should occur when there is an economic benefit to refinance the mortgage. That is, when the current market interest rate for mortgages is less than the mortgage rate on the loan outstanding by an amount sufficient to cover refinancing costs. In this case, the option is said to be "in the money." Yet, there are homeowners who, for whatever reason, do not exercise this option when it is beneficial to do so from an economic point of view. The existence of 16% mortgages at a time when the current mortgage rate was 8% was evidence of this. Similarly, this occurred when mortgage rates were 16%, and some homeowners paid off their 8% mortgages. From an options' perspective, such mortgages were "out of the money" and should not have been exercised. For the other reasons cited above, the action of these homeowners to prepay their mortgage may have been rational from their point of view.

Cash Flow of Mortgage Pass-Through Securities

The cash flow from a mortgage pass-through security will depend on the cash flow of the underlying pool of mortgages. The amount and the timing of the cash flow from the pool of mortgages and the cash flow passed through to investors, however, are not identical. The monthly cash flow for a pass-through security is less than for the monthly cash flow of the underlying mortgages by an amount equal to servicing and other fees.[8] Typically, the coupon rate on a pass-through security is 0.5% less than the coupon rate on the underlying pool.

The timing of the cash flow is also different. The monthly mortgage payment is due from each mortgagor on the first day of each month. There is a delay in passing through the corresponding monthly cash flow to the security holders. The number of days that the payment is delayed varies by the type of pass-through security.

Types of Mortgage Pass-Through Securities

There are three major guarantors of mortgage pass-through securities: the Government National Mortgage Association, the Federal Home Loan Mortgage Corporation, and the Federal National Mortgage Association. The last two are federally sponsored credit agencies. The Government National Mortgage Association is a wholly owned U.S. government corporation within the Department of Housing and Urban Development (HUD). The securities associated with these three entities are known as *agency pass-through securities*. About 98% of all pass-through securities are agency pass-through securities. The balance are privately issued pass-through securities. These securities are called *conventional mortgage pass-through securities*.

The Government National Mortgage Association (GNMA), popularly known as "Ginnie Mae," guarantees the largest amount of pass-through securities of the three agencies.[9] Only FHA-insured mortgages and VA-guaranteed mortgages are contained in the pool. The two major types of Ginnie Mae securities are GNMA Is and GNMA IIs. Ginnie Mae securities can be further divided into GNMA ARMs, GNMA

---

[8]Servicing of the mortgage involves collecting monthly payments from mortgagors and forwarding proceeds to owners of the loan, sending payment notices to mortgagors, reminding mortgagors when payments are overdue, maintaining records of mortgage balances, furnishing tax information to mortgagors, administering an escrow account for real estate taxes and insurance purposes, and, if necessary, initiating foreclosure proceedings. The servicing fee is a fixed percentage of the outstanding mortgage balance. The other fees are those charged by the issuer or guarantor of the pass-through security for guaranteeing the issue. The servicer pays the guarantee fee to the issuer or guarantor.

[9]Ginnie Mae is often referred to as an issuer of pass-through securities. Technically, Ginnie Mae does not issue the securities; instead, an originator of mortgages files the necessary documents with Ginnie Mae and, if approved, issues pass-throughs guaranteed by Ginnie Mae.

Midgets, GNMA GPMs, GNMA Mobile Homes, GNMA Buydowns and GNMA FHA Projects. Unlike the other two agency pass-through securities, Ginnie Mae pass-throughs are guaranteed by the full faith and credit of the United States government with respect to timely payment of both interest and principal. Timely payment means that the interest and principal will be paid when due.

The second largest type of agency pass-through security is issued by the Federal Home Loan Mortgage Corporation, popularly known as "Freddie Mac." The securities issued by Freddie Mac are called *participation certificates*. Most pools of mortgages consist of conventional mortgages, although participation certificates with underlying pools consisting of FHA-insured or VA-guaranteed mortgages have been issued. There are participation certificates that guarantee the timely payment of both interest and principal. However, most Freddie Mac participation certificates only guarantee the timely payment of interest. The scheduled principal is passed through as it is collected, with Freddie Mac guaranteeing only that the scheduled principal will be paid no later than one year after it is due. A guarantee by Freddie Mac is *not* the guarantee of the U.S. government. That is one reason why Freddie Mac pass-throughs offer a higher yield than Ginnie Mae securities with the same coupon and remaining term. Yet, most market participants view the creditworthiness of the Freddie Mac participation certificates as similar, although not identical, to that of Ginnie Mae pass-throughs which are fully guaranteed by the U.S. government. The higher yield for Freddie Mac participation certificates is also due to the prepayment characteristics of the underlying pool of mortgages. Conventional mortgages tend to prepay more variably than FHA/VA mortgages, which are generally assumable and which collateralize Ginnie Mae pass-throughs.

The other issuer of agency pass-through securities is the Federal National Mortgage Association (FNMA), popularly known as "Fannie Mae." Its pass-through securities, called *mortgage-backed securities*, are similar in many respects to the Freddie Mac participation certificates. However, Fannie Mae guarantees the timely payment of both interest and principal on all its securities. Just as in the case of Freddie Mac participation certificates, the Fannie Mae mortgage-backed securities are not the obligation of the U.S. government.

Conventional pass-through securities, also called *private pass-through securities* or *private-label pass-through securities*, are issued by thrifts, commercial banks and private conduits who purchase non-conforming mortgages (that is, mortgages that do not qualify for pooling in agency pass-through securities) in order to package them to sell pass-through securities.

While conventional mortgage pass-through securities are not guaranteed by the U.S. government (as with Ginnie Maes) or the other agencies (Fannie Mae and Freddie Mac), they often are supported by credit enhancements. This takes the form of either (1) letters of credit or guarantees from commercial banks that provide for payment up to some specified percentage of the total outstanding balance of the mortgages, (2) pool insurance from a mortgage insurance company, or (3) subordinated interests. While agency pass-throughs are not rated by the rating agencies such as Moody's and Standard & Poor's (because they think it is inappropriate to do so), conventional mortgage pass-through securities are rated. As of late 1986, the credit enhancements have allowed more than 70% of all conventional mortgage pass-through securities to be rated double-A or better at the time of issuance.[10] Despite the credit enhancement, default risk is present when investing in these pass-through securities. The investor in a conventional pass-through security must therefore be compensated for accepting both prepayment risk and default risk.

Measuring Yields on Pass-through Securities

In the absence of prepayments and ignoring default risk, the only uncertainty about the return on a mortgage pass-through security would be due to reinvestment risk. That is, there would be the risk of reinvesting the monthly mortgage payments at a rate less than the yield offered on the security at the time of purchase. However, prepayments do occur. Thus, an investor in pass-through securities does not know what the cash flow will be and cannot determine a precise return on the security when contemplating purchase. Despite this, market conventions for quoting and measuring (and therefore comparing) yields have developed. These measures assume that the investor will hold the security until the last mortgage in the pool is fully repaid.

---

[10]Howard Altarescu, Erik Anderson, Mike Asay and Hal Hinkle, "The Conventional Mortgage Pass-Through Market," Chapter 8 in Frank J. Fabozzi (ed.), *The Handbook of Mortgage-Backed Securities*, Revised Edition (Chicago, IL: Probus Publishing, 1988).

An investor must make some assumption about prepayment rates for an individual pool in order to estimate the cash flow that can be expected from a pass-through security for which that pool is the underlying collateral. Based on the estimated cash flow, a yield can be computed. A yield computed in this manner is called a *cash flow yield*. Cash flow yields are typically based on one of the following benchmarks for projecting cash flows: FHA experience, constant prepayment rate, or PSA standard prepayment model.

At one time, the most commonly used benchmark for estimating prepayment rates was the prepayment experience on 30-year mortgages derived from a Federal Housing Administration (FHA) probability table of mortgage survivals. Using this FHA experience, cash flows are forecasted for a pool, assuming that the prepayment rate is the same as the FHA experience ("100% FHA") or some multiple of FHA experience (faster than FHA experience or slower than FHA experience). For example, taking the square root of the FHA experience is referred to as "50% FHA"; squaring the FHA experience for the prepayment rate is referred to as "200% FHA."

Despite their popularity, prepayment rate forecasts based on FHA experience are not necessarily indicative of the prepayment rate for a particular pool. The reason is that FHA experience represents an estimate of prepayments on all FHA-insured mortgages over various interest rate periods. Since prepayment rates are tied to interest rate cycles, what does one average prepayment rate over various cycles mean? To many market participants, not much. Consequently, since a cash flow forecast based on prepayments using FHA experience may be misleading, the resulting cash flow yield may not be meaningful for making investment decisions.

Another approach to estimating prepayments and cash flow yield is to assume that some fraction of the remaining principal in the pool is prepaid each month. The constant prepayment rate (CPR) assumed for a pool is based on the characteristics of the pool and the economic environment. The advantage of the CPR is its simplicity; what's more, changes in economic conditions that impact prepayment rates can be analyzed quickly. This method also accounts for the unique characteristics of a specific pool.

Although initially developed for the evaluation of collateralized mortgage obligations (discussed later in this chapter), the Public Securities Association (PSA) standard prepayment model can be applied to project cash flows for any mortgage-related security. The PSA model is expressed as a monthly series of annual prepayment rates. The basic PSA model assumes that prepayments will occur less frequently for newly originated mortgages and then will speed up as the mortgages become seasoned. More specifically, the PSA model assumes the following prepayment rates for 30-year mortgages: (1) an annualized rate of 0.2% for the first month, increased by 0.2% per annum each month for the next 2.5 years when it reaches 6% per year, and (2) 6% per year for the remaining years. This base benchmark is referred to as "100% PSA." Slower or faster speeds are then referred to as some percentage of PSA. For example, 50% PSA means one half the PSA prepayment rate; 150% PSA means one and a half times the PSA prepayment rate.

The PSA prepayment model is a benchmark, not a model for forecasting prepayments. While it has helped standardize quotations on mortgage-related securities and is easy for market participants to understand, it has several shortcomings that limit its usefulness as a tool for analysis.[11] Most importantly, it implicitly assumes that all mortgage-backed securities have the same pattern of prepayment. No recognition is given to the specific characteristics of the underlying pool. For example, discount, premium and current coupon pools will have different prepayment patterns, as will GNMAs and conventional pass-throughs securities and 15-year and 30-year securities.

COLLATERALIZED MORTGAGE OBLIGATIONS

There is considerable uncertainty about the maturity of any mortgage pass-through security. Consequently, market participants interested in purchasing a short-term security, say 1 to 3 years, find these securities unattractive; some long-term investors find these securities unattractive because a fast-pay pass-through security could substantially reduce its maturity. A collateralized mortgage obligation (CMO) reduces the uncertainty concerning the cash flow pattern of a mortgage-backed security and thereby provides a more predictable risk/return pattern not available with typical mortgage pass-through securities.

---

[11]For a more detailed discussion, see David J. Askin and William J. Curtin, "Unsafe at any Speed? Derivative Mortgage-Backed Securities and the PSA Prepayment Model," Drexel Burnham Lambert *Monthly Prepayment Report*, April 1987.

A CMO is a security backed by a pool of mortgages and/or by a portfolio of pass-through securities. Because CMOs derive their cash flows from the underlying mortgage collateral, they are referred to as "derivative" securities. CMOs are structured so that there are several classes of bondholders with varying *stated* maturities. The principal payments from the underlying collateral are used to sequentially retire the bonds.[12]

For example, in a typical CMO structure, there are four classes of bonds generally referred to as class-A, class-B, class-C and class-Z.[13] The first three classes, with class-A representing the shortest bond, receive periodic interest payments from the underlying collateral; class-Z (also called the Z-bond) is an accrual bond that receives no periodic interest until the other three classes are retired. When principal payments, both scheduled and prepayments, are received by the trustee for the CMO, they are applied to retire the class-A bonds. After all the class-A bonds are retired, all principal payments received are applied to retire the class-B bonds. Once all the class-B bonds are retired, class-C bonds are paid off from all principal payments. Finally, after the first three classes of bonds are retired, the cash flow payments from the remaining underlying collateral are used to satisfy the obligations on the Z-bonds (original principal plus accrued interest).

The cash flows for each class can only be derived by assuming some prepayment rate for the underlying mortgage collateral. The prepayment benchmark used by mortgage-backed securities dealers to quote CMO yields is the PSA standard prepayment model discussed in the previous section.

The spread over Treasuries for each class of this CMO issue represents compensation for prepayment risk and credit risk. The prepayment risk is lower than for a mortgage pass-through security, because of the cash flow structure.

The credit quality for most CMOs is high enough to be rated triple-A by the major commercial rating agencies. The credit risk is determined by the way in which the CMO is structured and by the quality of the

---

[12]In structuring a CMO, the issuer has to consider Federal income tax consequences which resulted in inefficient structures. The Real Estate Mortgage Investment Conduit (REMIC) provision of the 1986 tax act gave issuers greater flexibility in structuring CMOs.

[13]In a particular CMO issue the letters for each class may be different but the mechanics concerning the sequential retirement of the bonds for each class are the same. The classes are commonly referred to as *tranches*.

underlying mortgage collateral, and generally not the creditworthiness of the issuer. Most CMOs are backed by agency pass-through securities or FHA/VA guaranteed mortgages. For these CMOs, credit risk is minimal. The majority of those CMOs not backed by agency pass-throughs or FHA/VA guaranteed mortgages are issued by Freddie Mac. These issues therefore carry its guarantee and are perceived to have low credit risk. CMOs that do not fall into one of these two categories typically carry pool insurance that guarantees the timely payment of interest and principal.

Another key element in determining the credit quality of the CMO is the manner in which the cash flows are structured. In order to receive a triple-A quality rating, the cash flows must be sufficient to meet all of the obligations under any prepayment scenario. Also, the reinvestment rate assumed to be earned on the cash flow until it is distributed to bondholders must be low.

Because of the safeguards built into a CMO structure, a triple-A rating for a CMO is generally viewed as being of higher quality than most triple-A rated corporate securities. Yet CMOs typically offer a higher spread to comparable Treasury securities than do triple-A rated corporate bonds. The higher yield reflects the fact that there is greater relative prepayment risk for CMOs than there is call risk for callable corporate bonds.

Other CMO Structures

Several CMO structures have been introduced since the introduction of the first CMO issue in June 1983. In September 1986, Shearson Lehman Brothers introduced a CMO issue (SLB CMO Trust D, $150 million) where the first class received interest which was reset quarterly at a spread of 37.5 basis points over the three-month London Interbank Offer Rate (LIBOR). This floating rate CMO structure appealed to financial institutions and foreign investors who sought investments in which the yield on funds invested varied with the rate on their liabilities. The design of the floating rate CMO has been refined to make the floating rate class comparable in investment characteristics to other short-term instruments that attract funds from financial institutions.

The inverse floater, introduced in October 1986 with the CMO Trust 13 ($490 million), has two floating rate classes. One class is paid interest based on a fixed spread over LIBOR. The other class, the inverse floating rate class, has an interest rate that moves in the opposite direction to the change in LIBOR. Thus, if LIBOR increases (decreases), the coupon rate on the floating rate class increases (decreases) while the coupon rate on the inverse floating rate class decreases (increases). While there is still a cap on the coupon rate for the floating rate class, it is greater than the cap that would exist in the absence of the inverse floating rate class (due to cost savings from lower interest paid on inverse floaters when the benchmark increases).

In March 1987, the M.D.C. Mortgage Funding Corporation, CMO Series O, included a class of bonds referred to as "stablized mortgage reduction term" or "SMRT" bonds, and in its CMO Series P it included a class referred to as a "planned amortization class" or "PAC" bonds. The Oxford Acceptance Corporation III, Series C CMOs included a class of bonds referred to as a "planned redemption obligation" or "PRO" bonds. The common characteristic of these three types of bonds is that, within a wide range of prepayment rates, the cash flow pattern is more certain than it is in other classes of a typical CMO issue.

The greater predictability of the cash flow for these classes of bonds occurs because there is a sinking-fund schedule that must be satisfied in order to retire the obligations of this class. Therefore, these bondholders have priority over all other classes in the CMO issue in receiving principal payments from the underlying collateral. The greater certainty of the cash flow for this class of bondholders comes by increasing the prepayment risk of the other bondholder classes.

CMO Residual

The excess of the cash flow generated from the underlying collateral over the amount needed to pay interest, retire the bonds, and pay administrative expenses is called the *CMO residual*. Investors can purchase an equity position in the residual cash flow as it accumulates over time. The excess cash flow is not know with certainty and depends on several factors: (1) current and future interest rates, (2) the coupon rate on the underlying mortgage collateral, (3) the type of collateral, (4) the prepayment rate on the underlying collateral, and (5) the structure of the CMO issue.

The most significant source of excess cash flows is the spread between the net coupon on the underlying mortgage collateral and the weighted average coupon for the CMO issue. In an upward-sloping yield curve environment, the shorter term and intermediate term class bonds will require a lower yield than on the longer term bond classes and the underlying collateral. The second major source of residual cash flow is the difference between the actual reinvestment income earned on the cash flow invested before the payout to the bondholders and the assumed reinvestment rate. Recall from our earlier discussion on the rating determination of CMO issues that a conservative (low) reinvestment assumption is made. When the actual reinvestment rate is greater than the assumed rate, residual cash flow will result.

STRIPPED MORTGAGE-BACKED SECURITIES

Stripped mortgage backed securities, introduced by Fannie Mae in 1986, are another example of derivative mortgage securities. Mortgage pass-through securities divide the cash flow from the underlying pool of mortgages on a pro rata basis for distribution to the security holders. A stripped mortgage-backed security is created by altering the distribution of principal and interest from a pro rata distribution to an unequal distribution. By doing so, at least one of the securities created will have a price/yield relationship that is different from the price/yield relationship of the underlying mortgage pool.

The first generation of stripped mortgage-backed securities were "partially stripped" mortgage-backed securities. That is, some of the interest payment and principal payments were distributed to each of two classes of bondholders but not in equal proportions. For example, one-third of the interest payments from the underlying pool of mortgages may be distributed to Class A bondholders and two-thirds to the Class B bondholders. The principal received from the underlying collateral may or may not be divided equally between the two classes.

In early 1987, stripped mortgage-backed securities began to be issued in which all of the interest was allocated to one class (called the *interest only* or *IO* class), and all of the principal was allocated to the other class (called the *principal only* or *PO* class). Thus, the IO class receives no principal payments. The investor in an IO class wants the underlying mortgages to remain outstanding as long as possible since the interest is the only form of return that the IO class will receive and will be paid as long as the mortgages are outstanding. When mortgage rates fall and prepayments are expected to rise, the interest only class will decline in value. Thus, the price of an IO moves in the same direction as interest rates. In the extreme case where prepayments are much faster than anticipated when pricing the IO class, it is possible for the investor not to recover the amount invested in the IO class.

The PO class sells at a discount from par. Since investors benefit by faster recovery of the principal in the case of a discount security, a fall (rise) in mortgage rates will increase (decrease) expected prepayments and therefore increase (decrease) a PO's price. Thus, the price of a PO changes in the opposite direction of the change in interest rates. Both IOs and POs have substantial interest-rate risk.

SUMMARY

In this chapter we reviewed the securities traded in the bond and mortgaged-backed securities markets: Treasury securities, stripped Treasury securities, Federal sponsored credit agency securities, corporate bonds, municipal bonds, mortgage pass-through securities, collateralized mortgage obligations and stripped mortgage-backed securities. An investor in these securities may be exposed to one or more of the following risks: (1) interest-rate risk, (2) reinvestment risk, (3) default risk, (4) call risk (prepayment risk in the case of mortgage-backed securities), (5) inflation risk, (6) foreign-exchange rate risk, and (7) marketability/liquidity risk.

CHAPTER 12

Framework for Active Total Return Management of Fixed Income Portfolios

RAVI E. DATTATREYA, PH.D.
DIRECTOR
FINANCIAL STRATEGIES GROUP
PRUDENTIAL-BACHE CAPITAL FUNDING

FRANK J. FABOZZI, PH.D., CFA
VISITING PROFESSOR OF FINANCE
SLOAN SCHOOL OF MANAGEMENT
MASSACHUSETTS INSTITUTE OF TECHNOLOGY

Fixed income portfolio management can be classified as active strategies, passive strategies and structured portfolio strategies. Active strategies require forecasts of either the direction of interest rates, expected change in yield spreads, or expected future interest rate volatility. Passive strategies involve minimal expectational input. Structured portfolio strategies involve designing a portfolio to achieve the performance of some predetermined benchmark. When the benchmark is a

231

bond index, the strategy is referred to as indexing and is the subject of the next chapter. When the benchmark is to satisfy future liabilities regardless of how interest rates change in the future, the strategies available are immunization and cash flow matching. There are strategies that employ active portfolio strategies within a structured portfolio strategy.

Regardless of the strategy employed, a framework is needed to evaluate its potential performance. In this chapter we will present such a framework, focusing on the attributes of a bond or bond portfolio that will impact its performance. We begin with an overview of active fixed income portfolio strategies.

TYPES OF ACTIVE FIXED INCOME PORTFOLIO STRATEGIES

Historically, active fixed income portfolio management has been associated with three general types of strategies. The first type is forecasting interest rates and positioning the portfolio to capitalize on the direction of interest rate forecasted. This type of strategy is referred to as a *rate anticipation strategy*. The second type is based on anticipated changes (narrowing or widening) of yield spreads between market sectors. This type of strategy is referred to as a *sector swap strategy*. Examples include: (1) swaps between mortgage pass-through securities and Treasuries; (2) swaps between industrials and utilities of the same quality rating; and (3) swaps between utilities with different quality ratings. *Substitution swaps* are the third type of strategy. In a substitution swap a portfolio manager swaps one bond for another bond that is perceived to be identical in all risk characteristics but offers a higher yield.

The first two types of strategies—rate anticipation strategies and sector swaps—are based on forecasts. In rate anticipation strategies, the direction of future interest rates must be forecasted. This is admittedly a difficult (indeed, many would say impossible) task. A sector swap requires (1) an analysis of the historical yield spread, (2) an expectation of a normal yield spread that should prevail in the future, and (3) constructing a swap if the current yield spread departs from the normal yield spread expected by an amount sufficient to cover transaction costs. A substitution swap depends on a capital market imperfection. Such situations sometimes exist in the bond market due to temporary market imbalances.

In all three strategies, the portfolio manager faces considerable risk. With rate anticipation strategies, there is the risk that interest rates will move in the direction opposite that forecasted. With sector swaps, the yield spread may not change in the direction expected. The risk in a substitution swap is that the bond purchased may not be identical to the bond for which it is exchanged. For example, if credit quality is not the same, the bond purchased may be offering a higher yield due to higher risk rather than to a market imbalance.

Recently, active strategies to enhance portfolio performance based on expected future interest rate volatility have been employed. While it is not simple to forecast future interest rate volatility, many practitioners feel that it is simpler than forecasting future interest rates or yield spreads. In addition, these strategies may be designed so as to have low potential risk and, in some cases, a known maximum downside risk.

Implementing any of these strategies requires an understanding of three attributes of a bond or bond portfolio: horizon (or total) return, duration, and convexity. To understand these three attributes, the price/yield relationship of a bond must be understood. This is the subject of the next section.

PRICE/YIELD RELATIONSHIP

The price of a bond is equal to the present value of the cash flow expected from the bond. The cash flow is not always simple to project. In the case of noncallable bonds, barring default, the cash flow pattern is known. For bonds with embedded options such as callable bonds and mortgage-backed securities[1], the cash flow pattern is not known with certainty. The required rate that should be used to compute the present value of the expected cash flow will equal the yield on comparable Treasury securities plus a premium for risk plus the value of any options granted to the issuer minus an adjustment for any options the issuer grants to the bondholder.[2]

Let's begin with the price/yield relationship for an option-free bond,

---

[1] For a discussion of mortgage-backed securities, see Chapter 11.

[2] For a discussion of the risks associated with fixed income securities, see Chapter 11.

that is, a bond that does not have an embedded option. (Later in this chapter we shall discuss the price/yield relationship for bonds with embedded options.)

The price of an option-free bond moves in the opposite direction of a change in yield. The reason is that since the price is the present value of the cash flow, a higher (lower) yield will decrease (increase) the present value of the cash flow and therefore its price. Exhibit 1 illustrates this for a 20-year, 10% coupon bond.

If the price/yield relationship for this bond is graphed, it would have the bowed shape shown in Exhibit 2. This shape is referred to as *convex* and it is not unique to our hypothetical bond. The price/yield relationship for any option-free bond will have a convex shape.

While the relationship between price and yield shown in Exhibits 1 and 2 is for an instantaneous change in yield, over time three factors will change the price of a bond. First, as yields in the market change, the price of a bond will change. Second, the price of a bond selling at a discount or premium will change as it approaches maturity even if market yields do not change. More specifically, the price of a discount bond will increase while that of a premium bond will decrease. Third, as the perceived credit risk changes, the price of a bond will change.

EXHIBIT 1:
PRICE/YIELD RELATIONSHIP FOR 20-YEAR 10% COUPON BOND

Required Yield	Price (Par = 100)
7.00%	132.02
8.00	119.79
9.00	109.20
9.50	104.44
9.90	100.86
9.99	100.09
10.00	100.00
10.01	99.91
10.10	99.15
10.50	95.85
11.00	91.98
12.00	84.95
13.00	78.78

EXHIBIT 2:
GRAPH OF PRICE/YIELD RELATIONSHIP

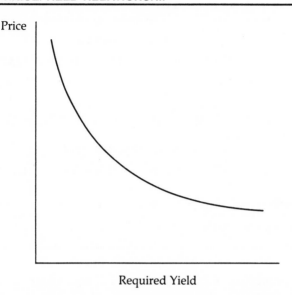

Price

Required Yield

PRICE VOLATILITY FOR AN OPTION-FREE BOND[3]

Exhibit 3 shows the percentage change in the price of our hypothetical 20 year, 10% coupon bond assuming (1) the initial yield is 10% and (2) the yield change is instantaneous.

From Exhibit 3 it can be seen that for small changes in required yield such as 10 basis points, the percentage price increase is the same as the percentage price decrease. However, for larger changes in the required yield, this is no longer true. In fact, the percentage price increase is greater than the percentage price decrease. An implication is that if an investor owns a bond, the price appreciation that will be realized if the required yield decreases is greater than the capital loss that will be realized if the required yield increases by the same number of basis points.[4]

---

[3]For a more detailed discussion of bond price volatility, see Frank J. Fabozzi, *Fixed Income Mathematics* (Chicago, IL: Probus Publishing 1988), Chapters 9-11.

[4]A basis point is equal to .01% (.0001). 100 basis points are equal to to 1%.

EXHIBIT 3:
PERCENTAGE PRICE CHANGE FOR A 20-YEAR 10% COUPON BOND
SELLING AT PAR TO YIELD 10%

	Increase in Required Yield					
Required yield	10.01%	10.10%	10.50%	11.00%	12.00%	13.00%
Change (in basis points)	1	10	50	100	200	300
% change in price	−0.09	−0.85	−4.15	−8.02	−15.05	−21.22

	Decrease in Required Yield					
Required yield	9.99%	9.90%	9.50%	9.00%	8.00%	7.00%
Change (in basis points)	−1	−10	−50	−100	−200	−300
% change in price	0.09	0.86	4.44	9.20	19.79	32.03

These properties of an option-free bond, which are due to the convex shape of the price/yield relationship, can be summarized as follows:

Property 1: Changes are approximately symmetric for small changes in yield.

Property 2: Price changes are not symmetric for large changes in yield.

Property 3: Percentage price increases are greater than percentage price decreases for the same change in yield.

While all option-free bonds exhibit the price/yield and bond price volatility characteristics just described, all bonds do not change by the same percentage for a given change in basis points. There are two characteristics of a bond that will determine its price volatility: coupon and maturity. The impact of these two characteristics on a bond's price volatility are summarized below:

Characteristic 1: Holding maturity and yield constant, the price volatility of a bond is greater the lower the coupon rate.

Characteristic 2: Holding the coupon rate and yield constant, the price volatility of a bond is greater the longer the maturity.[5]

---

[5]The exception is some deep discount coupon bonds.

Measuring Bond Price Volatility

In addition to knowing how the coupon rate and maturity of a bond will influence its price volatility, a measure that quantifies the combined impact of coupon rate and maturity is also needed to implement portfolio strategies. Such a measure is Macaulay duration[6], which is defined below for a semiannual pay bond whose next cash flow is exactly six months from now[7]:

$$\text{Macaulay duration (in years)} = \frac{\dfrac{1\ CF_1}{(1+y/2)^1} + \dfrac{2\ CF_2}{(1+y/2)^2} + \cdots + \dfrac{n\ CF_n}{(1+y/2)^n}}{2\ \text{Price}}$$

where

CF_t = cash flow in period t

y = yield (annual and in decimal form)

n = number of six month periods

Macaulay duration for a zero-coupon bond is equal to its maturity.

Exhibit 4 shows how to compute the Macaulay duration for the 20-year, 10% coupon bond selling at par (100) to yield 10%.

The link between Macaulay duration and percentage price change is:

$$\text{percentage price change} = -\frac{\text{Macaulay duration}}{(1+y/2)} \times \text{Yield change} \times 100$$

---

[6]Frederick R. Macaulay, *Some Theoretical Problems Suggested by the Movements of Interest Rates, Bond Yields and Stock Prices in the United States Since 1865* (National Bureau of Economic Research, 1938).

[7]For a semiannual pay bond between coupon dates, the formula for Macaulay duration must be adjusted as follows. First, instead of multiplying the cash flows by the time period (t = 1, 2 . . . n) , they are multiplied by:

$$\text{time period} + \frac{\text{time (in days) remaining to the next cash flow}}{\text{total time (in days) between cash flows}} - 1$$

Second, the above expression is used in the present value formula rather the time period to compute the present value of each cash flow. Third, the numerator is divided by price plus accrued interest not just price.

EXHIBIT 4:
CALCULATION OF MACAULAY DURATION FOR A 20-YEAR,
10% COUPON BOND SELLING AT PAR TO YIELD 10%

Period	Cash Flow*	PV of $1 @5%	PV of CF	Period × PV
1	5	0.952380	4.76190	4.761
2	5	0.907029	4.53514	9.070
3	5	0.863837	4.31918	12.957
4	5	0.822702	4.11351	16.454
5	5	0.783526	3.91763	19.588
6	5	0.746215	3.73107	22.386
7	5	0.710681	3.55340	24.873
8	5	0.676839	3.38419	27.073
9	5	0.644608	3.22304	29.007
10	5	0.613913	3.06956	30.695
11	5	0.584679	2.92339	32.157
12	5	0.556837	2.78418	33.410
13	5	0.530321	2.65160	34.470
14	5	0.505067	2.52533	35.354
15	5	0.481017	2.40508	36.076
16	5	0.458111	2.29055	36.648
17	5	0.436296	2.18148	37.085
18	5	0.415520	2.07760	37.396
19	5	0.395733	1.97866	37.594
20	5	0.376889	1.88444	37.688
21	5	0.358942	1.79471	37.688
22	5	0.341849	1.70924	37.603
23	5	0.325571	1.62785	37.440
24	5	0.310067	1.55033	37.208
25	5	0.295302	1.47651	36.912
26	5	0.281240	1.40620	36.561
27	5	0.267848	1.33924	36.159
28	5	0.255093	1.27546	35.713
29	5	0.242946	1.21473	35.227
30	5	0.231377	1.15688	34.706
31	5	0.220359	1.10179	34.155
32	5	0.209866	1.04933	33.578
33	5	0.199872	0.99936	32.978
34	5	0.190354	0.95177	32.360
35	5	0.181290	0.90645	31.725
36	5	0.172657	0.86328	31.078
37	5	0.164435	0.82217	30.420
38	5	0.156605	0.78302	29.755
39	5	0.149147	0.74573	29.083
40	105	0.142045	14.91479	596.591
			Total	1801.704

$$\text{Macaulay duration} = \frac{\$1801.704}{2\,(100)} = 9.01$$

*Per $100 par.

The Macaulay duration divided by $(1 + y/2)$ is called modified duration; that is,

$$\text{Modified duration} = \frac{\text{Macaulay duration}}{(1 + y/2)}$$

Using modified duration, the percentage price change can be expressed as:

percentage price change = - Modified duration x Yield change x 100

For the 20-year, 10% coupon bond selling at par to yield 10%, modified duration is:

$$\text{modified duration} = \frac{9.01}{(1 + .10/2)} = 8.58$$

Exhibit 5 shows the percentage price change based on duration for our hypothetical bond and compares it to the actual price change as shown in Exhibit 3. Note the following three points. First, for small changes in yield, Macaulay duration (modified duration) does a good job approximating the actual percentage price change. Second, for a large change in yield, the approximation is off. The error is greater the larger the change in yield. Finally, the percentage price change based on duration is less than the actual percentage price change when yields decline but greater when yields increase. This implies that the estimated price based on duration will always be less than the actual price.

For a 100 basis point change in yield (that is, a yield change of 0.01), the percentage price change based on duration will be:

$$\begin{aligned} \text{percentage price change} &= \; - \text{ Modified duration x } (.01) \text{ x } 100 \\ &= \; - \text{ Modified duration} \end{aligned}$$

Thus, modified duration is the percentage price change for a 100 basis point change in yield.

While we have focused on the percentage price change, the properties discussed earlier are also applicable to the dollar price change. The relationship between the dollar price change of a bond and modified duration is:

EXHIBIT 5:
ESTIMATED PERCENTAGE CHANGE IN PRICE USING MODIFIED DURATION FOR A 20-YEAR 10% COUPON BOND SELLING AT PAR TO YIELD 10%*

	Increase in Required Yield:					
Required yield	10.01%	10.10%	10.50%	11.00%	12.00%	13.00%
Change (in basis points)	1	10	50	100	200	300
Estimated % change	−0.09	−0.86	−4.29	−8.58	−17.16	−25.74
Actual % change	−0.09	−0.85	−4.15	−8.02	−15.05	−21.22

	Decrease in Required Yield					
Required yield	9.99%	9.90%	9.50%	9.00%	8.00%	7.00%
Change (in basis points)	−1	−10	−50	−100	−200	−300
Estimated % change	0.09	0.86	4.29	8.58	17.16	25.74
Actual % change	0.09	0.86	4.44	9.20	19.79	32.03

*Modified duration = 8.58.

Dollar price change =
        − Price x Modified duration x Yield change x 100

The product of the price and modified duration is called *dollar duration*. That is,

Dollar duration = Price x Modified duration

Therefore the dollar price change can be expressed as:

Dollar price change = − Dollar duration x Yield change x 100

We now know that duration (Macaulay, modified, dollar) provides a good approximation for the change in a bond's price for small changes in yield but not for large changes. We've also seen that by using duration the new price of a bond will be understated. To see why, let's take a closer look at the graph of the price/yield relationship for the 20-year, 10% coupon bond.

Exhibit 6 is the same graph as Exhibit 2 except that there is a tangent line drawn at a yield of 10%, the yield we assume this bond is offering. The tangent line is used to estimate what the new price will be if yield changes. Take note of three things. First, for small changes in yield the tangent line deviates little from the price/yield curve. Thus, for small changes in yield the tangent line does a good job approximating the new price. Second, for large changes in yield the tangent line departs much more from the price/yield curve. In fact, as we move further and further from the 10% yield, the difference between the price estimated from the tangent line and the actual price as given by the price/yield curve increases. Third, regardless of whether the yield increases or decreases, the tangent line is below the price/yield curve. Thus, the estimated price will be less than the actual price.

EXHIBIT 6:
CONVEX CURVE WITH TANGENT LINE

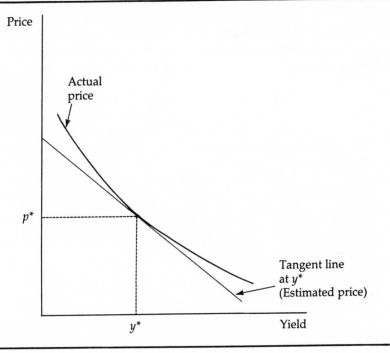

What does the tangent line represent? The slope of the tangent line represents the dollar duration of a bond. Thus, our earlier observations concerning the use of duration to approximate price or percentage price change are due to the convex shape of the price/yield curve.

Convexity

Let's examine what happens to the tangent line when yield changes. As the yield increases, the slope of the tangent line flattens (becomes smaller). The slope of the tangent line steepens (becomes larger) when yield decreases. Since the slope of the tangent line represents dollar duration, this means that when yield increases, dollar duration gets smaller and when yield decreases, dollar duration gets larger. For an investor who is long a bond, an increase in dollar duration when yield decreases and a decrease in dollar duration when yield increases is an attractive investment feature.

While all option-free bonds share this feature, the rate at which dollar duration increases when yield decreases and decreases when yield increases differs for each bond. It is possible to measure the rate of change of dollar duration. The measure is popularly known as *convexity* and is measured as follows for a semiannual pay bond whose next coupon payment is exactly six months from now[8]:

$$\text{Convexity (in years)} = \frac{\dfrac{(1)^1 \, CF_1}{(1+y/2)^1} + \dfrac{(2)^2 \, CF_2}{(1+y/2)^2} + \cdots + \dfrac{(n)^2 \, CF_n}{(1+y/2)^n}}{4 \text{ Price}}$$

Exhibit 7 illustrates the calculation of convexity for our 20-year, 10% coupon bond selling at par to yield 10%.

---

[8]Technically, the formula for convexity is:

$$\text{Convexity (in years)} = \frac{\dfrac{1 \, (2) \, CF_1}{(1+y/2)^1} + \dfrac{2 \, (3) \, CF_2}{(1+y/2)^2} + \cdots + \dfrac{n(n+1) \, CF_n}{(1+y/2)^n}}{4 \text{ Price}}$$

However, the formula in the text provides almost identical values.

EXHIBIT 7:
CALCULATION OF CONVEXITY FOR A 20-YEAR,
10% COUPON BOND SELLING AT PAR TO YIELD 10%

Period	Cash Flow*	PV of $1 @5%	PV of CF	Period^2 × PV
1	5	0.952380	4.76190	4.761
2	5	0.907029	4.53514	8.140
3	5	0.863837	4.31918	8.872
4	5	0.822702	4.11351	5.816
5	5	0.783526	3.91763	7.940
6	5	0.746215	3.73107	134.318
7	5	0.710681	3.55340	174.116
8	5	0.676839	3.38419	216.588
9	5	0.644608	3.22304	261.066
10	5	0.613913	3.06956	306.956
11	5	0.584679	2.92339	353.730
12	5	0.556837	2.78418	400.922
13	5	0.530321	2.65160	448.121
14	5	0.505067	2.52533	494.966
15	5	0.481017	2.40508	541.144
16	5	0.458111	2.29055	586.382
17	5	0.436296	2.18148	630.448
18	5	0.415520	2.07760	673.143
19	5	0.395733	1.97866	714.299
20	5	0.376889	1.88444	753.778
21	5	0.358942	1.79471	791.467
22	5	0.341849	1.70924	827.276
23	5	0.325571	1.62785	861.136
24	5	0.310067	1.55033	892.995
25	5	0.295302	1.47651	922.821
26	5	0.281240	1.40620	950.593
27	5	0.267848	1.33924	976.307
28	5	0.255093	1.27546	999.967
29	5	0.242946	1.21473	1021.589
30	5	0.231377	1.15688	1041.198
31	5	0.220359	1.10179	1058.827
32	5	0.209866	1.04933	1074.514
33	5	0.199872	0.99936	1088.305
34	5	0.190354	0.95177	1100.250
35	5	0.181290	0.90645	1110.402
36	5	0.172657	0.86328	1118.820
37	5	0.164435	0.82217	1125.561
38	5	0.156605	0.78302	1130.690
39	5	0.149147	0.74573	1134.270
40	105	0.142045	14.91479	23863.670
			Total	50006.190

$$\text{Convexity} = \frac{50,006.190}{4\,(100)} = 125.02$$

*Per $100 par

Given the convexity of a bond, modified convexity and dollar convexity are computed as follows:

$$\text{Modified convexity} = \frac{\text{Convexity}}{(1 + y/2)^2}$$

and

$$\text{Dollar convexity} = \text{Modified convexity} \times \text{Price}$$

The percentage price change of bond due to convexity can be estimated using the following equation:

percentage price change due to convexity =

$$\frac{1}{2} \times \text{Modified convexity} \times (\text{Yield change})^2 \times (100)^2$$

Exhibit 8 shows the percentage price change due to convexity for our hypothetical bond.

Combining the price change due to duration and the price change due to convexity gives a considerably better approximation to the percentage change in price. This can be seen in Exhibit 8.

The properties of convexity are summarized below without proof:

Property 1: As the yield increases (decreases) the dollar duration of a bond decreases (increases).

Property 2: For a given yield and maturity, the lower the coupon rate, the greater the convexity of a bond.

Property 3: For a given yield and modified duration, the lower the coupon rate the smaller the convexity.

Property 4: The convexity of a bond increases at an increasing rate as duration increases.

Property 2 implies that a zero-coupon bond will have greater convexity than a coupon bond with the same maturity. However, Property 3 implies that a zero-coupon bond will have lower convexity than a coupon bond with the same duration.

EXHIBIT 8:
PERCENTAGE PRICE CHANGE USING MODIFIED DURATION AND CONVEXITY FOR A 20-YEAR, 10% COUPON BOND SELLING AT PAR TO YIELD 10%*

Increase in Required Yield

Required yield	10.01%	10.10%	10.50%	11.00%	12.00%	13.00%
Change (in basis points)	1	10	50	100	200	300
Estimated % – duration	– 0.09	– 0.86	– 4.29	– 8.58	– 17.16	– 25.74
Estimated % – convexity	0.00	0.01	0.14	0.57	2.27	5.10
Total % estimated	– 0.09	– 0.85	– 4.15	– 8.01	– 14.89	– 20.64
Actual % change	– 0.09	– 0.85	– 4.15	– 8.02	– 15.05	– 21.22

Decrease in Required Yield

Required yield	9.99%	9.90%	9.50%	9.00%	8.00%	.00%
Change (in basis points)	– 1	– 10	– 50	– 100	– 200	– 300
Estimated % – duration	0.09	0.86	4.29	8.58	17.16	25.74
Estimated % – convexity	0.00	0.01	0.14	0.57	2.27	5.10
Total % estimated	0.09	0.87	4.43	9.15	19.43	30.84
Actual % change	0.09	0.86	4.44	9.20	19.79	32.03

*Modified duration = 8.58.
Modified convexity = 125.002.

HORIZON RETURN

There are two yield measures that are commonly used in the bond market — yield to maturity and yield to call. The yield to maturity of a bond is the interest rate that will make the present value of its cash flow to maturity equal to its price (plus accrued interest). The yield to call is the interest rate that will make the present value of its cash flow to call equal to its price (plus accrued interest)[9]

These yield measures are often used to assess the relative value of bonds. Unfortunately, it is only under very limited circumstances that these measures offer any insight into the relative attractiveness of bonds.

[9]The calculation of these two yield measures is illustrated in Fabozzi, *Fixed Income Mathematics*, Chapter 6.

There are two drawbacks to these measures. First, yield to maturity assumes that the bond will be held to maturity. In the case of yield to call, the assumption is that the bond will be held to the call date. Since an active bond portfolio manager may sell a bond prior to maturity or call, this assumption is not realistic. Second, the yield to maturity will only produce a return at the maturity date equal to the yield to maturity if all coupon payments can be reinvested at an interest rate equal to the yield to maturity. For the yield to call all coupon payments must be reinvested at an interest rate equal to the yield to call. The risk that coupon payments may be reinvested at an interest rate below the required interest rate is called *reinvestment risk*. How important is this risk? For some bonds, the interest income that must be generated to produce the accumulated value necessary to realize the yield to maturity (or yield to call) may constitute as much as 80% of the bond's total dollar return.

Because of the limitations of yield to maturity and yield to call for assessing the performance of a bond in a portfolio and the relative value of bonds, an alternative measure must be developed. The measure must take into consideration the three sources of dollar return from holding a bond over some investment horizon: (1) coupon interest, (2) interest from reinvesting coupon interest over the investment horizon, and (3) any capital gain or loss. This requires that a portfolio manager specify: (1) the investment horizon, (2) an interest rate that the coupon payments can be reinvested, and (3) the price that the bond can be sold at the end of the investment horizon. The last assumption is effectively equivalent to projecting what the required yield on the bond will be at the end of the investment horizon.

The rate of return computed using this framework is called the *horizon return*. Other names used for horizon return are *total return*, *realized compound yield*[10], and *effective yield*. Horizon return when the cash flows are semiannual is calculated as follows:

$$\left[\frac{\text{Total coupon payments} + \text{Reinvestment income} + \text{Price at end of investment horizon}}{\text{initial price plus accrued interest}} \right]^{2/h} - 1$$

---

[10]This term was first used by Sidney Homer and Martin Leibowitz in *Inside the Yield Book* (Englewood Cliffs, NJ: Prentice Hall 1972).

Of course, the horizon return will depend on the investment horizon and the underlying assumptions. A portfolio manager will want to investigate the sensitivity of these assumptions on a bond's horizon return. For short-term investment horizons, the horizon return is not sensitive to changes in the reinvestment rate. However, it will be sensitive to the assumed yield at the end of the horizon.

APPLICATIONS[11]

In this section we will apply the concepts discussed thus far in this chapter.

Dumbbell-Bullet Analysis

A *dumbbell* is a combination or a portfolio of two bonds. In our application we select the bonds and their holdings such that the duration of the dumbbell is equal to that of a third bond, known as the *bullet*. We want to compare the relative attractiveness of the dumbbell and the bullet.

There are two unknowns in the creation of a dumbbell: the par holdings of each of the two bonds that comprise the dumbbell. We need two conditions to determine these two unknowns. The first condition is that the total dollar duration of the dumbbell equals that of the bullet. By equating the dollar durations, we equate the interest rate risk of the two positions. A common second condition is to equate the total market value of the dumbbell to that of the bullet. This ensures that the proceeds from the sale of the bullet (or dumbbell) can be used to purchase the dumbbell (bullet) with no cash left over after the transaction.

A comparison of the yield to maturity of the bullet to the weighted average yield to maturity of the dumbbell to determine whether a portfolio manager can enhance portfolio performance poses several problems. First, the yield for a portfolio is not simply the weighted average of the yields of the bonds in the portfolio. Instead, it is the internal rate of return of the cash flow of the portfolio. Second, as we explained in the previous section, the yield to maturity measure is a

---

[11]The illustrations in this section are adapted from Ravi E. Dattatreya and Frank J. Fabozzi, *Active Total Return Management of Fixed Income Portfolios* (Chicago, IL: Probus Publishing, 1989).

poor measure of relative value because it assumes that the bonds will be held to maturity and that the coupon payments will be reinvested at the yield to maturity. Finally, bond price performance depends not only on duration but convexity. The following illustration demonstrates these points.

Exhibit 9 compares a dumbbell consisting of a 5-year, 8.5% bond and a 20-year, 9.5% bond blended in the ratio of 50.2% and 49.8% to a bullet of 10-year maturity and 9.25% coupon. All bonds are initially priced at par.

The yield to maturity of the bullet is 9.25%. The weighted average yield to maturity of the dumbbell is 9%. A naive analysis would suggest that there is a yield pickup of 0.25% or 25 basis points by buying the bullet and selling the dumbbell. However, while the dollar duration for the bullet and dumbbell is equal, the dollar convexity of the two is not. The dumbbell has higher dollar convexity. Thus, while there is a yield to maturity pickup by investing in the bullet, there is a convexity give-up by investing in the bullet. The yield giveup can be viewed as the cost of improving convexity.

However, if the yield on the dumbbell is properly computed based on the cash flow from the two bonds, there is a much smaller yield pickup by investing in the bullet (6.3 basis points).

We're not yet finished with this story. We still have not properly assessed whether the bullet or dumbbell is more attractive because the yield — whether computed as a weighted-average yield or cash flow yield — is not a meaningful measure of potential return. To assess relative value a horizon return must be computed over some holding period.

Exhibit 10 presents the horizon return for the performance of the bullet and dumbbell over a six-month horizon for a parallel shift in the yield curve (i.e. the yield for all maturities changes by an equal number of basis points). The first column of the exhibit shows the change in yield. The next three columns show the price corresponding to that change in yield. The fifth and sixth columns show the total dollars at the end of six months (which in our illustration represents the price plus coupon interest) for the dumbbell and bullet, respectively. Since the strategy under consideration is to sell the dumbbell and buy the bullet, the seventh column shows the difference in the total dollars at the end of six months. The last three columns provide the same information based on horizon return rather than total dollars.

EXHIBIT 9:
DUMBBELL-BULLET ANALYSIS

Three bonds used in analysis:

Bond	Coupon	Maturity (Years)	Price Plus Accrued	Dollar Yield	Dollar Duration	Convexity
A	8.50	5	100	8.50%	4.00544	19.8164
B	9.50	20	100	9.50%	8.88151	124.1702
C	9.25	10	100	9.25%	6.43409	55.4506

Bullet: Bond C

Dumbbell: Bonds A and B
 Composition of dumbbell: 50.2% of Bond A; 49.8% of Bond B
 Dollar duration of dumbell =
  .502 x 4.00544 + .498 x 8.88151 = 6.434
 Average yield of dumbbell =
  .502 x 8.50 + .498 x 9.5 = 8.998

Strategy: Sell the dumbbell and buy the bullet

Analysis based on average yield
 Yield pickup = Yield on bullet − Average yield of dumbbell
  = 9.25 − 8.998 = .252 or 25.2 basis points

Analysis based on duration, convexity and average yield
 Dollar convexity of dumbell =
  .502 x 19.8164 + .498 x 124.1702 = 71.7846

 Yield pickup = Yield on bullet − Average yield of dumbbell
  = 9.25 − 8.998 = .252 or 25.2 basis points

 Convexity giveup = Convexity of dumbbell − Convexity of bullet
  = 71.7846 − 55.4506 = 16.334

Analysis based on duration, convexity and cash flow yield

 Cash flow yield of dumbbell* =

$$\frac{(8.5 \times .502 \times 4.00544) + (9.5 \times .498 \times 8.88151)}{6.434} = 9.187$$

 Yield pickup = Yield on bullet − Cash flow yield
  = 9.25 − 9.187 = .063 or 6.3 basis points

 Convexity giveup = Convexity of dumbbell − Convexity of bullet
  = 71.7846 − 55.4506 = 16.334

*The calculation shown is actually a dollar-duration-weighted yield, a very close approximation to cash flow yield.

EXHIBIT 10:
DUMBBELL-BULLET ANALYSIS BASED ON HORIZON RETURN: PARALLEL SHIFT IN YIELD CURVE ASSUMED

Yield Change	Price of Bond			Dollar Value of			Horizon Return		
	A	B	C	Dumbbell	Bullet	Difference	Dumbbell	Bullet	Difference
−5.000	124.90124	169.20719	143.37301	146.96915	143.37301	−3.59613	93.94	86.75	−7.19
−4.750	123.75147	164.71523	141.01688	144.15470	141.01688	−3.13782	88.31	82.03	−6.28
−4.500	122.61503	160.39327	138.71132	141.43162	138.71132	−2.72030	82.86	77.42	−5.44
−4.250	121.49174	156.23402	136.45514	138.79617	136.45514	−2.34103	77.59	72.91	−4.68
−4.000	120.38141	152.23050	134.24717	136.24480	134.24717	−1.99764	72.49	68.49	−4.00
−3.750	119.28389	148.37606	132.08625	133.74412	132.08625	−1.68787	67.55	64.17	−3.38
−3.500	118.19901	144.66438	129.97128	131.38088	129.97128	−1.40960	62.76	59.94	−2.82
−3.250	117.12661	141.08938	127.90117	129.06199	127.90117	−1.16081	58.12	55.80	−2.32
−3.000	116.06652	137.64531	125.87487	126.81448	125.87487	−0.93962	53.63	51.75	−1.88
−2.750	115.01858	134.32665	123.89133	124.63554	123.89133	−0.74421	49.27	47.78	−1.49
−2.500	113.98264	131.12812	121.94956	122.52246	121.94956	−0.57291	45.04	43.90	−1.15
−2.250	112.95854	128.04473	120.04857	120.47267	120.04857	−0.42410	40.95	40.10	−0.85
−2.000	111.94612	125.0716	118.18741	118.48369	118.18741	−0.29628	36.97	36.37	−0.59
−1.750	110.94525	122.20432	116.36515	116.55317	116.36515	−0.18802	33.11	32.73	−0.38
−1.500	109.95576	119.43836	114.58088	114.67886	114.58088	−0.09798	29.36	29.16	−0.20
−1.250	108.97752	116.76960	112.83371	112.85860	112.83371	−0.02489	25.72	25.67	−0.05
−1.000	108.01038	114.19403	111.12279	111.09033	111.12279	0.03245	22.18	22.25	0.06
−0.750	107.05420	111.70785	109.44727	109.37209	109.44727	0.07518	18.74	18.89	0.15
−0.500	106.10883	109.30741	107.80632	107.70198	107.80632	0.10434	15.40	15.61	0.21
−0.250	105.17415	106.98924	106.19916	106.07821	106.19916	0.12095	12.16	12.40	0.24

0.000	104.25000	104.75000	104.62500	104.49904	104.62500	0.12596	9.00	9.25	0.25
0.250	103.33626	102.58651	103.08308	102.96283	103.08308	0.12025	5.93	6.17	0.24
0.500	102.43280	100.49574	101.57265	101.46799	101.57265	0.10466	2.94	3.15	0.21
0.750	101.53949	98.47477	100.09300	100.01301	100.09300	0.07999	0.03	0.19	0.16
1.000	100.65619	96.52083	98.64342	98.59645	98.64342	0.04698	−2.81	−2.71	0.09
1.250	99.78278	94.63125	97.22323	97.21691	97.22323	0.00632	−5.57	−5.55	0.01
1.500	98.91913	92.80350	95.83174	95.87306	95.83174	−0.04132	−8.25	−8.34	−0.08
1.750	98.06513	91.03515	94.46830	94.56364	94.46830	−0.09533	−10.87	−11.06	−0.19
2.000	97.22065	89.32385	93.13229	93.28741	93.13229	−0.15512	−13.43	−13.74	−0.31
2.250	96.38556	87.66740	91.83207	92.04322	91.82307	−0.22015	−15.91	−16.35	−0.44
2.500	95.55976	86.06366	90.54003	90.82994	90.54003	−0.28991	−18.34	−18.92	−0.58
2.750	94.74312	84.51058	89.28259	89.64650	89.28259	−0.36391	−20.71	−21.43	−0.73
3.000	93.93553	83.00623	88.05017	88.49186	88.05017	−0.44169	−23.02	−23.90	−0.88
3.250	93.13687	81.54872	86.84219	87.36504	86.84219	−0.52285	−25.27	−26.32	−1.05
3.500	92.34704	80.13627	85.65612	86.26510	85.65812	−0.60698	−27.47	−28.68	−1.21
3.750	91.56592	78.76718	84.49742	85.19112	84.49742	−0.69370	−29.62	−31.01	−1.39
4.000	90.79341	77.43979	83.35955	84.14224	83.35955	−0.78268	−31.72	−33.28	−1.57
4.250	90.02939	76.15253	82.24402	83.11761	82.24402	−0.87358	−33.76	−35.51	−1.75
4.500	89.27377	74.90391	81.15032	82.11643	81.15032	−0.96611	−35.77	−37.70	−1.93
4.750	88.52643	73.69248	80.07796	81.13793	80.07796	−1.05997	−37.72	−39.84	−2.12
5.000	87.78727	72.51685	79.02647	80.18138	79.02647	−1.15491	−39.64	−41.95	−2.31

Note: Starting value for each bond is 100.

Our horizon analysis suggests that if yields change by more than 100 basis points, the dumbbell will outperform the bullet. This would generate a loss if we pursued a strategy of buying the bullet and selling the dumbbell. In contrast, a gain would be produced if yields change by 100 basis points or less. The better performance of the dumbbell for large changes in yield is due to its better convexity.

While we have restricted our analysis thus far to a parallel shift in the yield curve, Exhibits 11 and 12 show the same information as Exhibit 10 for nonparallel shifts. In Exhibit 11, we assumed that if the yield on Bond C (the intermediate-term bond) changes, Bond A (the short-term bond) will increase by 25 basis point while Bond B (the long-term bond) will decrease by 25 basis points. Under this scenario, the dumbbell will always outperform the bullet. In Exhibit 12, the nonparallel shift assumes that for a change in Bond C's yield, the yield on Bond A will decrease by 25 basis point while that on Bond B will increase by 25 basis points. In this case, the bullet would outperform the dumbbell only if the yield on Bond C does not rise by more than 250 basis points or fall by more than 325 basis points.

Thus, horizon analysis tells us that by looking at measures such as yield (yield to maturity, average-weighted yield or cash flow yield), duration and convexity can be misleading because the performance of a security or a portfolio of securities depends on the magnitude of the change in yields over some investment horizon and how the yield curve changes.[12]

Break-even Reinvestment Rate

Horizon return analysis can be used to compare the attractiveness of two bonds over some predetermined investment horizon. A concept that is useful in the analysis is the *break-even reinvestment rate*. The break-even reinvestment rate between two bonds is the reinvestment rate at which the horizon returns for two bonds over a given horizon are equal.

---

[12]There's even more to this story. See Chapter 5 of Dattatreya and Fabozzi, *Active Total Return Management of Fixed Income Portfolios*, for an illustration of dumbbell-bullet analysis within an internally and externally consistent framework.

Depending on the maturities, coupons and prices of the two bonds, the horizon return of one of the bonds is expected to be greater than that of the other if the reinvestment rate is below the break-even rate, and smaller if it is above the break-even rate. Therefore, depending on interest rate expectations, it is possible to conclude whether one bond is relatively more attractive than another. Confidence in such a conclusion is especially high if the break-even rate is extreme, i.e., much higher or much lower than current or expected interest rates. Sometimes the break-even rate is within the expected interest rate band, in which case the analysis may be inconclusive as to the determination of the more attractive bond.

Exhibit 13 compares Bond 1, a five-year 15% bond priced at 120, and Bond 2, a five-year 5% bond priced at 80, for a horizon of five years (the same as the maturity of the bonds). Bond 2 has the greater horizon return if an 8% reinvestment rate is assumed. On the other hand, if a 16% reinvestment rate is assumed, Bond 1 would have a higher horizon return. Both bonds have higher returns as reinvestment rate assumptions climb, yet they do not increase at the same rate.

Exhibit 14 shows this relationship, which is a sloping curve for each bond with the curve for Bond 1 being steeper. It also illustrates the point at which the two curves intersect. This point is called the *break-even point*, and the corresponding reinvestment rate is the *break-even reinvestment rate*. If the expected cash flows from the bonds are reinvested at this rate, both bonds would generate the same horizon return.

By examining the location of the break-even reinvestment rate between two bonds, one can determine the more attractive bond. If an investor's expectation of future rates is higher than the break-even reinvestment rate, then the 15% bond will achieve a greater horizon return than the 5% bond, as shown in Exhibit 14. Conversely, if an investor's expectation of future rates is lower than the break-even reinvestment rate, then the 5% bond will achieve a greater horizon return.

A break-even reinvestment rate does not always exist for any two bonds. It may be that one bond will always have a higher horizon return than another bond for any assumed reinvestment rate. Exhibit 15 shows a comparison between the same five-year bonds as in Exhibit 13; however, Bond 2 is now priced at 90. Over any range of selected reinvestment rates, Bond 1 will always generate higher horizon returns

EXHIBIT 11:
DUMBBELL-BULLET ANALYSIS BASED ON HORIZON ANALYSIS: NON-PARALLEL SHIFT IN YIELD CURVE

Yield Change*	Price of Bond			Dollar Value of			Horizon Return		
	A	B	C	Dumbbell	Bullet	Difference	Dumbbell	Bullet	Difference
-5.000	123.75147	173.87681	143.37301	148.71790	143.37301	-5.34489	97.44	86.75	-10.69
-4.750	122.61503	169.20719	141.01688	145.82165	141.01688	-4.80478	91.64	82.03	-9.61
-4.500	121.49174	164.71523	138.71132	143.02049	138.71132	-4.30917	86.04	77.42	-8.62
-4.250	120.38141	160.39327	136.45514	140.31052	136.45514	-3.85538	80.62	72.91	-7.71
-4.000	119.28389	156.23402	134.24717	137.68801	134.24717	-3.44084	75.38	68.49	-6.88
-3.750	118.19901	152.23050	132.08625	135.14942	132.08625	-3.06316	70.30	64.17	-6.13
-3.500	117.12661	148.37606	129.97128	132.69134	129.97128	-2.72005	65.38	59.94	-5.44
-3.250	116.06652	144.66438	127.90117	130.31054	127.90117	-2.40937	60.62	55.80	-4.82
-3.000	115.01858	141.08938	125.87487	128.00393	125.87487	-2.12906	56.01	51.75	-4.26
-2.750	113.98264	137.64531	123.89133	125.76854	123.89133	-1.87721	51.54	47.78	-3.75
-2.500	112.95854	134.32665	121.94956	123.60156	121.94956	-1.65201	47.20	43.90	-3.30
-2.250	111.94612	131.12812	120.04857	121.50029	120.04857	-1.45173	43.00	40.10	-2.90
-2.000	110.94525	128.04473	118.18741	119.46216	118.18741	-1.27475	38.92	36.37	-2.55
-1.750	109.95576	125.07165	116.36515	117.48469	116.36515	-1.11954	34.97	32.73	-2.24
-1.500	108.97752	122.20432	114.58088	115.56553	114.58088	-0.98465	31.13	29.16	-1.97
-1.250	108.01038	119.43836	112.83371	113.70243	112.83371	-0.86872	27.40	25.67	-1.74
-1.000	107.05420	116.76960	111.12279	111.89324	111.12279	-0.77046	23.79	22.25	-1.54
-0.750	106.10883	114.19403	109.44727	110.13591	109.44727	-0.68864	20.27	18.89	-1.38
-0.500	105.17415	111.70785	107.80632	108.42845	107.80632	-0.62213	16.86	15.61	-1.24
-0.250	104.25000	109.30741	106.19916	106.76900	106.19916	-0.56984	13.54	12.40	-1.14
0.000	103.33626	106.98924	104.62500	105.15574	104.62500	-0.53074	10.31	9.25	-1.06
0.250	102.43280	104.75000	103.08308	103.58695	103.08308	-0.50387	7.17	6.17	-1.01

0.500	101.53949	102.58651	101.57265	102.06099	101.57265	-0.48834	4.12	3.15	-0.98
0.750	100.65619	100.49574	100.09300	100.57627	100.09300	-0.48327	1.15	0.19	-0.97
1.000	99.78278	98.47477	98.64342	99.13129	98.64342	-0.48786	-1.74	-2.71	-0.98
1.250	98.91913	96.52083	97.22323	97.72459	97.22323	-0.50136	-4.55	-5.55	-1.00
1.500	98.06513	94.63125	95.83174	96.35479	95.83174	-0.52305	-7.29	-8.34	-1.05
1.750	97.22065	92.80350	94.46830	95.02056	94.46830	-0.55225	-9.96	-11.06	-1.10
2.000	96.38556	91.03515	93.13229	93.72063	93.13229	-0.58834	-12.56	-13.75	-1.18
2.250	95.55976	89.32385	91.82307	92.45378	91.82307	-0.63071	-15.09	-16.35	-1.26
2.500	94.74312	87.66740	90.54003	91.21884	90.54003	-0.67881	-17.56	-18.92	-1.36
2.750	93.93553	86.06366	89.28259	90.01470	89.28259	-0.73212	-19.97	-21.43	-1.46
3.000	93.13687	84.51058	88.05017	88.84029	88.05017	-0.79012	-22.32	-23.90	-1.58
3.250	92.34704	83.00623	86.84219	87.69457	86.84219	-0.85237	-24.61	-26.32	-1.70
3.500	91.56592	81.54872	85.65612	86.57655	85.65812	-0.91843	-26.85	-28.68	-1.84
3.750	90.79341	80.13627	84.49742	85.48530	84.49742	-0.98788	-29.03	-31.01	-1.98
4.000	90.02939	78.76718	83.35955	84.41991	83.35955	-1.06035	-31.16	-33.28	-2.12
4.250	89.27377	77.43979	82.24402	83.37950	82.24402	-1.13548	-33.24	-35.51	-2.27
4.500	88.52643	76.15253	81.15032	82.36324	81.15032	-1.21292	-35.27	-37.70	-2.43
4.750	87.78727	74.90391	80.07796	81.37033	80.07796	-1.29237	-37.26	-39.84	-2.58
5.000	87.05620	73.69248	79.02647	80.40000	70.02647	-1.37352	-39.20	-41.95	-2.75

Note: Starting value for each bond is 100.

*Change in yield for Bond C. Nonparallel shift as follows:
yield change bond A = yield change bond C + 25 basis points
yield change bond B = yield change bond C − 25 basis points

EXHIBIT 12:
DUMBBELL-BULLET ANALYSIS BASED ON HORIZON ANALYSIS: NONPARALLEL SHIFT IN YIELD CURVE

Yield Change*	Price of Bond			Dollar Value of			Horizon Return		
	A	B	C	Dumbbell	Bullet	Difference	Dumbbell	Bullet	Difference
−5.000	126.06449	164.71523	143.37301	145.31565	143.37301	−1.94264	90.63	86.75	−3.89
−4.750	124.90124	160.39327	141.01688	142.57911	141.01688	−1.56223	85.16	82.03	−3.12
−4.500	123.75147	156.23402	138.71132	139.93038	138.71132	−1.21906	79.86	77.42	−2.44
−4.250	122.61503	152.23050	136.45514	137.36590	136.45514	−0.91076	74.73	72.91	−1.82
−4.000	121.49174	148.37606	134.24717	134.88228	134.24717	−0.63511	69.76	68.49	−1.27
−3.750	120.38141	144.66438	132.08625	132.47627	132.08625	−0.39002	64.95	64.17	−0.78
−3.500	119.28389	141.08938	129.97128	130.14477	129.97128	−0.17349	60.29	59.94	−0.35
−3.250	118.19901	137.64531	127.90117	127.88483	127.90117	0.01635	55.77	55.80	0.03
−3.000	117.12661	134.32665	125.87487	125.69360	125.87487	0.18126	51.39	51.75	0.36
−2.750	116.06652	131.12812	123.89133	123.56840	123.89133	0.32293	47.14	47.78	0.65
−2.500	115.01858	128.04473	121.94956	121.50664	121.94956	0.44291	43.01	43.90	0.89
−2.250	113.98264	125.07165	120.04857	119.50585	120.04857	0.54271	39.01	40.10	1.09
−2.000	112.95854	122.20432	118.18741	117.56368	118.18741	0.62373	35.13	36.37	1.25
−1.750	111.94612	119.43836	116.36515	115.67786	116.36515	0.68729	31.36	32.73	1.37
−1.500	110.94525	116.76960	114.58088	113.84624	114.58088	0.73464	24.69	29.16	1.47
−1.250	109.95576	114.19403	112.83371	112.06676	112.83371	0.76695	24.13	25.67	1.53
−1.000	108.97752	111.70785	111.12279	110.33744	111.12279	0.78534	20.67	22.25	1.57
−0.750	108.01038	109.30741	109.44727	108.65641	109.44727	0.79086	17.31	18.89	1.58
−0.500	107.05420	106.98924	107.80632	107.02184	107.80632	0.78448	14.04	15.61	1.57
−0.250	106.10883	104.75000	106.19916	105.43203	106.19916	0.76714	101.86	12.40	1.53
0.000	105.17415	102.58651	104.62500	103.88530	104.62500	0.73970	7.77	9.25	1.48
0.025	104.25000	100.49574	103.08308	102.38008	103.08308	0.70300	4.76	6.17	1.41

0.500	103.33626	98.47477	101.57265	100.91485	101.57265	0.65780	1.83	3.15	1.32
0.750	102.43280	96.52083	100.09300	99.48817	100.09300	0.60484	-1.02	0.19	1.21
1.000	101.53949	94.63125	98.64342	98.09863	98.64342	0.54479	-3.80	-2.71	1.09
1.250	100.65619	92.80350	97.22323	96.74492	97.22323	0.47830	-6.51	-5.55	0.96
1.500	99.78278	91.03515	95.83174	95.42576	95.83174	0.40598	-9.15	-8.34	0.81
1.750	98.91913	89.32385	94.46830	94.13992	94.46830	0.32839	-11.72	-11.06	0.66
2.000	98.06513	87.66740	93.13229	92.88623	93.13229	0.24606	-14.23	-13.74	0.49
2.250	97.22065	86.06366	91.82307	91.66357	91.82307	0.15949	-16.67	-16.35	0.32
2.500	96.38556	84.51058	90.54003	90.47087	90.54003	0.06916	-19.06	-18.92	0.14
2.750	95.55976	83.00623	89.28259	89.30709	89.28259	-0.02450	-21.39	-21.43	-0.05
3.000	94.74312	81.54872	88.05017	88.17125	88.05017	-0.12109	-23.66	-23.90	-0.24
3.250	93.93553	80.13627	86.84219	87.06239	86.84219	-0.22020	-25.88	-26.32	-0.44
3.500	93.13687	78.76718	85.65812	85.97961	85.65812	-0.32149	-28.04	-28.68	-0.64
3.750	92.34704	77.43979	84.49742	84.92203	84.49742	-0.42462	-30.16	-31.01	-0.85
4.000	91.56592	76.15253	83.35955	83.88882	83.35955	-0.52927	-32.22	-33.28	-1.06
4.250	90.79341	74.90391	82.24402	82.87917	82.24402	-0.63515	-34.24	-35.51	-1.27
4.500	90.02939	73.69248	81.15032	81.89230	81.15032	-0.74198	-36.22	-37.70	-1.48
4.750	89.27377	72.51685	80.07796	80.92748	80.07796	-0.84952	-38.15	-39.84	-1.70
5.000	88.52643	71.37571	79.02647	79.98400	79.02647	-0.95752	-40.03	-41.95	-1.92

*Change in yield for Bond C. Nonparallel shift as follows:
yield change bond A= yield change bond C -25 basis points
yield change bond B= yield change bond C +25 basis points

EXHIBIT 13:
BREAK-EVEN REINVESTMENT RATE ANALYSIS BETWEEN TWO FIVE-YEAR BONDS

Settlement 10/01/1987
Horizon 10/01/1992

	BOND 1	BOND 2
Calendar	Treasury	Treasury
Coupon:	15.000	5.000
Maturity:	10/01/1992	10/01/1992
Price:	120	80
Yield:	9.84	10.21

Horizon Returns

Reinvestment Rate:	8	9	10	11	12	13	14	15	16
BOND 1:	9.41	9.64	9.88	10.12	10.36	10.61	10.86	11.12	11.37
BOND 2:	9.95	10.07	10.18	10.30	10.42	10.55	10.67	10.80	10.93

Break-Even Rate: 12.49

Note: The horizon is five years, the same as the maturity of the bonds.

EXHIBIT 14:
BREAK-EVEN REINVESTMENT RATE ANALYSIS BETWEEN TWO FIVE-YEAR BONDS

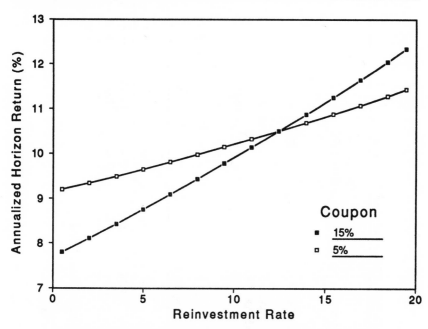

Note: The 15% bond is priced at 120, and the 5% bond is priced at 80.

than Bond 2, and therefore no break-even point exists between them. At these prices, Bond 1 is inherently cheaper.

EXTENDING THE ANALYSIS TO CALLABLE SECURITIES

Most corporate bonds are callable prior to the maturity date at the option of the issuer. Mortgage pass-through securities may be repaid in whole or part by the homeowner prior to the maturity of the mortgage loan. Thus, mortgage pass-through securities will exhibit price/yield characteristics similar to callable corporate bonds. We will focus our attention on callable corporate bonds.

Exhibit 16 shows the price/yield relationship for both a noncallable bond and the same bond if it is callable. The convex curve a-a′ is the

EXHIBIT 15:
BREAK-EVEN REINVESTMENT RATE ANALYSIS BETWEEN TWO FIVE-YEAR BONDS

Settlement 10/01/1987
Horizon 10/01/1992

	BOND 1	BOND 2
Calendar		
Coupon:	Treasury	Treasury
Maturity:	15.000	5.000
Price:	10/01/1992	10/01/1992
Yield:	120	90
	9.84	7.43

Horizon Returns

Reinvestment Rate:	6	7	8	9	10	11	12	13	14
BOND 1:	8.96	9.18	9.41	9.64	9.88	10.12	10.36	10.61	10.86
BOND 2:	7.28	7.38	7.49	7.61	7.72	7.84	7.96	8.08	8.21

Break-Even Rate: None

Note: The horizon is five years, the same as the maturity of the bonds.

EXHIBIT 16:
OPTION-FREE AND CALLABLE BOND PRICE/YIELD RELATIONSHIP

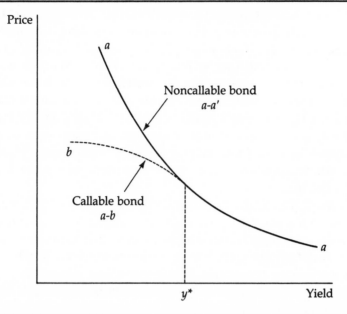

price/yield relationship for the noncallable (option-free) bond. The unusual shaped curve denoted by a-b is the price/yield relationship for the callable bond.

The reason for the shape of the price/yield relationship for the callable bond is as follows. When the prevailing market yield for comparable bonds is higher than the coupon interest on the bond, it is unlikely that the corporate issuer will call the bond. For example, if the coupon rate on a bond is 8% and the prevailing yield on comparable bonds is 16%, it is highly improbable that the corporate issuer will call in an 8% bond so that it can issue a 16% bond. In option terminology, the call option is deep out-of-the money. Since the bond is unlikely to be called when it is deep out of the money, a callable bond will have the same price/yield relationship as a noncallable bond. However, even when the option is near the money (the coupon rate is just below the market yield) investors may not pay the same price for the bond if it is callable because there is still the chance the market yield may drop further, making it beneficial for the issuer to call the bond.

As yields in the market decline, the likelihood increases that yields will decline further so that the issuer will benefit from calling the bond. We may not know the exact yield level at which investors begin to view the issue likely to be called, but we do know that there is some level. In Exhibit 16, at yield levels below y^*, the price/yield relationship for the callable bond departs from the price/yield relationship for the noncallable bond. Suppose, for example, the market yield is such that a noncallable bond would be selling for 109, but since it is callable it would be called at 104 — investors would not pay 109. If they did and the bond is called, investors would receive 104 (the call price) for a bond they purchased for 109. Notice that for a range of yields below y^*, there is price compression — that is, there is limited price appreciation as yields decline.

To develop an analytical framework for assessing relative value and evaluating the potential performance of callable bonds over some investment horizon, it is necessary to understand the components of the bond. A callable corporate bond is a bond in which the bondholder has sold the issuing corporation a call option that allows the issuer to repurchase the bond from the time the bond is first callable until the maturity date.

Effectively, the owner of a corporate callable bond is entering into two separate transactions. First he buys a corporate noncallable bond from the issuer, for which he pays some price. Then he sells the issuer a call option for which he receives the option price from the issuer. Therefore, we can summarize the position of a corporate callable bondholder as follows:

long a callable bond = long a noncallable bond + short position in call

or equivalently,

callable bond = noncallable bond − call option

The minus sign in front of the call option means that the bondholder has sold (written) the call option.

In terms of price, the price of a callable corporate bond is therefore equal to the price of the two components parts. That is,

callable bond price = noncallable bond price − call option price

The call option price is subtracted from the price of the noncallable bond. The reason is that when the bondholder sells a call option, he receives the option price. Graphically this can be seen in Exhibit 16. The difference between the price of the noncallable bond and the callable bond is the price of the embedded call option.

As explained in Chapter 1, the price of a call option increases when the expected price volatility of the underlying instrument increases. Since the price of a call option on a bond depends on its interest rate, the price of a callable bond will depend on expected interest rate volatility.

Call-Adjusted Yield

Given the above relationship for the callable bond, a portfolio manager wants to know if the noncallable bond is correctly priced in the sense that he is being adequately rewarded for the call risk associated with owning the bond. The price that the noncallable bond should sell for can be computed as follows:

noncallable bond price = callable bond price + call option price

The price of the callable bond can be observed in the market. The price of the call option can be estimated using an option pricing model. Adding the two prices gives the implied price of the noncallable bond.

Given the implied price of the noncallable bond, it is then simple to compute the yield on this bond. The yield computed is referred to as the *call-adjusted yield*. The call-adjusted yield is the implied yield on the noncallable bond.

A noncallable bond is priced fairly if the call-adjusted yield for a callable bond is the proper yield for a noncallable bond with the same features and of the same issuer. A bond is rich or overvalued if the call-adjusted yield is less; it is, cheap or undervalued if the call-adjusted yield is more.

Bond Price Volatility of a Callable

As explained earlier, the two parameters of a bond that determine price volatility are duration and convexity. The duration of a callable bond after adjusting for the call option, is commonly referred to as the *call-adjusted (modified) duration*.[13] It depends on three factors: (1) the duration of the underlying noncallable bond; (2) the ratio of the price of the noncallable bond to the callable bond; and (3) the sensitivity of the price of the call option to the change in the price of the underlying noncallable bond. The last factor is commonly referred to as the *delta* of an option and measures how the option price will change if the price of the underlying noncallable bond changes by $1.

For a callable bond in which the coupon rate is substantially above the current market rate, its call-adjusted duration will be close to 0. In contrast, for a callable bond in which the coupon rate is substantially lower than the current market rate, its call-adjusted duration will be the same as the duration of the noncallable bond. Thus, the call-adjusted duration for a callable bond will range between 0 and the duration of the noncallable bond.

The call-adjusted convexity of a bond can also be computed. It will depend on the same three factors that determine call-adjusted duration plus (1) the convexity of the noncallable bond and (2) the convexity of the call option.

Recall that convexity measures the rate of change of dollar duration. For an option-free bond, the convexity measure is always positive. Dollar duration, which is the slope of the tangent to the price/yield relationship, increases when yield decreases and decreases when yield increases. As can be seen in Exhibit 16, the slope of the tangent line to the price/yield relationship for a callable bond would flatten when yield decreases. Thus, dollar duration gets smaller as yield decreases. This is feature of a noncallable bond is referred to as *negative convexity* and causes the price compression that we referred to earlier.[14]

Horizon Return for a Callable Bond

The call-adjusted yield suffers from the same drawbacks as the yield to maturity: it assumes that the bond will be held to the maturity date and the coupon payments can be reinvested at an interest rate equal to the

---

[13]The formula for the call-adjusted duration is given in Fabozzi, *Fixed Income Mathematics*, Chapter 13.

[14]A call-adjusted convexity can be computed for a callable bond. See Fabozzi, *Fixed Income Mathematics*, Chapter 13.

call-adjusted yield. Instead, the horizon return framework should be employed. The assumptions necessary to compute the horizon return for a callable bond over some investment horizon are the same as those necessary to compute the horizon return for a noncallable bond. However, to compute the price of the callable bond at the end of the investment horizon it is necessary to project both the yield on a noncallable bond and the value of the embedded call option. The latter, in turn, depends on the expected interest rate volatility at the end of the investment horizon.

For a mortgage pass-through security, two additional assumptions are required. First, the prepayment rate between the time of purchase and the end of the investment horizon must be projected in order to obtain the cash flow from the mortgage pass-through security. Because the cash flow includes coupon interest and principal repayment (scheduled and prepayments) and the payments are received monthly, the reinvestment assumption becomes more critical than for a Treasury or corporate bond. The second assumption is the prepayment rate that is expected at the end of the investment horizon. The assumed prepayment rate will determine the cash flow of the mortgage pass-through security and therefore its price.

SUMMARY

In this chapter we reviewed the attributes of both option-free bonds and bonds with an embedded call option (i.e., callable corporate bonds and mortgage pass-through securities) that determine their price performance. These attributes are the bond's duration and convexity.

Conventional yield measures such as yield to maturity and yield to call do not provide insight as to the potential return from owning a bond over some predetermined investment horizon, nor the relative value of bonds. Instead, because it takes into account all sources of potential dollar return expected to be realized from investing in a bond over some investment horizon, the horizon return framework should be used.

CHAPTER 13

Understanding and Evaluating Index Fund Management

SHARMIN MOSSAVAR-RAHMANI, CFA
SENIOR VICE PRESIDENT
FIDELITY MANAGEMENT TRUST COMPANY, BOSTON

Indexing the performance of fixed income assets to match that of a market benchmark has become widespread in portfolio management. Between 1980 and late 1986, assets under index fund management grew from only $40 million to over $40 billion, with both small and large pension funds accounting for the tremendous growth. Indeed, some of the nation's largest pension funds have begun to index a significant portion, if not all, of their fixed income assets. Among the public funds, all $17 billion of the fixed income assets of the New York City Retirement System and some seven billion dollars of the fixed income assets of the California State Teachers Retirement System have been indexed. In the corporate sector, American Telephone & Telegraph Co. has indexed some $3.5 billion. Smaller funds have also indexed assets through either separate index funds or co-mingled index funds.

Growth in the size of indexed assets has brought with it a prolifera-tion of indices, index fund managers, and index fund management models and software services. In recent years, three broad market indices were introduced in rapid succession—the Merrill Lynch Do-mestic Master Index, the Salomon Brothers Broad Investment-Grade Bond Index, and the Shearson Lehman Aggregate Index. Several spe-cialized fixed-income indices have also been introduced. The number of major investment advisors offering index fund management during this period grew from six to over 20, and several index fund optimiz-ation models were developed by investment houses and software vendors.

This chapter provides a detailed review of indexing, starting with a discussion of the motivations for setting up index funds. An evaluation of the disadvantages of indexing is discussed in the second section, followed by an examination of current indexing methodologies. The fourth section reviews "enhanced indexing" and the requisite use of value-added strategies. The chapter then examines the more recent interest in customized index funds and the role of the Financial Ac-counting Standards Board Statements 87 and 88 to the development of such funds. The last section concludes with a discussion of the implica-tions of indexing for fixed income management and for the fixed income securities market overall.

MOTIVATIONS FOR SETTING UP INDEX FUNDS

Four key factors account for the increased interest in indexing of pension funds. The first motivation for indexing has been the poor past performance of investment advisors as a group. In the past several years, 75% of active fixed income managers have underperformed market benchmarks, as illustrated in Exhibit 1. Indexing of assets improves relative performance inasmuch as the returns of an index fund closely track those of a market index; the risk of underperforming an index to the extent illustrated in Exhibit 1 is therefore eliminated by definition.

A second motivation for indexing has been the reduction of advisory fees. Advisory fees for active management normally range from 15 basis points to as much as 50 basis points. Advisory fees for index fund management range from a low of one basis point up to 20 basis points for enhanced and customized index funds, with 10 basis points repre-

EXHIBIT 1:
ANNUALIZED TOTAL RETURN FOR FIXED INCOME FUNDS
(FOR PERIODS ENDING JUNE 30, 1987)

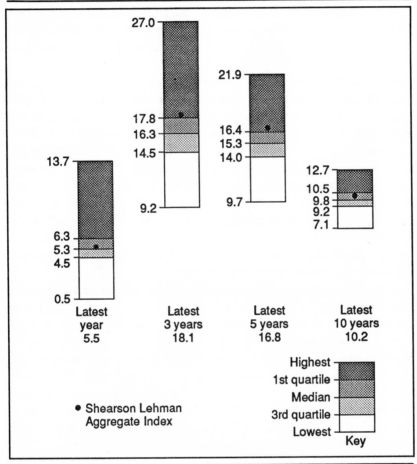

Source: PIPER report © Crain Communications, Inc.

senting the mode. The consequent savings in management fees, particularly in the case of very large pension funds, can be substantial. It is interesting to note that the advisory fees for indexing are now generally lower for many pension funds than the associated custodian and master trustee fees.

A third and less obvious motivating factor for indexing has been the growth of the nation's pension assets. Between September 1981 (which marked the peak in interest rates) and September 1986, the fixed income market produced a total return of 147.6% as measured by the Salomon Brothers Broad Investment-Grade Bond Index, and 149.4% as measured by the Shearson Lehman Aggregate Index (the equities market returned a total of 150.8% over the same period as measured by the Standard & Poor's 500 Index). The consequent increases in the size of many pension funds have led to increases in the costs associated with the maintenance of these funds. The number of investment advisors hired to manage each fund, for example, has increased, resulting not only in greater advisory fees, but also in greater hidden costs associated with multiple managers. Custodian costs and master trustee costs increase with the number of managers as do the time and effort required for supervision and coordination of multiple managers. Indexing reduces many such hidden costs by reducing the number of advisors responsible for managing any one fund. The size of assets given to any single advisor of an index fund is generally much larger than the size of assets given to any single advisor for active management. In the summer of 1986, for example, the State Universities Retirement System of Illinois transferred fixed income assets from four active and passive managers to a single index fund manager.

A fourth factor behind indexing of fixed income assets has been the increased interest in "structured management." Structured management de-emphasizes interest rate forecasts on the part of investment advisors, and emphasizes instead risk control relative to a market benchmark. Both the benchmark and acceptable risk parameters are specified by the plan sponsor. Examples of structured management are indexing and enhanced indexing, duration-controlled management, management with respect to a normal portfolio, and immunization. It is important to note that all forms of structured management reflect a gradual shift in control away from the active manager to the plan sponsor.

DISADVANTAGES OF INDEXING

The rapid growth in its popularity notwithstanding, indexing does have its doubters and detractors. One key criticism voiced is that while indexing matches the performance of a market benchmark, that benchmark might not reflect optimal performance. Indeed, for the five-year period ending in September 1981, the Shearson Lehman Government/ Corporate Index measured a return lower than that of 50% of active managers, as shown in Exhibit 2.

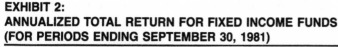

EXHIBIT 2:
ANNUALIZED TOTAL RETURN FOR FIXED INCOME FUNDS
(FOR PERIODS ENDING SEPTEMBER 30, 1981)

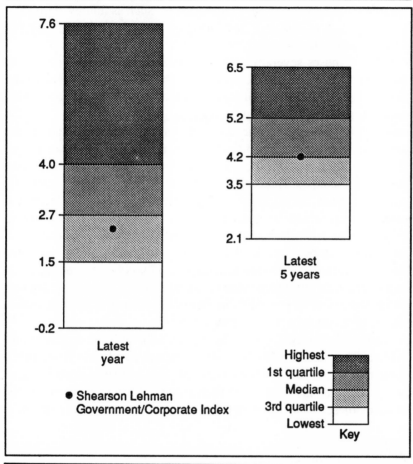

Source: SEI Corporation

Another criticism is that indexing against a broad market benchmark may not meet the specific requirements and objectives of a particular fund, e.g., matching pension assets with pension liabilities.

Index funds are also criticized for lacking flexibility. True (also called "straight" or "vanilla" index funds) do not invest in instruments outside the benchmark universe. For example, non-federal agency conventional mortgage pass-throughs such as those issued by Citibank and Sears Mortgage Securities are not included in any of the broad market benchmarks. Excluding this small but growing sector of the market—thereby giving up as much as 25 to 50 basis points of additional yield—is an unnecessary constraint. Among other instruments excluded from the benchmark universes are synthetic assets such as futures, derivative securities such as collateralized mortgage obligations, and Strips and other Treasury zero-coupon bonds.

Indexing poses several logistical problems. Pricing of securities in the index universe is one such problem. The fixed income market is an over-the-counter market without a centralized exchange from which reliable closing prices could be obtained. Thus, at a given time, the same securities might be priced very differently from one dealer to the next, as illustrated in Exhibit 3. Even in the more efficient and more liquid Treasury market, prices can vary significantly; at a given time, the 10.75% coupon Treasury maturing on August 15, 2005, could be purchased from Dealer B at $128-05 (five thirty-seconds) while the same security could be purchased from Dealer D at $128-09 (nine thirty-seconds). Such pricing differences create two potential problems: first, the benchmarks that represent the same market may produce very different data (see Exhibit 4), and second, the returns of an index fund may not match those of the benchmark. An index fund that purchased a Treasury bond from Dealer B will not match the performance of a benchmark priced by Dealer D.

Another difficulty is caused by the illiquidity of the corporate bond market. The Salomon Brothers Broad Investment-Grade Bond Index contains over 3,700 corporate issues, and the Shearson Lehman Aggregate Index contains over 5,400 such issues. Not only is the pricing of many of these issues unreliable but many cannot be readily found.

EXHIBIT 3:
PRICE SPREADS

	TSY10.75% 8/15/05	HCA* 8% 4/15/96	GNSF** 12%
Dealer A	128^2-6***	$97\frac{1}{4}-\frac{3}{8}$	108^2-4
B	128^3-5	$97\ -\frac{3}{8}$	$108\ -4$
C	128^4-8	$97\frac{1}{8}-\frac{3}{8}$	108^1-5
D	128^5-9	$97\frac{3}{8}-\frac{1}{2}$	108^4-8
E	128^6-8	$97\frac{1}{4}-\frac{1}{2}$	Passed

*Hospital Corporation of America
**GNMA Single Family
***This quote represents a bid price of 128^2 and an ask price of 128^6.

EXHIBIT 4:
VARIATION IN MONTHLY RETURNS OF MARKET INDICES (PERCENT)

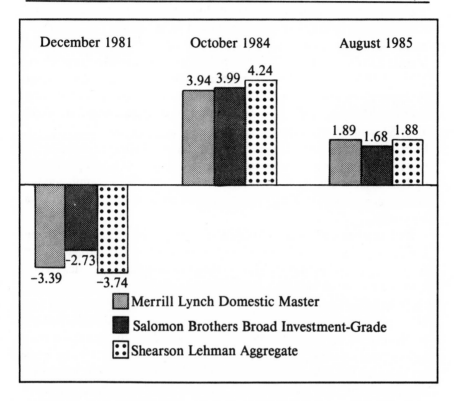

A third logistical problem is specific to indexing of the mortgage-backed securities component of these indices. The three major market indices include the pass-through securities of the Government National Mortgage Association (GNMA or Ginnie Mae), of the Federal National Mortgage Association (FNMA or Fannie Mae), and of the Federal Home Loan Mortgage Corporation (FHLMC or Freddie Mac). Together, these three agencies have issued well over 200,000 specific pools. The indices, however, have consolidated these pools into several hundred issues. There are 8,000 GNMA pools with a 12% coupon; yet in the indices, these pools are "collapsed" into only one hypothetical issue whose profile characteristics are intended to reflect the market value weighted average characteristics of all 8,000 pools. Locating pools that precisely match the performance of the hypothetical issue could be extremely difficult.

This problem is compounded by the differences in the risk and reward measurements in mortgage-backed securities indices. The duration and yield-to-maturity of the three major mortgage indices (the Merrill Lynch Mortgage Master, Salomon Brothers Mortgage Pass-Through Index, and the Shearson Lehman Mortgage-Backed Securities Index) vary by a wide margin. The effective duration of the Salomon Brothers Mortgage Pass-Through Index, for example, was 3.20 years as of September 30, 1986, whereas the duration of the Merrill Lynch Mortgage Master was 5.04 years. The difference in the durations of the two indices can be attributed to different prepayment assumptions and options evaluations; nevertheless, these differences do complicate the task of correctly matching the duration of an index fund to that of a benchmark.

Still another logistical problem of indexing stems from the pricing biases of the market benchmarks. The securities in all broad market indices are priced at the "bid side"—the price at which securities can be sold to a broker. Bond index funds, however, purchase securities at the "offer side" or "ask side." The spread between purchase price and sale price, referred to as transaction cost, is not incorporated in the pricing mechanism of the broad market indices. Therefore, the market indices have a total return advantage relative to index funds that can be measured by the bid-ask spread of individual securities. Exhibit 3 provides an example of such spreads in the Treasury, corporate, and mortgage-backed securities market.

KEY METHODOLOGIES

There are currently three approaches to managing an index fund: the stratified sampling or the cellular approach; the optimization approach using linear programming; and the variance minimization approach using quadratic programming.

The *stratified sampling method* is the most straightforward and the most flexible of the three approaches. In the stratified sampling method, an index is divided into subsectors, i.e., the index is stratified into "cells." The divisions are made on the basis of such features as sector, coupon, maturity and quality. For example, one cell might contain all

Treasury securities with maturities between five and 10 years and coupon rates between nine and 12%. Another cell might contain all AA Industrial bonds with maturities greater than 15 years and coupon rates between 10 and 15%.

The cells can be defined in much broader terms as well. A market index can be divided into four cells: a Treasury cell that accounts for all the Treasury securities; an agency cell that accounts for all the agency securities; a corporate cell for all the corporate issues; and a mortgage cell for all mortgage-backed securities. Alternatively, the index can be divided into as many cells as there are issues in the index, so that each cell contains only one issue.

Of the factors that determine the number of cells in an index fund, the size of the fund is the most critical. Larger asset size enables the index fund manager to divide the benchmark into a greater number of cells. Indeed, one of the problems with small index funds (under $50 million) is that the fund can be divided into only a few cells, thereby limiting the diversification in the fund.

The next step in the stratified sampling method is the selection of securities to represent each cell. Securities are chosen such that the total return and the profile characteristics (such as yield and duration) of each "sample" of securities representing a particular cell match the average characteristics of all the securities in that cell. The selection of securities enables the index fund manager to impose certain biases on the fund; securities with higher yields but lower convexity may be selected over securities with lower yields and greater convexity.

The product of this approach is a portfolio whose characteristics match those of the index. These characteristics include duration, yield-to-maturity, convexity, maturity and coupon distribution, quality, callability and sinking fund exposure, and, ideally, prepayment risk.

The second methodology, the *optimization approach,* builds on the stratified sampling approach. There are two components to the optimization: the first component is an objective function in which one comprehensive bias is specified, and the second component is a series of constraints in which the cellular breakdown described above is implemented and the portfolio characteristics are forced to match those of the index. Some widely used objective functions are the maximization of yield, convexity, or expected total returns. Typical constraints include cell specifications and duration targets.

The third approach, or the *variance minimization methodology,* is a form of optimization where the objective is to minimize the variance of the tracking error. Tracking error is defined as the total return deviation of the portfolio from the index. This methodology relies on historical data to generate multi-variate price functions for every bond in the index universe. These price functions are, in turn, used to estimate the variance of returns based on the variance of the term structure of interest rates and of some 80 factors that determine the value of a bond. This optimization model selects a series of bonds whose risk exposure to interest rate changes and to changes in the 80 or so valuation factors will closely match that of the index. As a result of the optimization, the returns of the portfolio will closely match those of the index and minimize the tracking error.

The Relative Merits and Pitfalls of the Methodologies

Of the three approaches, stratified sampling is the most flexible. Attractive yield spread swaps can be implemented within specific cells without affecting the rest of the index fund. Value-added strategies can be implemented without re-optimizing and rebalancing the entire portfolio. Swaps that take advantage of long or short positions of the broker/dealer community can be readily implemented. Yield and convexity biases can be implemented with greater focus; for example, convexity can be maximized in some of the Treasury cells, while yield can be maximized in some of the corporate cells. In addition, strategies that involve sectors outside the index universe (such as CMOs, Strips, and futures) can also be implemented. And, the index fund can be partially rebalanced, resulting in less turnover and hence lower transaction costs. In contrast, in a true optimization, rebalancing can impact the entire portfolio.

The optimization approach is less flexible in other ways as well. A strict implementation of optimization implies use of the model to select issues from a universe of securities, and the purchase and sale of securities according to the solution of the optimization. The problem with such an approach is that it relies completely on a database of bond prices from which the model can choose securities. As mentioned earlier, bond prices in these databases can be very unreliable, due to the over-the-counter nature of the fixed income market. Thus, the model's selection of securities may not be readily traded in the market or, at least, may not be available at prices indicated in the databases. One recourse would be to substitute the securities chosen by the optimization. Such substitution, in effect, results in greater use of the stratified sampling approach and lesser use of an optimization model. Another recourse would be to work with dealers who offer smaller databases (that only contain their own inventories or securities they believe are available in the market) in order to circumvent this pricing problem. The key disadvantage of these databases is the requisite reliance on only one dealer whose major objective is the sale of house inventory or of securities that the dealer can locate and re-sell at a profit. Securities available through another dealer at a lower price are therefore excluded.

Still, the optimization approach does have its advantages. An investment advisor with little or no index fund management experience can readily acquire some index fund management capabilities through access to such a model. Optimization also requires less time and effort on the part of the index fund manager since the model selects all attractive swaps and combinations of securities.

The variance minimization model is the least flexible of the three approaches. Bond swaps, value-added strategies, yield or convexity biases, and partial rebalancings cannot be implemented in this approach. The model can be forced to select various securities by imposing constraints and by limiting the securities in the universe. Again, such tactics imply a move away from the variance minimization model, towards a sampling technique. Complete dependence on historical issue-specific pricing data is another drawback; as mentioned earlier, the pricing of some of the securities may be unreliable and their availability uncertain. Finally, the variance minimization model is based on the assumption that past performance of individual securities is a good indication of future performance; such an assumption is not valid in all market environments. It is also important to note that since the model relies on historical data, new instruments with innovative features cannot be incorporated into the universe, irrespective of their potential value.

Tracking Error

Tracking error is the difference between the total return of an index fund and that of the benchmark. What is acceptable tracking error? And does large positive tracking error imply large negative error (i.e., is tracking error normally distributed)? Salomon Brothers Inc maintains an index optimization system which can be used to generate historical data on the tracking error between an optimal portfolio and the Salomon Brothers Broad Investment-Grade Bond Index or any of its components. A two-year historical analysis found that tracking error varies according to the type of fund (e.g., corporates, mortgage-backed securities, or Treasuries) and the size of assets under management. The corporate component of the Salomon Brothers Broad Investment-Grade Bond Index was the most difficult to track; as shown in Exhibit 5, the standard deviation of the monthly tracking error was 17 basis points, with the largest monthly positive error at 40 basis points and the largest monthly negative error at 26 basis points. However, over the 23-month horizon, the corporate component of the index fund outperformed its respective benchmark by 3.01%. Such tracking error in the corporate sector, can be attributed to event risk, call risk, illiquidity, and higher transaction costs.

In the mortgage-backed securities market, tracking error was less volatile with a standard deviation of 3 basis points, a high of 6 basis points and a low of negative 7 basis points. The mortgage-backed securities component outperformed its benchmark by 6 basis points over a two-year period. In this sector, prepayment risk and the task of matching the performance of some 200,000 pools account for the tracking error.

EXHIBIT 8:
TRACKING ERROR OF MONTHLY RETURNS IN BASIS POINTS (1984-1985)

| Sector | Standard | | | | Total | |
	Deviation	Mean	High	Low	Cumulative	Annualized
Broad market	5	2	13	−6	69	34
Governments	2	2	5	−1	63	31
Corporates*	17	9	40	−26	301	156
Mortgages	3	0	6	−7	6	3
Broad market (Including transaction costs)	5	0	11	−8	−12	−6

*Analysis between January 1985 and November 1986.
Source: Salomon Brothers Inc, based on Salomon Brothers Broad Investment-Grade Bond Index and its component.

Tracking error volatility was lowest in the government sector with a standard deviation of monthly errors of only 2 basis points, a high of 5 basis points, and low of negative 1 basis point. Like the corporate component of the fund, government securities also significantly outperformed their benchmark, albeit by a smaller amount. Yield curve twists and varying spreads between current coupon Treasuries and off-the-run Treasuries underlie most of the tracking error.

In the analysis above, the objective of the optimal portfolio or index fund was to track a specific subsector. For example, the mortgage-backed securities data reflect the tracking error of a portfolio designed to track the mortgage-backed securities component of the Salomon Brothers Broad Investment-Grade Index. Similarly, the data on corporates reflect the tracking error of a portfolio designed to track the corporate component of the Salomon Index. Such a strategy of managing index funds by specialized sectors has, in fact, been implemented by the New York City Retirement System.

The data on the broad market reflect the tracking error of a portfolio designed to track the entire Salomon Brothers Broad Investment-Grade Bond Index. The tracking error statistics of the broader index fund fall between the extreme volatility of the corporate index fund and the relative stability of the government index fund. The cumulative performance of the broader portfolio relative to its benchmark is closer to the cumulative performance of the government portfolio relative to its respective benchmark. Such similarity partly reflects the 60% weighting of government securities in the broader benchmark.

When transaction costs are included in the analysis, the broader index fund underperforms the Salomon Brothers Broad Investment-Grade Bond Index by 12 basis points.

Finally, it should be noted that the tracking error of each individual subsector in a portfolio designed to track the entire market will be greater than the tracking error of an individual subsector designed to track its respective benchmark.

ENHANCED INDEXING

The purpose of straight or "vanilla" indexing is to closely track the performance of a benchmark. The purpose of enhanced or "index plus" indexing, on the other hand, is to outperform the benchmark without incurring additional long-term risk. In the short-term, additional risk, defined as greater positive and negative tracking error, is inevitable. Over a longer time horizon, however, the index fund is expected to outperform its benchmark by a small percentage. Three types of strategies can be used to outperform a benchmark while maintaining similar long-term risk exposure as the benchmark: value-added strategies using securities included in the benchmark, value-added strategies using securities and instruments excluded from the benchmark, and trading and execution strategies.

Exhibit 6 illustrates a strategy based on the relative value of specific maturities in the September 1986 current coupon Treasury yield curve. The 5-year current coupon Treasury security is sold and replaced with a 4-year and a 7-year current coupon Treasury security. The swap is implemented such that the duration of the assets sold equals the market value-weighted duration of the assets purchased. In this specific example, the swap results in 15 basis points of additional yield, and a small increase in convexity of 0.01. Furthermore, since the four to seven year spread of 46 basis points is at historically wide levels, the expected flattening of the yield curve provides additional value to the index fund. This strategy would be implemented in a cell with a 4- to 7-year maturity range.

Exhibit 7 illustrates the potential value of derivative securities that are not included in the index universe. Similar coupon and weighted average life GNMA-backed collateralized mortgage obligations have outperformed GNMA counterparts in six out of the past 7 quarters.

The returns of an index fund can also be enhanced through efficient trading and execution. Transaction costs can be reduced by taking

EXHIBIT 6:
TREASURY YIELD CURVE STRATEGY (BARBELLS VERSUS BULLETS)

Issue			Yield	Duration	Convexity
Sell: TSY	6.50	11/15/91	6.706	4.186	.109
Buy: TSY	6.75	9/30/90	6.637	3.364	.070
TSY	7.25	7/15/93	7.098	5.124	.169
Value Added					
Yield Pick-Up		0.15			
Convexity Gain		0.01			
4-7 Year Spread		46			

EXHIBIT 7:
QUARTERLY TOTAL RETURNS OF CURRENT COUPON GNMAs AND
GNMA-BACKED COLLATERALIZED MORTGAGE OBLIGATIONS

Yaer/Quarter	Current Coupon GNMA (%)	Quarterly Total Returns (%)	CMO Returns Tranche III (%)
1985	12	2.90	4.00
II	12½	7.95	8.56
III	11	2.06	2.94
IV	11	9.41	10.41
1986 I	9½	5.76	6.04
II	8½	−0.45	2.60
III	9½	4.33	2.75

Source: The First Boston Corporation

advantage of long and short positions in the market, by knowing each dealer's particular expertise, or simply by adept placement of buy and sell orders.

CUSTOMIZED BENCHMARKS

As mentioned earlier, indexing against one of the three broad market benchmarks may not meet the objectives of a particular fund. A long duration benchmark may be more suited for a pension fund with long duration liabilities, while an intermediate duration benchmark may be more suited for an endowment fund concerned with capital preservation. Customized benchmarks to meet the specific requirements and objectives of a fund offer an alternative to the more standard market benchmarks.

Customized benchmarks are constructed in three steps. First, a duration level is selected. The duration level may be a function of the duration levels of broad benchmarks or of the liabilities of a pension fund. For example, a customized benchmark may have a duration that is 75% of the duration of the Shearson Lehman Aggregate Index. Second, the weightings of market sectors are specified. Such weightings are determined by a fund's liquidity and quality preferences and overall risk tolerance. Treasuries may be overweighted relative to the Treasury component of the broad benchmarks while corporates may be underweighted. And third, an information system must be established to measure the performance and the profile characteristics of the customized benchmark and to ensure that the parameters (such as the weighting of Treasuries and the target duration) are internally consistent and practical.

In December 1986, Salomon Brothers Inc. introduced a new benchmark, the Salomon Brothers Large Pension Fund Baseline Bond Index, for large pension funds designed to match the long duration of pension liabilities while taking advantage of the higher yields of corporates and mortgage-backed securities. The motivation in developing such an index was to offer a benchmark that was more suited to the objectives of large long-term oriented pension funds.

Following the introduction of the Large Pension Fund Baseline Bond Index, Salomon Brothers, Inc. introduced a matrix of indices in August 1987. The matrix was designed to allow customization of benchmarks by providing a menu of duration levels and market sector weightings. For example, a pension fund sponsor can select a benchmark with an effective duration of 6 years, a 50 percent allocation to Treasuries, and 50% allocation to corporates and mortgage-backed securities.

Two factors distinguish the indices based on this matrix from all other market benchmarks introduced to date. Unlike other market benchmarks, the durations of these matrix-based indices do not change in response to changes in interest rates; instead, the duration of each index is maintained at a fixed level by restructuring the universe of securities in the matrix on a monthly basis. For example, a 6-year duration is fixed at six years, regardless of whether interest rates are at 8% or 18%. Such restructuring implies high turnover relative to the more traditional capitalization-weighted market benchmarks. Typically, turnover in market benchmarks is determined by the addition of new issues and by removal of securities that have been called by the issuer, downgraded to below investment-grade securities or aged such that they have less than one year remaining to maturity; turnover in the matrix-based indices, however, is determined by the monthly restructuring required to adjust the duration levels to their initial fixed levels.

Customized benchmarks designed to match or outperform the present value of pension liabilities will become widespread also as companies incorporate FASB Statements 87 and 88 in their income statement and balance sheet reporting by 1987.

FASB Statements No. 87 and 88 have imposed new standards for calculating and reporting pension expense on the income statement and for measuring and reporting pension liabilities in excess of the market value of pension plan assets on the balance sheet. The new standards require the use of market interest rates to evaluate liabilities and hence pension expenses; the Standards, therefore, introduce market-related volatility to the income statement and balance sheet as interest rates fluctuate from one reporting period to another. The interest in controlling market-related volatility of pension expenses and in maintaining stable and favorable asset-liability ratios has prompted many corporate pension plan sponsors to consider indexing pension assets against a customized benchmark that fluctuates with their liabilities.

IMPLICATIONS FOR THE FIXED INCOME MARKET

The trend towards indexation has several implications for the investment community. First and foremost, the level of transaction activity will decrease since index funds have less turnover than actively managed funds. In addition, most of the transaction activity will be concentrated at month end when the majority of index funds are rebalanced.

The fixed income market will also witness a decrease in the turnover of each plan sponsor's investment advisors. It is unlikely that plan sponsors will terminate an index fund manager as frequently as they have terminated active portfolio managers in the past; an index fund manager is less likely to underperform a fund benchmark by the magnitudes that result in termination. Furthermore, as the duration of more portfolios, both active and indexed, are clustered around the duration of the broad market indices, the range in the performance of investment advisors will narrow; and the performance of the median manager, the performance of the managers around the mode, and the performance of the broad market indices will all converge.

CHAPTER 14

Liability Funding Strategies

LLEWELLYN MILLER
VICE PRESIDENT
FIXED INCOME RESEARCH
DREXEL BURNHAM LAMBERT

UDAY RAJAN
ASSOCIATE
FIXED INCOME RESEARCH
DREXEL BURNHAM LAMBERT

PRAKASH SHIMPI
ASSOCIATE
FIXED INCOME RESEARCH
DREXEL BURNHAM LAMBERT

INTRODUCTION

Liability funding refers to the process of selecting and managing asset portfolios to offset liabilities undertaken by institutions. The goal is to ensure that the assets are sufficient to pay off the liabilities as they come due.

Fixed income securities are commonly used for liability funding. These securities provide periodic cash flows, thereby avoiding the need for frequent liquidation of assets. Portfolios formed to fund liabilities often include stocks as well, in an effort to increase overall return. This chapter, however, will focus exclusively on fixed income portfolio strategies.

Defining "Liability"

For the purposes of this discussion, a liability is considered to be a contractually promised stream of future cash outflows. These outflows arise from financial obligations underwritten by institutions. Life insurance policies and guaranteed investment contracts issued by insurance companies, employee retirement benefits promised by pension plans, and bond defeasances undertaken by corporations are all examples of contractual obligations to meet some future cash outflows.

The nature of the liabilities can differ vastly across institutions, depending on the nature of the underlying financial contracts, as the following cases illustrate.

Case I: The state lottery is won by an individual who is entitled to receive payment in the form of a fixed monthly annuity over ten years. In this case, the institution that has issued the liability, i.e. the state, knows exactly what its cash outflow will be every month for the next ten years.

Case II: An insurance company has just issued a new block of universal life policies. A policyholder is entitled to:
1. each month, choose the amount of premium she wishes to pay, and
2. withdraw part or all of her investment at any time for a nominal fee.

The insurance company can influence her decisions by changing, within certain stated constraints, the rate of interest which her accounts earn. In this case, the exact dates of payment and the amounts of the cash inflows and outflows are not known, so the insurance company will have to estimate them.

In Case I, both the timing and the amounts of the liability cash flows are fixed, and are known in advance by the issuing institution. In contrast, the cash flows in Case II are variable and unknown. A simplifying assumption would be that all liabilities are like those in Case I. However, of late, several of the new liabilities undertaken by institutions resemble those in Case II. The ability to distinguish between the various types of liabilities is therefore critical.

Types of Liabilities

The preceding cases suggest that liabilities can be classified by the extent of uncertainty in timing or amount or both. However, by allowing for borrowing or lending for short time periods at the prevailing short term rates, all cash flows can be analyzed as though their timings are known. For example, in Exhibit 1, the cash outflow of $1,000 that actually occurs between the predicted dates 1 and 2 can be offset by borrowing $1,000 till the next predicted date, 2, and adding the $1,000 plus the cost of borrowing to the liability at date 2. Therefore, it is uncertainty in the amounts of the liability outflows that is of primary concern.

To some extent, most liabilities have some elements of uncertainty. For example, pension fund payouts depend on future salaries and on mortality rates. It is more useful to focus on the inherent uncertainty which arises when the receiver of the liability outflow has the option of deciding when he would like to receive those cash flows. The exercise of the option generally depends on current interest rates. For example, when rates are rising, investors tend to withdraw their money quicker, in search of the higher returns that are available elsewhere.

Throughout this chapter, liabilities with such option features will be referred to as "interest sensitive" or "variable." All option-free liabilities will be referred to as "fixed." Examples of fixed liabilities would

EXHIBIT 1:
ANALYZING A LIABILITY WHICH FALLS BETWEEN PREDICTED DATES

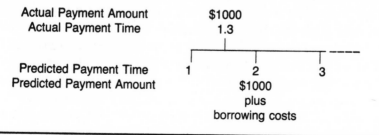

be accrued pension fund obligations, bond defeasances, and state lottery payouts, while several insurance company liabilities, such as single premium deferred annuities and single premium whole life policies would be classified as interest sensitive.

The Asset Side

As with the liabilities, fixed income securities purchased by a funder can also have option features which give the issuers of the securities the right to redeem them at specified prices and times in the future. Callable bonds and mortgage-backed securities are primary examples of this. A putable bond is an example of an asset where the funding institution, as the purchaser, has an option to sell the security back to the issuer at some future time for a pre-specified price. Hence, asset cash flows can also be classified as "fixed" or "interest sensitive/variable," depending on the presence of option features.

The Funding Problem

Liability funding is complicated by the risks faced by a funding institution in managing its asset portfolio. One of these risks is default risk, which is common to several fixed income portfolios, and is controlled through diversification and allocation among quality categories. There are also some risks specific to liability funding problems. Since the goal is to match the cash flows from the assets to the liability outflows, these risks stem from differences in amounts and timings of asset and liability cash flows, and can be classified as market risk and reinvestment risk.

Market risk is incurred whenever assets have to be marked to market, either for reporting purposes or when liquidated to meet a liability. With fixed income securities, this refers to assets maturing *after* the liability is due. Reinvestment risk refers to the situation where asset cash flows occur *before* the liability is due, and must be reinvested at prevailing interest rates for the interim.

When asset receipts and liability outflows are interest sensitive, both risks are accentuated. If an unexpectedly large liability becomes due, the investor may have to sell off some assets to meet it, thereby incurring market risk. If interest rates fall and a callable bond is unexpectedly called, the investor faces reinvestment risk, since the resulting proceeds will have to be reinvested at the lower interest rates.

Types of Strategies

Conventionally, liability funding strategies have tended to assume that both assets and liabilities have fixed cash flows. Under such assumptions, strategies based on cash matching and immunization could be used. These are discussed separately below.

The first complication that can be introduced is interest-sensitivity in asset cash flows. This is facilitated by the use of option-adjusted parameters in the immunization of liabilities.

Finally, when both assets and liabilities are interest sensitive, the conventional funding methods are of little use, since so many of the assumptions they rely on do not apply. A newly developed scenario based approach called *realized return optimization* is more appropriate. This is discussed towards the end of the chapter.

Exhibit 2 summarizes the various funding strategies.

EXHIBIT 2:
LIABILITY FUNDING STRATEGIES

	Asset Cash Flows	
	Fixed	Variable
Liability Fixed Cash Flows	Cash Matching Immunization Hybrids of Immunization	Immunization with Option-Adjusted Parameters
Variable	Realized Return Optimization	

FUNDING FIXED LIABILITIES WITH FIXED ASSETS

There are two methods commonly used to fund liabilities when both asset and liability cash flows are fixed or can safely be assumed to be fixed (as in the case of a callable bond that is extremely unlikely to be called). The first, cash matching, is virtually riskless since it involves arranging the asset cash flows to coincide with the liability cash flows. The second, immunization, selects an asset portfolio which is protected from the effects of changes in the interest rate environment. One variation of immunization combines the elements of cash matching for the near term liabilities and immunization for the later ones. Another immunization related strategy, contingent immunization, permits active portfolio management until an immunized portfolio is deemed to be necessary, and is therefore the riskiest of these methods.

Cash Matching

Cash matching is conceptually the simplest liability funding method. It is a buy and hold strategy which requires that the assets be held to maturity.

The coupon flows and maturities of the assets are structured to meet the known liability payments on the due dates. The funding ability is unaffected by changes in the interest rate environment for two reasons. First, only assets with no serious default risk and no option features, such as non-callable Treasury and agency issues are used. Second, reinvestment risk is eliminated by assuming a very conservative reinvestment rate (often zero) for asset cash flows. Market risk is eliminated since assets are held to maturity.

The strategy works as follows. First consider the last liability, and find a bond maturing on or before the liability due date. An amount of the bond is purchased that will completely offset that liability. Then, all previous liabilities are reduced by the amount of the coupon income on that bond. Now, the entire process is repeated with the next last liability, and so on till all liabilities have been met.

In carrying out this exercise, all cash flows earned before a liability is due are typically assumed to be carried forward to the liability date at a constant reinvestment rate. Often, to be conservative, the reinvestment rate is assumed to be zero. This can result in very expensive portfolios being chosen. As a practical matter, assuming a higher, though still conservative, rate such as 5% can help reduce the cost of the initial portfolio.

It is possible that more than one portfolio of assets is able to match the liabilities. Mathematical programming is used to select the optimal portfolio which achieves cash matching at the least cost. For taxable investors, the portfolio may be chosen on the basis of after-tax cost, by adding on the present value of future taxes payable to the cost of the portfolio. Alternatively, all cash flows from the assets could be computed on an after-tax basis. If a fixed sum of money has to be invested, the selected portfolio could be the one which provides the maximum balance after the last liability has been paid.

Cash matching is commonly used to fund liabilities such as lottery payouts, where the timing and amounts of the liability outflows are known, or those arising out of bond defeasances, where statutory regulations require that the liabilities be cash matched with Treasury securities. It is a purely passive strategy—once the portfolio has been purchased, it is held till all assets have matured. No rebalancings or liquidations are necessary, provided that the liabilities do not change.

As an illustration of the strategy, consider the following funding problem. On June 25, 1987, X contracts to pay Y $100,000 on July 1 each year from 1988 to 1992. Since both the amount and timing of the payments are known, X decides to adopt a cash matching strategy. Only Treasury securities are used, in order to eliminate default risk. The asset portfolio selected is described in Exhibit 3. The cost of the assets is $401,028.

EXHIBIT 3:
CASH MATCHED PORTFOLIO FOR FIXED LIABILITIES

Treasury Bond/Strip			
Maturity	Coupon %	Par Amount $	Market Value $
Jun 30 1988	7.000	70,209	72,530
Jun 30 1989	9.625	85,054	92,251
Jun 30 1990	7.250	93,240	95,153
May 15 1991	0.000	100,000	73,547
May 15 1992	0.000	100,000	67.547
Total		448,503	401,028

EXHIBIT 4:
PROOF OF CASH MATCHING

Treasury Bond/Strip	Payment Date - July 1				
	1988 $	1989 $	1990 $	1991 $	1992 $
1988—Coupon	7,371				
Par	70,209				
1989—Coupon	12,280	8,186			
Par		85,054			
1990—Coupon	10,140	6,760	6,760		
Par			93,240		
1991—Coupon	0	0	0	0	
Par				100,000	
1992–Coupon	0	0	0	0	0
Par					100,000
Total	100,000	100,000	100,000	100,000	100,000

The securities are held to maturity, with the par amount received at maturity being used to pay the next liability. In 1988, for instance, the final coupon and par amount of the maturing asset plus the two other coupons are used to make up the $100,000 payable on July 1. As proof that the liabilities have been matched, Exhibit 4 sets out the coupon and principal flows of the asset portfolio and shows that $100,000 is available at each liability date.[1]

Immunization

Immunization attempts to match assets and liabilities by ensuring that changes in the present values of the liabilities are offset by even more favorable changes in the present values of the assets. This is achieved by locking in a rate of return over a specified horizon by balancing market and reinvestment risk around the horizon date.

The concepts behind the theory of immunization have been discussed

---

[1]In order to highlight the differences between the strategies, the portfolio selection processes in this and subsequent examples ignore the fact that there is an advantage to trading assets in round lots. The strategies work just as well with round lots as they do with odd lots; round lot solutions only represent another level of complexity.

EXHIBIT 5:
IMMUNIZATION CONDITIONS

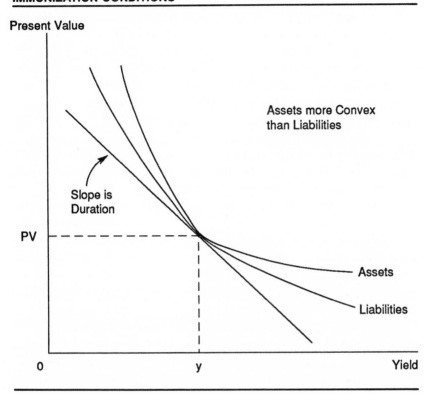

at length in the finance literature. Briefly, there are three conditions necessary for immunization. In order that the assets have a value at least equal to the value of the liabilities when interest rates change:

1. The present value of the assets must equal the present value of the liabilities.
2. The duration of the assets must equal the duration of the liabilities. This makes the price sensitivity to changes in interest rates the same for both assets and liabilities.
3. The convexity of the assets must be greater than or equal to the convexity of the liabilities. When this condition is satisfied, a fall in interest rates will result in asset values increasing by more than the increase in the value of the liabilities, and a rise in interest rates will cause asset values to fall by less than the fall in the value of the liabilities.

Exhibit 5 represents the price-yield relationships of the assets and liabilities under immunization.

Two measures of duration are commonly used—Macaulay duration and modified duration. The Macaulay duration of a stream of payments is the weighted average time to receipt of the payments, where the weights are the present value of each payment. Modified duration measures the price sensitivity of the payment stream to interest rate changes. Immunization is concerned with matching movements in the values of assets and liabilities, so *modified duration* is used as the immunizing criterion. However, the horizon date referred to earlier is determined by the Macaulay duration of the liabilities. When the payment stream is free of options, there is a close algebraic relationship between Macaulay and modified duration.

Convexity measures the change in duration when interest rates change. Using calculus terminology, modified duration represents the first order derivative, and convexity the second order derivative of price with respect to yield. Referring to Exhibit 5, the modified duration of the assets (or liabilities) at any point is given by the slope of the tangent to the price-yield line, and convexity by the degree of curvature of the line.

When immunizing a single liability, the convexity condition is redundant because, of all fixed streams of cash flows with the same present values and durations, a single cash flow has the least convexity. With multiple liabilities, the convexity condition forces the assets to be at least as dispersed over the horizon as the liabilities. Until recently, convexity has tended to be ignored in the asset selection and only the durations equated, giving the strategy its other name, duration matching.

As with cash matching, there may be a number of portfolios which meet the three stated conditions. The chosen portfolio is the one that achieves some specified investment objective, such as earning the highest yield.

Referring to the problem described earlier, of funding a $100,000 payment on July 1 from 1988 to 1992, X decides to immunize the liabilities. The asset portfolio selected is described in Exhibit 6. The assets cost $395,079 which is $5,949 cheaper than the cash matching solution. The duration of both the assets and liabilities is 2.76 years. The asset duration is the result of averaging the durations of long dated securities with short dated ones. This portfolio also satisfies the convexity condition.

EXHIBIT 6:
IMMUNIZED PORTFOLIO FOR FIXED LIABILITIES

Treasury Bond/Strip		Par			Market
Maturity	Coupon	Amount	Yield	Duration	Value
	%	$	%		$
Oct 31 1987	8.875	77,438	6.76	0.34	79,016
Jul 15 1988	14.000	69,805	7.02	0.93	79,018
Jul 31 1988	6.625	77,421	7.19	1.02	79,013
Jan 15 1991	11.750	11,829	7.95	2.79	13,815
Feb 15 1992	0.000	94,673	8.20	4.46	65,201
Nov 15 1995	0.000	149,700	8.54	7.33	79,016
Total		480,866	8.18	2.76	395,079

The assets can be liquidated before maturity to meet the liabilities, but immunization does not specify the order in which the assets should be sold. Therefore, unlike cash matching, the coupon and principal flows of the assets cannot be projected in order to prove the adequacy of the funding. The only proof of immunization lies in the soundness of the underlying theory.

Immunization appears very attractive in theory, since it guarantees the impossibility of a deficit. Exhibit 7 shows that the surplus (difference between asset and liability values) is never negative, regardless of whether rates rise or fall. However, the method has a few disadvantages, which stem mainly from its assumptions:

1. Duration and convexity drift: Duration and convexity are local measures; they are valid only for very small changes in interest rates. Furthermore, they are static, because they are computed at a particular point in time, and their values change from day to day. Liability and asset durations and convexities can respond differently to the passage of time, resulting in a mismatch. If the portfolio is mismatched to the liabilities for a significantly long period, there is a danger that the funding ability may be irreparably impaired. Generally, rebalancing is done periodically, perhaps every three or six months.

2. Parallel shifts of yield curve: Conventional immunization works perfectly only under parallel shifts of the yield curve. Historically, however, the yield curve has often experienced changes in slope, with short-term rates being more volatile than long-term ones.

EXHIBIT 7:
EFFECT OF RATE CHANGE ON IMMUNIZED POSITION

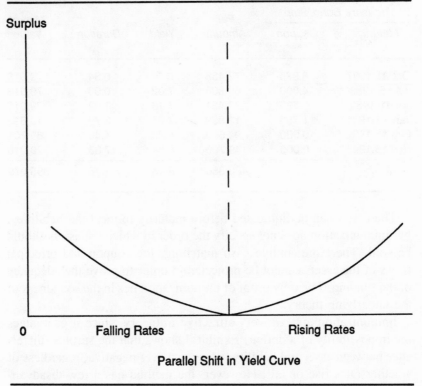

Parallel Shift in Yield Curve

3. Reinvestment: The theory implicitly assumes that all cash flows from the assets can be reinvested at the spread or yield to maturity of the portfolio until used to meet a liability. In practice, short term cash is rarely reinvested in the same portfolio; instead it earns the prevailing short term rate of interest, which may be higher or lower than the yield on the portfolio. Any immunizing portfolio with intermediate cash flows being consistently reinvested at a rate lower than that earned by the portfolio is, in fact, underfunded.

4. Inflexibility: Another assumption behind immunization is that no new cash inflows or outflows occur once the portfolio has been chosen. The portfolio may need to be re-immunized if this condition is violated. This assumption proves to be particularly restrictive when dealing with interest sensitive assets or liabilities.

EXHIBIT 8:
IMMUNIZATION SURPLUS

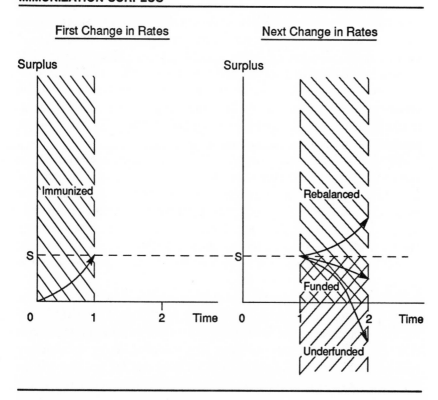

The effect on surplus when rates change is shown in Exhibit 8. Starting from an immunized position at time 0, funding can always be assured up to the first change in rates. In this case, a change in rates has resulted in a surplus of S. If the portfolio is rebalanced immediately at time 1, the portfolio is immunized again; the next change in rates will assure that the total surplus will not fall below S. If the portfolio is not rebalanced at time 1, the portfolio may or may not be funded at time 2; the next change in rates could push the total surplus above S, below S, or in the worst case, below 0.

When implemented properly, and when the required assumptions hold, immunization can be an excellent method to reduce funding risk. It is riskier than cash matching, but, as compensation, offers higher returns. It is a strategy typically used by institutions such as pension funds.

Hybrids of Immunization

One hybrid strategy combines cash matching for the shorter term liabilities with immunization for the longer term ones. The short term liability cash flows are explicitly matched, and a riskier strategy (immunization) is used to meet the long term ones. This hybrid is based on the notion that the liabilities in the near term can be forecast with greater certainty and accuracy than those further out in time. Alternatively, liquidity is paramount in meeting the short term liabilities, while the long term ones are market value concerns.

Another derivative called contingent immunization is essentially the same as immunization, except that the investment manager is permitted to hold an active, non-immunized position until it is necessary to immunize. Active management can increase the overall return on a portfolio. However, since it is riskier, there is a chance that the return on the portfolio will actually decrease. The ability to switch to the immunized mode protects the return on the portfolio in adverse conditions.

The decision to move to the immunized mode is determined by some set of indicators or triggers. These are generally poor investment performance or unfavorable investment potential. When immunization is deemed appropriate, the portfolio is rebalanced along the lines of multiple liability immunization. It is unlikely that the position will be switched back to the active mode once the immunized mode is entered, unless there are some substantial favorable changes in the assets or liabilities. Exhibit 9 shows the asset return profile that can be achieved through contingent immunization. The practical objective of the investment manager is to avoid activating the trigger by earning a return above some minimum such as the return on an immunized portfolio.

The ability to change from the active to the immunized state and, possibly, back again requires constant monitoring of the assets and the liabilities to determine whether the position held at any time is appropriate. Furthermore, some safety zone has to be established below which the value of the freely managed assets cannot fall without jeopardizing the ability to immunize.

Contingent immunization enables the investment manager to defer immunization till the ability to exceed the immunized rate of return is exhausted. The strategy exposes the liabilities to the risk of underfunding through adverse performance on assets when they are not immu-

EXHIBIT 9:
RETURN ON PORTFOLIO MANAGED BY CONTINGENT IMMUNIZATION

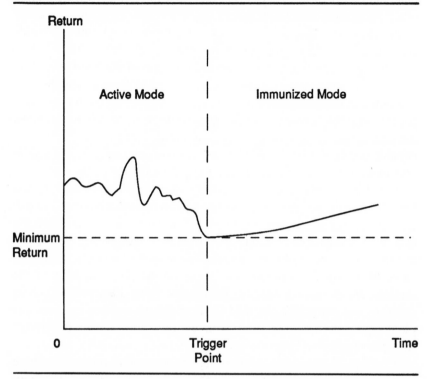

nized. When immunized, the portfolio is subject to all the advantages and disadvantages of immunization discussed earlier.

FUNDING WITH INTEREST SENSITIVE ASSETS

Proper Evaluation of Assets

The interpretation of duration depends on the assumption that all asset cash flows are non-callable and have no default risk, which applies to a very limited subset of available assets. For assets with options, the stated maturity is an inappropriate measure of the actual term or productive life, since the true term may be shorter. For example, when rates fall, some callable corporate bonds may get called well before their stated maturity date.

In the case of callable bonds, one way to account for this would be to compute the yield to maturity and the yield to call, and then compute other parameters such as duration and convexity based on the lower yield. However, this is also somewhat arbitrary—all callable bonds with yield to call lower than yield to maturity will not be called on their first call dates. Actually, the yield and duration of the bond should lie somewhere between the measures as computed to maturity and those as computed to call. Moreover, for an asset like a pass-through mortgage-backed security, no measure analogous to the yield to call exists, since the call option is now held not by one entity (such as the issuer of a callable bond), but by each different house owner, and different people will make different decisions regarding the exercise of the option.

A useful way to evaluate a security with option features is to try and break it up into an option free security and an option component, and to use option pricing techniques to value the latter. Doing this permits accurate parameter estimation for both parts of the security (the option and the option free asset) and thereby of the overall security itself. The value of the option component depends on the price volatility of the security which in turn depends on interest rates. Parameters such as duration and convexity obtained from an analysis which involves explicit separation and evaluation of the option component are referred to as "option-adjusted" parameters.

A further complication when using securities with interest sensitive cash flows for immunization is that these securities often exhibit negative convexity. Assets with no option features lengthen (i.e., experience an increase in duration) when interest rates fall, and shorten when interest rates rise. An asset with negative convexity behaves in an exactly opposite manner—it lengthens when rates rise and shortens when rates fall. Premium callable bonds and mortgage-backed securities often behave in this manner. When rates fall, the higher probability of the asset being called reduces the duration, and when rates rise, the lower call probability raises it.

Negative convexity can be a severe problem when trying to fund a fixed liability, which will always exhibit positive convexity. Any movement in interest rates, regardless of direction, can result in a deficit, with the value of the portfolio being less than the value of the liabilities. This hazard can be mitigated if option-adjusted parameters are used in choosing the portfolio, since any negative convexity in the assets will be explicitly identified.

To sum up, in order to use immunization with a greater degree of reliability when assets have option features, option-adjusted parameters should be used. The durations and convexities so derived provide a much better estimate of how the price of the security will react to changing interest rates.

FUNDING INTEREST SENSITIVE LIABILITIES

Proper Evaluation of Liabilities

As with assets, liabilities may include options which make cash flows sensitive to interest rates. The insurance industry, for instance, has seen the steady growth of interest sensitive products such as universal life and the single premium deferred annuity (SPDA). These produce cash outflows that are strongly dependent upon changes in the interest rate environment over the life of the insurance contract.

A brief description of some SPDA features will demonstrate why the options can be problematic. Under a typical contract a policyholder pays a single premium to the insurance company. This premium is invested so that at maturity, the entire premium plus investment earnings are applied towards securing an annuity. Each policy is credited with interest at a rate determined by the insurance company. During the contract's life the policyholder has the option of withdrawing at any time part or all of the accumulated premium, thereby reducing the amount available at maturity. If the insurance company exercises its option to reduce the crediting rate so that it is no longer competitive, the policyholder may exercise the option to withdraw funds. The interaction of these options presents the first difficulty that arises in valuing the liabilities.

There are two further complications. As in the case of mortgage-backed securities, the options are often exercised when seemingly financially sub-optimal and therefore less predictably. Unlike the case with the assets, there is no secondary market for these liabilities to facilitate accurate pricing.

Need for New Approach

When liabilities have options, measures like duration and convexity no longer have the economic interpretation as when they pertain to default free, option free bonds. Pricing such a liability is itself difficult. Determining the price response to interest rate changes is much more complex, unless several unrealistically restrictive assumptions are made. Moreover, even if these parameters can be computed, the liability cash flows may be so volatile that the estimates would be valid merely for small changes in interest rates.

For these liabilities the funding strategy used should not depend on marginal measures such as duration and convexity. Instead, strategies which explicitly consider the effect of different interest rate environments on liability cash flows recommend themselves. The ability to measure the liability response to rate environment will still be important. However, new strategies must afford a greater margin of error for measurement of value than does immunization.

The dependence of immunization on duration and convexity can lead to the exclusion of some profitable funding opportunities. Exhibit 10 demonstrates how an asset portfolio with negative convexity and yield $y(A)$ can be used to meet positively convex liabilities which require a lower yield, $y(L)$, for funding. Two immunization conditions are met; the present values (PV) are equal and the durations are equal. The convexity condition, however, is violated, so the asset portfolio would not be given further consideration. In this instance, however, the return offered by the assets implies that negative convexity can be used to the benefit of the investor. Exhibit 10 also illustrates that, if the assets are earning more than the accrual rate on the liabilities, it is not necessary to match durations in order to be fully funded.

Instead of using duration and convexity to summarize the effects of interest rates, a scenario-based approach is used. A range of interest rate paths is generated, with an interest rate environment being specified at each point in time along a path. The asset and liability cash flows and prices are projected for each stage along each path. Pricing models based on the term structure and, where necessary, option pricing theory may be used to project the future asset prices and liability values.

Both asset and liability cash flows are *path dependent*. That is the cash flow at any time in the future depends not only on the interest rate environment then, but also on the interest rates at all preceding points. This is because for both assets and liabilities, the exercise of an option at any point may affect all future cash flows.

The asset portfolio selected by a scenario-based strategy should try to ensure full funding under all scenarios considered. Realized return optimization, described below, uses this approach.

EXHIBIT 10:
PROBLEM WITH IMMUNIZATION WHEN ASSETS
HAVE NEGATIVE CONVEXITY

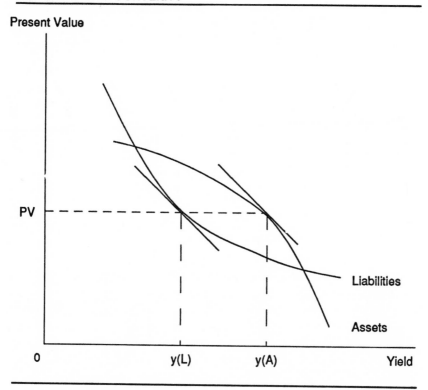

Example of an Interest Sensitive Liability

Exhibit 11 provides a simplified demonstration of how interest rate scenarios over ten years can be generated using a binomial process. To keep the example small, branching along the binomial tree occurs at the end of every year for the first three years, and the last step represents the change in rates during the final seven years. At each branch along the binomial tree, interest rates are allowed to go up or come down 150 basis points in the first three years and 300 basis points over the final seven years. In this example, the interest rate environment is summarized by one rate (r).

The numbers within the brackets identify nodes on the binomial tree.

EXHIBIT 11:
PROJECTED INTEREST RATE SCENARIOS

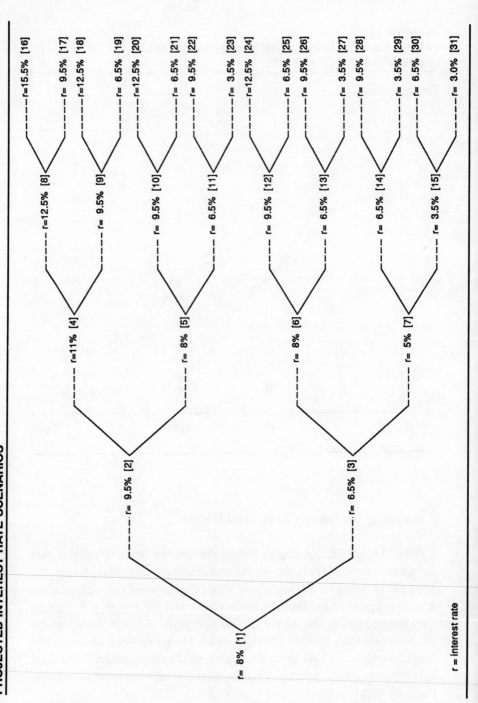

r = interest rate

The nodes refer to the status of the asset and liability portfolios. Because asset and liability cash flows are path dependent more than one node on the tree can have the same interest rate at the same point in time. For example, both node [5] and node [6] have the same rate, 8%. A distinction is drawn between them because they are on different interest rate paths. Node [5] is on the path [1] - [2] - [5] with rates 8%, 9½%, and 8% whereas Node [6] is on the path [1] - [3] - [6] with rates 8%, 6½% and 8%. Exhibit 12 shows that the liability cash flows are different at these nodes; $134 million at node [5] and $200 million at node [6].

The liability used in this example is a block of simplified SPDA policies with a total purchase price of $1,000 million and annuities payable from the end of the 10th year. The option features of an SPDA contract, briefly described earlier, make it suitable to demonstrate the interest sensitive nature of the liability cash flows. In this example, interest is credited to each of the policyholder accounts at the end of each year. Policyholders can withdraw cash from their accounts once a year at the end of the year. In rising rate scenarios, the rate at which cash is withdrawn increases since the issuer adjusts the crediting rate at a slower pace than alternative investments available to policyholders. The opposite holds for falling rate scenarios. The dollar amount withdrawn, however, increases or decreases depending on how much interest has been credited and how much cash has been withdrawn previously. In duration terms, the liability is shorter in the rising rate scenarios than in the falling rate scenarios. (See Exhibit 12.)

To meet these liabilities, a portfolio is selected from eight available assets, five callable bonds and three Treasury strips. The prices, yields and call-adjusted durations are set out in Exhibit 13.

The selection of assets for funding depends on the method used. The next method described is recommended for such liabilities. To make comparisons, however, a portfolio is first selected using the standard method, duration matching. Exhibit 14 sets out the assets selected.

Realized Return Optimization

Realized return optimization (RRO) is an asset selection strategy which ensures that the return earned on the assets is at least equal to the return

EXHIBIT 12:
PROJECTED CASH FLOWS OF INTEREST SENSITIVE LIABILITY IN FIRST THREE YEARS

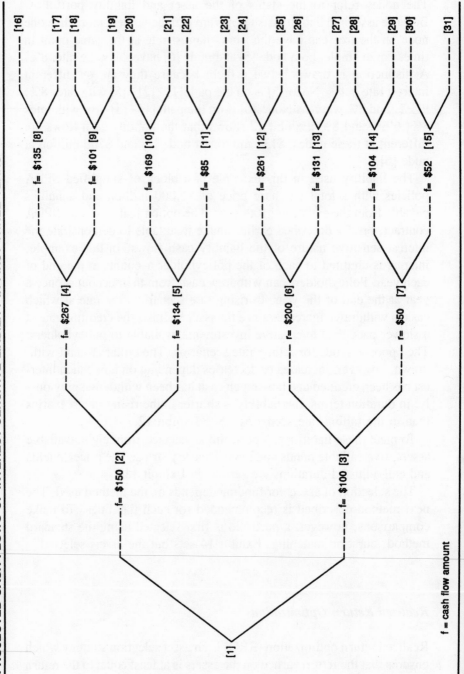

f = cash flow amount

EXHIBIT 13:
ASSETS AVAILABLE FOR FUNDING INTEREST SENSITIVE LIABILITY

Asset (abbreviation)	Maturity	Coupon %	Price $	Yield %	Modified Duration
Treasury Coupon Strip (TCS1)	May 15 1988	0	92.86	7.57	0.90
Treasury Coupon Strip (TCS2)	May 15 1989	0	85.24	8.16	1.92
Treasury Coupon Strip (TCS3)	May 15 1990	0	78.02	8.45	2.88
Atlantic Richfield Co. (ARC)	Oct 15 1995	10.500	108.50	8.13	4.59*
George Power Co (GAP)	May 01 2008	9.625	91.85	9.67	6.00*
General Electric Cr Co (GEC)	Nov 01 2001	5.500	68.63	9.29	7.72*
Southern Bell Tel Co (SBT)	Nov 01 2024	8.750	88.50	8.68	6.67*
Tenneco Inc (TGT)	May 15 2013	11.125	102.75	9.11	4.07*

*Option-Adjusted Modified Duration.

EXHIBIT 14:
IMMUNIZED PORTFOLIO FOR INTEREST SENSITIVE LIABILITIES

Assets	Par Amount	Market Value
GAP	$792.24*	$ 732.09
TCS1	288.51	267.91
Total asset value		1,000.00
Liability value		1,000.00

*All figures in millions.

required in order to fund the liabilities.[2] It can be applied to all liability funding problems, but is particularly useful when the liabilities are sensitive to changes in interest rates.[3]

The strategy can be framed in terms usually applied to immunization. Immunization promises that on the horizon date, the value of the assets will be greater than or equal to the value of the liabilities. Since

---

[2]For a complete discussion of RRO, see Llewellyn Miller, Uday Rajan, and Prakash Shimpi, "Realized Return Optimization," in Frank J. Fabozzi (ed.), *Institutional Investor Focus on Investment Management* (Cambridge: Ballinger Publishing, 1989).

[3]See Llewellyn Miller and Nancy Roth, "Funding SPDA Liabilities," in Frank J. Fabozzi (ed.), *Fixed Income Portfolio Strategies* (Chicago: Probus Publishing, 1989).

the initial condition of immunization is that the present value of assets and liabilities are equal, this is equivalent to ensuring that the rate of return on the assets exceeds the rate implied by the liabilities.

The first step requires selecting a range of interest rate scenarios over a specified period of time. This is done as described earlier. The next step involves the calculation of two types of return measures, realized return for the assets and required return for the liabilities.

The realized return (RR) on an asset over a specified period of time depends on the value of the asset at the beginning and end of the period, the cash flows received during the period, and the reinvestment income earned on the cash flows received during the period. These amounts depend on the interest rate environments at each point in time along a scenario. The RR can be calculated for any specified period under any scenario.

For example, consider a 10% bond priced at par maturing in 10 years. We wish to compute the realized return under a rising rate scenario over 1 year. The bond pays a coupon of 5% in 6 months, with another coupon being paid at the end of the year. The first coupon is reinvested for 6 months at the prevailing short term rate of 8%. The price of the bond falls to 95 by the end of the year. The details of the realized return computation are set out in Exhibit 15a. In this example, the realized return is 5.20%.

The return that must be earned on the assets in order to successfully discharge the liabilities is referred to as required return (RQ). Since the liability cash flows depend on the scenario under consideration, the required returns are also scenario dependent. As with the RR, an estimation of the RQ can be calculated for any specified period under any scenario.

As an example, consider an interest sensitive liability funded with assets worth $100 million. Under a falling rate scenario, the cash outflow at the end of the year is projected to be $5 million, and the present value of the liability $110 million. Exhibit 15b shows the computation of required return, which works out to be 15%.

Given the capability to estimate RR and RQ over any specified period, only those returns necessary for a solution need to be computed. Ideally, each one period realized return should exceed the corresponding one period required return (a one period return is the return earned between consecutive "event" dates, where an event is defined as either a rebalance or a liability outflow). However, it is sufficient to specify some selected return requirements.

EXHIBIT 15:
REALIZED AND REQUIRED RETURNS

a. Realized Return

Price of bond at end of year	=	95.00*
Coupon income over the year	=	10.00*
Reinvestment income (= 5 × .04)	=	0.20*
Total accumulated value over 1 year	=	105.20
Price of bond at beginning of year	=	100.00

Reazlied return = 5.20 / 100.00 = 5.20%

(Note: All figures are quoted as a percentage of par.)

b. Required Return

Market value of asset portfolio today	=	$100 million
Cash flow at end of one year	=	$ 5 million*
Liability value at end of one year	=	$110 million*
Total estimated liability at end of year	=	$115 million
Required return = $15 million / $100 million	=	15%

*Projected value.

To ensure the feasibility of a successful rebalance, the realized return on the assets must exceed the required return over the period till the next rebalancing. This is illustrated in Exhibit 16. The liabilities are fully funded so long as the RR in each time period remains on or above the RQ line, but are underfunded otherwise. For the strategy itself to be successful, the RR to the last liability date must also exceed the RQ to that date. In other words, the RR must exceed the RQ over a short horizon as well as the long haul.

Of all portfolios which satisfy the return conditions, the one with the highest expected realized return over some selected period is purchased. Alternative objectives are:

1. Increase the expected spread between RR and RQ over a specified period.
2. Reduce overall variance of the spread in each scenario between RR and RQ over a specified period. This restricts both upside potential and downside losses.
3. Reduce downside variance of the spread in each scenario between

EXHIBIT 16:
REALIZED RETURN OPTIMIZATION—REQUIREMENT FOR FUNDING

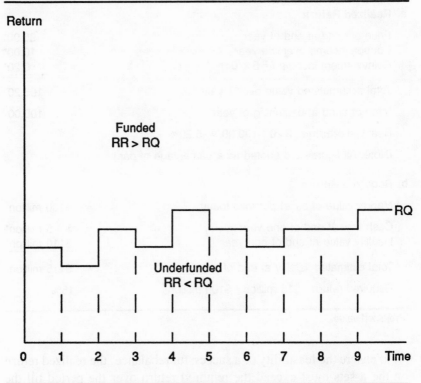

RR and RQ over a specified period. This restricts downside losses only, without controlling variations in the gains.

The last objective points out another useful feature of RRO—an explicit measure of risk is used. Risk is controlled through minimizing the downside deviation of the spread between RR and RQ in specified scenarios and periods.

Modern portfolio theory uses the overall variance of the returns on the portfolio as a measure of risk. However, in a situation where the investor has a target return, risk more realistically refers to the likelihood of not meeting that target. Hence, a risk measure which captures just the instances where the actual return falls below the target is appropriate. This feature of RRO is also a major improvement over immunization, which presumes that funding with the selected portfolio is riskless.

In cases where there is some risk, RRO explicitly identifies the situations which can lead to underfunding. Advance knowledge of these situations facilitates the development of specific hedging strategies to mitigate any losses. Immunization, as mentioned before, assumes away the possibility of underfunding.

Finally, in contrast to immunization, RRO explicitly ensures that the chosen portfolio will earn enough to achieve full funding under all scenarios considered. At each rebalance, sufficient funds will be available to pay the immediate liability and to rebalance to the new optimal asset portfolio. Even if the market value of assets is initially less than the market value of the liabilities, full funding can be achieved since the RQ's take that factor into account. Also, transaction costs required for rebalancing can be covered if the required returns are appropriately increased.

Exhibit 17 demonstrates how surplus can arise from RRO whenever an "event," e.g. liability payment or periodic rebalancing date, occurs. Starting with equal asset and liability values (although not an essential condition), the liabilities are fully funded and, in this example, realize a surplus of S at time 1. If time 1 coincides with an anticipated rebalancing date, then the assets are rebalanced thereby assuring a surplus of at least S. If time 1 does not coincide with a rebalancing date, but time 2 does, then the return conditions of RRO ensure that the surplus will not be negative at time 2; it may be on, above or below S, but never negative. The primary objective that the liabilities are always funded will be met.

The long and short term conditions imposed when selecting the assets can be modified to incorporate the notion of spread. Instead of simply ensuring that the RR be at least equal to the RQ, the requirement can be that the RR exceeds the RQ by some specified minimum spread. This spread can be constant or variable over different periods and scenarios.

To illustrate this method, a portfolio of assets is selected to fund the SPDA liabilities described earlier. The asset selection specifies that realized return on the chosen portfolio must exceed the required return over one year (the time to the next rebalance) and ten years (the life of the liability). The portfolio selected maximizes the expected value of

EXHIBIT 17:
SURPLUS UNDER REALIZED RETURN OPTIMIZATION

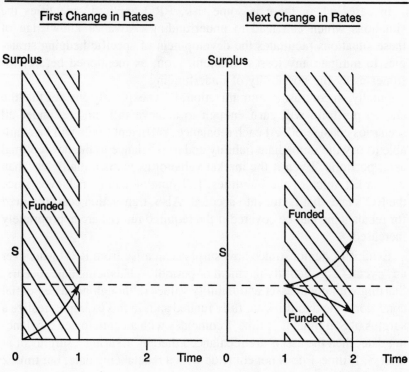

EXHIBIT 18:
RRO PORTFOLIO FOR INTEREST SENSITIVE LIABILITIES

Assets	Par Amount	Market Value
GAP	$230.87*	$ 213.43
TCS1	86.80	80.60
TCS3	904.85	705.97
Total asset value		1,000.00
Liability value		1,000.00

*All figures in millions.

the realized return over the first three years, during which time, the risk of policyholders withdrawing cash is highest.

Exhibit 18 lists the composition of the portfolio selected by RRO.

Evaluation of Scenario Based Methods

In general, scenario based methods such as RRO provide greater flexibility than immunization, which attempts to summarize all interest sensitivity in the parameters of duration and convexity. Some of the advantages of RRO are:

1. The scenarios chosen can be based on the investment manager's expectations, or be generated by some mathematical technique, or be specified by legislation. The wider the range of scenarios selected, the more robust the solution.
2. Unlike conventional immunization, these methods are not restricted to considering only parallel shifts in the yield curve. They are flexible enough to consider any type of change in the interest rate environment.
3. Variables other than interest rates can be used in specifying scenarios. For example, if an insurance company is uncomfortable with predictions about the lapse rates on its new Universal Life policies (a "lapse" refers to an investor exercising the option to withdraw), different lapse rates could be modeled for each scenario, to accommodate all likely cases.
4. The scenarios can be probability weighted to reflect the expectations of the investment manager. For example, in a high interest rate environment, the manager may feel that the rates are more likely to fall than to rise. The probabilities can be allocated accordingly.

Some of the disadvantages of such methods are:

1. The set of scenarios used may not be sufficiently representative. The goal in choosing scenarios is *not* to examine every possible interest rate change that can occur. Instead, a subset of scenarios should be created that account for the likely *volatility* of interest rates, since the values of the asset and liability options depend largely on rate volatility.

2. Scenario based techniques exchange the risk of miscalculation or improper use of parameters under immunization for errors introduced by mispricing in the future. However, for interest sensitive cash flows, parameters like duration are often computed using the binomial option pricing model, which requires the ability to price the cash flows in the future under different interest rate scenarios.

In general, scenario based methods offer a trade-off between greater flexibility and errors caused by bad choice of scenarios. The flexibility afforded assumes greater importance when asset and liability cash flows are interest sensitive.

Comparison of Immunization and RRO

Each of the two strategies has been used to select an asset portfolio to fund interest sensitive liabilities. The goal of each portfolio is to ensure that the liabilities are fully funded regardless of changes in interest rates.

In order to compare these strategies, the performance of each portfolio is evaluated at the end of one year. Performance is measured by the accumulated *surplus* earned by a portfolio at the end of one year under various interest rate scenarios. The surplus, at any point in time, is the difference between the market value of the portfolio, net of transactions costs, and the present value of the liabilities.

The first comparison is based on portfolio performance when interest rates move either up or down by 150 basis points. The next comparison is based on how the portfolios perform if rates take a path not explicitly considered in the asset selection process, rising by either 100 or 200 basis points. The rising rate environment is chosen because this is the situation which can lead to disintermediation by policyholders. Cash is withdrawn and invested elsewhere, and the liability issuer has to liquidate assets at depressed market values.

(i) **Rates rise or fall by 150 basis points:** Exhibit 19 shows the value of the surplus at the end of the first year. The accumulated cash flow and the new market value of the portfolio determine how much is available to pay the liability and rebalance to the new portfolio.

With RRO, the assets produce a surplus in each scenario. The objectives of the strategy are therefore achieved in the short term. Since the

EXHIBIT 19:
SURPLUS AT REBALANCE WHEN RATES RISE OR FALL
150 BASIS POINTS

Rates rise 150bp:

	IMM	RRO
Market value of liabilities	$ 880.00*	$ 880.00
Available from initial assets	1025.47	$1040.00
Liability payment	150.00	150.00
Market value of new portfolio	880.00	880.00
	−4.53	10.00
Minus transactions costs	−2.70	−2.41
Surplus at rebalance	−7.23	7.59

Rates fall 150bp:

	IMM	RR0
Market value of liabilities	$ 980.00*	$ 980.00
Available from initial assets	1141.73	1117.52
Liability payment	100.00	100.00
Market value of new portfolio	980.00	980.00
	61.73	37.52
Minus transactions costs	−1.29	−3.65
Surplus at rebalance	60.44	33.87

*All figures in millions.

long term objectives can be considered the product of a series of short term objectives, this result leads to confidence that the strategy works. RRO still manages to produce a surplus in both scenarios; $7.59 million when rates rise and $33.87 million when rates fall. The surplus in the rising rate environment can be increased by raising the required return, although this will result in a lower surplus in the down scenario.

Immunization produces a large surplus of $60.44 million when rates fall and a deficit of $7.23 million when rates rise. Comparing this with RRO, it appears that the RRO surplus in the up scenario has been achieved at the expense of a large reduction in surplus in the down scenario. In choosing the assets, it was assumed that the issuer wished to be fully funded at all times, without trading off deficits in one scenario with surpluses in another. However, RRO does provide the flexibility to make such trade-offs, and averaging out the surplus across scenarios would have led to a different portfolio being chosen.

(ii) Rates rise by 100 basis points: If rates rise by 100 rather than 150 basis points, the liability cash flow is $145 million, and the present value of the liabilities is $900 million. Exhibit 20 shows that the portfolios selected by both strategies produce more accumulated income and market value than when rates rise by 150 basis points, but the greater liability value provides an offsetting effect.

The immunized portfolio is underfunded by $1.32 million. The RRO portfolio produces a surplus of $4.20 million.

EXHIBIT 20:
SURPLUS AT REBALANCE WHEN RATES RISE BY 100
OR 200 BASIS POINTS

Rates rise 100bp:

	IMM	RRO
Market value of liabilities	$ 900.00*	$ 900.00
Available from initial assets	1046.20	$1053.10
Liability payment	145.00	145.00
Market value of new portfolio	900.00	900.00
	1.20	8.10
Minus transactions costs	−2.52	−3.90
Surplus at rebalance	−1.32	4.20

Rates rise 200bp:

	IMM	RRO
Market value of liabilities	$ 860.00*	$ 860.00
Available from initial assets	1004.74	1026.81
Liability payment	155.00	155.00
Market value of new portfolio	860.00	860.00
	−10.26	11.81
Minus transactions costs	−2.90	−1.77
Surplus at rebalance	−13.16	10.04

*All figures in millions.

(iii) Rates rise by 200 basis points: The liability cash flow is higher at $155 million when rates rise by 200 basis points. However, the value of the liabilities is lower at $860 million, and asset values are also depressed.

The assets chosen by RRO produce enough to rebalance and provide a surplus of $10.04 million. The assets held by the immunized portfolio do not produce enough to meet the rebalancing costs, resulting in a deficit of $13.16 million.

(iv) Appropriateness of the strategies: This example, although limited in its size, demonstrates that immunization is an inappropriate strategy for funding interest sensitive liabiliites. As shown in Exhibit 21, the immunized portfolio in this example incurs large deficits under rising rates, though the goal is to ensure funding regardless of how interest rates change.

EXHIBIT 21:
SURPLUS EARNED OVER ONE YEAR WHEN RATES CHANGE

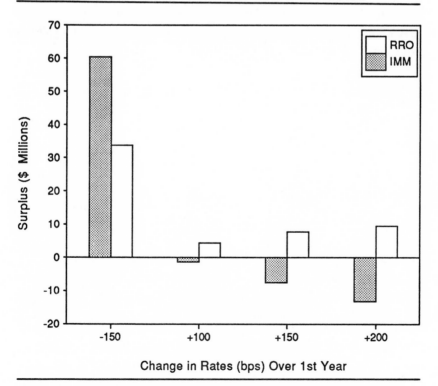

In this example, immunization does not result in successful funding because the interest sensitivity of the liabilities cannot be summarized by static parameters like duration and convexity. RRO proves to be a better strategy because it accounts more explicitly for changes in the cash flows and values of the assets and liabilities.

CONCLUSION

With the wide diversity in available assets and liabilities, the practitioner must be careful not to use a liability funding strategy in situations where it may not be valid. Using an inappropriate strategy can lead to underfunding. For example, duration matching should not be used when assets and liabilities have option features. In order to choose the best method in any situation, it is useful to know the assumptions that underlie each funding strategy.

Strategies can be classified according to the assumptions they make about the nature of the liability and asset cash flows. The first step in liability funding should be a complete evaluation of the liabilities, in order to determine which funding technique is most suitable in the given context. The actual selection of the asset portfolio then follows with the implementation of the strategy.

CHAPTER 15

Managing Fixed Income Assets Using Futures Contracts, Put Options, and Call Options*

FRANK J. JONES, PH.D.
MANAGING DIRECTOR
KIDDER, PEABODY & CO., INC.

BETH A. KRUMHOLZ
VICE PRESIDENT
KIDDER, PEABODY & CO., INC.

Hedging Treasury, corporate, and mortgage-related bonds and portfolios of such bonds with Treasury bond futures contracts has become common in recent years. The advent of options on the Treasury bond futures contract, however, makes available new types of transactions that can be used in conjunction with holding such bonds and that affect the gain and loss potentials of the bonds.

This chapter discusses some of the possible transactions involving

*The authors wish to thank Frank Fabozzi for his assistance in the preparation of this chapter.

319

Treasury bond futures options that can be used to change the gain/loss profiles of holding bonds and compares the outcomes of these option transactions combined with bonds with those of hedging the bonds with short Treasury bond futures contracts and holding the bonds unhedged. The options transactions considered are put buying and call writing (selling).

The next three sections discuss selling futures, buying puts, and selling calls, respectively, in conjunction with holding bonds. The last two sections compare the results of these three strategies and discuss the reasons for selection among them.

As a benchmark throughout this chapter, assume that the underlying cash Treasury bond is initially priced at 96. The gain/loss profile of this bond, considering only the market price of the bond is shown in Exhibit 1.

Exhibit 1 shows the gain/loss profile of only the market price component of the bond. But while it is held, the bond also accrues interest due to its coupon. The amount of accrued interest depends on the time the bond is held.

Assume that the holding period of the bond is six months and that the market price of the bond on the horizontal axis of Exhibit 1 refers to the price of the bond at the end of the holding period. Given the coupon of

EXHIBIT 1:
GAIN/LOSS PROFILE ON LONG TREASURY BOND

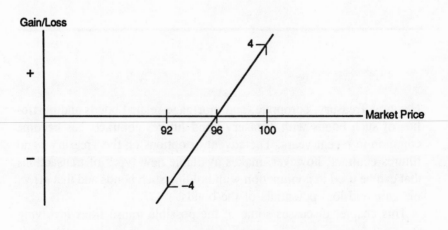

the bond and this holding period, the amount of interest accrued while holding the bond should be added to the gain/loss profile of the bond.

Assume that the annual coupon on the bond is 14 and, thus, the amount of interest accrued on the bond during the six-month holding period is 7. For the bond initially purchased at 96, the accrued interest of 7 should be added to the gain/loss profile shown in Exhibit 1 to provide the complete gain/loss profile of the bond, as shown by the dotted line in Exhibit 2.

In general, the return on the bond over a holding period can be thought of as the initial gain/loss profile, shown in Exhibit 1 without including accrued interest, moved upward by the accrued interest, which equals $(N/365) \times C$, where C is the annual coupon and N is the length of the holding period.[1] This general case is shown in Exhibit 3, on which the "Market Price" on the horizontal axis is the market price at the end of the holding period N.

EXHIBIT 2:
GAIN/LOSS PROFILE ON LONG TREASURY BOND,
INCLUDING ACCRUED INTEREST

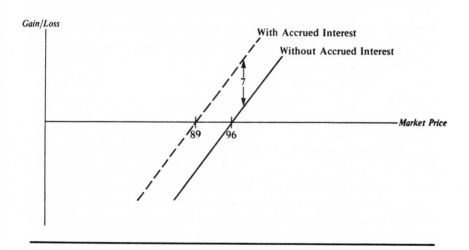

---

[1] In practice, coupons are paid on a semiannual basis. Accrued interest then depends not only on the number of days the bond is held but also on the number of days in the specific half year of the coupon payment.

EXHIBIT 3:
GAIN/LOSS PROFILE ON LONG TREASURY BOND,
INCLUDING ACCRUED INTEREST

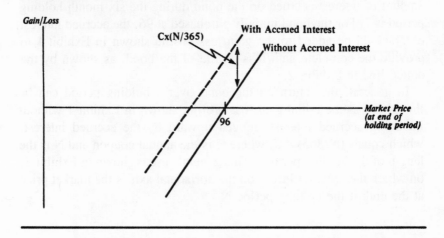

SHORT FUTURES—THE HEDGE

Hedging bonds with Treasury bond futures contracts has been done since the advent of the Treasury bond futures contract in 1977.

A hedge is defined as a transaction whose gain or loss *offsets* the loss or gain on a related cash market transaction. A perfect hedge, thus, results when a dollar gain on the hedge position is offset by an equal dollar loss on the cash market position and vice versa.

The gain/loss profile of a short futures position is shown in Exhibit 4. Assume for now that the initial futures price is the same as the initial bond price, 96. A more realistic assumption is made later in this section. The short futures position obviously provides an offset to the bond shown in Exhibit 1. The gain/loss profile of the bond described in Exhibit 1 when perfectly hedged with a short futures position is shown in Exhibit 5. The net gain/loss is zero at any bond price.

Several comments are appropriate. The first is related to the cost of a hedge. The advantage of a perfect hedge is that it eliminates the possibility of capital loss. The disadvantage is that it also eliminates the potential for capital gain. Thus, the cost or "price" of a hedge, the cost

EXHIBIT 4:
GAIN/LOSS ON SHORT TREASURY BOND FUTURES

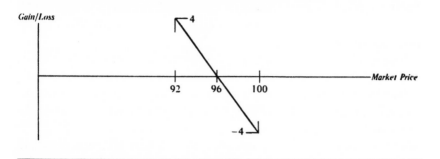

EXHIBIT 5:
BOND PERFECTLY HEDGED WITH SHORT FUTURES

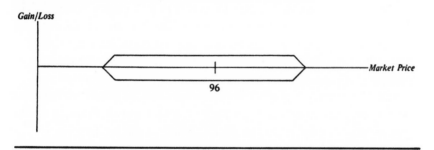

or price of eliminating the possibility of a loss, is the potential gain.[2] Uncertainty is eliminated on both the upside and the downside.

Is this "price" high or low? The answer to this question depends initially on the hedger's expectations and, after the fact, on the actual outcome. Initially, if the hedger is very bearish, sacrificing the upside potential to avert downside potential may seem cheap. If the hedger is not particularly bearish or is bullish, sacrificing the upside may seem quite expensive.

After the fact, if the market moves against the cash instrument and for the hedge, the hedger will think it was a "good hedge." But if the cash market moves for the cash instrument and against the hedge, the

---

[2] There are also commissions and the cost of initial. and potentially. variation margin.

hedger will be less pleased. This reaction is particularly likely if the gain is a book gain rather than a realized gain, as may be the case in holding a bond, since the hedge or futures loss is always a cash, or out-of-pocket, loss. But this is the nature of a hedge. It sacrifices upside potential to avert downside loss.

The second comment is related to a common futures market phrase, "basis risk." In a perfect hedge the gain on one side of a hedge perfectly offsets the loss on the other. However, for various technical reasons the gain on one side of a hedge may be greater or less than the loss on the other side. Among the reasons are: 1) The instrument being hedged is not the same as the instrument underlying the futures contract (specifically, the cheapest deliverable instrument underlying the futures contract), as is the case, for example, if corporate bonds are being hedged with the Treasury bond futures contract or if the 13¼% Treasury bond of 5/15/14 is being hedged with the Treasury bond futures contract whose cheapest deliverable bond is a different Treasury bond. 2) The hedge is taken off on a day that is not a futures contract delivery day and/or on a day on which the futures contract is not fully converged to the price of the cheapest deliverable bond. In this case, there may be less-than-full convergence of the bond to the futures contract.

And on imperfect hedges the gain or loss may be greater or less than the loss or gain on the cash instrument, a fact that, depending on the circumstances, may be to the disadvantage of the hedger.

The third comment is related to the rate of return realized on a hedged bond. Among newcomers to hedging there are two extreme views with regard to this return, both erroneous. The negative view is that since there is no capital gain or loss there is a zero return on the hedged bond. The actual outcome is not that bad.

The positive view is that by hedging a Treasury bond with a short futures position an investor can earn the Treasury bond coupon (current) yield with no capital risk, since the capital risk is hedged away. Earning a long-term return on an investment with no capital risk seems too good to be true. And it is.

What is the return on a hedged bond? What one should realistically expect to earn on an investment with no capital risk is a short-term capital-risk-free rate of return. And that is typically approximately what is earned. The return on a perfectly hedged Treasury bond is the Treasury bond financing rate, which is the repurchase agreement rate (repo rate) over the period of the hedge. Thus, if a futures contract with three or six months to maturity is sold against a Treasury bond, the return on a perfect hedge over the corresponding three- or six-month holding period is approximately the three- or the six-month term repo rate, respectively.

This conclusion can be demonstrated by considering the assumption made earlier that the initial bond and futures prices are the same, 96 in the example. In general, the futures price should equal the bond price on the day the bond is bought and the futures contract is sold, plus the net cost of carrying the bond from the day on which the bond is bought and the futures contract is sold until delivering the bond on the short futures position. Arbitrage will assure that this is approximately true. The net cost of carrying a bond equals the financing cost (a cost) less the accrued interest earned while holding the bond (a return). On this basis the following relationship between the futures price and the bond price results:

$$\text{Futures Price (PF)} = \text{Bond Price (PC)} + \text{Financing Cost (FC)} - \text{Accrued Interest (AI)}$$

where the Financing Cost (denoted by FC) and the Accrued Interest (denoted by AI) refer to the amounts over the holding periods of the bond and the futures contract.

Thus, the futures price and the bond price will differ by an amount equal to the difference between the financing cost and the accrued interest, that is:

$$PF - PC = FC - AI$$

The term $FC - AI$, the difference between the financing cost (a short-term rate) and the accrued interest (a long-term rate), depends on the slope of the yield curve. With the positive yield curve AI is greater than FC, and, thus, PC will be greater than PF. With negative yield curve FC is greater than AI, and, thus, PF will be greater than PC.

But, regardless of the slope of the yield curve, FC and AI are both dollar amounts and, thus, depend not only on the financing *rate* and the coupon *rate*, respectively, but also on the number of days, N, the bond is held. Thus, the closer to the maturity of the futures contract, that is, the smaller N, the smaller in magnitude is $FC - AI$, and the smaller in magnitude is $PF - PC$, that is, the closer PF and PC are to each other.

On the delivery day of the futures contract there is no further financing cost or accrued interest; hence $FC - AI$ is zero, and the futures price (PF) will equal the bond price (PC). This is called *convergence*.

Prior to delivery on the futures contract, however, the futures price and the bond price differ by an amount equal to the dollar value of the difference between the financing cost and the accrued interest over the period until delivery on the futures contract.[3]

For the following discussion assume a positive yield curve, which implies that the financing cost is less than the accrued interest. Thus, the futures price will be less than the cash price by this difference. Exhibit 6 shows the difference between PF and PC as the time to maturity (N) decreases for a positive yield curve. For example, given an annual coupon of 14 and an annual financing cost of 6 given the initial price of the bond, the amount by which the futures price is less than the cash price for various times before the maturity of the futures contract is:

- 8 for one year to maturity;
- 4 for six months to maturity;
- 2 for three months to maturity;
- 0 at maturity;

as illustrated in Exhibit 6.[4]

Thus, in this example, if the bond price remained at 96 for the last year prior to the maturity of the futures contract, the futures price would be: 88 $(96 - 8)$ one year prior to maturity; 92 $(96 - 4)$ six months prior to maturity; 94 $(96 - 2)$ three months prior to maturity; and 96 at maturity. The bond itself, at a market value of 96, would have accumulated accrued interest of 3.5 over three months, accrued interest of 7 over six months and accrued interest of 14 over one year.

The outcome of a bond hedged with short futures over a holding period can now be determined. First consider the net return to this combined long bond/short futures position on a conceptual basis. As-

---

[3]This convergence equality will exist only for the cheapest deliverable bond adjusted for its conversion factor. The other cash price/futures price relationships discussed in this section must also be adjusted by their conversion factors.

[4]Of course, even at a constant point in time (N fixed) $FC - AI$ and, thus, $PF - PC$, may change because FC changes relative to AI. This term may change because, among other reasons, the slope of the yield curve changes or the cheapest deliverable bond changes.

EXHIBIT 6:
FUTURES/BOND PRICE RELATIONSHIP (FOR POSITIVE YIELD CURVE)

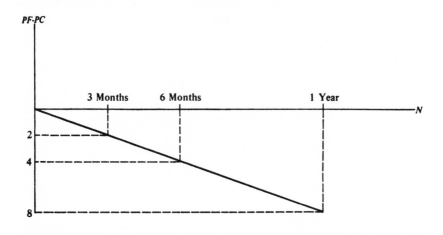

sume a constant bond price. Over a holding period the gain on the bond is the accured interest AI. With a positive yield curve (and a constant bond price), the futures price increases relative to the bond price by an amount equal to the change in the difference between the financing cost (FC) and the accrued interest (AI). Since a hedge requires a short futures position, this increase in the futures price represents a loss of equal amount.

In summary, there is a gain on the bond equal to AI and a loss on the short futures position equal to AI − FC over the holding period. The net gain on the long bond/short futures combination position is, thus, FC, the financing cost. The gain on a bond hedged with a short futures position, thus, equals the financing cost over the holding period, which represents a risk-free rate of return (in this application the term repo rate). The actual gain over the holding period is the dollar value of the financing rate over the holding period; the rate of return over the holding period is the financing rate.

This result can also be shown graphically in the context of this example, as shown in Exhibit 7. Consider the gain/loss profiles at various points in time for a bond initially purchased at 96 and a futures position sold at the corresponding futures price of 88 one year prior to the maturity. (The annual coupon is 14 and the annual financing cost is 6.)

EXHIBIT 7:
**GAIN/LOSS PROFILE ON BOND, SHORT FUTURES AND COMBINED
BOND/SHORT FUTURES POSITIONS**

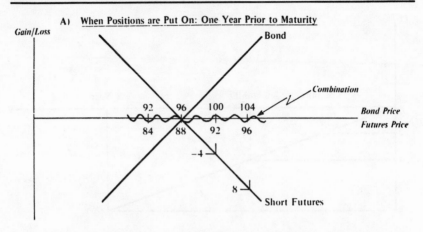

A) When Positions are Put On: One Year Prior to Maturity

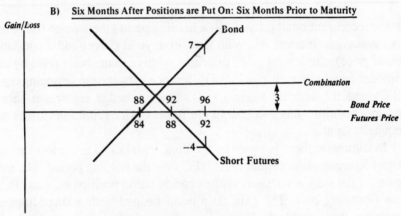

B) Six Months After Positions are Put On: Six Months Prior to Maturity

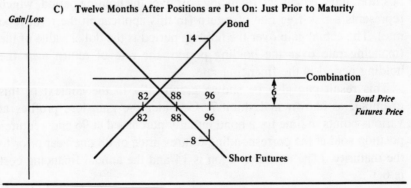

C) Twelve Months After Positions are Put On: Just Prior to Maturity

Immediately after the bond is bought and the futures contract is sold, there is not yet any accrued interest earned on the bond or any convergence loss on the short futures position. Exhibit 7A shows the gain/loss profile of the two individual positions and the combination of these two positions at this time. To illustrate these three gain/loss profiles on the same graph, the horizontal axis shows the bond price on the upper portion of the axis and the *corresponding* futures price on the lower portion of the axis. Initially a futures price of 88 corresponds to a bond price of 96, and so they are shown at the same position on the horizontal axis. And futures prices of 87 and 89 correspond to bond prices of 95 and 97, respectively.[5]

Note that in Exhibit 7A, the short futures position shows a loss of 4 at a futures price of 92 and a loss of 8 at a futures price of 96. These relationships are used in the following discussion.

As shown in Exhibit 7A, for an immediate change from the initial bond price of 96 to any other bond price, there will be zero net gain or loss on the combined bond/short futures position. The gain/loss profile for the net position is shown by the wavy line on the horizontal axis. This result is consistent with the preceding conceptual discussion because over a holding period of zero there is no financing cost.

Consider the same positions six months later, which is also six months prior to the maturity of the futures contract. After six months the bond has accrued interest of 7. Thus, the gain/loss profile of the bond after six months is 7 higher than when the bond was purchased as shown in Exhibit 7B. After six months the futures price has also increased by 4 relative to the bond price. For example, at a constant bond price of 96 the futures price will have increased from 88 to 92, as indicated earlier. Thus, in Exhibit 7B the futures price of 92 is shown below the corresponding bond price of 96. But at a futures price of 92, as indicated earlier, there is a loss of 4 (92 − 88) on the short futures position, as shown in Exhibit 7B. The combined bond/short futures positon ("Combination"), thus, has a gain of 3 at all bond prices, as shown in Exhibit 7B. This amount of 3 is equal to the financing cost of 6 over six months.

Exhibit 7C shows the gain/loss profiles of the bond, the short futures, and the combined position just prior to maturity of the futures contract. At this time the bond will have accrued interest of 14. And the

---

[5]These relationships are only approximate.

futures price will have increased from its initial level of 8 below the bond price to a level equal to the bond price. For example, if the bond price remains 96 at the maturity of the futures contract, the futures price will also be 96. Thus, the bond and futures prices on the horizontal axis are the same. And at a futures price of 96 there is a loss of 8 on the short futures, as indicated earlier.

The combination of the gain of 14 at a constant bond price of 96 and the loss of 8 on the short futures price at this bond price provides a net gain of 6. Combining the bond and short futures gain/loss profiles shown in Exhibit 7C also provides a gain of 6 at all other bond prices. This amount, 6, represents the amount of the financing cost of 6 over a year.

The table below summarizes the results of Exhibit 7.

Time (Prior to Maturity of Futures Contract)	Bond Price	Corresponding Futures Price	Accrued Interest on Bond	Loss on Short Futures Contract	Net Gain on Bond/Short Futures
1 yr.	96	88	0	0	0
6 mos.	96	92	7	4	3
0	96	96	14	8	6

Note that at each time the accrued interest on the bond is based on the coupon return over the holding priod (the coupon is 14). The loss on the short futures position equals the difference between the coupon (14) and the financing cost (6) over the holding period. And the net gain on the basis of the net bond/short futures position is, thus, the financing cost over the holding period.

Exhibit 8 shows the gain/loss profile for a combined bond/short futures position, in general, for various holding priods.

The results described in this section are for a perfect hedge. Imperfect hedges result from basis changes, as indicated earlier, or from the fact that the initial futures price is too high or too low given the initial bond price, that is, the cash and futures prices differ by an amount not equal to net carry costs. If the hedge is better or worse than perfect, the return on the hedge will be greater or less than the financing cost (term repo rate) over the holding period. A complete discussion of this topic

EXHIBIT 8:
GAIN/LOSS ON COMBINED BOND/SHORT FUTURES POSITION
GENERAL CASE

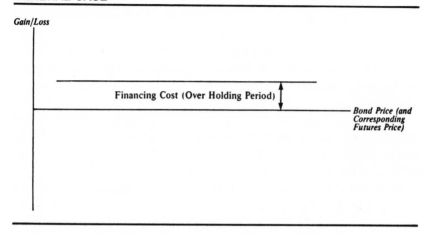

is not appropriate here. Recently, however, the return on hedges has been somewhat below the corresponding financing (repo) rate.

LONG PUTS—INSURANCE

In hedging with short futures the price paid to avert loss is the sacrifice of potential gains. This is not the same type of protection provided by standard insurance, wherein a fee or premium is paid to protect against losses of a certain specified type (in some cases protection against losses in excess of a certain specified amount, the "deductible" amount). Thus, the loss to the insured is limited to the amount of the premium (plus the amount of the deductible, if any). But, except for the amounts of the premium and deductible, any profit derived from the insured property is retained.

Such standard insurance differs from hedging with short futures in two ways:

- In hedging there is no necessary loss, whereas in insurance the premium is necesarily lost.
- In hedging potential gains are sacrificed, whereas in insurance potential gains are retained.

There are now instruments available in the financial markets that provide protection for bonds that is basically "insurance" of this type. These instruments are Treasury bond futures put options. Such insurance can be obtained by buying a put option on the Treasury bond futures contract.

A put option is an instrument that permits the buyer to sell, or "put," the specified instrument, at his option, to the put's seller at the put's strike price. The buyer initially pays the put premium to the seller for this option.

The gain/loss profile of a long put with a strike price of 96 and an initial premium of 3 when the price of the underlying bond is 96 (the put is at the money) is shown in Exhibit 9. This gain/loss profile applies to the time of expiration of the put.

Note that if the market price is 96 or above at expiration the loss on the put will be 3. In this case the buyer of the put will not exercise it, and the premium of 3 will be lost. On the other hand, if the market price is below 96 at expiration the buyer will exercise the put, and the profit on the long put will be the amount by which the market price is below 96, less the premium of 3.

Assume that an at-the-money put is purchased in conjunction with the purchase of the underlying bond, also purchased at 96. The gain/loss profile of the combination is shown in Exhibit 10. For comparison, the gain/loss profile of the bond alone is shown as a dotted line.

EXHIBIT 9:
GAIN/LOSS PROFILE ON LONG PUT

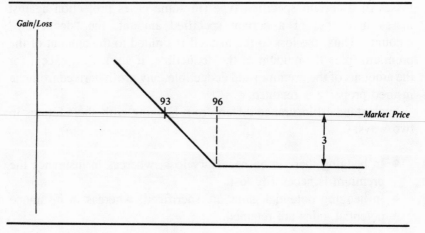

EXHIBIT 10:
GAIN/LOSS PROFILE OF LONG PUT/LONG BOND

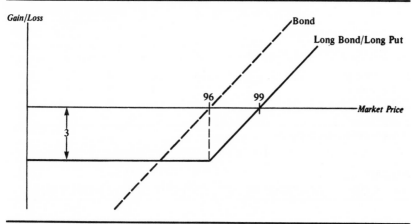

At all prices below the initial bond price of 96 the loss on the combination position is 3, the amount of the initial premium. Thus, on the downside the loss is limited to 3. At prices above 96, however, the outcome is the gain on the cash market bond minus the premium of 3. Thus, the combination position breaks even at 99 and shows a net profit above this break-even level. And, of course, if the market remains constant at 96, the premium of 3 is lost.

In general, this outcome is the same as for standard insurance. On the downside the loss is limited to the amount of the insurance premium, and on the upside there is a profit equal to the gain on the cash market bond less the initial premium of 3. Specifically, this is the same as standard insurance with no deductible.

In this discussion the outcome for the purchase of an at-the-money put is considered, that is, a put whose strike price equals the initial bond price. Now consider the purchase of in-the-money puts (puts whose strike prices are above the initial bond price) and out-of-the-money puts (puts whose strike prices are below the initial bond price). Assume, as summarized in Exhibit 11, that an in-the-money 100-strike-price put is selling at 6 (4 for intrinsic value and 2 for time value) while a 92-strike-price put is selling at 2 (all time value).

The gain/loss profiles of these in- and out-of-the-money puts and the at-the-money put previously considered are shown in Exhibit 12.

The time value of these puts is greatest, 3, for the at-the-money put

EXHIBIT 11:
IN-, AT-, AND OUT-OF-THE-MONEY LONG PUTS

	Strike Price	Premium	Intrinsic Value	Time Value	Maximum Loss Amount	At or Above	Break-even*
In-the-money	100	6	4	2	6	100	94
At-the-money	96	3	0	3	3	96	93
Out-of-the-money	92	2	0	2	2	92	90

*Equals strike price minus premium.

EXHIBIT 12:
GAIN/LOSS PROFILES OF IN-, AT-, AND OUT-OF-THE MONEY PUTS

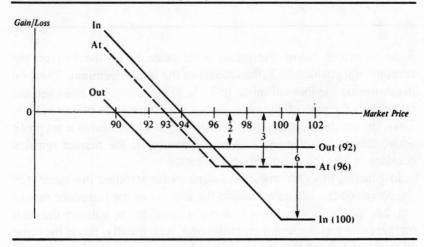

and is 2 for the 4-point in- and out-of-the-money puts. The premium of the in-the-money put is the time value of 2 plus the intrinsic value of 4, that is, 6. Exhibits 11 and 12 summarize the trade-offs between in-the-money and out-of-the-money puts. The in-the-money put, 100 strike price, has a greater maximum loss, at a price of 100 or higher but generates a profit at prices below only 2 points under the initial market level, at 94. The out-of-the-money put, 92 strike price, has a smaller maximum loss, 2, but begins to generate a profit only at 6 points below the market, at 90.

Note that if the bond price remains constant at 96, each put loses its initial time value, 2 for the in- (100) and out-of-(92) the-money puts and 3 for the at-the-money (96) put. If the bond price increases, each put can lose its full premium value (at the expiration of the put):

- 6 for the in-the-money (100) put above a price of 100, at which prices the 100 put has no intrinsic value;
- 3 for the at-the-money (96) put above the initial price of 96, at which prices the 96 put has no intrinsic value; and
- 2 for the out-of-the-money put (92) above the price of 92, at which prices the 92 put has no intrinsic value.

But at prices below the initial price of 96, the 96 and 100 strike price puts are in the money, and the premiums of the 96 and 100 puts both increase with the decline in the value of the bond because of an increase in intrinsic value. (The intrinsic value of an at- or in-the-money put at expiration has a delta, or hedge ratio, of 1.0, that is, increases dollar for dollar with the underlying bond price.) But the 92 strike price put is still out of the money at prices between 96 and 92, and the premium increases because of intrinsic value only after a decrease in the bond price below 92, that is only after the bond price has decreased by more than 4.

Thus, the in-the-money put can lose its entire premium, which includes intrinsic value, with a bond price increase, but for price decreases it shows the greatest profit (because it has a lower time value than an at-the-money put) and begins to show an incremental profit at a higher price than an out-of-the-money put.

The out-of-the-money put shows a smaller loss for a bond price increase because, although it loses its entire premium, that premium consisted only of time value—there was no intrinsic value. But for a bond price decrease, the out-of-the-money put shows a smaller profit because its incremental profits begin only at a lower bond price.

Exhibit 13 shows the combination of a bond purchased at 96 with these in, out- and at-the-money long puts that result from the gain/loss profiles of long puts shown in Exhibit 11 and bonds shown in Exhibit 1. Exhibit 13 shows, in effect, the type of insurance provided by long puts to bond positions. Exhibit 14 summarizes these results.

For the in-the-money put (100), the loss on the bond/long put portfolio can be no greater than 2, the initial time value of the put. But if the bond price increases, the entire put premium may be lost, and the profit on the bond/long put is less than on a naked bond by the entire amount of the put premium.

EXHIBIT 13:
IN-, AT-, AND OUT-OF-THE-MONEY PUTS WITH A BOND

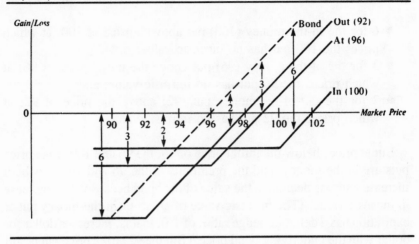

For the out-of-the-money put (92), the loss on the bond/long put portfolio can be greater than the put premium, a maximum loss of 6 in this example. This maximum loss of 6 is the result of buying a put 4 points below the initial bond price (4 points out of the money) for a premium of 2 points (all time value). Thus, an out-of-the-money put ensures a lower minimum level, 6 points below the initial price, than an in-the-money put.

But if the bond price increases, the out-of-the-money put can lose only its premium, which is composed only of time value (the more out of the money the put the lower the time value). Thus, the out-of-the-money put will have less opportunity loss when the bond price increases.

Buying out-of-the-money puts locks in a lower price but costs less and, thus participates more fully in market price increases. The more out of the money the put, the lower the level of the price locked in but the less the initial premium and the less sacrificed if the market price increases. Thus, deep out-of-the-money puts can be viewed as disaster insurance. The price for disaster insurance is low, but the insurance is only against fairly large losses.

On the other hand, in-the-money puts ensure a higher price, that is, if the market moves down, the loss on the bond/long put portfolio will be only the initial time value of the put (and the more in the money

EXHIBIT 14:
IN-, AT-, AND OUT-OF-THE-MONEY LONG PUTS WITH BOND

| | Strike Price | Premium | Time Value | Maximum Loss | | | Breakeven Level (4) | Opportunity Loss in Profit Range (5) |
				Amount (1)	Minimum Level Locked In (2)	At or Below (3)		
In-the-money	100	6	2	2	94	100	102	6
At-the-money	96	3	3	3	93	99	99	3
Out-of-the-money	92	2	2	6	90	98	98	2

(1) Equals out-of-the-money amount, if any, plus time value.
(2) Equals strike price minus in-the-money amount minus time value (or strike price minus premium).
(3) Equals strike price.
(4) Equals strike price plus time value plus out-of-the-money amount.
(5) Equals time value plus the initial in-the-money amount (initial premium).

the put the less the initial time value). But if the market moves up, the entire put premium, which also includes the intrinsic value, will be lost, and thus the sacrifice relative to a naked bond will be great. In-the-money puts lock in high prices, but the cost is high.

Overall, the opportunity loss when bond prices increase and there is a profit is the put premium. (If the market moves up, the long put, which is a bear position, loses its entire premium.) obviously this opportunity loss is larger the more in the money (or less out of the money) the put. For a decrease in the bond price, the level locked in is the strike price minus the premium, which is higher the more in the money (less out of the money) the put. Thus, there is a trade-off between the level locked in if the bond price decreases and the opportunity loss if the bond price increases. Overall, the choices are between a low level of insurance (disaster insurance) for a low price and a high level of insurance for a high price—not an unexpected choice combination.

In general, for long puts a fixed premium is paid for protection against losses greater than a certain initial amount. But participation in an upward market move remains (less the initial premium, of course). This is a familiar type of insurance. The purchase of an at-the-money put provides insurance with no deductible. The purchase of an out-of-the-money put provides insurance with a deductible; the deductible amount is the amount by which the put is out of the money.

One issue addressed in hedging bonds with short futures not yet addressed in this section is accrued interest. When a put is bought against a bond, the bond holder continues to earn interest. Thus, to include accrued interest in the gain/loss profile of a bond and a long put, the gain/loss profile must be moved upward by the amount of accrued interest over the holding period, as shown in Exhibit 15. The maximum net loss is, thus, not the put premium but the put premium minus the accrued interest over the holding period. And for high coupon rates and low put premiums, the maximum loss on the combined position may actually be a gain.

SELL CALLS (COVERED CALL WRITING)—YIELD ENHANCEMENT

Holding a bond is a bull position. To provide protection against market declines for a bull position requires a bear position. Short futures and

EXHIBIT 15:
GAIN/LOSS PROFILE FOR BOND AND LONG PUT, INCLUDING ACCRUED INTEREST

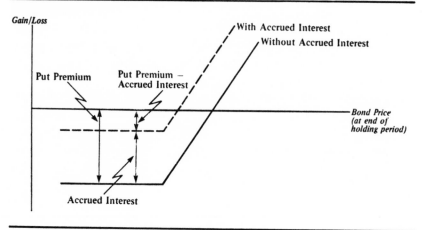

long puts, discussed earlier, are both bear positions. The types of protection these positions afford has been discussed.

In this section a third type of bear position that can be used against a bond position, a call position, is discussed. A call option is an instrument that permits the buyer to demand delivery, or "call," the specified instrument, at his option, from the call seller at the call's strike price. As with puts, the buyer pays the seller a premium for this option.

Exhibit 16 shows the gain/loss profiles for a long and a short 96 call with an initial premium of 3 when the bond price is 96, that is, for an at-the-money call. Buying a call, as shown, is a bull position, and selling a call is a bear position.

Selling (or writing) a call provides a profit equal to the initial premium of 3 if the market remains constant at 96. For market price decreases the call expires worthless, and the seller retains the initial premium collected, that is, the profit on the short call is the initial premium, 3. If the market price increases and is above 96 at the option's expiration, however, the call has (intrinsic) value at expiration, and the call seller loses dollar for dollar the amount by which the bond price is above 96.

Thus, although a long put is a bear strategy with limited loss and unlimited gain, a short call is a bear strategy with the opposite gain/loss profile, that is with unlimited loss and limited gain.

EXHIBIT 16:
GAIN/LOSS PROFILE FOR LONG AND SHORT CALL

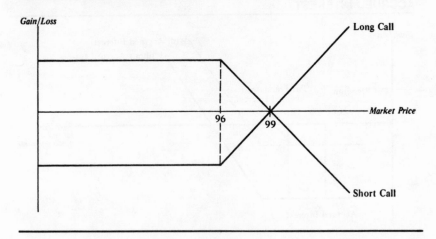

What happens when an at-the-money short call, a bear strategy, is combined with a long bond position? The gain/loss profile for this combination is shown in Figure 17 along with a profile for a naked bond.

The purchase of an at-the-money call does not limit the downside loss to any specified amount, as do short futures and long puts. For bond price decreases the loss on the bond/short call position is the amount lost on the bond less 3, the initial premium collected. Of course this outcome is better than that for the naked bond position itself, even though the loss is not limited to a specific amount.

At a stable price of 96 the combined bond/short call portfolio provides a gain of 3, the call premium initially collected.

For increases in bond prices the gain is limited to 3, the amount of premium collected. This is because at a bond price above the strike price of 96 the short call will be exercised at the strike price, and no additional gain will result from further price increases. Thus, the gain on a bond/short call portfolio is limited to the premium collected.

As shown in Exhibit 17, above a bond price of 99 the combined portfolio will show a smaller gain than a naked bond position. Below a bond price of 99 the combined portfolio has a greater gain/smaller loss than a naked bond position.

In summary, the sale of an at-the-money call against a bond does not

EXHIBIT 17:
GAIN/LOSS PROFILE FOR LONG BOND/SHORT CALL

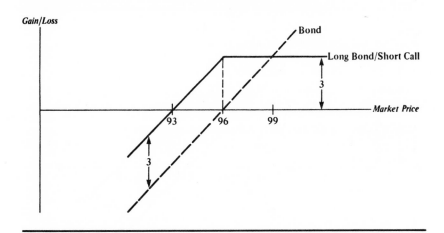

EXHIBIT 18:
IN-, AT-, AND OUT-OF-THE-MONEY SHORT CALLS

					Maximum Profit		
	Strike Price	Premium	Intrinsic Value	Time Value	Amount	At or Below	Break-even*
Out-of-the-money	100	2	0	2	2	100	102
At-the-money	96	3	0	3	3	96	99
In-the-money	92	6	4	2	6	92	98

limit the loss when the price decreases but reduces it by the amount of the premium. Gains are limited for a bond price increase to the amount of the premium. With stable markets, however, selling a call against a bond provides a gain. These results are opposite from those for combining a long put with a bond.

What effects do selling in- and out-of-the-money calls have on combined bond/short call positions? To answer this question, consider the gain/loss profiles of in- and out-of-the-money short calls. The gain/loss profiles of the in- (92 strike price) and out-of-the-money (100 strike price) short calls described in Exhibit 18 are shown in Exhibit 19.

EXHIBIT 19:
GAIN/LOSS PROFILE OF IN-, AT-, AND OUT-OF-THE-MONEY SHORT CALLS

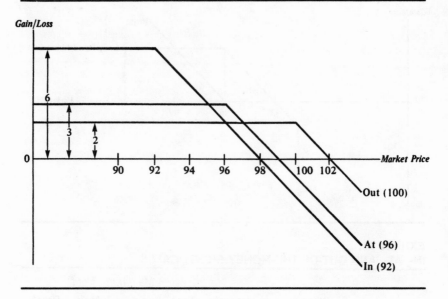

At a constant bond price, 96, the gain on both the in- and the out-of-the-money calls equals 2, their initial time value. As indicated earlier, at constant bond prices the gain in the at-the-money call is also its initial time value, in this case, 3.

For decreases in the bond price, however, the in-the-money call will provide a greater gain because the initial intrinsic value of the call will decrease. At a bond price below 92 the total intrinsic value of the 92 call will collapse (and the call will not be exercised), resulting in a gain of 6 on the short call. Of course, the at-the-money (96) and out-of-the-money (100) calls do not have any initial intrinsic values, and their maximum gains, which equal their premiums (which are all time value), are achieved at any market price below the strike price. In any case, for a bond price decrease the maximum gain on in-, at-, and out-of-the-money short calls is the initial premium collected.

For bond price increases, if the final bond price is above the strike price, the call will be exercised by the long and must be delivered on by the short. Thus, above the call's strike price the gain will decrease. The break-even price for the short call will then be the strike price plus the premium initially collected. The break-even points for the three calls considered in this example are:

In-the-money (92):	98 (92 + 6)
At-the-money (96):	99 (96 + 3)
Out-of-the-money (100):	102 (100 + 2)

What are the results of writing in- and out-of-the-money calls against a bond? The gain/loss profiles of the combinations are shown in Exhibit 20 along with the results for the at-the-money call and a naked bond. Exhibit 21 summarizes the results.

For at-the-money calls, as discussed earlier, for a constant bond price the bond/short call combination provides a gain of 3, the premium, whereas the naked bond position breaks even. For price increases this combination provides a maximum effective bond price of 99, the strike price plus the premium, because at any market price above the strike price the bond will be called away.

Similarly, for in- and out-of-the-money calls combined with a bond, for bond price decreases, the opportunity gain for combined bond/short

EXHIBIT 20:
GAIN/LOSS PROFILE OF IN-, AT-, AND OUT-OF-THE-MONEY SHORT CALLS AND BOND

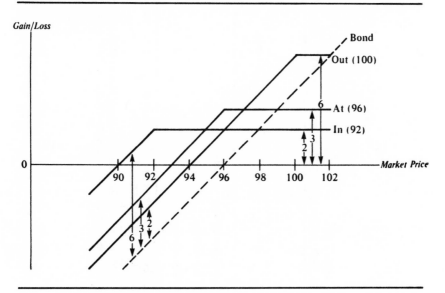

EXHIBIT 21:
IN-, AT-, AND OUT-OF-THE-MONEY SHORT CALLS WITH BOND

	Strike Price	Premium	Intrinsic Value	Time Value	Maximum Profit			Break-even Level (4)	Opportunity Loss in Loss Range (5)
					Amount (1)	Maximum Level (2)	At or Above (3)		
Out-of-the-money	100	2	0	2	6	102	100	94	2
At-the-money	96	3	0	3	3	99	96	93	3
In-the-money	92	6	4	2	2	98	92	90	6

(1) Equals out-of-the-money amount, if any, plus time value of premium.
(2) Equals strike price plus premium.
(3) Equals strike price.
(4) Equals strike price minus time value minus out-of-the-money amount.
(5) Equals premium collected (time value plus in-the-money amount).

call portfolios is the initial call premium, since it is the profit on the short call for a market decline (below its strike price). For bond price increases, however, the maximum effective bond price that can be achieved equals the strike price of the call (above the strike price the bond will be called away) plus the initial premium, which is retained. Of course, the higher the strike price the lower the premium.

Over all, then, if a high-strike-price (out-of-the-money) call is sold, there is a large maximum potential gain, but because the premium will be low there is little downside opportunity gain. Or if a low-strike-price (in-the-money) call is sold, there is little upside potential (the maximum effective price will be the strike price plus the initial premium, which equals the initial market price plus the initial time value of the call), but there is a high downside opportunity gain. Again, this is a typical trade-off.

In the same manner in which accrued interest is earned while a bond is hedged with a short future or insured with a long put, accrued interest is also earned while carrying a bond covered with a short call. Thus, to include accrued interest the gain/loss profile of a bond combined with a short call should be moved upward by the amount of accrued interest over the holding period, as shown in Exhibit 22.

EXHIBIT 22:
GAIN/LOSS PROFILE FOR BOND AND SHORT CALL, INCLUDING
ACCRUED INTEREST

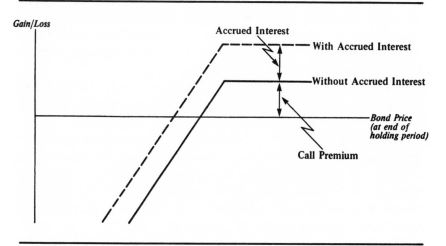

SIMULATION RESULTS

The three previous sections of this chapter discuss three types of bear strategies that can be combined with holding a bond or a bond portfolio. Of course, the bond could also be carried naked. This section provides results of simulations of buying puts and selling calls of varying strike prices against the 10⅜% Treasury bond of 11/15/12 for various changes in the price of the bond from minus 10 to plus 10 and compares these results with those of carrying the bond hedged with short futures contracts and unhedged.

Exhibits 23 and 24 show the rates of return for buying puts and selling calls of various strike prices, respectively, in conjunction with holding the bond. Each exhibit also shows the results for carrying the bond hedged with short futures and unhedged.

Note that the rate of return from hedging the bond with short futures is essentially independent of market moves. This return is approximately 7.4%, the surrogate for the risk-free rate of return. And, of course, the rate of return on the unhedged bond varies widely, from a negative 48.7% for a decrease in the price of the 10⅜% bond to a positive 74.8% for a price increase of 10. This lack of symmetry, that is, the greater gain than loss for the same price change, results from accrued interest on the bond.

Several observations on buying puts against bonds can be made on the basis of Exhibit 23. First, note that the losses are limited for all strike prices. This is demonstrated by the fact that the rates of return for all strike prices are approximately the same for market declines of 8 and 10. And the rate of return would be the same for all greater price decreases. However, given this similarity across strike prices, there are three important differences among the strike prices.

First, the magnitude of the minimum return is smallest for the lowest (most out-of-the-money) strike price and greatest for the highest (most in-the-money) strike price.

Second, the market price at which the minimum return is achieved is lower the lower the strike price (the more out of the money). For example, for the 56 strike price the minimum return of minus 30.5% is achieved with a decline of 8, while for 58 strike price the minimum return of minus 18.4% is achieved with a decline of 5. Exhibit 25 summarizes these results for all strike prices.

Third, for any given bond price increase the rate of return is higher

EXHIBIT 23:
T-BOND FUTURES OPTIONS
PROTECTIVE PUT BUYING STRATEGY
RATE OF RETURN SUMMARY

		Change in Price of Bond (in points)														
Puts		−10	−8	−5	−4	−3	−2	−1	0	+1	+2	+3	+4	+5	+8	+10
Premium	*Strike*															
0.23	56	−30.59	−30.52	−20.48	−14.34	−8.19	−2.05	4.09	10.23	16.37	22.52	28.66	34.80	40.94	59.37	71.66
0.50	58	−18.37	−18.30	−18.32	−17.45	−11.35	−5.25	0.85	6.95	13.05	19.15	25.26	31.36	37.46	55.76	67.96
1.32	60	−8.51	−8.45	−8.47	−8.55	−8.40	−8.48	−4.57	1.46	7.49	13.53	19.56	25.59	31.62	49.72	61.79
2.35	62	−1.32	−1.25	−1.27	−1.35	−1.21	−1.29	−1.37	−1.22	−0.38	5.55	11.49	17.42	23.36	41.16	53.03
3.57	64	3.47	3.53	3.52	3.44	3.58	3.50	3.42	3.56	3.48	3.40	3.55	7.32	13.13	30.58	42.21
5.38	66	5.48	5.55	5.53	5.45	5.59	5.51	5.43	5.57	5.50	5.42	5.56	5.48	5.62	17.76	29.10
Short Futures @ 60-19																
(SEP 84)		7.42	7.49	7.47	7.39	7.54	7.45	7.37	7.52	7.43	7.35	7.50	7.42	7.57	7.55	7.38
Unhedged		−48.71	−36.36	−17.83	−11.65	−5.47	0.71	6.88	13.06	19.24	25.42	31.60	37.77	43.95	62.48	74.84

Assumptions:

- Date of calculation: 6/11/84.
- Bond hedged: 10⅜% of 11/15/12 (also the cheapest deliverable bond).
- Initial bond price 76-30
- Initial futures price (SEP 84 futures contract): 60-19.
- The hedge ratio is the conversion factor for the 10⅜% bond, the cheapest deliverable.

EXHIBIT 24:
T-BOND FUTURES OPTIONS
COVERED CALL WRITING STRATEGY
RATE OF RETURN SUMMARY

Calls								Change in Price of Bond (in points)								
Premium	Strike	−10	−8	−5	−4	−3	−2	−1	0	+1	+2	+3	+4	+5	+8	+10
4.44	56	−13.60	−0.24	8.86	8.77	8.94	8.84	8.75	8.92	8.82	8.73	8.89	8.80	8.97	8.95	8.76
3.17	58	−24.84	−11.80	7.76	13.26	13.42	13.33	13.24	13.40	13.31	13.22	13.38	13.29	13.46	13.44	13.25
2.04	60	−33.94	−21.16	−1.99	4.40	10.79	17.18	19.33	19.49	19.40	19.31	19.47	19.38	19.54	19.52	19.34
1.11	62	−40.44	−27.85	−8.96	−2.66	3.63	9.93	16.23	22.52	27.84	27.75	27.90	27.82	27.97	27.96	27.78
0.37	64	−44.67	−32.20	−13.49	−7.26	−1.02	5.21	11.45	17.48	23.92	30.16	36.39	38.49	38.65	38.63	38.45
0.17	66	−46.87	−34.46	−15.85	−9.64	−3.44	2.77	8.97	15.18	21.38	27.58	33.79	39.99	46.20	51.50	51.33
Short Futures @ 60-19																
(SEP 84)		7.42	7.49	7.47	7.39	7.54	7.45	7.37	7.52	7.43	7.35	7.50	7.42	7.57	7.55	7.38
Unhedged		−48.71	−36.36	−17.83	−11.65	−5.47	0.71	6.88	13.06	19.24	25.42	31.60	37.77	43.95	62.48	74.84

Assumptions:

- Date of calculation: 6/11/84.
- Bond hedged: 10⅜% of 11/15/12 (also the cheapest deliverable bond).
- Initial bond price 76-30
- Initial futures price (SEP 84 futures contract): 60-19.
- The hedge ratio is the conversion factor for the 10⅜% bond, the cheapest deliverable.

EXHIBIT 25:
SUMMARY OF EXHIBIT 23—PUT BUYING

Price	Minimum Return	Price Below Which Minimum Return Is Achieved
56	− 30.5%	− 8
58	− 18.4	− 5
60	− 8.5	− 2
62	− 1.3	− 1
64	3.5	+ 3
66	5.5	+ 5

the lower the strike price (provided the bond price is above the put's strike price).

Thus, as discussed in the second section, there is a tradeoff across strike prices, that is, for a given strike price the higher the minimum return locked in the lower the rate of return for a market price increase. Exhibit 26, which plots the rates of return shown in Exhibit 23 for selected strike prices against various market moves, illustrates these observations. These results are consistent with the discussion in the second section.

The simulation results for writing covered calls of varying strike prices against the 10⅜% bond, shown in Exhibit 24, are also consistent with the discussion in the third section. For covered call writing a maximum rate of return is achieved for all strike prices. Note specifically that the rate of return for each strike price is approximately the same for price increases of 8 and 10.

But for covered call writing there are also three differences across strike prices. First, the higher the strike price (the more out of the money) the higher the maximum return. Second, the lower the strike price (the more in the money), the lower the price at which the maximum return is achieved. For example, for a 56 strike price the maximum return of 8.8% is achieved at − 5, while for a 58 strike price the maximum return of 13.3% is achieved at − 4. Exhibit 27 summarizes these results across strike prices. Third, for any given market price decrease (for which losses on covered calls are unlimited) the loss is less the lower the strike price.

Exhibit 28 shows a plot of the rates of return of selected strike prices against various market moves based on Exhibit 24.

RATES OF RETURN OF VARIOUS STRIKE PRICES
BOND/LONG PUT POSITIONS

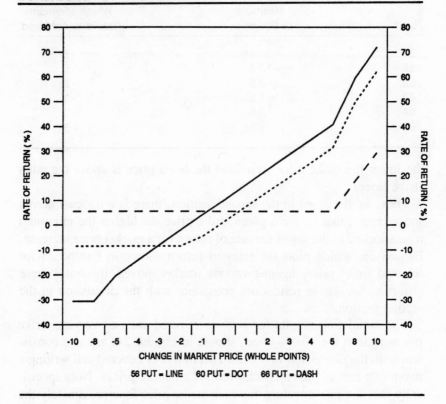

56 PUT = LINE   60 PUT = DOT   66 PUT = DASH

EXHIBIT 27:
SUMMARY OF EXHIBIT 24—CALL WRITING

Price	Maximum Return	Price Above Which Maximum Return Is Achieved
56	8.8%	−5
58	13.4	−4
60	19.4	−1
62	27.8	+1
64	38.6	+4
66	51.5	+8

EXHIBIT 28:
RATES OF RETURN OF VARIOUS STRIKE PRICES
BOND/SHORT CALL POSITIONS

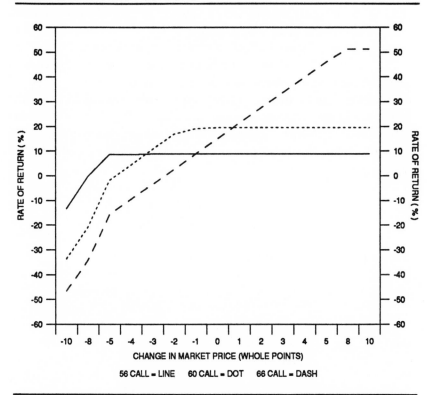

56 CALL = LINE   60 CALL = DOT   66 CALL = DASH

Thus, as discussed in the third section, there is also a trade-off for covered calls across strike prices: The higher the strike price of the call (that is, the more out of the money) the higher the maximum return (because the price at which the bond will be called away is higher) but the smaller the rate of return for price decreases (because the premium collected for the out-of-the-money call will be less).

As indicated earlier, accrued interest is included in these simulations.

In evaluating the gain/loss profiles of bond/long put and bond/short call combinations two relationships or equivalencies should be recognized. The bond/long put gain/loss profile, shown in Exhibit 10, is equivalent to that of a long call, as is evident from Exhibit 16. In addition, the bond/short call gain/loss profile shown in Exhibit 17 is equivalent to that of a short put, as is evident from Exhibit 9 (the gain/loss profile of the short put is the negative of that for the long put shown). So insuring a bond with a long put is equivalent to buying a call and covering a bond with a short call. The rate of return profiles in Exhibits 26 and 28 are indicative of these equivalencies.

Prior to considering the joint role of buying puts and selling calls in bond portfolio management, as is done in the next section, two types of observations can be made. The first type of observation concerns the difference in the behavior of bonds combined with long puts and short calls. These differences, discussed in detail above, are summarized in the table below for bond prices decreasing, remaining constant and increasing.

| | Bond Price Change | | |
	Decrease	**Constant**	**Increase**
Bond and long put	Loss limited	Loss	Gain limited but reduced by premium
Bond and short call	Loss not limited but reduced by premium	Gain	Gain limited

The second type of observation concerns the difference between the behavior of different strike prices of either bonds covered with long puts or short calls in terms of the aggressiveness of the strategy.

Obviously a naked bond is a very aggressive strategy—it maximizes gain if bond prices increase and maximizes loss if bond prices decrease. And a bond hedged with a short futures position is least aggressive—it minimizes both gain and loss. How do the strike prices of puts and calls affect the aggressiveness of bonds combined with long puts and short calls?

Consider long puts first. As shown in Exhibits 23 and 26, for bonds combined with long puts the lower the strike price, that is the more out of the money the put, the greater the gain if bond prices increase and the greater the loss if bond prices decrease, that is the more aggressive the outcome. Thus, the more out of the money the put the more the outcome of the bond combined with the put is like that of a naked bond.

But the higher the strike price of the put, that is the more in the money the put, the less the gain if bond prices increase and the less the loss if bond prices decrease, that is the less aggressive the outcome. Thus, the more in the money the put the more the outcome of the bond combined with the put is like that of a bond hedged with a short futures.

As shown in Exhibits 24 and 28, for bonds covered with short calls the higher the strike price of the call, that is the more out of the money the call, the greater the gain if bond prices increase and the greater the loss if bond prices decrease, that is the more aggressive the outcome. And the lower the strike price of the call, the less aggressive the outcome. So for bonds combined with short calls, the more out of the money the call the more the outcome is like that of a naked bond and the more in the money the call the more the outcome is like that of a bond hedged with a short futures position.

These observations are summarized in Exhibit 29.

In determining the strike price of a put bought or a call sold in conjunction with a bond or bond portfolio, the aggressiveness of the outcome desired should be considered in selecting the strike price.

SELECTION OF OPTIMAL STRATEGY

This chapter discusses three different strategies that can be combined with a bond. Which is the optimal strategy? The answer to this question is an unequivocal "It depends." The answer depends largely on two issues, both related to the cost of the strategy. The two types of costs are out-of-pocket costs and opportunity costs.

The three types of strategies have different out-of-pocket costs. For a short futures position, there is no out-of-pocket cost (other than the commission). The initial margin is simply earnest money, which will be returned if the futures price remains the same.

For the long put the out-of-pocket cost is the premium, which must be paid in cash. This premium has two components: the intrinsic value and the time value. The premium varies with the strike price of the put, and the purchaser of the put can select the strike price. But the premium also depends on other factors over which the put purchaser has no control, such as the volatility of the underlying bond and the short-term interest rate. Obviously, the higher the put premium the less likely a bond holder is to buy a put to provide downside protection.

On the other hand, since a call writer collects the call premium, the

EXHIBIT 29:
AGGRESSIVENESS OF BONDS COMBINED WITH LONG PUTS AND SHORT CALLS BY STRIKE PRICE

Most aggressive		Naked bond
	Bond combined with short call	
Bond combined with long put	Out-of-the-money (high strike price)	
Out-of-the-money (low strike price)	At-the-money	
At-the-money	In-the-money (low strike price)	
In-the-money (high strike price)		
Least aggressive		Bond hedged with short futures

out-of-pocket cost to a call writer is negative. And the higher the premium the more likely it is that a bond holder will sell a call against his bond.

So the higher the premium the more likely it is that a bond holder will sell a call and collect the premium, and the lower the premium the more likely it is that the bond holder will pay the premium and buy a put.[6]

In the intermediate premium range a bond holder may decide neither to pay the premium and buy a put nor collect the premium and sell a call, but rather to sell a futures contract at a zero out-of-pocket cost.

The second type of cost that may affect the selection of the strategy is the opportunity cost of the strategy. The opportunity cost is the potential profit forgone by selecting the strategy if the bond price increases. As discussed, the opportunity cost of a short futures contract is the total potential gain (in excess of the risk-free rate of return). The bond holder could also avert all capital risk by selling the bond and buying a risk-free instrument, a strategy equivalent to a short futures hedge.[7]

The opportunity cost of the put buyer is the initial premium paid. The opportunity cost of a call writer equals all gains in excess of the strike price less the initial call premium.

Based on opportunity cost, or the foregone potential for gain, the ranking of the potential strategies by aggressiveness, that is the degree of bullishness or bearishness, is as shown below:

Most Aggressive (Most bullish; least bearish)
   (1) Hold bond
   (2) Hold bond and buy put
   (3) Hold bond and sell call
   (4) Hold bond and sell futures
       (or sell bond and buy risk-free instrument)
Least Aggressive (Least bullish; most bearish)

Thus, the bond holder's market view will affect the strategy chosen. A bullish investor is most likely to choose strategy (1) and least likely

---

[6]The put and call premiums with the same strike price are related by a concept called "put-call parity."

[7]Some technical factors related to the pricing of the futures contract, indicated above, could modify this conclusion somewhat.

to choose strategy (4). And a bearish investor is most likely to choose strategy (4) and least likely to choose strategy (1).

In general, both the level of the put/call premium and the view of the bond holder will determine the appropriate strategy for the bond holder.

The gain/loss profiles of strategies for varying market views by the initial bond holder that are, in fact, vindicated, are shown in Exhibit 30. Exhibit 30 which excludes accrued interest, is a combination of Exhibit 1, a long bond excluding accrued interest; Exhibit 5, a bond hedged with a short futures position excluding accrued interest (assuming the initial futures price equals the bond price); and Exhibit 17, a bond covered by a short (at-the-money) call excluding accrued interest. For an expected large increase in market price the bond holder will optimally hold the bond naked, that is, without any corresponding bear instrument (short futures, long put, or short call). For an expected large market decline the bond holder will optimally hedge the bond with a short futures contract (or, equivalently, sell the bond and buy a risk-free instrument). For an expected stable market, or a market in which prices are expected to increase or decrease only slightly, selling a call for which a premium is collected is optimal.

EXHIBIT 30:
GAIN/LOSS PROFILES FOR OPTIMAL STRATEGIES

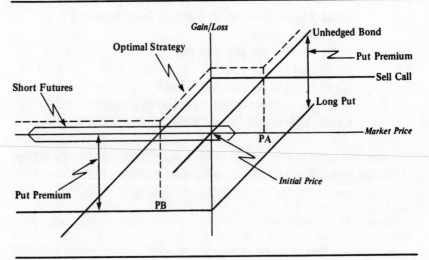

For a final market price above PA in Exhibit 30 the unhedged bond would be optimal. For a final price below PB selling a futures contract against the bond would be optimal. For the final market prices between PB and PA selling a call against the bond would be optimal. The optimal outcome across all expected views or outcomes is shown by the dotted line in Exhibit 30. This line could be viewed as the return due to perfect market timing.

Note that buying a put is not yet considered an optimal strategy for any specific market view in Exhibit 30. How does buying a put compare with these optimal strategies? This is shown by the "Long Put" curve in Exhibit 30 for an at-the-money put. Accrued interest is not included in the optimal strategy gain/loss profile for the bond/long put gain/loss profile (as in Exhibit 10).

Note that for final prices above PA and below PB in Exhibit 30 the amount by which the return to a put buyer is inferior to that to a bond manager who selected the optimal strategy (unhedged bond or bond hedged with short futures) is the initial put premium. Between PB and PA the advantage of the optimal strategy (bond covered with short call) over a put buyer exceeds the put premium by a variable amount.[8]

Exhibit 30 does not include accrued interest. Accrued interest over the holding period is, however, included in Exhibit 31. In Exhibit 31 the gain/loss profiles for the unhedged bond and the bond covered with a short call are moved upward by the accrued interest over the holding period. And the gain/loss profile for the bond hedged with a short futures contract is moved upward by an amount equal to the financing cost over the holding period. (It is also assumed that the initial futures price does not equal the bond price but differs by the net carry cost.) Specifically, Exhibit 31 is the combination of Exhibit 2, for the naked bond; Exhibit 22, for the bond covered with short calls; and Exhibit 8, for a bond hedged with short futures. The optimal strategies over actual or expected final prices are shown by the dotted line in Exhibit 31. The choice of the optimal strategy excluding accrued interest, Exhibit 30, and including accrued interest, Exhibit 31, is similar.

The gain/loss profile for the bond/long put combination including accrued interest (Exhibit 15), is also shown in Exhibit 31. This gain/

---

[8]Theoretically, the return to a bond portfolio manager who has perfect market timing should equal the amount of the advantage of the optimal strategy over the bond/long put strategy weighted by the probability of the final market prices.

EXHIBIT 31:
GAIN/LOSS PROFILES FOR OPTIMAL STRATEGIES VS. BUYING PUT—
INCLUDING ACCRUED INTEREST

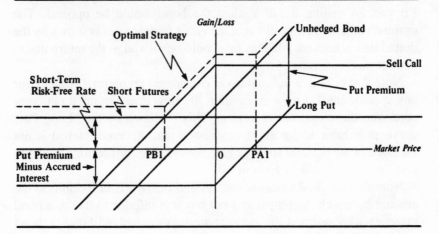

loss profile is that for the long put shown in Exhibit 30 moved up by the amount of accrued interest.

Again, the outcome of the bond/long put combination is inferior to that of the optimal strategy (unhedged bond, bond covered with short call or bond hedged with short futures position) for any bond price change but is superior to the results of these strategies for price changes for which they are not the optimal strategy.

An interpretation of this observation is that, although carrying the bond unhedged, hedging with short futures, or selling calls against the bond may be optimal for specific market outcomes, buying a put against the bond may be the optimal strategy when no view is firmly held or, alternatively, may be the optimal strategy across all views.

CONCLUSION

This chapter summarizes the types of Treasury bond futures and option transactions that can be executed in conjunction with holding a bond or a bond portfolio and that alter the gain/loss profile of the bond or portfolio.

Typically bond portfolio managers who pursue active strategies alter the gain/loss profiles of their portfolios due to changing market views by changing the maturity (or duration) of their portfolios. The transactions described in this chapter provide alternative ways to alter the gain/loss profile of a bond or a portfolio of bonds, often more quickly and less expensively than can be accomplished by maturity/duration changes.

As discussed in this chapter, for a bullish market view carrying the bond or bond portfolio naked is optimal. For a bearish market view hedging the bond or bond portfolio with futures, which is equivalent to swapping into a bill, is optimal. For a neutral market view selling calls against the bond or bond portfolio provides the greatest return.

Finally, if no view is held, buying a put against the bond or portfolio may provide the highest return against all market outcomes. In this context, thus, put buying against a bond portfolio could be considered a passive strategy alternative to other commonly used passive strategies.

On the other hand, changing among carrying the bonds with no related futures or options position, selling calls against the bonds and hedging the bonds with short futures, depending on the portfolio manager's market view, may be the ultimate in market timing, that is active management, an alternative to altering the maturity/duration of the portfolio.

Thus, Treasury bond futures and options can be used in implementing either active or passive bond portfolio strategies.

CHAPTER 16

Decreasing the Financial Risk of Pension Plans*

JO ANN CORKRAN
VICE PRESIDENT
PORTFOLIO STRATEGIES DEPARTMENT
THE FIRST BOSTON CORPORATION

MICHAEL PESKIN
VICE PRESIDENT
MORGAN STANLEY

Since the appearance of FASB No. 87, there has been much publicity concerning the potentially adverse effects of the new rules on corporate financial statements. Currently, many new investment strategies are being proposed to alleviate the impact of the statement. While some of these strategies may be appropriate, there is a danger that many plan sponsors will focus solely on smoothing accounting results at the expense of long-term economic performance. Although plan sponsors

*The authors would like to thank the following individuals for their contribution to this chapter: Jonathan Lieber, Doris Meister, and Buddy Powers.

361

should review the extent of their new exposure due to FASB 87, most sponsors can use simple adjustments to investment and accounting policies to control financial statement risks effectively enough. Sponsors who do need more control should consider a fundamental change in investment strategy *only* after careful analysis of the risk/return tradeoffs inherent in their particular plan.

This chapter is designed to help plan sponsors consider how best to respond to FASB 87. The following concerns are addressed:

- Implications of FASB 87 on financial statements.
- Other implications of FASB 87 on the corporate level.
- Corporations likely to be affected by FASB 87.
- Risks involved with changing asset allocation.
- Prudent response to FASB 87.

IMPLICATIONS OF FASB 87 ON FINANCIAL STATEMENTS

One key stipulation of FASB 87 is that pension plan liabilities must now be valued each year using a "market" discount rate. Since sponsors have previously used a variety of discount rates to value their liabilities, this rule will make asset/liability ratios much more comparable among companies as well as more realistic. Further, prior to FASB 87, plan sponsors could use the discount rate to regulate asset/liability ratios, or surplus, and expense. Without control over the discount rate, asset/liability ratios and plan surpluses will become more volatile. These changes could have several effects on sponsors' financial statements.

(1) Most sponsors will have larger swings in reported annual pension expense, because yearly changes in plan surpluses will be more quickly reflected in annual cost calculations under FASB 87.

Exhibit 1 shows changes in a typical plan's assets and liabilities since 1973. The assets were assumed to be invested in a 60%-40% stock-bond portfolio structured using market capitalization weightings. Liabilities are discounted at the then current long-term Treasury yield. Exhibit 2 shows the asset/liability or funded ratio over the same time period.

Exhibit 3 shows how the funded ratio changes above could have translated into annual expense changes under pre-FASB 87 accounting standards and under the FASB rules. Under FASB 87, changes in the

EXHIBIT 1:
PENSION PLAN ASSETS AND LIABILITIES—
JANUARY 1973-AUGUST 1987

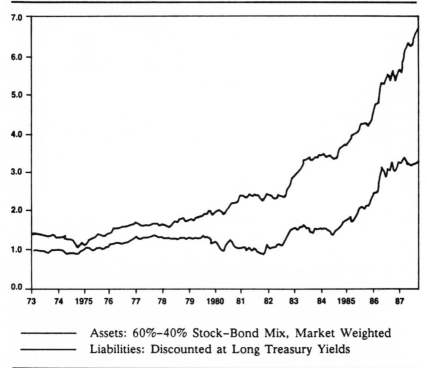

——————— Assets: 60%–40% Stock–Bond Mix, Market Weighted
——————— Liabilities: Discounted at Long Treasury Yields

funding ratios are very quickly reflected in changes in expense. The decline in the ratio in 1982 and 1985-1986 is reflected in sharply rising expense in 1983 and 1986-1987. The increase in ratio from 1979-1981 and in 1983 would have been mirrored by declines in expense in the following periods. The old rules, which allowed major smoothing of asset and liability changes, bear almost no relationship to the ratio of assets to liabilities. In addition, the magnitude of expense changes would have been significantly greater under the FASB standard in most years.

(2) Some sponsors will have a potential balance sheet liability, if their ratio of the market value of plan assets to the Accumulated Benefit Obligation (ABO)[1] falls below 100%.

---

[1]For a definition of terms and a brief discussion of FASB 87, see Appendix A.

EXHIBIT 2:
FUNDED RATIOS—JANUARY 1973-AUGUST 1987

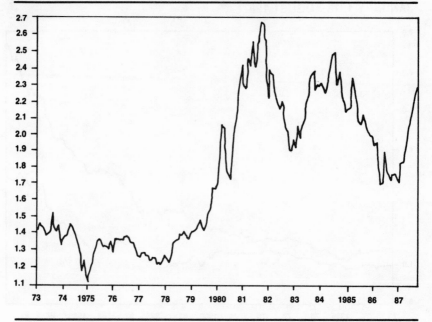

(3) Those sponsors with visibly deteriorating surpluses (and the increased expenses and potential liabilities these imply) may face increased corporate borrowing costs.

OTHER IMPLICATIONS OF FASB 87 ON THE CORPORATE LEVEL

FASB 87 has implications for more than financial statements. The more realistic and timely calculations of pension expense and balance sheet liabilities required under FASB 87 will serve to highlight the effects of sponsoring a pension plan that have previously been disguised. These effects include:

An increase in corporate interest rate exposure. Under FASB 87, the impact of pension plans on a corporation's financial statements can be extremely interest rate sensitive. Where pension plans are large relative

EXHIBIT 3:
CHANGES IN EXPENSE—FASB 87 STANDARD VERSUS
PRIOR ACCOUNTING RULES

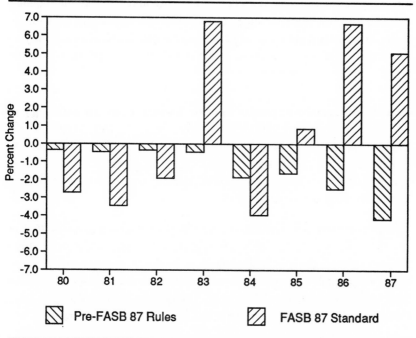

to the assets of the corporation, this sensitivity can fundamentally alter the interest-rate sensitivity of the entire corporation. Fortunately, this interest rate sensitivity is adjustable, and sponsors can act to control the effects of rate exposure.

Earlier indication of trends in cash costs. FASB 87 will change the way pension expense is *reported*; increased or decreased expense on the statements will not force sponsors to alter contributions immediately if sponsors continue to fund the pension plan on former principles. Nevertheless, the realistic calculations on the financial statement will provide early information about contribution requirements. If assets are not keeping pace with the value of liabilities, expenses will rise immediately; a greater infusion of cash may be postponable, but it will not be avoidable forever. Conversely, expenses considerably below cash contributions signal future declines in allowable deductions.

Direct pension plan impact on competitive position. Plan surpluses under FASB 87 will be comparable between companies. Changes in these surpluses translate quickly into expense and possibly into balance sheet liabilities. Thus, changes in earnings and financial ratios due to the relative performance of a plan's assets and liabilities may play an important role in evaluating a corporation's competitive position among comparable entities.

CORPORATIONS LIKELY TO BE AFFECTED BY FASB 87

Some companies will be far more vulnerable to the financial statement effects we have just described than others. Pension sponsors should consider the potential effects of FASB 87 if their company falls into one of these two categories:

15% of the current service cost plus 1% of plan assets exceeds 10% of pre-tax earnings. Although it is very difficult to generalize on what is a reasonable expected annual change in expense, experience suggests that a reasonable change in expense can be approximated by adding 15% of the current service cost to 1% of plan assets. Clearly, cash flows could be substantially affected under these circumstances.

Pension assets are greater than or equal to net worth. Where surplus is limited, a decline in assets relative to liabilities could put the plan in or near a disclosure position of substantial size. Even where surplus is large, such a decline could affect market valuation given the increasing sophistication of the marketplace.

RISKS INVOLVED WITH CHANGING ASSET ALLOCATION

FASB 87 increases the risk of sponsoring a pension plan. Much of this risk is interest rate risk, which can be easily managed. Other risks, however, are more complex to manage and attempting to do so could incur unexpected long-term costs.

For example, if a plan sponsor's goal were only to smooth changes in expense and balance sheet liability disclosures, the sponsor would want plan assets and liabilities to move exactly in tandem, since changes in asset/liability ratios and plan surplus cause the annual fluctuations. Over the short term, the value of liabilities is closely related to interest rates and is largely unaffected by other factors. A sponsor, therefore, would invest all assets in a portfolio of securities that has a price sensitivity to interest rates (i.e., a duration) similar to that of the liabilities. Pension plan liabilities, whether measured by the Projected Benefit Obligation (PBO) or Accumulated Benefit Obligation (ABO), are very sensitive to changes in interest rates. A bond portfolio matching these liabilities could have a duration two or three times greater than that of a traditional pension plan bond portfolio. Even bond portfolios matched (or dedicated) against retiree liability will need to be lengthened. This portfolio restructuring, along with the accounting considerations suggested in the next section, would smooth financial statement numbers as much as possible.

Unfortunately, other less desirable results could also be expected from the switch from equity to bonds. Since equities have historically outperformed bonds over extended time periods, this strategy would be expected to eventually lower total returns. Lower total returns on assets will result in lower funded levels and higher expense.

Exhibit 4 shows the funded ratios since 1980 of a pension plan with assets invested in the traditional 60%-40% stock-bond asset mix. Exhibit 5 shows the results for the same period if the plan's assets had been invested in an all bond portfolio with duration matched to that of the liabilities. The ratios of assets to liabilities in Exhibit 4 vary erratically from 150% to 250%, while those in Exhibit 5 are near constant at 145%.

On the other hand, the exposure to stocks in Exhibit 4 allows the value of the plan's ratio to quickly exceed that of the all bond portfolio since stocks returned more than bonds over the period shown. Hence, expenses of the plan in Exhibit 4 will eventually be less than those of the plan in Exhibit 5. Although the relationships between stocks and bonds in the period shown are not meant to be indicative of future expectations, it is important to remember that cumulative stock returns in excess of bond returns will eventually cause lower expense levels independent of the volatility of those expenses.

PRUDENT RESPONSE TO FASB 87

1. Simple Investment Change to Control Interest Rate Exposure

Plan sponsors can balance the short-term goal of limiting annual statement fluctuations and the long-term goal of maintaining or even lowering cost by making a simple investment policy change. Sponsors

EXHIBIT 4:
FUNDED RATIOS, TRADITIONAL PORTFOLIO—
JANUARY 1980-AUGUST 1987

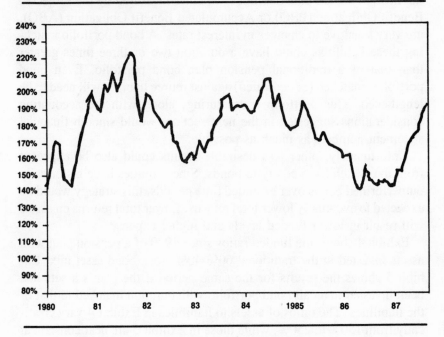

should match the interest rate sensitivity of their investment portfolio to that of their entire pension plan liability. In most cases, this can be accomplished by changing the interest rate sensitivity, or *duration*, of the fixed income portion of the fund only and leaving the allocation between fixed income, equity, and other assets intact. This will help control the new interest rate risks injected into plan sponsorship due to FASB 87 by insuring that changes in the market value of liabilities due to interest rate changes are mirrored by changes in the market value of assets. Equity exposure through asset allocation, which most sponsors have spent considerable time and effort developing, remains unchanged. This technique is generally known as "dollar duration matching," and is demonstrated in Appendix B.

Exhibits 6-9 show the assets, liabilities, and ratios of a pension plan with assets invested in a 60%-40% stock mix. Exhibits 6 and 7 have a

EXHIBIT 5:
FUNDED RATIOS, ALL BOND DURATION MATCHED PORTFOLIO—
JANUARY 1980-AUGUST 1987

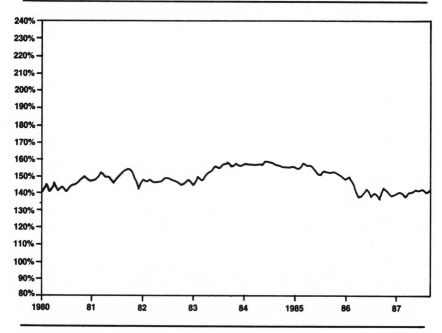

traditional bond portfolio invested according to market capitalization weightings. Exhibits 8 and 9 have a bond portfolio that has been "dollar duration matched" to the plan's PBO. The path of the ratio of assets to liabilities, and hence expenses, in the matched case are substantially smoother than in the traditional bond case.

Exhibit 10 shows the difference in changes in expense, under FASB 87 standards, for the plans in Exhibits 6-9. The plan with the dollar duration matched bond portfolio has significantly smaller changes in expenses from year to year.

In some cases, where there is little exposure to bonds in the current asset mix, it will be difficult or impossible to match the plan's interest-rate sensitivity even using dollar duration matching. Sponsors with heavy equity exposure will tend to be those who have determined that they are not averse to possible fluctuations in asset values. Now, under

EXHIBIT 6:
PENSION PLAN ASSETS AND LIABILITIES, TRADITIONAL
PORTFOLIO—JANUARY 1973-AUGUST 1987

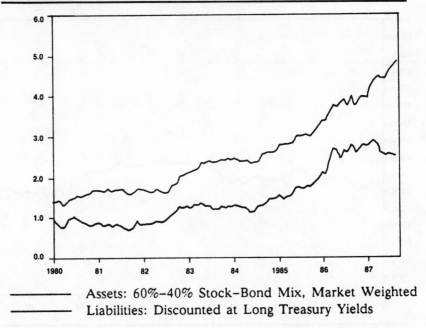

———————— Assets: 60%–40% Stock–Bond Mix, Market Weighted
———————— Liabilities: Discounted at Long Treasury Yields

FASB 87, however, these fluctuations in asset values translate quickly into increased expense volatility. Where this is a concern, an increased exposure to bonds may be appropriate.

In addition to controlling pension plan interest rate exposure, dollar duration matching can be useful in hedging other corporate interest rate exposure. Under FASB 87, market value changes in fixed income assets pass quickly through to the income statement. A plan sponsor could deliberately mismatch and take interest rate risk in the plan in order to offset interest rate exposure in the corporation. For instance, as shown in Exhibit 11, a sponsor could increase the interest rate sensitivity of plan assets to help stabilize the effect of short-term corporate borrowing costs.

In the first part of the exhibit, the pension plan cost is only moderately sensitive to interest rates. Borrowing costs are, however, very sensitive to changes in rates. The pension expense response to rate changes

EXHIBIT 7:
FUNDED RATIOS, TRADITIONAL PORTFOLIO—
JANUARY 1980-AUGUST 1987

is in the opposite direction to the changes in borrowing cost, thus the pension cost acts as a partial hedge. In the second part of the exhibit, the pension plan sensitivity to rate changes has been increased through adjustments in investment policy so as to almost entirely offset the sensitivity of borrowing costs.

2. Use Accounting Flexibility to Smooth Expense Further

The investment recommendations above can greatly reduce pension plan interest rate exposure and the annual expense instability it causes. Nevertheless, there will be some residual interest rate risk. In addition, there will be expense volatility due to plan experience other than interest rate volatility, especially equity experience. While FASB 87 removes much of the accounting freedom sponsors have had in the past to control accounting fluctuations, some flexibility still remains. In

EXHIBIT 8:
PENSION PLAN ASSETS AND LIABILITIES
DOLLAR DURATION MATCHED PORTFOLIO
JANUARY 1980-AUGUST 1987

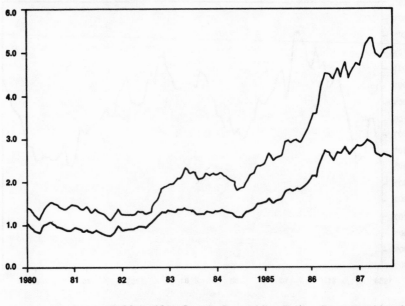

—————— Assets" 60%–40% Stock–Bond Mix, Dollar Duration Matched
—————— Liabilities: Discounted at Long Treasury Yields

particular, the following techniques can provide some additional year-to-year smoothing of expense without any detraction from the intent or realism of the accounting standard.

Choice of discount rate. FASB 87 requires the use of a market-based rate for valuing liabilities but does not specify which one. In any year, there will be a range of acceptable rates. Although wholesale changes from one index to another will probably not be allowed, careful choice among the acceptable rates from year to year can ameliorate the effect of the market on the valuation of liabilities.

Smoothing techniques for the valuation of non-fixed income assets. Although, as demonstrated earlier, averaging fixed income market

EXHIBIT 9:
FUNDED RATIOS, DOLLAR DURATION MATCHED PORTFOLIO—
JANUARY 1980-AUGUST 1987

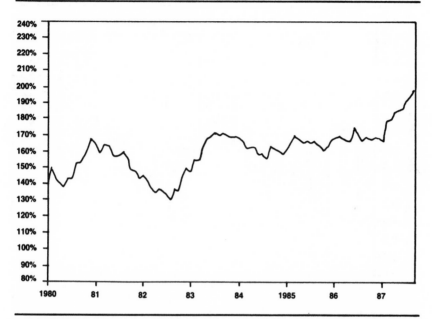

values should not be done when attempting to control expense volatility, averaging equity-related market values will generally serve to decrease that volatility.

Choice of assumed return on assets. This is a highly leveraged assumption. Even a 10 basis point change can have a significant impact on expense. Although there are guidelines for this assumption, they are not as restrictive as the "mark to market" rules for the discount rate.

These and other accounting techniques will be helpful only under certain circumstances. They can reduce pension expense volatility around a long-term mean, but they will not hide a long-term trend. The best accounting strategies can do is smooth the rough edges off a long-term increase or decrease in pension plan expense. As seen in Exhibit 12, accounting techniques can help smooth the erratic patterns of the unadjusted expense numbers, but the trend in expense from 5% of pay toward 7% of pay is not affected.

EXHIBIT 10:
CHANGE IN EXPENSE—TRADITIONAL PORTFOLIO VERSUS DOLLAR
DURATION MATCHED PORTFOLIO

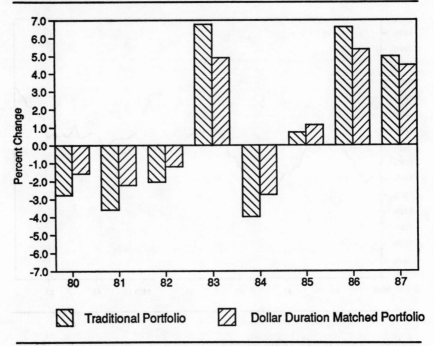

Traditional Portfolio   Dollar Duration Matched Portfolio

3. Analyze Further Changes

Even after the above two steps, some sponsors will still find the financial volatility of pension expense and balance sheet liabilities to be unacceptable. These sponsors will need to reassess their entire investment strategy, especially the risk/return profile of their current asset allocation.

The simplest solution to further decrease financial statement volatility is to increase bond exposure at the expense of equities. This strategy, as shown above, can lower returns. Such a change should be undertaken only after all the consequences, especially higher expenses and required contributions in the long run, are reviewed and deemed acceptable.

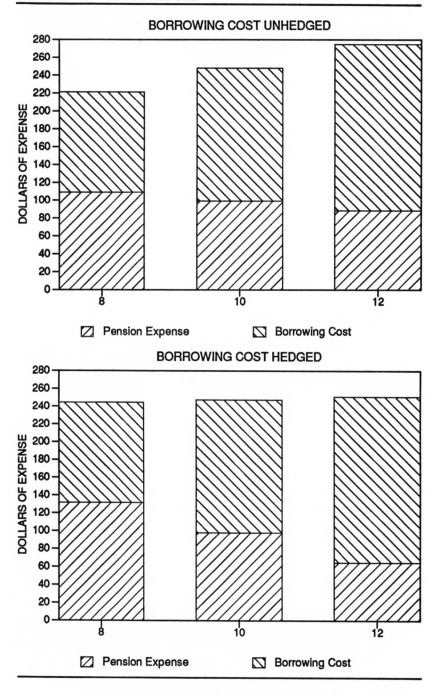

EXHIBIT 12:
SMOOTHING EXPENSE WITH ACCOUNTING FLEXIBILITY

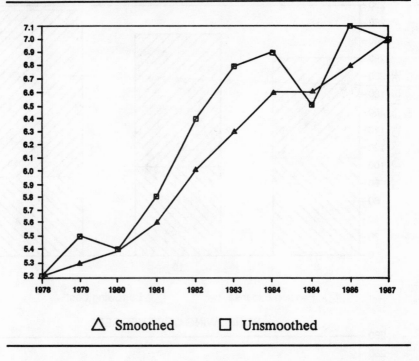

△ Smoothed   □ Unsmoothed

Other solutions, such as various forms of surplus insurance, promise to limit risk without lowering returns. These strategies use dynamic trading to effectively change asset mix as asset/liability ratios change. Theoretically, this allows plans to enjoy equity exposure when equities are outperforming liabilities. Although these strategies have intuitive appeal, they are largely untested, require substantial trading and daily monitoring, and should be adopted only after extensive modeling of the true costs relative to the benefits.

CONCLUSION

There has been concern over the negative impact FASB 87 might have on plan sponsors. However, FASB 87 will force plan sponsors to match the interest rate sensitivity of assets and liabilities more closely. This is an appropriate investment technique that should have already been considered as a part of an effective investment strategy.

APPENDIX A: FASB 87 DEFINITIONS

Plan Liabilities

FASB 87 defines two types of plan liabilities.

The Accumulated Benefit Obligation (ABO) An approximate measure of the liability of the plan in the event of a termination at the calculation date. The ABO includes the present value of:

- benefits currently being paid to retired employees,
- benefits payable in the future to vested ex-employees, and
- benefits payable in the future to employees who are currently active.

The benefits for active employees are based on their service and compensation on the calculation date. This liability is the same as the disclosure numbers that were required under previous accounting rules.

The Projected Benefit Obligation (PBO) This is also a measure of the liability of the plan at the calculation date. The PBO, however, assumes that the plan is ongoing and will not terminate in the foreseeable future. This ongoing plan assumption has no effect on the liability for retired employees or vested ex-employees. For these employees, the same present value is used in calculating both the ABO and PBO.

In plans where benefits are accumulated as a function of salary, however, the ongoing plan assumption increases the amount of the benefits attributed to employees who are currently active. Therefore, for those plans in which benefits are based on salary, the PBO exceeds the ABO. This is due to the assumption that salary level will grow over time and thus increase the plan liability when benefits are based on salary. Typically, the ABO will be 50% to 80% of the PBO.

The difference between the ABO and PBO due to the calculation for active employees is best described by an example. Suppose a pension plan pays annual benefits at retirement equal to 2% of an employee's final year compensation times the number of years of service. For an active employee with five years of service and annual compensation of $25,000 the annual benefit used in the ABO calculation would be $2,500 (2% × 5 × $25,000).

The PBO calculation would, however, be based on the salary the employee is projected to have at retirement. If retirement is ten years away and salaries are projected to increase 3% per year, the annual benefit used in the PBO calculation would be $3,360 ($2\% \times 5 \times \$25,000 \times (1.03)^{10}$). The difference between the benefits used in the PBO and ABO calculations is largest for young employees. The difference decreases to zero as employees approach retirement age.

Plan Assets

FASB 87 describes the way Plan Assets must be valued to determine the amount of pension expense each year. Under FASB 87 plan sponsors may choose to set Plan Assets equal to the market value of assets, a market-related value, or a combination of the two, by asset class. Market-related values under FASB 87 must recognize all changes in market values smoothly, consistently, and rationally over no more than five years. Since expenses under FASB 87 reflect the difference in Plan Assets and the present value of liabilities, market-related values may help to dampen year-to-year fluctuations in expenses. This approach was used precisely for this purpose under previous accounting rules. Under the new rules, plan sponsors may want to use market value for fixed income securities and market-related values for equity types of investment. This will allow smoothing of equity returns, but will immediately reflect changes in bond values, which may be structured to move in tandem with the liabilities.

The Use of PBO, ABO, and Plan Assets

To show how the PBO, ABO, and Plan Assets are used under the Statement, consider a pension plan in which the PBO is $100 million, the ABO is $60 million, the market value of Plan Assets is $80 million, and Plan Assets are $75 million.

Balance Sheet Disclosure For the purpose of balance sheet disclosure, the market value of assets is compared to the ABO. Since the market value of assets exceeds the ABO in this particular case, it is unnecessary to record an unfunded pension liability on the balance sheet.

Plan Expense   For the purpose of computing annual plan expense, the market value of Plan Assets are compared to the PBO. In this case, the shortfall of $25 million will effectively be amortized over time and will constitute a component of plan expense.

Interest Calculations

FASB 87 requires best estimates of the following important interest assumptions:

- The *discount rate* used in computing the ABO, the PBO, and the service component of plan expense should reflect market rates. For example, plan sponsors may look at the rates implicit in the current prices of annuity contracts that could be purchased by the plan to settle its liabilities. Alternatively, the rates provided by "high-quality fixed income investments . . . available during this period to maturity of the pension benefits" could be used.
- The *expected return on assets* should reflect the return expected on investments held by the pension plan to fund the PBO liabilities. Since this rate and the discount rate are based on assets available to fund the same benefits, it is anticipated that many sponsors will set the two rates equal. It should be noted, however, that the relationship of the expected return on assets to the discount rate can have a substantial effect on the annual overall expense. Careful selection of these two interest rates may be used by some plan sponsors to help manage the volatility of pension expense.

APPENDIX B: DOLLAR DURATION MATCHING

Dollar duration matching is a technique used to structure fixed income asset portfolios. The structure is used to insure that changes in the price of corresponding liabilities due to interest rate changes will be matched by changes in the market price of the asset portfolio. Duration is an index of price sensitivity due to interest rate changes that can be calculated for any fixed payment asset or liability. For example, a duration of 7 years means that for a change in interest rates of plus 100 basis points (bp), the price of the asset or liability can be expected to decline by approximately 7%.

A dollar duration matched portfolio of fixed income assets structured against a liability would be developed as follows:

Liability

Current Market Value = $50 million
Duration = 10 years
Price change for +100 bp yield change = −$5 million (−10 × 50)

Dollar Duration Matching Assets

$50 million fixed income portfolio with overall duration of 10 years.
Price change for +100 bp yield change = −$5 million (−10 × 50)

or,

$25 million fixed income portfolio with overall duration of 20 years.
Price change for +100 bp yield change = −$5 million (−20 × 25)

or,

$40 million fixed income portfolio with overall duration of 12.5 years.
Price change for +100 bp yield change = −$5 million (−12.5 × 40)

Note that each portfolio would be constructed differently; as rates changed, the portfolios would need to be adjusted to maintain the target duration.

CHAPTER 17

Normal Portfolios and Their Construction

JON A. CHRISTOPHERSON, PH.D.
ASSISTANT VICE PRESIDENT
RESEARCH AND DEVELOPMENT
FRANK RUSSELL COMPANY

For many years, investment professionals have understood the importance of comparing manager returns against benchmarks composed of securities in the same asset class from which the manager was selecting. Investment managers, though, will often specialize in subsets of a universe of securities in an asset class, rather than consider the entire universe. Within the group of managers who invest primarily in U.S. equities, we call this specialization investment style. The differences in managers' returns can often be explained by differences in the average return within their respective subuniverses.

One method of improving one's understanding of the differences in managers' returns is to develop specialized benchmarks for a specific manager or a class of managers. A normal portfolio is a specialized benchmark (or an index) for a specific manager.

While some work has been published that describes how to create a

381

normal portfolio,[1] the exact method is somewhat vague. Our purpose in this chapter is to discuss not only how to create normal portfolios but how to use them. We will show how to identify one that is well-constructed and how properly to apply it to fund management. The examples that follow are taken primarily from U.S. equities; however, the framework for developing normal portfolios presented here is applicable to other asset classes or to funds of different classes. Most of the normal portfolio work to date has been in U.S. equities because the large amounts of historical and current data required for building normal portfolios are not readily available for other asset classes.

DEFINITION OF A NORMAL PORTFOLIO

The notion of a normal portfolio was first introduced by Barr Rosenberg and the BARRA organization. The choice of the word *normal* to describe a portfolio is intended to capture the idea that for each money manager there exists a habitat of securities whose composition is very similar to the manager's average portfolio over time. In this sense the normal portfolio is "typical" or "average." Normal portfolios can be defined in the following way:

A normal portfolio is a set of securities that contains all of the securities from which a manager normally chooses, weighted as the manager would weight them in a portfolio. As such, a normal portfolio is a specialized index.

Using a normal portfolio as a benchmark is an attempt to further refine one's understanding of a manager's activities. This is done by comparing the manager's performance against that of the subset of securities from which he actually selects. Similarly, the aggregate of the normal portfolios of a manager mix can be used to manage the total exposure of a plan. It is simple to identify over- or underexposed sectors or risks by comparing such a set of normal portfolios to a market benchmark. This use of normal portfolios also allows one to create a passive investment strategy that can be replicated over time.

---

[1]Mark Kritzman, "How to Build a Normal Portfolio in Three Easy Steps." *Journal of Portfolio Management* (Summer 1987), pp. 212–23.

Thus, a properly constructed normal portfolio may be used as a performance measurement benchmark and as a tool for constructing manager mixes. Let us examine each of these purposes in turn.

NORMAL PORTFOLIOS AS MANAGER PERFORMANCE BENCHMARKS

The normal portfolio is normal or neutral because it includes all of the stocks in the manager's investment habitat. Although the Russell 3000® Index or the S&P 500 could be a manager's normal portfolio, this is often not the case. Managers tend to specialize in different segments of the market, and broad market indicators are not generally useful for evaluating their stock selection and sector allocation skill. Broad market indexes are also inadequate as benchmarks for most managers because they contain many stocks managers of a given style would normally not even consider, much less choose. They also contain stocks in proportions managers normally would not hold. As a result, the average equity characteristics of many managers' portfolios can be quite different from a broad market index.

In fact, broad market indexes can cause us to make incorrect judgments regarding a manager's skill. For example, a manager who specializes in defensive stocks will often outperform a broad market index during bear markets and underperform it during bull markets. The manager may exhibit either good or bad stock selection within his universe, but his stock picking ability does not show up in performance attribution based on a broad market index comparison. The measurement of his skill is muted by other broad market factors. In other words, when a manager's style is in favor he appears to be skillful, and when the style is out of favor his returns indicate a lack of skill. Without an adequate normal, it is difficult to determine the source of his skill.

Therefore, to produce useful performance benchmarks, we must create a portfolio whose characteristics can be used to determine a manager's stock selection capability and, if appropriate, sector allocation skill.

Presumably, the manager adds value by selecting the better performing stocks and/or the better performing sectors of his normal universe. If his portfolio return is worse than his universe return, then the manager made mistakes in choosing stocks, in departing from his normal weighting scheme, in choosing sectors, or all three.

The normal portfolio will also be useful if it is representative of the universe of securities that constitute the manager's "normal habitat" (i.e., the securities from which the manager typically chooses), and if it holds these in proportions the manager normally holds. Furthermore, the normal portfolio's equity profile should closely resemble the manager's typical equity profile over time. Note, however, that a manager's observed portfolio may vary considerably over time, so that deviations from the normal are not unusual. This latter point is a constant source of difficulty because we are never really quite sure whether the observed current portfolio's deviation from the normal portfolio is merely the result of the manager's short-term tactical bets or a sign of major change in his investment philosophy and style.

HOW TO CREATE A NORMAL PORTFOLIO

Approaches to Normal Portfolio Construction

The methods used for creating a normal portfolio are relatively straightforward. A stock list based on an analysis of the manager's behavior is the approach most commonly used, and the approach endorsed by Russell and BARRA. In this approach, a broad universe of securities, such as the Russell 3000 Index, is screened on characteristics which capture a manager's investment process. The result is a subset of the broad universe. The list of stocks is then weighted appropriately to produce a normal portfolio. The benchmark that emerges can be used for performance evaluation and risk control.

Although BARRA and Russell agree on the basic philosophy of normal portfolio construction, they take slightly different approaches to the process. BARRA tends to rely on their E2 multiple factor model of equity risk (E2 Model) as a basis for determining the normal screens, whereas Russell advocates obtaining screening criteria from the manager directly, from his written materials, and from the information contained in his equity portfolio statistics. BARRA is especially inclined toward using the E2 model in a case where the plan sponsor is constructing a normal portfolio on behalf of an external manager and has limited access to the manager as a source of information. However, in all cases both Russell and BARRA attempt to combine an evaluation of the manager's historial behavior with a description of the investment process taken directly from the manager.

While BARRA and Russell may at times select different normal screens for a manager, they both agree that the screens chosen should closely represent the manager's investment process. Since there are often several ways of representing a particular investment concept, non-uniqueness of normal screen selection can be expected. BARRA feels an added benefit of using their E2 model for normal screen selection is that it serves as a common language simplifying the comparison of diverse managers. The Russell approach is somewhat easier to understand and implement (no E2 factor model is necessary), and this approach will be used for the purposes of this chapter.

The Beginning Universe of Securities

Regardless of how one arrives at the normal's stock list, the central goal is to capture stocks from which the manager normally chooses and on which one can obtain information reliably and readily. One could begin with all possible U.S. equities, which number over 6,000. The difficulty with this strategy is that insufficient data is available for many of the small capitalization stocks in this group. Furthermore, few investors in the U.S. actively trade the very small stocks which make up the tail end of the equity market.

There are a number of ways of isolating the beginning universe. Choosing subsets on the basis of capitalization is an easy first cut. A practical starting list is the stocks in the Russell 3000. Using the Russell 3000 Index stock list will provide coverage of nearly all U.S. stocks with capitalization above $20 million. One could also choose the stock list of the S&P 500 or some other major index. Most of these are subsets of the Russell 3000.

Choosing the Securities for the Normal

Assuming that the chosen universe contains all or most of the stocks from which the manager is likely to select, the next step is to reduce the list of stocks to those from which the manager actually does select. This is usually accomplished by subsetting the universe using screening criteria consistent with the manager's stock selection habit patterns.

Decision rules are required for this process, i.e., it is necessary to have a numeric basis for deciding whether or not a stock belongs in the normal. Exhibit 1 is an example of the kind of information needed in order to build a normal portfolio. This example comes from materials distributed by a well-known money management firm with a growth orientation. Obviously, it makes the sponsor's task much easier. Most firms do not publish this sort of information.

The screens (as shown in Exhibit 1, Section A) must accurately capture the subuniverse of stocks from which the manager actually chooses. These screens may be determined through communication with the manager (as in Exhibit 1) or developed independently, based on the plan sponsor's assessment of the manager's key selection criteria. In either case, the content of the screens is critical. Since, in our example, the manager will choose among large rather than small capitalization stocks, we would choose the broad, large capitalization market as the beginning universe on such criteria as those listed in Exhibit 1, Section A.

Of course, "average" can mean either the mean or median of the distribution, depending on the skewness of the underlying distribution. At Russell we usually use the equity portfolio statistics of the Russell 1000 or 3000 as market values. These are capitalization-weighted means. One could divide the universe in half by using the median, since the distributions of many characteristics are skewed, but here the problem arises of whether to use weighted or unweighted medians. Where possible, we want to set breakpoints on the basis of the manager's behavior, either as described by the manager or as we have observed it. If the manager's decision criteria are not known, it may very well be desirable to try several screening values and examine how representative the resulting sub-universes are.

There are no unambiguous rules about setting screening values. The only good check is the reasonableness of the resulting subuniverse given the manager's style of investing. The reasonableness of a subuniverse should be judged by how well the manager's return patterns fit the normal and how well the normal fits the manager's portfolio characteristics. If we had to choose between the two criteria, we should be more concerned with the portfolio characteristics than with similarity of performance. However, we would expect to find significantly higher correlations of the manager's performance with the normal than with the broad market, and there should be a lower residual variance relative

EXHIBIT 1:
EXAMPLE OF NORMAL PORTFOLIO SPECIFICATION

A. *Screening Procedure*

    1. Capitalization   ≥ $350,000,000
                                                (i.e., large caitalization)

    2. Yield   ≤ 5.00%

    3. Book Price   ≤ 0.5 Std. Deviation
                                                (translates to Price/Book
                                                Ratio 1.00)

    4. Dividend Payout Ratio   ≤   Std. Deviation
                                                  (translates to less than or
                                                  equal to the mean of the
                                                  distribution)

    5. Historical Beta   ≥ 0.85

    6. Earnings Variability   ≥ (0.5) Std. Deviation
                                                  (translates to one-half
                                                  standard deviation below the
                                                  mean of the distribution)

B. *Weight Scheme*

        Equal Weight Within the Following Parameters

	% of Portfolio
$350 Million–$1 Billion	15%
$1 Billion–$3 Billion	30%
$3 Billion–$6 Billion	35%
$6 Billion and up	15%
IBM	5%

C. *Rebalancing*

Previously, we ran the screens semi-annually and rebalanced position sizes monthly. In the future, we will not rebalance monthly, letting positions run for the full six months.

to the normal than relative to other indexes. The size of these differences is a function of the differences between the normal universe and the broad market as well as the size of the bets the manager makes relative to his normal.

Weighting the Securities

Once the normal subuniverse of stocks has been specified, the critical problem of how to combine them into an index remains—i.e., the weights that should be applied to each stock. Broad market indexes such as the Russell Indexes and the S&P 500 are capitalization-weighted indexes. Managers, on the other hand (as clearly demonstrated in Exhibit 1, Section B), often do not capitalization-weight their portfolios. A short example will demonstrate the importance of choosing a correct weighting scheme when creating normal portfolios.

Let us assume that we screen our universe in such a way that we end up with the same four stocks held in the manager's portfolio and the normal portfolio. Assume also that we choose to weight the normal portfolio on a capitalization basis even though our manager chooses an equal-weighted basis. Finally, let us assume that at the end of the quarter, the security return numbers shown in Exhibit 2 emerge.

As can be seen, the normal portfolio has a much higher return than the manager's portfolio even though their holdings are identical. This example highlights the importance of the choice of weighting schemes. It always makes a significant difference in total performance. Generally, the normal portfolio and the manager's current portfolio will not have all the same stocks, so the weighting scheme can easily become a source of confusion and/or contention.

Bear in mind that while one wants to choose a weighting scheme that fairly reflects the manager's behavior, the plan sponsor also needs to evaluate other aspects of the manager's behavior, such as sector weighting and other bets, that can affect overall performance. Note that when a manager equal-weights his portfolio there is an implicit bias against large capitalization stocks and toward smaller capitalization stocks. There will be more on this subject later.

Weighting Alternatives

One can choose from a variety of candidate weighting schemes. Here are three examples of weighting schemes based on capitalization:

EXHIBIT 2:
EFFECTS OF CAPITALIZATION WEIGHTING ON PORTFOLIO RETURNS

Stock	Cap Weight	Security Return	Stock Impact on Return	Manager Weight	Security Return	Stock Impact on Return
A	50%	15%	7.50%	25%	15%	3.75%
B	30	10	3.00	25	10	2.50
C	15	5	0.75	25	5	1.25
D	5	5	0.25	5	5	1.25
Total Return			11.50%			8.75%

1. Equal weighting—the same portfolio percentage for each stock regardless of stock capitalization
2. Capitalization weighting—each stock weighted according to its percentage of the total market value of the portfolio
3. Capitalization weighting with break points—each stock weighted according to its percentage of the total market value of the portfolio, up to a certain capitalization size; above the breakpoint each stock is equal-weighted (e.g., equal weight above $1 billion in market capitalization)

Other weighting schemes are also feasible, such as the complex scheme shown in Exhibit 1, Section B, which equal-weights stocks in the same size category and roughly capitalization-weights the size categories. One might assign percentage weightings based on the log of capitalization to compensate for the high degree of skewness in the distribution of capitalization—i.e., to give the smaller companies a larger percentage. Other mathematical transformations of capitalization are appealing as well.

Of course, one is not confined to assigning portfolio percentages on the basis of capitalization. Weighting could be a function of other data. The treatment of such stocks as IBM often causes membership and weighting problems for normal portfolios; notice how it is given special treatment by the manager in Exhibit 1. No maybe's are allowed in portfolio membership—a stock is either in or out—but partial weighting can be obtained by allowing a stock into the portfolio and then reducing its weight.

Advantages and Disadvantages of Capitalization Weighting

When choosing a weighting scheme for normal portfolios, one should be aware that capitalization weighting has certain advantages and disadvantages. A passive capitalization-weighted normal portfolio need not be rebalanced because of fluctuations in the price of the stocks in the portfolio. Also, since one is purchasing a percentage of each company, in a capitalization-weighted portfolio, liquidity problems tend to be minimized. Because capitalization-weighted stock portfolios can be purchased more readily, due to liquidity they are also easier to replicate passively, if desired. Capitalization weighting also makes a buy and hold strategy easier to pursue.

The disadvantages of capitalization weighting are not inconsequential. As mentioned earlier, managers often do not capitalization-weight their portfolios for a variety of reasons. Often the reluctance to capitalization-weight a portfolio is related to the manager's aversion to putting too much money in any one basket (such as IBM). When compared to a capitalization-weighted portfolio, this aversion can be seen as a bet against certain sectors and stocks. As demonstrated in our earlier example, capitalization weighting tends to magnify the impact of large capitalization equities on the portfolio's characteristics and performance. Finally, capitalization weighting tends to weight some sectors of the market more than the average institutional money manager would. In our experience, capitalization weighting will cause differences between the average characteristics of the manager's portfolio and his normal portfolio, as well as differences in performance.

Note, however, that weighting other than by capitalization is fraught with theoretical difficulties. For example, not every investor can purchase such portfolios. As well, these types of benchmarks make a passive alternative difficult, and in some cases impossible, to implement. Furthermore, if one creates a noncap-weighted normal portfolio, a cap-weighted portfolio will also have to be created so that the user can determine the performance effect of underweighting large capitalization stocks relative to market valuations. This is not a moot point. In the fourth quarter of 1986, the large cap stocks performed much better than the overall market; managers who did not cap-weight their portfolios were negatively affected by their capitalization bets. It seems reasonable that the plan sponsor would want to know the extent of this bet against large cap stocks. As a general rule, to simplify passive management and to retain all market opportunities available to investors, we recommend capitalization weighting unless there is good reason not to do so.

ISSUES TO CONSIDER WHEN CREATING NORMAL PORTFOLIOS

Limitations of the Stock List Model

There are certain implicit assumptions about normal portfolios that one should bear in mind when creating and using normals. For example, the assumption inherent in the methodology described above is that the universe of securities from which a manager chooses can be determined by the fundamental stock characteristics used in screens. Hence, some styles of management such as market timing behavior would represent bets against a normal portfolio. If a manager has the discretion to move funds out of equities and into cash or other assets, this cannot be captured in a normal portfolio of equities only. A normal portfolio for market timers must also have a "normal" weight in the type of securities which the manager uses in market timing (e.g., cash).

Communication Prior to Measurement

It is important to choose a normal portfolio in advance of the performance measurement period so that the manager and the sponsor both know the investment objective. The manager may be unclear concerning his most appropriate equity style. One should negotiate or otherwise determine before the performance period what characteristics the manager feels are a "fair" description of his universe. Such an *a priori* agreement can go a long way toward avoiding the "it doesn't fit me" argument.

Arbitrariness of Screening

When setting decision rules about including or excluding stocks, one should realize that decision rules such as above/below market mean values are arbitrary. Hence, they will arbitrarily include or exclude stocks with large capitalizations or other characteristics. This may cause the performance of the normal portfolio to vary considerably depending on whether certain stocks (such as IBM) or groups of stocks (such as energy) are included or excluded.

As can be seen from the foregoing, normals can be difficult to create and use as benchmarks due to data requirements and lack of necessary information to do them well. However, normals can provide the sponsor with evaluation tools that give the manager few places to hide.

NORMAL PORTFOLIOS AS INVESTMENT STRATEGY TOOLS

So far, we have examined how to create and use normals for the purpose of manager performance measurement. We will now turn to the second purpose of normals—the use of normals as investment strategy tools.

Normal Portfolios and the Policy Portfolio

The aggregate of the normal portfolios can be used to show the total equity exposure of the plan—the "policy portfolio." For example, a comparison of total exposure in the normal portfolios to a market benchmark such as the Russell 3000 will help identify over- or under-exposed sectors or factors. Passively managed "completeness" funds can be created to fill the gaps in exposure if needed. Of course, each of the multiple normal portfolios can be matched against one or more managers to help effectively mix multiple managers. Note also that normal portfolios can be seen as policy portfolios at the manager level.

Difficult Management Questions

While combining normals to achieve a policy portfolio appears simple on the surface, the decision to use normals presupposes the answers to several difficult and interrelated management questions.

- *Why Do We Create Normal Portfolios?*
  We create normals to provide an *ideal benchmark* against which to measure individual manager performance. In other words, we want to see how well he picks stocks within the group from which he normally chooses. We also want to see how well he allocates funds across industrial sectors and company sizes, and perhaps how well he covers a portion of the market.

  Another equally valid reason is to provide a tool for plan management. The sum of our normal portfolios across a plan can tell us what portion of the market has been covered. The sum of the normals plus a completeness fund can tell us how close we are to our policy portfolio or target portfolio. In this way, normal portfolios can be used to guide our selection of managers and control the plan's exposure to market risks—i.e., to manage the plan.

  These two answers are in conflict in certain ways. For example, in creating an ideal benchmark we would weight stocks in the normal portfolio exactly the way the manager does, but in using normals to manage a plan, cap weighting is desirable to minimize plan complexity and to determine the effects of cap bets. We may also cap-weight the normal because we may like to think of it as an investable alternative, in which case cap weighting is essential. So the sponsor's purpose in creating normal portfolios is crucial to how they are constructed.

As for "ideal benchmarks," highly customized normal portfolios may provide much less useful tools for measuring performance than generic normals. It may very well be that the manager's returns may correlate as highly as or more highly with a generic style index than with a customized normal. In such a case the question naturally arises about whether or not the expense and effort of creating individual normal portfolios are worthwhile. Furthermore, as benchmarks go, an ideal normal portfolio may not be able to explain a high percentage of the variance in a manager's return history because of variations in normal manager behavior. These departures may result from variations in weighting, oscillating poor/outstanding stock picking, and poor/outstanding sector bets. So, over time, the ideal normal portfolio may fail to provide much information as a predictor of performance.

- *For What Should a Manager Be Given Credit?*
The second question is related to the first. If a manager, through intuition or research, arrives at the contrarian investment strategy in which he buys only out-of-favor or undervalued stocks, then how much value added over a broad market benchmark should the manager be accorded—all of the contrarian style performance above or below the benchmark or only that portion not explained by a contrarian normal portfolio? This question, of course, moves the previous question of why we hire active managers in the first place: because we think managers can add value over a passive alternative. To the extent that active managers cannot or do not over time add excess return above their normal portfolios, the plan sponsor should create a passive portfolio of the securities in the style normal and save a portion of the active management fees. Managers, of course, want all of the credit and none of the blame for the wisdom of their styles of investing, so giving credit is obviously a way of preserving feelings of fairness.

- *How Close to the Manager's Ideal Portfolio Do We Wish to Come?*
Does the sponsor want a customized normal portfolio that matches the manager's style as closely as possible, or a more generic normal that captures the manager's general style or substyle of

management? The virtue of a close match is that it allows us to know more precisely where the manager added value—i.e., how well he chose securities. The virtue of the more generic normal is that we can judge how well the manager's variation on a theme—his skill in security weighting, sector allocation, and security selection—added value. A more generic normal portfolio also makes it possible to judge the skill of other managers of a similar style. The broader the normal portfolio, the more useful it will be for measuring opportunity costs, i.e., answering the question of how much better off the sponsor would be with Manager A rather than Manager B (given that the generic normal portfolio fairly accurately captures the investment style of both). The answer to this third question falls out of the answer to the first two, but it might very well be the first issue a plan sponsor decides.

- *How Much Cooperation Is Necessary from the Manager?*
The fourth question is more of a personnel management issue. Does the plan sponsor need and want the cooperation of the manager in creating the normal portfolio? This decision is the plan sponsor's call, not the manager's. If we know the securities from which a manager tends to choose, and we do not care much whether or not the manager likes being compared to a normal that we feel represents his universe and/or strategy, then we can proceed without the manager's cooperation. The virtue of this approach is that it allows greater flexibility in plan management. The sponsor can define a set of "target" normals that come close to a policy portfolio and hold managers accountable for doing or not doing their part. In this context, normals may be seen as analogous to management by objective.

On the other hand, developing a customized normal for performance measurement usually requires the close cooperation of the manager to obtain the correct subset of securities for the normal and the correct weighting rules; hence, the closer we want to fit the normal to the manager's investment behavior, the more cooperation from the manager is required. Furthermore, a manager must know the basis of his evaluation, and to force a normal portfolio upon a manager can be seen as an arrogant, presumptive, and unfriendly act.

The resolution of this last question has implications for all of the other questions. If we decide that the generic normal is close enough for our plan management purposes, then the manager's cooperation is less critical. This decision, in turn, is related to the question of giving credit for a manager's style. The more credit the sponsor wants to give the manager for his style and active management within his style, the less closely the normal will fit the manager's portfolio, and the more closely it will fit the broad market. And, of course, the further away the normal is from the manager's typical portfolio, the less useful it is as a benchmark to measure manager skills within his universe—bringing us back to the question of what purpose the sponsor has in mind.

In summary, how the plan sponsor intends to use normal portfolios in plan management has much to do with the critical decisions the sponsor must make about the nature of each normal portfolio. Making any one decision has implications for all the other decisions, and the cumulation of them determines the overall usefulness of the normal portfolios.

CONCLUDING REMARKS

As we have seen, normal portfolios provide useful tools for plan sponsors to evaluate their money manager's performance and behavior as it relates to the overall plan structure. Some users of normal portfolios advocate producing normal portfolios that mirror as closely as possible the average portfolios of their managers. While this is a perfectly legitimate purpose for normal portfolios, we should also consider the merits of using normal portfolios to manage the plan structure. We believe that this provides a better basis for creating a set of normal portfolios. In other words, in addition to providing a close benchmark for performance measurement, the normal should also be created with opportunity costs in mind. This decision means that we will not require strict cooperation from the manager, and it also means that we are giving the manager credit for the nuances of his implementation of his investment style. It also recognizes that so long as the normal is reasonably close, it will be an effective benchmark for measuring not only security selection, but also sector allocation and capitalization bets.

While one could create normals that model a management firm so precisely that they can pick up the differences between portfolio managers within one shop, it is more realistic to create normal portfolios that reflect the average portfolios of managers who could have been chosen instead of the manager selected. In this way, the plan sponsor can evaluate the opportunity cost of hiring one manager rather than another or buying a passively managed alternative. At the same time, the sponsor can create a flexible instrument for plan management purposes.

CHAPTER 18

Performance Measurement and Evaluation

RONALD J. SURZ
PRINCIPAL
BECKER, BURKE ASSOCIATES INC.

In the mid-1960s a new field of financial services was born—the measurement and evaluation of retirement fund performance. Prior to that date, fund sponsors had no means of and little interest in understanding the performance of their pension assets. No one had conducted any serious study of fund performance, the size of the assets was relatively small, and there was only minor governmental supervision of the industry. Sponsors were content to let their funds be placed in balanced portfolios managed by their bank or in contracts with insurance companies.

The results of the initial performance evaluation studies showed that there was a wide range of performance being generated by professional investment managers. Sponsors saw that plan assets were growing substantially and that performance would impact their future costs. They began to analyze investment returns, question their managers, and diversify plan assets. All of this caused an explosion in the performance measurement industry. Dozens of firms began to offer services to measure, compare, and evaluate fund performance.

Standardized formulas and methodologies were developed to measure the returns and analyze the characteristics of portfolios. Total return, the income received on an investment plus or minus appreciation or depreciation, became the accepted measure of performance. Terms and phrases like beta, alpha, R^2, standard deviation and modern portfolio theory were added to the lexicon of the industry.

Independent investment counselors began to open their doors, and managers at banks and insurance companies joined the performance game. Although the stock market declined in 1969 and early 1970, managers continued to become more and more aggressive. Little attention was paid to risk. By the end of the "Nifty-fifty" rally of 1971 and 1972, the average retirement fund had 80% of its assets in stocks. Suddenly, markets collapsed in 1973 and 1974—stocks declined 50% and interest rates soared. ERISA was passed on Labor Day 1974 and sponsors became keenly aware of their financial and fiduciary obligations.

In response to this new awareness, long range planning models were developed that looked at the emerging liabilities and assets of plans under a variety of scenarios. Goals and objectives were established that focused on the needs of the plan rather than on the desire to outperform the other guy.

Investment managers were given these guidelines and told to adhere to the policies. Specialty managers were hired to play specific roles in the overall manager structure and were evaluated against other managers with similar styles or characteristics.

Today, plan sponsors are using more sophisticated performance measures and evaluations to analyze their plans and managers. Certain fundamental elements form the foundation upon which these tools are built. This chapter will address those elements.

MECHANICS

Performance evaluation is judging whether performance has been good or bad. To make this judgment, the evaluator needs two essential pieces of information: a performance measurement, and a context for locating this measurement relative to the opportunities that were available. Performance evaluation always has a historical perspective. Attempts to project good or bad performance into the future must be coupled with judgment and understanding of the factors that produced the performance. In this chapter, we concern ourselves exclusively with historic determinations.

The first ingredient of performance evaluation—a performance measurement—is fairly easy to obtain. The *time-weighted rate of return* is the accepted measure of performance for purposes of evaluation. This performance measurement minimizes the effects of cash flows to and from a portfolio. This is important because the plan sponsor, not the manager, controls cash flow. For purposes of measuring the growth of wealth rather than performance evaluation, the appropriate measure is the *dollar-weighted*, or *internal*, rate of return. This measure takes full account of cash flows, and, as such, accords more weight to time periods during which greater monies were invested. Since performance evaluation is the focus of this chapter, attention is directed to calculation and evaluation of time-weighted returns.

The second ingredient of performance evaluation—a context for locating performance relative to the opportunities—is much more complex. Placing performance in context requires both the identification of certain portfolio characteristics and the construction of an opportunity set for portfolios with similar characteristics. The primary objective is to determine whether the performance result is good or bad in light of the risks that were taken to achieve the result. The evaluator must consider several dimensions that pertain to who is being evaluated—the sponsor or the manager. Sponsor evaluation is achieved by locating total plan performance relative to other plans with similar risk, as measured, for example, by return variability. Two aspects of evaluation are provided in this fashion: the effect of the sponsor's risk decision, and his success or failure at structuring a management team to take that risk. Manager evaluation is achieved by comparing the manager's performance result to other funds operating under similar sponsor-directed guidelines and to other managers who espouse a similar investment "style." Risk is the issue for manager evaluation as it is for sponsor evaluation. However, care must be taken to attribute only discretionary risk to the manager.

The following text provides the computational tools required for measuring performance and risk. It then concludes with a discussion of how performance is evaluated relative to the risk.

PERFORMANCE AND RISK MEASUREMENT

Rates of Return

The foundation of performance evaluation is the time-weighted return. Time-weighted return is analogous to the return that is reported by mutual funds. Mutual funds exclude the effects of purchases and redemptions on return calculations by carrying unit values. A unit value tracks the growth of the value of one share of the mutual fund held continuously for the entire time period. To calculate this unit value, the mutual fund must be valued at market each time there is a cash flow into or out of the fund. This is necessary in order to segregate performance-based growth from cash-flow-based growth. Ideally, the time-weighted return for an investment portfolio is calculated in the mutual fund fashion—the portfolio is evaluated at market each time there is a cash flow, where cash flows include purchases, sales, and dividend and coupon payments. In this way, a series of wealth ratios are developed as follows:

$$w_d = \frac{V_d + D_d}{V_{d-1} + C_{d-1}}$$

where d = cash flow date

w_d = wealth change from the previous cash flow date to the current cash flow date

V_d, V_{d-1} = portfolio value at the time of the current, and previous, cash flows, *before* the cash flow is added in

D_d = dividends and coupons payable on the cash flow date

C_{d-1} = previous flow

To calculate the time-weighted return over an entire time period, these wealth ratios are compounded as follows:

$$r = \left(w_1 \cdot w_2 \cdots w_n \right) - 1$$

where r = (unannualized) time-weighted return

w_i = wealth change during period i

N = number of subperiods covering the measurement period

If the measurement period is not a year, the return can be transformed into an annually compounded equivalent; this is called annualization. Annualization is accomplished as follows:

$$r_a = (1 + r_u)^{1/T} - 1$$

where r_a = annualized return

r_u = unannualized return

T = length of measurement period, expressed in years

Not many service providers calculate the exact time-weighted rate of return described above. This is due to the many complexities involved in valuing a portfolio each time there is a cash flow.

Stock portfolios are becoming easier to value on demand, but other types of investments, such as bonds, real estate, and private placements, cannot realistically be priced at the time of each cash flow. As a practical matter, an approximation known as the *linked internal rate of return method* is used to estimate the time-weighted return. Under this method, the portfolio is valued at pre-specified dates, normally monthly. Then dollar-weighted, or internal, rates are calculated for each of these specified time periods; these internal rates *approximate* the wealth ratios used in the exact calculation. These internal rates are then compounded ("linked" in the jargon of performance measurement) to calculate the approximate time-weighted rate for the period.

$$R = (1 + r_1)(1 + r_2)\cdots(1 + r_N) - 1$$

where r_i = dollar-weighted return for (prespecified) period i

N = number of subperiods

R = (unannualized) approximation to the time-weighted return

An illustration of how to calculate a time-weighted return is presented in Exhibit 1. The internal, or dollar-weighted, return is the rate of appreciation that equates beginning value plus cash flows to ending value. It is the solution, r, to the following equation.

$$V_0(1 + r) + \sum_{i=1}^{n} C_i(1 + r)^{T_i} = V_E$$

where V_0 = beginning market value

C_i = cash flow number i

T_i = fraction of the time period remaining when cash flow occured (e.g., if the flow occured on 31 March, and a calendar year calculation is made, T would be .75, since three quarters of the year would be remaining)

V_E = ending market value

EXHIBIT 1:
TIME-WEIGHTED CALCULATION

Time Period	Time-weighted Return, or Approximation
1	−5.97
2	6.62
3	−7.96

$R = (1 + r_1)\cdot(1 + r_2)\cdot(1 + r_3) - 1$

$= (1 - .0597)\cdot(1 + .0662)\cdot(1 - .0796) - 1$

$= (.9403)(1.0662)(.9205) - 1 = -.077 = -7.7\%$

This equation is non-linear, and requires a non-linear numerical computer method to solve for a solution. A discussion of one such method is provided in the appendix to this chapter. As a first approximation, some providers have substituted the following estimate:

$$(1 + r)^{T_i} \cong 1 + T_i r$$

With this estimate, an *approximate* rate is calculated as follows:

$$r \cong \frac{V_E - V_0 - \sum C_i}{V_0 - \sum T_i C_i}$$

This approximation is fairly accurate for returns near zero.

Most service providers capture market value data monthly. Transactional data (cash flows) are usually captured daily. This means that time-weighted returns are approximated by linking exact monthly dollar-weighted returns. However, some providers do not use daily transactions, which results in inexact dollar-weighted rates. The resultant error may be significant if large cash flows (relative to assets measured) have occurred during the time period. Some providers aggregate all cash flows into the middle of the month. This saves on computer storage and computer time. With mid-month cash flows, the rate equation becomes a quadratic function that is readily solved as follows:

$$r = \left[\frac{-C + \sqrt{C^2 + 4V_0 V_E}}{2V_0} \right]^2 - 1$$

Exhibit 2 shows how a monthly dollar-weighted return may be approximated, and calculated exactly.

Some providers aggregate all cash flows and try to place this aggregate at the most appropriate place within the month. This saves on computer storage but generally does not save much computer time. A couple of methods may be used to locate an aggregate cash flow within the month the individual cash flows occurred. One method, known as *day-weighted flows*, simply takes the value-weighted average of the remaining times (the T_i's in the rate equation) as the single transaction date; here there is one date for inflows and another date for outflows. Another method, which may be called *reverse engineering*, first calculates the exact dollar-weighted return and then solves for the time location that will result in an identical return when the aggregate net (inflows minus outflows) flow is used. A problem with this technique is that it occasionally has a time location solution that is outside the actual transaction period (a single T that is less than 0 or greater than 1).

EXHIBIT 2:
DOLLAR-WEIGHTED RETURN CALCULATION

Beginning value (V_0): $1,000

Mid-period cash flow (C): $420

Ending value (V_E): $1,800

Approximate Rate:

$$\frac{V_E - V_0 - C}{V_0 + C/2}$$

$$= \frac{1,800 - 1,000 - 420}{1,000 + 210}$$

$$= 31\%$$

Exact Rate:

$$r = \left[\frac{-C + \sqrt{C^2 + 4V_0 V_E}}{2V_0} \right]^2 - 1$$

$$= \left[\frac{-420 + \sqrt{(420)^2 + 4(1,000)(1,800)}}{2(1,000)} \right]^2 - 1$$

$$= \left[\frac{-420 + 2,716}{2,000} \right]^2 - 1$$

$$= 32\%$$

Potential Problems in Calculating Returns

There are several problems that can arise in calculating time-weighted rates of return. A major problem exists in deciding when a return should be calculated. This problem arises most frequently in actively traded fund segments, such as short-term debt investments. It is common for some managers to hold a position in short term for only a few days in a month. If exact dollar-weighted rates are calculated for the month, the resulting rate is a "monthlyized" version of a few-day rate; in other words, the rate equation in effect converts a few-day rate to a monthly rate. If inexact dollar-weighted rates are calculated, the resulting rate is frequently nonsense. The correct approach to use when a fund segment is not held throughout the measurement period is simply not to calculate a return for that segment. However, some providers of performance data have adjudged that it is preferable to report a potentially erroneous result rather than to report no result at all. Cash flows for fund segments are purchases minus sales minus income.

Another problem that can arise relates to the redeployment of assets. Many investment managers in 1975 had total fund rates of return that were less than both their equity return and their bond return. This was because many managers were underweighted in equities when the S&P 500 recovered from the 1973–74 bear market to post a 12.5% return for just the month of January. Managers subsequently re-entered equities, but for 1975 it was too late. To see how this type of redeployment anomaly occurs, consider the following example:

Time Period	% Equities	% Bonds	Equity Return	Bond Return	Total Fund Return
1	20%	80%	10%	5%	6%
2	80%	20%	5%	10%	7%
TOTAL			15.5%	15.5%	12.4%

As can be seen from this example, there was a significant redeployment out of bonds and into equities, just before equities materially underperformed bonds. This is an example of adverse redeployment; good redeployment occurs when a favored segment is moved into.

Another problem that can occur relates to accruals. The concept of market value is one of liquidation value—it is what would be received if an asset is sold. Since bond accruals and dividends due past the ex-date would be paid to the seller, these accruals must be incorporated into market values (V_0 and V_E) to calculate an accurate return. The claim that the errors of ignoring accruals cancel over time is simply not true.

A final problem relates to the issue of trade versus settlement date for establishing the timing of cash flows. Current accounting and banking practices allow the manager to behave as if capital and securities change hands on the trade date. That is, since only a very small percentage of trades fail to settle, modern accounting procedures treat the transactions as complete on trade date. This is particularly important for trades that occur near month end; for all practical purposes the transaction should be reflected in the ending asset value, but it might not be under settlement date accounting. Accordingly, trade date is the preferred date for locating transactions.

Risk Measurement

There are several measurements of risk that are helpful in evaluating performance. Some of these measurements are (1) average allocation, (2) return variability, (3) income yield, and (4) beta.

For evaluating historic performance, these risk measurements represent historic averages over the evaluation period, which is usually one to five years. *Average allocation* (or *average commitment*) to an asset category, such as equities, is calculated as follows:

$$A = \frac{\sum v_m}{\sum V_m}$$

where A = average allocation

v_m = market value of the asset category at the end of month "m"

V_m = total portfolio market value at the end of month "m"

Exhibit 3 shows how to calculate an average allocation (commitment) for a quarter.

EXHIBIT 3:
AVERAGE ALLOCATION (COMMITMENT) CALCULATION

| Time | Dollars Invested | |
Period	Fund Segment (v_m)	Total Fund (V_m)
0	$750	$1,000
1	$1,070	$1,300
2	$1,250	$1,550
3	$1,450	$1,800
$\Sigma v_m =$	$4,520	$\Sigma V_m =$ $5,650

$$A = \frac{\Sigma v_m}{\Sigma V_m} = \frac{4,520}{5,650} = 80\%$$

Return variability is calculated as the standard deviation of monthly returns over the measurement period, as follows:

$$RV = \frac{\Sigma (r_m - \bar{r})^2}{n-1}$$

where

RV = return variability

r_m = return in month m

$\bar{r}$ = $\dfrac{\Sigma r_m}{n}$

n = number of months

This may be annualized if desired by multiplying by $\sqrt{12}$, which is 3.46.

Exhibit 4 shows how to calculate the variability for a one-year time period.

EXHIBIT 4:
RETURN VARIABILITY CALCULATION

Time Period	Return (r_m)	Return Minus Mean $(r_m - \bar{r})$	Return Minus Mean Squared $(r_m - \bar{r})^2$
1	−5.7%	−7.7	59.29
2	7.5	5.5	30.25
3	−8.2	−10.2	104.04
4	5.6	3.6	12.96
5	2.6	0.6	0.36
6	−2.7	−4.7	22.09
7	13.4	11.4	129.96
8	4.1	2.1	4.41
9	2.7	0.7	0.49
10	−0.9	−2.9	8.41
11	1.0	−1.0	1.00
12	5.0	3.0	9.00

$$\sum r_m = 24.4 \qquad\qquad \sum (r_m - \bar{r})^2 = 382.26$$

$$\bar{r} = \sum \frac{r_m}{n}$$

$$= 24.4/12$$

$$= 2.0\%$$

$$RV = \frac{\sum (r_m - \bar{r})^2}{n-1} = \frac{382.26}{11} = 5.9\%$$

$$\text{Annualized } RV = \sqrt{12}\,(5.9\%) = 20.4\%$$

Income yield is calculated as the compounded growth of dollar-weighted income yields; this maintains comparability to time-weighted returns. Time-weighted income returns are calculated as:

$$Y = \left(1 + y_1\right)\left(1 + y_2\right)\cdots\left(1 + y_n\right) - 1$$

where

$$y_i = \frac{y + A_i - A_{i-1}}{V_0 + (P - S)/2}$$

Y = income yield

y_i = income rate for month i

y = income receipt

A_i = accrual at the end of month i

V_0 = beginning market value

P = purchases during month

S = sales

n = number of months

Exhibit 5 shows how to calculate a quarterly income yield.

Beta, or sensitivity to market movements, is the slope of the regression line of portfolio return premiums against market return premiums. A return premium is the actual return minus the Treasury bill return. The market is commonly represented by the S&P 500. The usefulness of beta has recently been called into question. The theory from which beta evolved described the market as all risky assets, not just stocks. Unfortunately, this total market portfolio is not knowable. Also, beta can only be applied to equities as a practical matter. As a result, many

EXHIBIT 5:
INCOME YIELD CALCULATION

Time Period	Beginning Value	A Beginning Accrual	Intra-Period		
			I Income	P Purchase	S Sales
0	$1000	$20	5	100	50
1	1050	25	20	50	100
2	1100	10	5	0	0
3	1110	15			

$$y = \frac{y + A_i - A_{i-1}}{V_0 + (P-S)/2}$$

$$y_1 = \frac{5 + 25 - 20}{1,000 + (100-50)/2} = .010 = 1.0\%$$

$$y_2 = \frac{20 + 10 - 35}{1,050 + (50-100)/2} = .005 = 0.5\%$$

$$y_3 = \frac{5 + 15 - 10}{1,100 + 0/2} = .009 = 0.9\%$$

$$Y = (1 + y_1)(1 + y_2)(1 + y_3) - 1$$
$$= (1.010)(1.005)(1.009) - 1$$
$$= 1.024 - 1 = .024 = 2.4\%$$

evaluators tend not to rely on beta very much. The formula for beta is as follows:

$$\beta = \frac{\dfrac{\sum\limits_{m} R_m S_m}{n} - \bar{R}\bar{S}}{\dfrac{\sum\limits_{m}(S_m - \bar{S})^2}{n}}$$

where

$$R_m = r_m - t_m$$

$$S_m = s_m - t_m$$

$$\bar{R} = \frac{\sum\limits_{m} R_m}{n}$$

$$\bar{S} = \frac{\sum\limits_{m} S_m}{n}$$

r_m = portfolio return for month m

s_m = market return for month m

t_m = return on Treasury bill for month m

R_m = portfolio return premium for month m

S_m = market return premium for month m

$\bar{R}$ = average portfolio return

$\bar{S}$ = average market return

n = number of months

Exhibit 6 shows how to calculate a one-year beta using monthly data. These risk measurements are used to evaluate whether or not performance has been acceptable relative to the risks, which brings us to our next topic.

PERFORMANCE EVALUATION

Performance is evaluated by placing the performance measurement into the context of available opportunities. This can be achieved with or without regard to risk. When risk is ignored, a total opportunity set can be examined. When the risk dimension is added, the evaluation determines whether or not risk was rewarded in general, and whether the particular portfolio had good or bad performance relative to portfolios with similar risk. Opportunity sets can be assembled from actual fund data collected by monitoring firms, or from theoretical data created by new methodologies known as simulation technologies. Simulation technologies create random portfolios that conform to rules regarding security selection and portfolio construction. Monitoring firms collect data on several thousand funds and array the performance of these funds into background distributions. To evaluate performance relative to risk, a monitoring firm divides its thousands of funds into risk groups, and constructs subdistribuions within each group. Simulation technologies can be applied to mirror these distributions and subdistributions of monitoring firms. But simulation technologies can also go beyond the monitoring firms by creating distributions that focus on a particular risk dimension of interest; it is this flexibility that can make simulation technologies preferable in many contexts.

With the appropriate context identified, the performance number is assigned a ranking. Convention has it that a performance ranking of 1% is good, meaning that performance is in the top 1% of the reference background, whereas a 99% percentile ranking is bad, meaning that 99% of the background funds performed better. Median, or middle, performance is assigned a ranking of 50%.

The former A. G. Becker Company is responsible for introducing the format that has become the accepted standard for performance evaluation. The so-called "Becker bar" is shown in Exhibit 7. The top of the bar shows the 5th percentile result, while the bottom shows the 95th. The solid line in the middle of the bar is the median result, while

EXHIBIT 6:
CALCULATION OF BETA

m Month	r_m Portfolio Return	S_m Market Return	t_m Treasury Bill Return	$R_m = r_m - t_m$ Portfolio Premium	$S_m = s_m - t_m$ Market Premium	$R_m S_m$ Portfolio X Market	$(S_m - \bar{S})^2$ Market Minus Mean Squared
1	-6.0%	-5.7%	0.5%	-6.5%	-6.2%	40.30	59.8
@	6.6	7.5	0.5	6.1	7.0	42.70	29.9
3	-8.0	-8.5	0.4	-8.4	-8.9	74.76	108.9
4	5.0	5.6	0.4	4.6	5.2	23.92	13.4
5	1.5	2.6	0.4	1.1	2.2	24.20	0.4
6	-2.5	-2.7	0.5	-3.0	-3.2	9.60	22.4
7	12.8	13.4	0.5	12.3	12.9	158.67	129.2
8	4.9	4.1	0.5	4.4	3.6	15.84	4.3
9	2.4	2.7	0.5	1.9	2.2	2.28	0.4
10	-1.7	-0.9	0.5	-2.2	-1.4	3.08	8.6
11	0.6	1.0	0.5	0.1	0.5	0.05	1.1
12	4.5	5.0	0.5	4.0	4.5	18.00	8.8
				14.4	18.4	413.40	387.2

$$\bar{R} = \frac{14.4}{12} = 1.2 \quad \bar{S} = \frac{18.4}{12} = 1.5 \quad \beta = \frac{\dfrac{\sum\limits_m R_m S_m}{n} - \bar{R}\bar{S}}{\dfrac{\sum\limits_m (S_m - \bar{S})^2}{n}} = \frac{\dfrac{413.4}{12} - (1.2)(1.5)}{\dfrac{387.2}{12}} = \frac{32.65}{32.27} = 1.01$$

EXHIBIT 7:
ABC COMPANY—CUMULATIVE PERFORMANCE COMPARISONS
TOTAL RETURNS OF BALANCED PORTFOLIOS—PERIODS ENDING 3/86

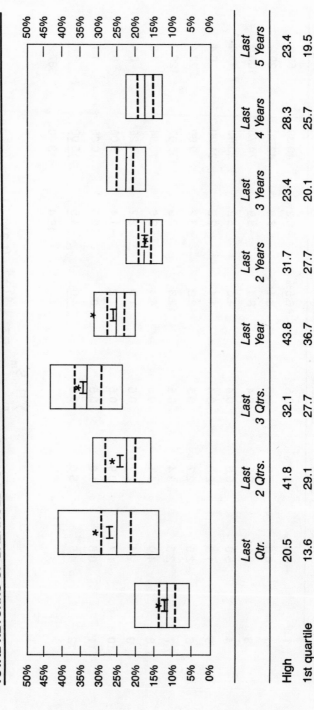

	Last Qtr.	Last 2 Qtrs.	Last 3 Qtrs.	Last Year	Last 2 Years	Last 3 Years	Last 4 Years	Last 5 Years
High	20.5	41.8	32.1	43.8	31.7	23.4	28.3	23.4
1st quartile	13.6	29.1	27.7	36.7	27.7	20.1	25.7	19.5
Median	11.6	24.9	23.1	32.7	25.0	18.2	23.0	17.4
3rd quartile	9.7	21.2	20.4	29.2	22.8	16.0	21.3	15.3
Low	5.8	14.8	16.6	24.1	20.1	13.1	18.1	13.2

the dashed lines depict the 25th and 75th percentiles. The asterisk in the bar locates the portfolio's relative performance. To evaluate performance relative to risk, three approaches can be used: (1) "effects of . . . ," (2) scatter diagrams, or (3) customized backgrounds.

"Effects of . . ." exhibits divide a total population into subsets on the basis of risk. The total population can be obtained from a monitoring service or from a portfolio simulator. Typically, four subsets are constructed corresponding to risk quartiles. For example, a universe can be ranked on the basis of return variability, broken into variability quartiles, and performance backgrounds constructed within each variability quartile. Exhibit 8 exemplifies this form of analysis. To evaluate a portfolio in this context, its risk quartile is identified and then its performance within the corresponding Becker bar is located. "Effects of . . ." exhibits tell the evaluator simultaneously whether or not the particular measure of risk was rewarded in general, and whether or not the portfolio in particular was rewarded relative to the risk. A problem with this exposition is that the extremes of the performance subdistributions are typically populated by funds with extreme risk characteristics. For example, the extremes of a low variability return distribution will be populated by very low variability funds and by funds that are almost low-middle variability. These edge condition problems are reduced when either scatter diagrams or customized backgrounds are used.

Scatter diagrams array all funds in risk-return space, and locate the fund being evaluated in this space. Exhibit 9 shows how scatter diagrams are used to evaluate performance. The risk-return space is usually divided into quadrants, with the "less risk, more return" quadrant being most desirable, and the "more risk, less return" quadrant being the least desirable. The background observations for the scatter can be actual (monitoring service) or theoretical (portfolio simulator).

Finally, a portfolio-specific background can be tailored to reflect the "essence" of the manager being evaluated. In this way, the portfolio's unique opportunity set is identified, and its performance ranking is strictly interpretable as the probability that value was actually added, rather than luck. Also, the tailored background can be contrasted to an unconstrained background to determine whether or not the portfolio's characteristics were generally in or out of favor. For most applications of this nature a portfolio simulator is required, because there are typically not enough funds in a monitoring service's population to meet the criteria.

EXHIBIT 8:
FIXED INCOME: RATES OF RETURN—COMPARED TO FUNDS WITH SIMILAR DURATION

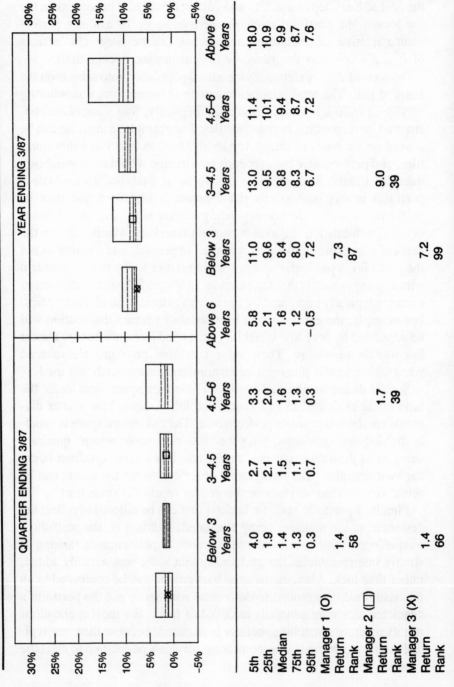

| | QUARTER ENDING 3/87 | | | | YEAR ENDING 3/87 | | | |
	Below 3 Years	3–4.5 Years	4.5–6 Years	Above 6 Years	Below 3 Years	3–4.5 Years	4.5–6 Years	Above 6 Years
5th	4.0	2.7	3.3	5.8	11.0	13.0	11.4	18.0
25th	1.9	2.1	2.0	2.1	9.6	9.5	10.1	10.9
Median	1.4	1.5	1.6	1.6	8.4	8.8	9.4	9.9
75th	1.3	1.1	1.3	1.2	8.0	8.3	8.7	8.7
95th	0.3	0.7	0.3	−0.5	7.2	6.7	7.2	7.6
Manager 1 (O)								
Return	1.4				7.3			
Rank	58				87			
Manager 2 (□)								
Return		1.7				9.0		
Rank		39				39		
Manager 3 (X)								
Return	1.4				7.2			
Rank	66				99			

EXHIBIT 9:
ABC COMPANY—TOTAL RETURN VS. RISK—BALANCED PORTFOLIOS
3 YEARS ENDING 12/86

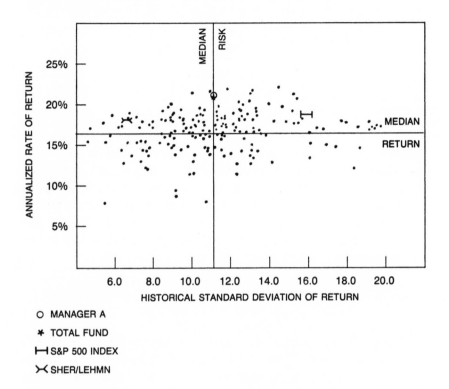

O MANAGER A

✳ TOTAL FUND

⊢⊣ S&P 500 INDEX

⋊⋉ SHER/LEHMN

CONCLUSION

Performance evaluation is part science and part art. The science aspect lies in measuring performance; current computer technology and the ready availability of security data make this so. The art aspect lies in assessing the performance number; the multiplicity of factors involved in managing a portfolio necessitates a blending of both qualitative and quantitative judgments to reach a conclusion regarding the acceptability of performance. New, creative evaluation techniques continue to be introduced. These will help, but the human aspects of judgment will never be entirely eliminated from the evaluation process.

APPENDIX—SOLVING THE RATE EQUATION

The dollar-weighted rate r is the solution to:

$$V_0(1+r) + \sum_i C_i(1+r)^{T_i} = V_E$$

$$V_0(1+r) + \sum_i C_i(1+r)^{T_i} - V_E = 0$$

The most commonly used numerical computer method for solving this equation is the Newton-Raphson method. This is a fairly simple one-point numerical method that typically finds the return solution in less than five iterations. To program your computer to solve for r, efficiency is improved by transforming the rate equation into continuously compounded form. Substituting $e^x = 1 + r$ results in the following functional relationship:

$$f(x) = V_0 e^x + \sum_i C_i e^{T_i x} - V_E = 0$$

To solve for x, a point of tangency on the function $f(x)$ is traced to the abscissa, as shown in Exhibit 10. A good first guess for this iterative process is to let $x_1 = 0$. As can be seen from the exhibit, the Newton-Raphson requires that the derivative of the function be calculated. For the rate function, this derivative is:

$$f'(x) = V_0 e^x + \sum_i C_i T_i e^{T_i x}$$

Successive estimates for the solution are:

$$x_{i+1} = x_i - \frac{f(x_i)}{|f'(x_i)|}$$

where $|f'(x_i)|$ = absolute value of the derivative (taking the absolute value reduces the problem of locating an extraneous root for the rate function)

EXHIBIT 10

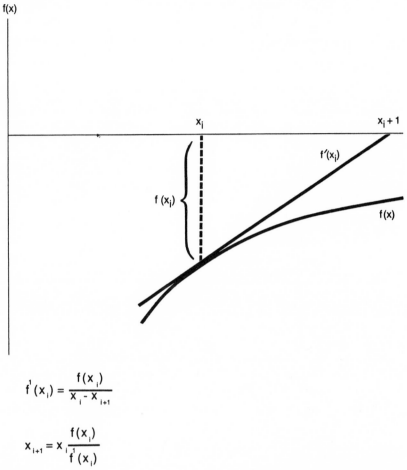

$$f'(x_i) = \frac{f(x_i)}{x_i - x_{i+1}}$$

$$x_{i+1} = x_i \frac{f(x_i)}{f'(x_i)}$$

A solution is located when the function $f(x)$ is acceptably close to zero. The last step is to convert the solution back to discrete compounding by setting r equal to $e^x - 1$.

CHAPTER 19

International Equities and Bonds

GARY P. BRINSON, CFA
PRESIDENT AND CHIEF INVESTMENT OFFICER
FIRST CHICAGO INVESTMENT ADVISORS

RICHARD C. CARR, CFA
MANAGING DIRECTOR
FIRST CHICAGO INVESTMENT ADVISORS

International equities and bonds are relatively new investments for American institutions and individuals, despite their very strong historical advantages in terms of risk reduction and return enhancement. The use of international securities is growing rapidly, though the proportion of U.S. institutional funds invested in the overseas markets is still small in relation to the large size of those markets.

In this chapter we provide a general introduction to the subject of international investments. Our focus is primarily on comparisons with the U.S. markets and the contributions of international securities to the total portfolio. We present the size of the aggregate markets, historical returns, risks, and correlations. In addition to discussing the advantages and disadvantages of investing outside the U.S., we examine the

423

composition of each asset class and the historical performance of the individual markets. Benchmark indexes, transaction costs, regulation, the role of currencies, and accounting information are also presented. Finally, we offer our views on expected returns, risks, and covariances that lead to an asset allocation policy for international investments.

THE INTERNATIONAL ASSET CLASSES

One of the most striking aspects of the international markets is their sheer aggregate size, particularly in relation to the size of the U.S. markets. The American investor is free to consider a wide range of wealth-generating forms of investments in the U.S. and across the globe. Exhibit 1 shows our estimate of the total value in U.S. dollar terms of all the investable capital markets that are available to the U.S. investor. It includes U.S. real estate and venture capital, but excludes those forms of investments in other countries due to a lack of acceptable data estimates and, in some cases, investment restrictions.

Non-U.S. equities are 20.8% of the total, or $3.4 trillion. Non-U.S. dollar bonds are 22.7% of the total, or $3.8 trillion. The non-U.S. dollar bond markets are larger than the U.S. bond market. The proportion of the U.S. markets in the total has declined over time due to the stronger relative performance of the other markets, the recent decline in the value of the dollar, and enormous bond issuance by other governments in the last decade. In terms of equities alone, the U.S. markets were 47% of the world market capitalization in 1970, but only 39% at the end of 1986.

The international markets clearly are large enough to command the interest of U.S. investors. Focusing only on securities inside the U.S. ignores more than half of the opportunities in the world markets.

Size alone, however, should not dictate investment policies. If investment characteristics of markets outside the U.S. are inferior, then there is no reason to consider international investing. Historically, however, returns from capital markets outside the U.S. have been at least equal to those in the U.S., and significantly different from them to provide important diversification benefits as well as active management opportunities.

Historical data on markets outside the U.S. are not as extensive as the data one finds in the U.S. There is nothing comparable to the U.S.

EXHIBIT 1:
TOTAL INVESTABLE CAPITAL MARKET
31 DECEMBER 1986—$16.5 TRILLION

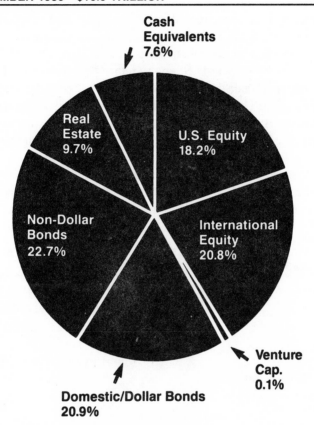

data series that begins in 1926, and the international data when available are often not as comprehensive.

For international equities, the longest time series that is calculated on a comparable basis across markets was developed by what is now the Morgan Stanley Capital International organization. The price data series begins at 31 December 1959, though the dividend series only go back to 31 December 1969.

For international bonds the data is even shorter. The most comprehensive series of returns on bond markets that is updated regularly and publicly available was developed by Salomon Brothers and dates back to 31 December 1977.

Returns from the international markets should be historically evaluated relative to returns from domestic markets and other alternative asset classes. Exhibit 2 presents returns and standard deviations from the investable capital markets in the period 31 December 1969 through 31 December 1986. Non-U.S. equity returns are from Morgan Stanley Capital International; they are constructed by taking the MSCI World Index minus the United States Index. Non-dollar bond returns utilize the Salomon Brothers data series. For earlier years, we use returns developed by First Chicago Investment Advisors, in conjunction with Roger Ibbotson.

The international equity market return of 14.3% in U.S. dollar terms was higher than the 10.7% return from U.S. equities, and the standard deviation of returns in U.S. dollar terms was modestly higher at 19.2%

EXHIBIT 2:
INVESTABLE CAPITAL MARKET PERFORMANCE CHARACTERISTICS
31 DECEMBER 1969–31 DECEMBER 1986

	In U.S. Dollar Terms	
	Annualized Returns	Standard Deviation*
Equities:		
U.S. Equity	10.7%	18.8%
Total Non-U.S. Equity	14.3	19.2
Venture Capital	12.6	36.9
Fixed Income Securities:		
Domestic Bonds	9.9	8.3
International Dollar Bonds	10.5	6.7
Non-Dollar Bonds	11.5	11.4
Real Estate (U.S.)	11.0	2.4
Cash Equivalents (U.S.)	7.7	1.4
Investable Capital Market Portfolio	10.6	9.2
Inflation (PCE)	6.1	1.2

*Annualized standard deviation of quarterly logarithmic data.

versus 18.8%. Non-dollar bonds also enjoyed a higher return than their domestic counterpart: 11.5% versus 9.9% during this period. The standard deviation of return, however, was significantly higher than that of U.S. bonds: 11.4% versus 8.3%. Thus, international markets in the past have provided higher returns but were more volatile asset classes from the standpoint of the U.S. investor.

The third key element in the evaluation of international markets is their correlation or lack thereof with the U.S. market. The returns from international equities and bonds were related to the U.S., but the correlation over the historical period in U.S. dollar terms was relatively low. Exhibit 3 shows the correlations between the returns of international assets and their domestic counterparts, each other, and other asset classes.

Historically, international investments provided higher returns, low correlations with the U.S. markets, and moderately greater risks in terms of volatility. U.S. investors who would have participated in the other markets over this time period would have increased the return and lowered the volatility of their total portfolio.

Despite the impressive historical results, U.S. institutions have not

EXHIBIT 3:
INVESTABLE CAPITAL MARKET PERFORMANCE CHARACTERISTICS
31 DECEMBER 1969–31 DECEMBER 1986 CORRELATION MATRIX*

	1	2	3	4	5	6	7	8	9
1. U.S. Equity	1.00								
2. Non-U.S. Equity	.66	1.00							
3. Venture Capital	.67	.52	1.00						
4. Domestic Bonds	.51	.39	.12	1.00					
5. International Dollar Bonds	.57	.48	.24	.96	1.00				
6. Non-Dollar Bonds	.40	.75	.29	.52	.57	1.00			
7. Real Estate	.05	−.05	.16	−.15	−.16	−.10	1.00		
8. Cash Equivalents	−.12	−.28	−.07	−.04	−.08	−.33	.56	1.00	
9. Investable Capital Market Portfolio	.87	.87	.59	.68	.73	.75	.01	−.20	1.00

*Based on Quarterly Logarithmic Returns.

EXHIBIT 4:
ERISA ASSETS INVESTED OVERSEAS

	ERISA Assets	
	Year End 1983	Year End 1986
Total Overseas ($billion)	$11.7	$45.2
As % of then ERISA Assets	1.8%	3.6%
% in Equity Oriented Portfolios	88%	87%

Source: InterSec Research Corporation.

historically allocated more than a small portion of their total assets to the non-U.S. markets. Exhibit 4 provides an estimate of U.S. institutional funds allocated to non-U.S. portfolios.

The reasons for the heretofore low use of international investments are historical, cultural, and legal. For many decades in the nineteenth century and the early part of the twentieth century, the U.S. economy imported capital. Historical returns from U.S. markets were adequate, particularly immediately after World War II. At that time, the foreign economies had been decimated by the war, and were rebuilding. The foreign markets were still small in the early 1960s when U.S. investors first began placing money overseas, primarily in Europe. That trend was extinguished by the Interest Equalization Tax, which started in 1964 and lasted until 1974. Two American institutions, Morgan Guaranty and First Chicago, began investing immediately after the IET was removed. Nonetheless, international investing was relatively minor in the 1970s and did not accelerate until the early 1980s. Lack of knowledge and experience, concern with currency risk, and a traditional bias toward American securities constrained potential use of the asset classes, notwithstanding their apparent benefits to portfolio diversification and performance.

INTERNATIONAL EQUITIES

As shown earlier, stock markets outside the U.S. have generated returns that exceeded those from the U.S. markets over the longer term. From 31 December 1969 through 31 December 1986, the compound annual return from the non-U.S. equity index was 14.3%, while the

EXHIBIT 5:
NON-U.S. EQUITIES VS. U.S. EQUITIES

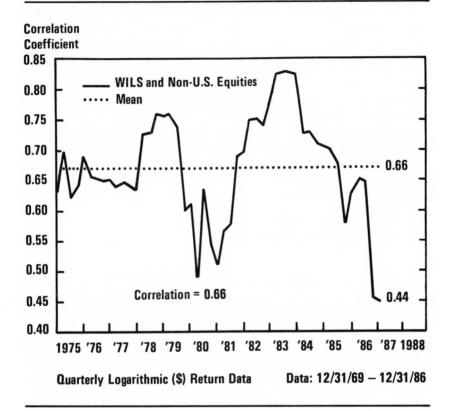

Correlation
Coefficient

Correlation = 0.66

0.66

0.44

1975 '76 '77 '78 '79 '80 '81 '82 '83 '84 '85 '86 '87 1988

— WILS and Non-U.S. Equities
····· Mean

Quarterly Logarithmic ($) Return Data   Data: 12/31/69 – 12/31/86

Wilshire 5000 Index provided a return over the same period of 10.7%. Exhibit 5 portrays a wealth index of returns from the indexes over the 1970 to 1986 period. The wealth index gives a visual indication of the relative volatility of the markets and their relationship.

The higher historical returns from the non-U.S. markets have been accompanied by somewhat higher volatility: the standard deviation of returns was 19.2% versus 18.8% from the Wilshire 5000 Index. The correlation was 0.66.

While the correlation of returns between the U.S. and non-U.S. equity markets has been relatively low, there is no historical evidence to indicate that the correlations are increasing. The statistical data, in fact, show that correlations have recently been decreasing, after a period in the early 1980s, when markets in dollar-adjusted terms exhibited higher covariance. That phenomenon was probably due to the reaction of world capital markets to higher U.S. interest rates and much tighter monetary policies imposed in 1980 by the Federal Reserve Board. An analysis of rolling five year correlations shown in Exhibit 6 helps to determine whether there are recent trends toward integration of markets. Clearly, the long-term and recent data support the hypothesis that international equities improve diversification and reduce the risk of the total portfolio.

The role of currency in creating dollar-adjusted returns from the international equity markets has been questioned by many observers. The fluctuations in the value of the U.S. dollar clearly have an impact

EXHIBIT 6:
WILSHIRE 5000 AND NON-U.S. EQUITIES
FIVE-YEAR TRAILING CORRELATION

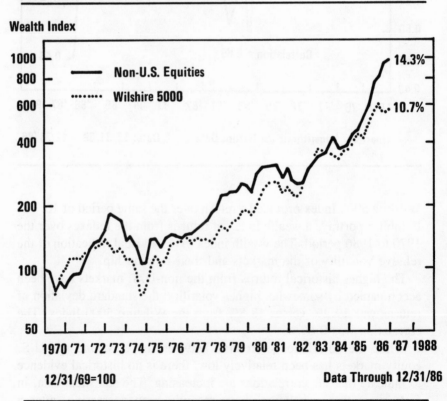

Wealth Index

1970 '71 '72 '73 '74 '75 '76 '77 '78 '79 '80 '81 '82 '83 '84 '85 '86 '87 1988

12/31/69=100   Data Through 12/31/86

on returns, and that impact can be significant over shorter time periods. Over longer term horizons, however, the impact of currency is minimal. The rise and fall of the U.S. dollar relative to a basket of other currencies washes out over time and becomes insignificant. The Non-U.S. Index in local currency terms is closely related to the Non-U.S. Index in dollar terms. From 1970 through 1986, the local currency returns from non-U.S. equities was 13.2%, quite close to the dollar-adjusted return of 14.3%. Exhibit 7 highlights the relationship of returns from the international equity markets in both dollar-adjusted and local currency terms.

While currency change is minor over time, the translation of returns into dollar terms does increase the risk of international equities. As can be seen from Exhibit 8, the standard deviation of returns from the Non-U.S. Index in local currency terms is lower than the standard deviation of returns in dollar terms.

EXHIBIT 7:
CURRENCY EFFECTS ON INTERNATIONAL EQUITIES

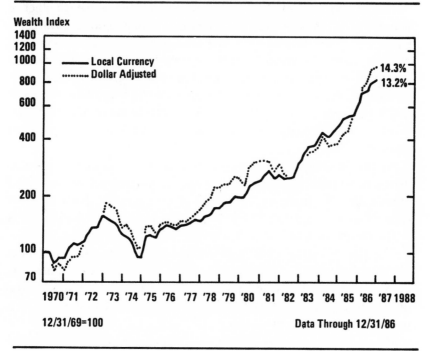

EXHIBIT 8:
CURRENCY EFFECTS ON EQUITY RISK

	31 December 1969–31 December 1986 Standard Deviation of Returns	
	In $ Terms	In Local Currency Terms
Non-U.S. Index	19.2%	13.9%
Wilshire 500 Index	18.8%	18.8

The returns from the individual markets have varied considerably. Exhibit 9 summarizes the annualized returns from the major non-U.S. markets as defined by Morgan Stanley Capital International. We show returns and standard deviations in both dollar-adjusted and local currency terms.

Japan has had the highest dollar-adjusted returns among the larger countries, though the volatility of that market has been surprisingly low. Australia has had the lowest return during the entire seventeen-year period.

The foreign stock markets are not well-correlated with each other or with the U.S., though there are sometimes strong regional covariance tendencies. (See Exhibit 10.) The low correlation across non-U.S. markets lowers the volatility of the aggregate index and provides important diversification benefits. This lack of homogeneity among international markets is very important for strategic investment decision-making but remains a largely overlooked factor in the planning of many investors who wrongly assess international investing as a single asset class segment.

As can be seen from Exhibit 11, the size of the stock markets also varies considerably. Japan is now the largest market in the world outside the U.S. It amounts to 50.8% of the aggregate dollar-adjusted capitalization of stock markets outside the U.S. The U.K. market is next in terms of size, but considerably smaller than Japan.

The size of markets has been defined by Morgan Stanley Capital International (MSCI). Their indexes have been used by most analysts because they are constructed in a consistent way across markets and the historical data series goes back to 1960. Local measures of stock markets are inconsistent in their methodology and coverage. Some are weighted by market value (like the S&P 500), and others are weighted

EXHIBIT 9:
GLOBAL EQUITY MARKETS PERFORMANCE CHARACTERISTICS

	Annualized Returns		*Standard Deviation**	
	In Local Currency Terms	*In $ Terms*	*In Local Currency Terms*	*In $ Terms*
Australia	10.6%	7.2%	24.1%	27.6%
Belgium	17.9	19.3	16.1	21.9
Canada	11.6	10.0	18.2	19.3
France	14.6	13.6	22.6	28.0
Germany	10.5	14.7	16.3	21.0
Hong Kong[1]	13.2	10.7	45.3	48.1
Italy	13.8	8.8	28.8	31.6
Japan	16.7	22.4	18.2	23.1
Netherlands	12.3	15.7	17.1	20.3
Norway	13.4	13.2	28.3	32.6
Singapore[1]	4.0	5.9	32.2	33.4
Spain	12.0	7.9	21.9	26.3
Sweden	18.0	16.1	20.0	21.4
Switzerland	7.1	13.4	16.4	21.9
U.K.	15.8	12.5	23.4	26.4
U.S.	10.7	10.7	18.8	18.8

*Annualized standard deviation of quarterly logarithmic returns data.
[1]Data for period 31 December 1972–31 December 1986.

by price (like the Dow Jones 30). Some national indexes are broad, while others include only a small number of large companies. Many national markets do not have a long history of index value.

Several new indexes of the international equity markets were recently introduced. The First Boston Index includes only "investable" companies—those stocks that can be purchased by foreign investors. As an example, Swiss Registered shares, which can only be purchased by Swiss residents, are excluded. The Financial Times has introduced a World Index in conjunction with the Institute of Actuaries in the U.K.,

EXHIBIT 10:
GLOBAL EQUITY MARKETS PERFORMANCE CHARACTERISTICS (U.S. DOLLAR RETURNS)
31 DECEMBER 1969–31 DECEMBER 1986—CORRELATION MATRIX

	1	2	3	4	5	6	7	8	9	10	11	12	13	14	15	16
1. Australia	1.00															
2. Belgium	0.43	1.00														
3. Canada	0.57	0.38	1.00													
4. France	0.38	0.79	0.28	1.00												
5. Germany	0.41	0.75	0.36	0.67	1.00											
6. Hong Kong*	0.38	0.27	0.30	0.26	0.41	1.00										
7. Italy	0.41	0.56	0.31	0.61	0.50	0.19	1.00									
8. Japan	0.46	0.54	0.41	0.45	0.54	0.49	0.52	1.00								
9. Netherlands	0.53	0.81	0.51	0.68	0.76	0.55	0.49	0.63	1.00							
10. Norway	0.37	0.59	0.33	0.50	0.34	0.22	0.35	0.20	0.52	1.00						
11. Singapore*	0.52	0.33	0.50	0.27	0.34	0.58	0.32	0.56	0.60	0.23	1.00					
12. Spain	0.32	0.43	0.17	0.33	0.33	0.28	0.47	0.49	0.36	0.23	0.14	1.00				
13. Sweden	0.39	0.58	0.40	0.41	0.53	0.17	0.54	0.55	0.58	0.27	0.43	0.38	1.00			
14. Switzerland	0.49	0.79	0.49	0.69	0.86	0.36	0.51	0.60	0.80	0.47	0.45	0.25	0.54	1.00		
15. U.K.	0.47	0.55	0.44	0.48	0.45	0.42	0.39	0.42	0.64	0.27	0.61	0.17	0.37	0.56	1.00	
16. U.S.	0.54	0.45	0.80	0.41	0.47	0.48	0.35	0.49	0.65	0.29	0.53	0.23	0.47	0.59	0.59	1.00

*Data for period 31 December 1972–31 December 1986.

EXHIBIT 11:
TOTAL MARKET VALUE OF COUNTRIES INCLUDED IN
MORGAN STANLEY CAPITAL INTERNATIONAL UNIVERSE—
31 DECEMBER 1986

	$ Billion	%
Austria	5.3	0.2%
Belgium	36.3	1.0
Denmark	15.1	0.4
France	149.5	4.4
Germany	245.9	7.2
Italy	140.8	4.1
Netherlands	73.3	2.1
Norway	9.6	0.3
Spain	41.6	1.2
Sweden	48.5	1.4
Switzerland	132.4	3.8
U.K.	439.5	12.8
Europe	1337.8	38.9
Australia	77.7	2.3
Hong Kong	53.1	1.5
Japan	1746.2	50.8
Singapore/Malaysia	32.6	1.0
Europe, Australia, Far East	3247.4	94.5
Canada	166.3	4.8
Mexico	6.5	0.2
South African Gold Mines	18.3	0.5
Total Non-U.S. Index	3438.5	100.0%

Goldman Sachs, and Wood Mackenzie. Salomon Brothers, in conjunction with the Frank Russell Company, has also created an international equity index.

All the new indexes include only investable stocks. Each index deals with the vexing problem of non-portfolio ownership in different ways. The foreign markets contain many common stocks that are partially owned by governments, banks or other corporations. As examples, the British Government owns 32% of British Petroleum, Toyota owns 21% of Nippon Denso, and Deutsche Bank holds 28% of Daimler Benz. To include the full value of the companies in any index, as several local indexes do, overstates both the size of that company and the national country market.

Double-counting from this ownership is eliminated by tallying only the market value of the company that is freely traded. The Financial Times Index excludes all companies with 75% or more control by other organizations. The First Boston Index excludes companies with 30% or more controlling ownership, and the Salomon Brothers Index takes out that portion of the market capitalization which is owned by governments, corporations, or other organizations when the proportion exceeds 10%, including the Japanese groupings such as Sumitomo or Mitsubishi, which total 10% or more.

The MSCI Index is composed of markets in the larger or more developed countries, and most of the newer indexes have the same feature. While Singapore and Hong Kong are included, other emerging markets such as Korea, Taiwan, Thailand, and India are not covered. These markets are either closed to foreign investment (Korea) or are difficult to repatriate money from (Brazil).

In addition, the indexes are measures of relatively large capitalization companies. There are no standardized measures of smaller companies like the American Stock Exchange, NASDAQ, the Unlisted Securities Market (in the U.K,), and the Tokyo Stock Exchange Index of Second Section companies.

Higher transaction costs are a disadvantage of the foreign stock markets. These arise from both the higher level of commissions and taxes imposed by some host countries. As an example, the U.K. charges 0.5% of market value on all stock exchange purchases. The Japanese government collects 0.35% on the value of all sales. Exhibit 12 shows estimated total transaction costs (commissions and taxes) as of mid-1987 for transaction amounts of $500,000.

Trends toward deregulation and greater internationalization of markets have led to declining transaction costs (e.g., commissions in the U.K. dropped from around 40 basis points to approximately 25 basis points after "Big Bang" in October 1986). Nonetheless, trading costs are higher outside the U.S.

Withholding taxes on income and dividends are another cost element of investing outside the U.S. The amount of tax withheld at source by governments depends upon the tax treaty with the investor's government, but is generally 15% net. The tax is often deducted from the dividend or coupon by the custodian bank. In a small number of

EXHIBIT 12:
EFFECTIVE TRANSACTION COSTS IN NON-U.S. EQUITY MARKETS
(BASIS POINTS)

(Size $500,00) Market	Buy	Sell	Average
Australia	80	80	80
Belgium	70	70	70
Canada	60	60	60
France	58	58	58
Germany	58	58	58
Hong Kong	107	107	107
Italy	72	72	72
Japan	45	100	73
Netherlands	40	40	40
Singapore	120	100	110
Spain	100	100	100
Sweden	136	136	136
Switzerland	55	55	55
U.K.	75	25	50
Weighted Non-U.S. Average	59	74	67
U.S.	20	20	20

countries a full tax of 30% is withheld at source, and the investor (through his custodian bank) must claim a refund such that the net amount of withholding becomes 15%.

Custodian costs are also somewhat higher than those in the U.S. Most securities owned by institutional investors are held with custodian banks in the local countries. Delivery of securities to and from custodian banks in the U.S. would be very slow, expensive, and unnecessary. Local subcustodians provide settlement, safekeeping, and income collection. The subcustodians are often monitored and controlled by a master custodian, who adds an additional fee.

The entire process of purchasing a security that trades in another country, arranging settlement, paying/receiving in another currency, collecting income, and handling withholding taxes is very complex as well as costly. The procedures and costs vary by country. As an example, settlement of stocks in Japan is in three days, twice a month in the U.K., and once a month in the cash market in France.

An alternative means of investing internationally in stocks is through American Depository Receipts (ADRs) which trade in America, are denominated in U.S. dollars, and pay dividends in U.S. dollars. These receipts are issued by U.S. banks as evidence of ownership of the underlying share of foreign corporations held by the same U.S. bank in the foreign country. One ADR usually represents five to ten shares of a foreign company.

An increasing number of companies is represented by ADRs in the U.S. and can be listed on the NYSE, AMEX or NASDAQ. However, the bulk of the more marketable ADRs has been Japanese, British, and South African. Continental European companies have not been well-represented in the ADR market. In addition to the narrow coverage and often low liquidity, there are costs associated with ADRs. The custodian bank charges for collection of income and other services. ADR investors are also not allowed to participate in rights issues, a frequent form of capital raising by European companies.

The American investor who trades outside the U.S. must also cope with markets that are not as regulated as the U.S. markets. There are government bodies in most foreign countries that are charged with supervising the local securities markets, but these organizations usually lack the power and resources of the Securities and Exchange Commission. As a result, there can be more opportunities for abuses and manipulation of stock prices.

Accounting information is often not as detailed or timely as it is in the U.S. Financial statements are usually semiannual rather than quarterly, and can sometimes be published long after the end of the accounting period. Accounting practices vary considerably across countries and are never identical with U.S. standards. However, accounting is often more conservative in other countries; restatement into U.S. practice usually produces higher earnings. The trend to greater interlisting of securities and capital raising in multiple markets is, however, leading to more accounting detail, greater disclosure, and financial statements using U.S. practice as well as local practice.

INTERNATIONAL BONDS

Non-dollar bonds have generated higher rates of return in U.S. dollar terms than U.S. dollar-denominated bonds over long time periods. Exhibit 13 is a wealth index of returns from 1970 for the two types of bonds. As described earlier, the annualized return over the 1970–1986 period was 11.5% from non-dollar bonds and 9.9% from U.S. domestic bonds. Returns differed significantly in many years. In the early 1970s, returns were similar when exchange rates were fixed. Non-dollar bonds performed well in the late 1970s when the U.S. dollar fell and U.S. interest rates rose. Non-dollar bonds benefited from currency appreciation and lower rates of inflation than those in the U.S. The cycles reversed in the early 1980s when U.S. bonds had the highest returns. Yields fell dramatically in the U.S., and the dollar strengthened considerably. The pattern of returns changed again in 1985 and 1986 when non-dollar bond returns exceeded 30% annually, thanks largely to another decline in the U.S. dollar.

EXHIBIT 13:
NON-DOLLAR BONDS VS. U.S. BONDS

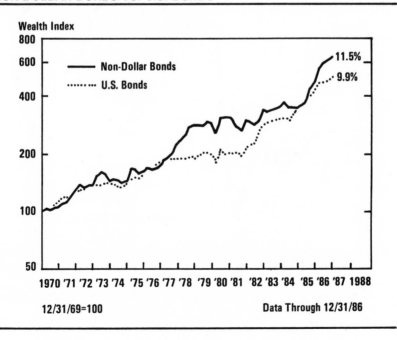

The correlation of returns in U.S. dollar terms between U.S. bonds and non-dollar bonds is low, and has been declining in recent years, just as in the case of equities. (See Exhibit 14.) Despite greater cross-border investing, there is no evidence to support the claim that the diversification benefits from international bonds have lessened.

The correlation of non-dollar bonds to U.S. domestic bonds is less than the historical correlation of non-U.S. equities to U.S. equities. In that sense, non-dollar bonds are a more powerful diversifier than are non-U.S. equities. The low correlations are, however, at least partially offset by proportionately higher standard deviations.

The role of currency in non-dollar bond returns is greater than it is in international equities: currency change is normally a higher proportion

EXHIBIT 14:
SALOMON BIG BOND AND NON-DOLLAR BONDS
FIVE-YEAR TRAILING CORRELATION

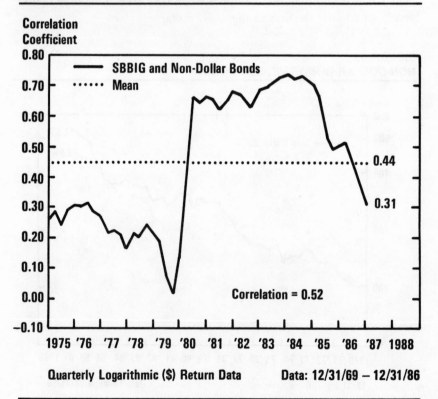

Quarterly Logarithmic ($) Return Data   Data: 12/31/69 – 12/31/86

EXHIBIT 15:
CURRENCY EFFECTS ON NON-DOLLAR BONDS

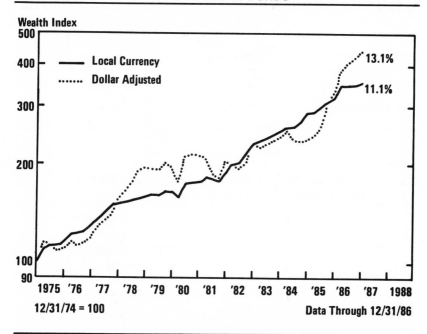

of dollar-adjusted international bond returns. Part of this is due to lower and more stable returns from bonds. The same currency changes become a smaller proportion of bigger swings in the equity markets. Currency change is also more related to bond market returns since they both are driven by inflation expectations. A strong currency often leads to lower interest rates and rising bond prices. The relationship between stock prices and currency changes is less strong, and firm currency values can sometimes produce declining stock prices when export prospects are damaged.

Exhibit 15 shows wealth indexes of returns from non-dollar bonds, expressed in dollar terms and local currency terms.

As with international equities, the addition of currency change to the local bond markets increases the volatility of returns. In local currency terms, the non-U.S. bond markets have been, in the aggregate, more stable than the U.S. bond markets. In dollar terms, their volatility becomes substantially greater. (See Exhibit 16.)

EXHIBIT 16:
CURRENCY EFFECTS ON BOND RISK

| | 31 December 1974–31 December 1986 Standard Deviation of Returns | |
	In $ Terms	In Local Currency Terms
Non-Dollar Bonds	11.4%	5.3%
U.S. Domestic Bonds	8.3	8.3

EXHIBIT 17:
GLOBAL FIXED INCOME PERFORMANCE CHARACTERISTICS
31 DECEMBER 1974–31 DECEMBER 1986

| | Annualized Returns | | Standard Deviation* | |
	In Local Currency Terms	In $ Terms	In Local Currency Terms	In $ Terms
Australia	10.7	7.7	13.9	16.1
France	12.1	8.7	7.8	15.9
Germany	9.8	11.7	5.1	14.7
Japan	11.2	17.3	4.7	14.4
Netherlands	9.6	10.8	6.6	15.3
Switzerland	7.7	11.8	6.1	17.2
U.K.	15.9	11.5	13.0	18.5
U.S.	11.0	11.0	9.2	9.2

*Annualized standard deviation of quarterly logarithmic returns data.

As with equities, the returns from the international bond markets vary considerably. Exhibit 17 shows the returns and standard deviations from the larger bond markets over the last thirteen years, in dollar-adjusted terms and local currency terms.

Japan was the best performing bond market in dollar-adjusted terms, while Canada had the lowest annualized returns during the period.

As with international equities, one finds low correlations between the non-U.S. bond markets except in continental Europe where Germany, Switzerland, the Netherlands, and France are in the same cur-

EXHIBIT 18:
GLOBAL FIXED INCOME MARKETS
PERFORMANCE CHARACTERISTICS (U.S. DOLLAR RETURNS)
31 DECEMBER 1974–31 DECEMBER 1986—CORRELATION MATRIX

	1	*2*	*3*	*4*	*5*	*6*	*7*	*8*
1. Canada	1.00							
2. France	0.30	1.00						
3. Germany	0.42	0.79	1.00					
4. Japan	0.42	0.64	0.68	1.00				
5. Netherlands	0.44	0.79	0.95	0.66	1.00			
6. Switzerland	0.46	0.69	0.85	0.75	0.80	1.00		
7. U.K.	0.38	0.37	0.37	0.36	0.39	0.38	1.00	
8. U.S.	0.91	0.36	0.49	0.41	0.51	0.48	0.33	1.00

EXHIBIT 19:
NON-U.S. GOVERNMENT BOND MARKETS
(REMAINING MATURITIES OF 1 YEAR OR MORE) 31 DECEMBER 1986

	$ Billion	*% of Total*
Japan	522.7	51.5
U.K.	164.7	16.2
Germany	99.2	9.8
France	68.3	6.7
The Netherlands	60.5	6.0
Australia	22.0	2.2
Canada	68.8	6.8
Switzerland	8.0	0.8
	1014.2	100.0

Source: Salomon Brothers

rency bloc. The returns from these markets are therefore highly correlated. The cross-correlations for bonds are even lower than those
between the international markets. (See Exhibit 18.)

The size of the international bond markets is calculated on an annual
basis by Salomon Brothers. Exhibit 19 describes the government bond
markets in dollar terms as of the end of 1986.

The Japanese bond market dominates the asset class, just as Japanese equities are an enormous part of the total non-U.S. equity markets.

Indexes of the international bond markets have been created by InterSec Research Corporation, Lombard Odier, and Salomon Brothers. The original Salomon Brothers World Bond Indexes have been supplemented by their World Government Bond Index, which has several advantages: maturities are one year or longer rather than five years (and are thus comparable to the domestic Salomon Brothers Broad Investment Grade Index). The Index is all inclusive of the government bond markets rather than based on a sample, and the country weights are changed monthly rather than annually. The new index contains only government bonds, whereas the previous index also included eurobonds and foreign bonds.

Salomon Brothers plans to add the latter two types of bond markets in 1987, but states that their exclusion is not critical since government bonds are 81% of the total non-U.S. bond markets. The historical data shown by Salomon Brothers are from their previous five-year maturity or more index. That index overstates the volatility of the bond markets because of its long maturity characteristic.

Corporate bonds are a very small part of the total fixed income markets in other countries. Most public debt is issued by governments, and corporations have relied heavily on the banks for fixed income financing.

Exhibit 20 lists the principal characteristics of the government bond markets at the end of 1986 as defined by Salomon Brothers. While maturities in some markets are less than those in the U.S., the average durations are surprisingly close to those in the U.S.

Transaction costs for bond trades are also higher outside the U.S. The markets are generally large and liquid, but spreads and commissions are significantly above normal U.S. levels.

Withholding taxes are also important considerations, though many countries have taken steps to eliminate the tax entirely (Western Europe) or to issue some bonds that are free of withholding tax (the U.K.). Eurobonds are free from withholding tax, and in domestic markets, such as Japan and Australia, bonds can be sold before the coupon date to avoid the tax, though Japanese rules relating to coupon avoidance transactions are under review.

Custody and settlement procedures and complexities are similar to those that the investor faces in the international equity markets. In

EXHIBIT 20:
SALOMON BROTHERS WORLD GOVERNMENT BOND MARKET
INDEXES: 31 DECEMBER 1986
(REMAINING MATURITIES OF AT LEAST ONE YEAR)

	Average Maturity (Yrs.)	Average Duration (Yrs.)
U.S. $ Government	8.4	5.0
Canadian $ Government	9.6	5.6
Deutschemark Government	6.5	5.0
Yen Government	5.2	4.3
Sterling Goverment	10.0[1]	5.5
15 + Years	19.5[1]	8.2
Swiss Franc Government	6.9	5.8
Dutch Florin Government	5.4[1][2]	4.3
French Franc Government	7.9	5.2
Australian $ Government	6.4	4.0
World Government Bond Index (Weighted)	7.5[1]	4.9

[1] Excludes a small number of perpetual issues in calculation of average maturity.
[2] Average remaining life of sample, rather than average final maturity.

some cases the requirements are even more stringent (U.K. government bonds settle next day, in pound sterling). Domestic bonds are normally held in the local country whereas eurobonds can normally be settled and held at Euroclear and Cedel, two European-based organizations. The number of government bonds that can be settled at Euroclear and Cedel is expanding rapidly.

THE FUTURE

A decision to participate in the international equity and bond markets should be based upon expected returns, risks, and covariances. Assumptions as to the long term charàcteristics of the non-U.S. markets ought to determine asset allocation policies. Shorter term forecasts of markets from their current price levels will provide the basis for global strategies and tactics.

Some analyses of the non-U.S. capital markets have simply projected historical trends into the future. We believe that the past has to be examined carefully, but forecasts must be made of the key characteristics that may differ from historical trends. Our research and analysis lead to the conclusion that the risks and covariances of the historical markets may be similar to what was seen in the past, but the returns are likely to be less impressive relative to the U.S. markets than they were in the past.

The non-U.S. equity markets performed better than the U.S. market in most of the periods since the data series began in 1960. We believe that this has been due to a more rapid growth of the foreign economies as they rebuilt from World War II, markets that were still somewhat cheap in global terms when the measurement period began, and a somewhat depressed U.S. dollar at the end of the measurement period. If market returns reflect economic returns in the long term, it is difficult to argue that U.S. growth and market return will be much less than the aggregate of the other countries. Japan, which represents more than half of the non-U.S. markets' capitalization, had very high growth in the 1950s and 1960s, but its growth has slowed and is unlikely to be much higher than that of the U.S. in the future. The European markets are unlikely to grow any faster than the U.S. market on a secular basis. There are a number of other countries that should exhibit above-average growth in the future, but most of these are small and constrained by physical size (Hong Kong, Singapore) or essentially closed to foreign investors (Korea, Taiwan).

We conclude that the dollar-adjusted returns from large capitalization equities outside the U.S. will be moderately higher than the returns from similar U.S. equities. As to small capitalization equities, there is no adequate measure outside the U.S. There is, as yet, no suitable index of the emerging markets.

As mentioned earlier, we believe that the risks of the foreign markets, largely for currency reasons, will remain moderately above that of the U.S. market. The correlation of returns should also remain low, though probably above what has been seen in the past. Most investors across the globe are biased toward their home markets. Cross-border investing has increased rapidly, but the markets are likely to be segmented for some time rather than integrated.

EXHIBIT 21:
LONGER-TERM EQUILIBRIUM ASSUMPTIONS FOR THE U.S. AND NON-U.S. EQUITY MARKETS

	Forecast Equilibrium Returns	Forecast Risk
U.S. Equities		
S&P 500	11.5%	16.5%
Intermediate Capitalization	12.8	21.0
Small Capitalization	15.0	30.0
International Equities	11.9	19.5

Exhibit 21 shows our longer-term equilibrium assumptions for the U.S. and non-U.S. equity markets. For the U.S., we include all sizes of companies, whereas the international equities forecast assumes large capitalization stocks. The proper comparison is between large capitalization U.S. (S&P 500) and large capitalization non-U.S. stocks.

What will be the long-term return from non-dollar bonds? Studies of only the Salomon Brothers data in the period 1977 to 1986 have concluded that non-dollar bonds are inferior to U.S. domestic bonds. Other studies that are based on seventeen and sometimes twenty-seven years of data have demonstrated that non-dollar bonds have had higher returns.

The historical analyses of international bonds are period-specific. Economic theory suggests that the dollar-adjusted returns from the two sets of markets will be equal in the long run. Bonds in countries with higher interest rates have higher inflation which leads to currency depreciation. Bonds in countries with low interest rates have lower inflation which leads to currency appreciation over time. Higher/lower rates of inflation and interest rates are offset over time by currency depreciation/appreciation. We believe that interest rate parity determines dollar-adjusted returns, particularly when markets are more open to cross-border flows of money.

The volatility of non-dollar bonds is likely to continue to be higher than that of U.S. domestic bonds because of the currency element. The correlation of returns with the U.S. bond market is likely to be low, in line with historical trends.

EXHIBIT 22:
ESTIMATED EQUILIBRIUM RETURNS AND RISKS

	Forecast Equilibrium Return	Forecast Risk
Domestic Bonds (Salomon BIG Index)	8.1%	7.5%
Non-Dollar Bonds	8.2	9.0

EXHIBIT 23:
LONG-TERM ASSET CLASS EQUILIBRIUM RETURNS—
CORRELATION FORECASTS*

	1	2	3	4	5	6	7
1. U.S. Equity	1.00						
2. Non-U.S. Equity	.60	1.00					
3. Venture Capital	.35	.15	1.00				
4. Dollar Bonds	.45	.25	.15	1.00			
5. Non-Dollar Bonds	.25	.60	.10	.30	1.00		
6. Real Estate	.35	.30	.25	.20	.15	1.00	
7. Cash Equivalents	−.10	−.15	−.10	−.05	−.10	.25	1.00

*Annual Return

Exhibit 22 shows our estimate of equilibrium returns and risks for U.S. bonds and non-dollar bonds.

We have examined the historical correlations between the international asset classes and all the major domestic asset classes. Based on the history, an analysis of trends, and judgments as to the future integration of global markets, we developed a matrix of expected correlations of returns from asset classes, shown as Exhibit 23.

Based upon the above forecasts, we believe that international equities and bonds should have an important role in U.S. portfolios. A minimum proportion should always be allocated to the international markets in order to gain the primary advantage of diversification. Ranges around a policy norm for international assets should be set for those institutions and individuals who can actively allocate assets across global markets.

Our research on asset allocations concludes that international equities should have a policy norm of 15% in an institutional portfolio, within a range of 5% to 25%. Non-dollar bonds should have a policy norm of 5% within a range of 2% to 12%.

SUMMARY

International equities and non-dollar bonds have historically provided longer term returns that were above those of the comparable U.S. asset classes. While the standard deviation of returns from international asset classes was also above that of the U.S., the correlation of returns has been low. Thus, the addition of international equities and/or bonds to a portfolio improved diversification by reducing total risk or volatility of return.

The disadvantages of international investing center on higher transaction costs, higher custody costs, financial information that is often not as comprehensive as in the U.S., and weaker regulation. Several of these features are changing, and the costs and problems are less than they were ten years ago.

Returns in the future are not likely to be as impressive as they were in the past, but should, in the long term, be at least equal to those in the U.S. for comparable asset classes. The risks of international investing will remain greater, but the low covariance of returns with the U.S. will ensure that the principal benefit of international investing—diversification—will remain in place for U.S. investors.

Index

451